THE UNCANNY

X-MEN

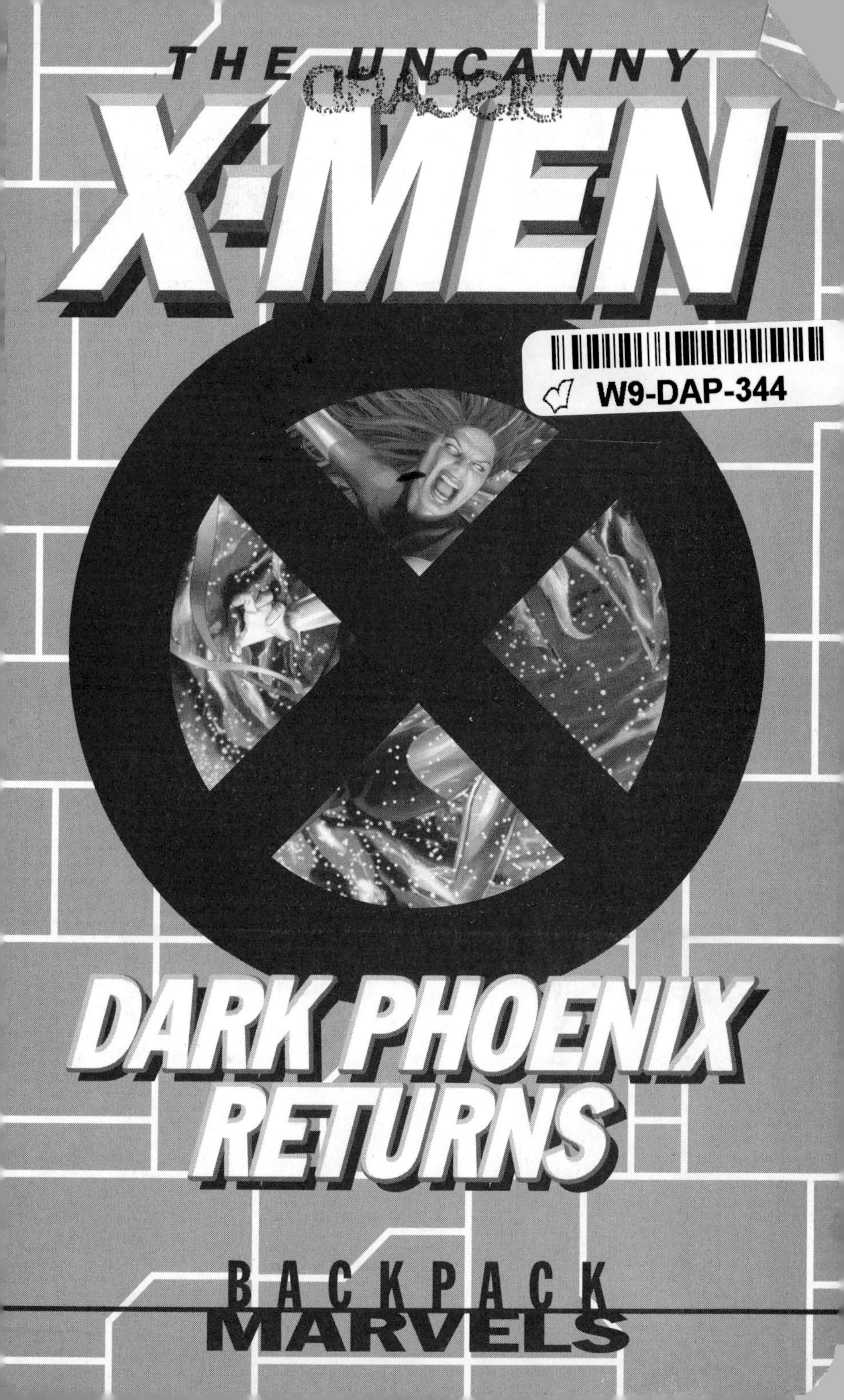

DARK PHOENIX RETURNS

BACKPACK MARVELS

TABLE OF CONTENTS

COVER ART: **GREG HORN**

BOOK DESIGN: **COMICRAFT**

REPRINT EDITOR: **POLLY WATSON**

EDITOR IN CHIEF: **JOE QUESADA**

BACKPACK MARVELS: X-MEN® Vol. 1 No. 2, November, 2000. Contains material original-
ly published in magazine form as UNCANNY X-MEN #'s 167-173. Published by MARVEL
COMICS, Bill Jemas, President; Frank Fochetta, Senior Vice President, Publishing; Joe
Quesada, Editor-in-Chief; Stan Lee, Chairman Emeritus. OFFICE OF PUBLICATION: 387 PARK
AVENUE SOUTH, NEW YORK, N.Y. 10016. Copyright © 1983, 2000 Marvel Characters, Inc.
All rights reserved. Price $6.95 per copy in the U.S. and $9.95 in Canada. BACKPACK
MARVELS: X-MEN (including all prominent characters featured in this issue and the dis-
tinctive likenesses thereof) is a trademark of MARVEL CHARACTERS, INC. No part of this
book may be printed or reproduced in any manner without the written permission of the pub-
lisher. Printed in Canada. First Printing, November, 2000. ISBN #0-7851-0763-0. GST.
#R127032852. MARVEL COMICS is a division of MARVEL ENTERPRISES, INC. Peter Cuneo,
Chief Executive Officer; Avi Arad, Chief Creative Officer.

10 9 8 7 6 5 4 3 2 1

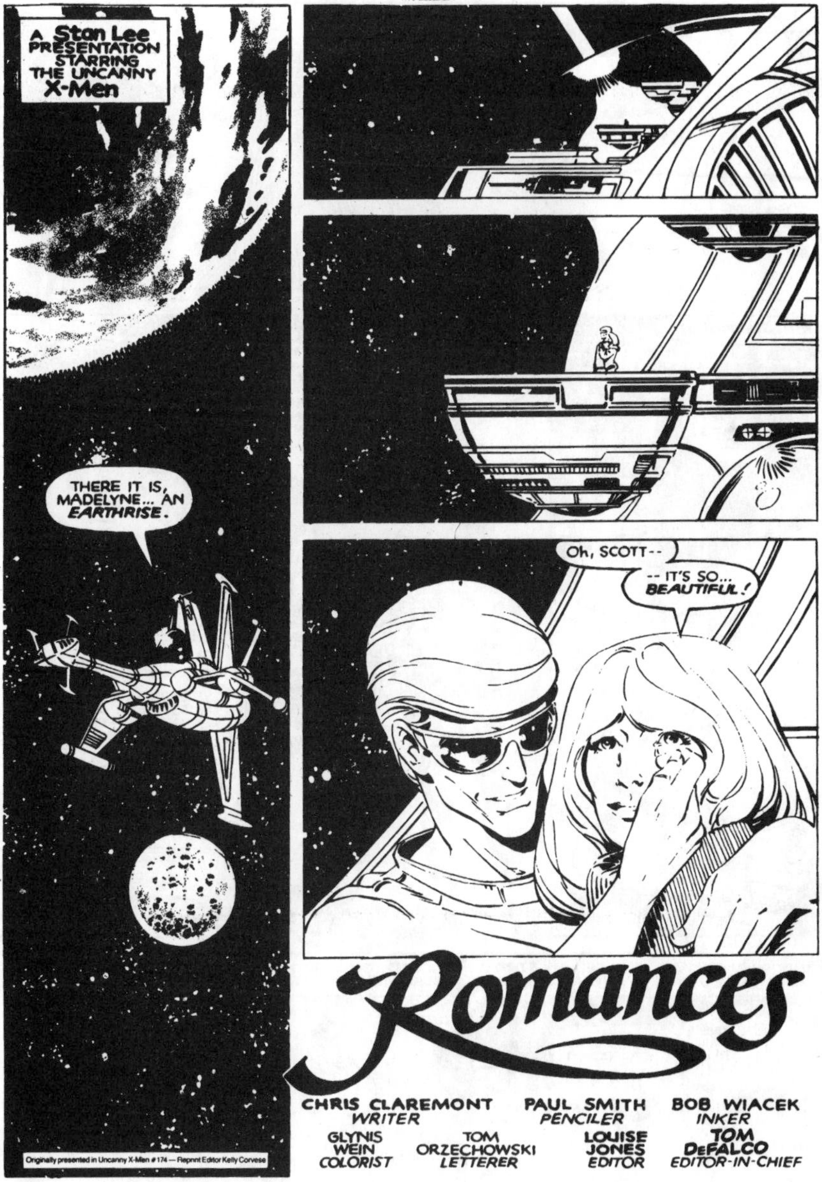
A Stan Lee PRESENTATION STARRING THE UNCANNY X-Men
THERE IT IS, MADELYNE... AN EARTHRISE.
Oh, SCOTT--
-- IT'S SO... BEAUTIFUL!

Romances

CHRIS CLAREMONT *WRITER* · PAUL SMITH *PENCILER* · BOB WIACEK *INKER*
GLYNIS WEIN *COLORIST* · TOM ORZECHOWSKI *LETTERER* · LOUISE JONES *EDITOR* · TOM DeFALCO *EDITOR-IN-CHIEF*

Originally presented in Uncanny X-Men # 174 — Reprint Editor Kelly Corvese

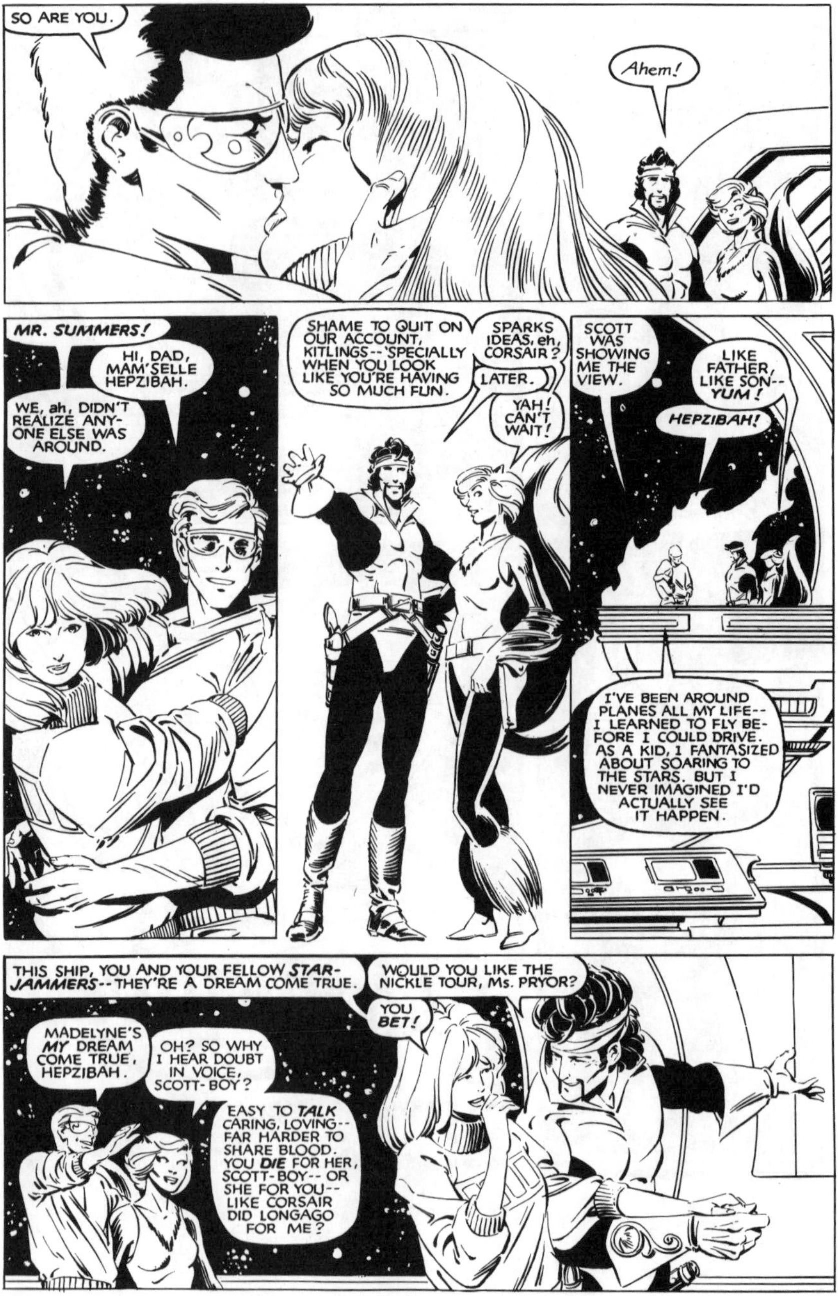
SO ARE YOU.
Ahem!
MR. SUMMERS!
HI, DAD, MAM'SELLE HEPZIBAH.
WE, ah, DIDN'T REALIZE ANY-ONE ELSE WAS AROUND.
SHAME TO QUIT ON OUR ACCOUNT, KITLINGS--'SPECIALLY WHEN YOU LOOK LIKE YOU'RE HAVING SO MUCH FUN.
SPARKS IDEAS, eh, CORSAIR?
LATER.
YAH! CAN'T WAIT!
SCOTT WAS SHOWING ME THE VIEW.
LIKE FATHER, LIKE SON-- YUM!
HEPZIBAH!
I'VE BEEN AROUND PLANES ALL MY LIFE-- I LEARNED TO FLY BE-FORE I COULD DRIVE. AS A KID, I FANTASIZED ABOUT SOARING TO THE STARS. BUT I NEVER IMAGINED I'D ACTUALLY SEE IT HAPPEN.
THIS SHIP, YOU AND YOUR FELLOW STAR-JAMMERS-- THEY'RE A DREAM COME TRUE.
WOULD YOU LIKE THE NICKLE TOUR, Ms. PRYOR?
YOU BET!
MADELYNE'S MY DREAM COME TRUE, HEPZIBAH.
OH? SO WHY I HEAR DOUBT IN VOICE, SCOTT-BOY?
EASY TO TALK CARING, LOVING-- FAR HARDER TO SHARE BLOOD. YOU DIE FOR HER, SCOTT-BOY-- OR SHE FOR YOU-- LIKE CORSAIR DID LONGAGO FOR ME?

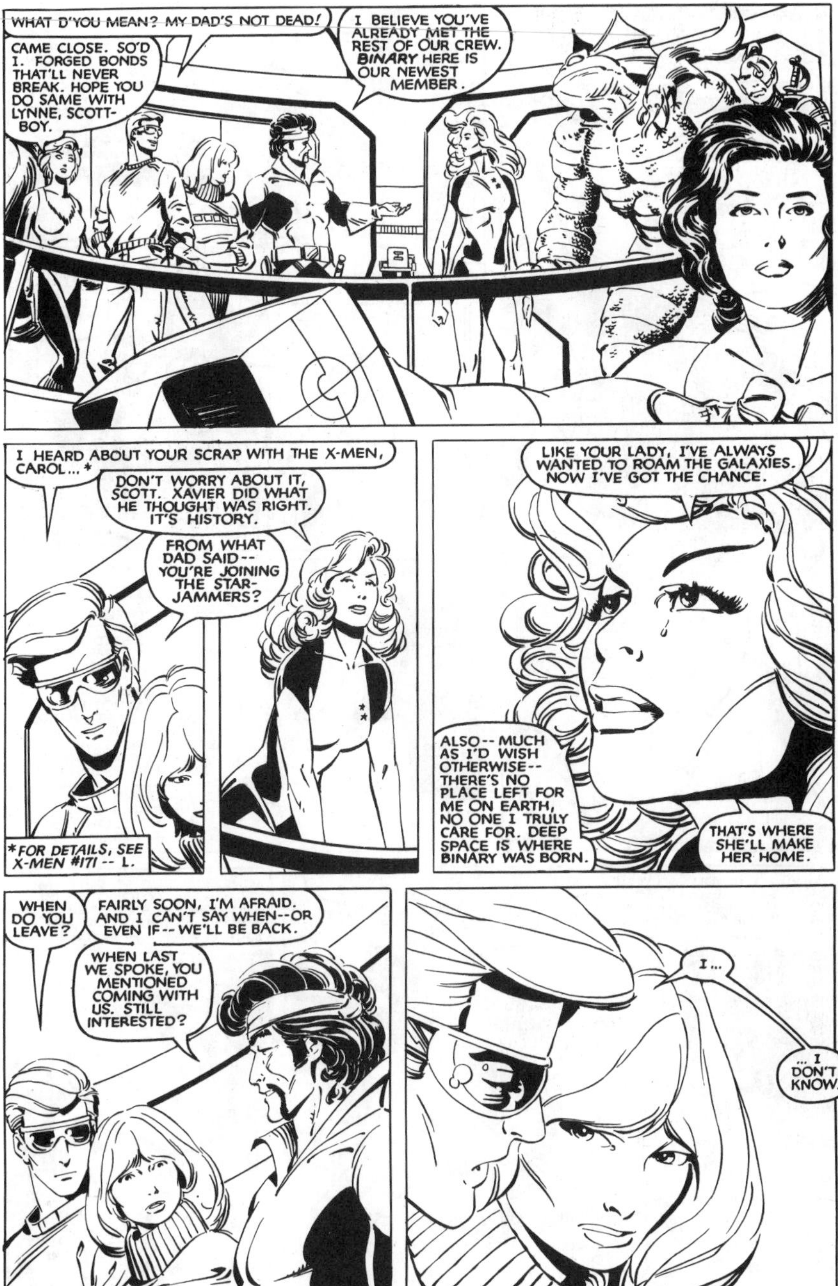
WHAT D'YOU MEAN? MY DAD'S NOT DEAD!
CAME CLOSE. SO'D I. FORGED BONDS THAT'LL NEVER BREAK. HOPE YOU DO SAME WITH LYNNE, SCOTT-BOY.
I BELIEVE YOU'VE ALREADY MET THE REST OF OUR CREW. BINARY HERE IS OUR NEWEST MEMBER.
I HEARD ABOUT YOUR SCRAP WITH THE X-MEN, CAROL...*
DON'T WORRY ABOUT IT, SCOTT. XAVIER DID WHAT HE THOUGHT WAS RIGHT. IT'S HISTORY.
FROM WHAT DAD SAID-- YOU'RE JOINING THE STAR-JAMMERS?
*FOR DETAILS, SEE X-MEN #171 -- L.
LIKE YOUR LADY, I'VE ALWAYS WANTED TO ROAM THE GALAXIES. NOW I'VE GOT THE CHANCE.
ALSO-- MUCH AS I'D WISH OTHERWISE-- THERE'S NO PLACE LEFT FOR ME ON EARTH, NO ONE I TRULY CARE FOR. DEEP SPACE IS WHERE BINARY WAS BORN.
THAT'S WHERE SHE'LL MAKE HER HOME.
WHEN DO YOU LEAVE?
FAIRLY SOON, I'M AFRAID. AND I CAN'T SAY WHEN--OR EVEN IF-- WE'LL BE BACK.
WHEN LAST WE SPOKE, YOU MENTIONED COMING WITH US. STILL INTERESTED?
I...
... I DON'T KNOW.

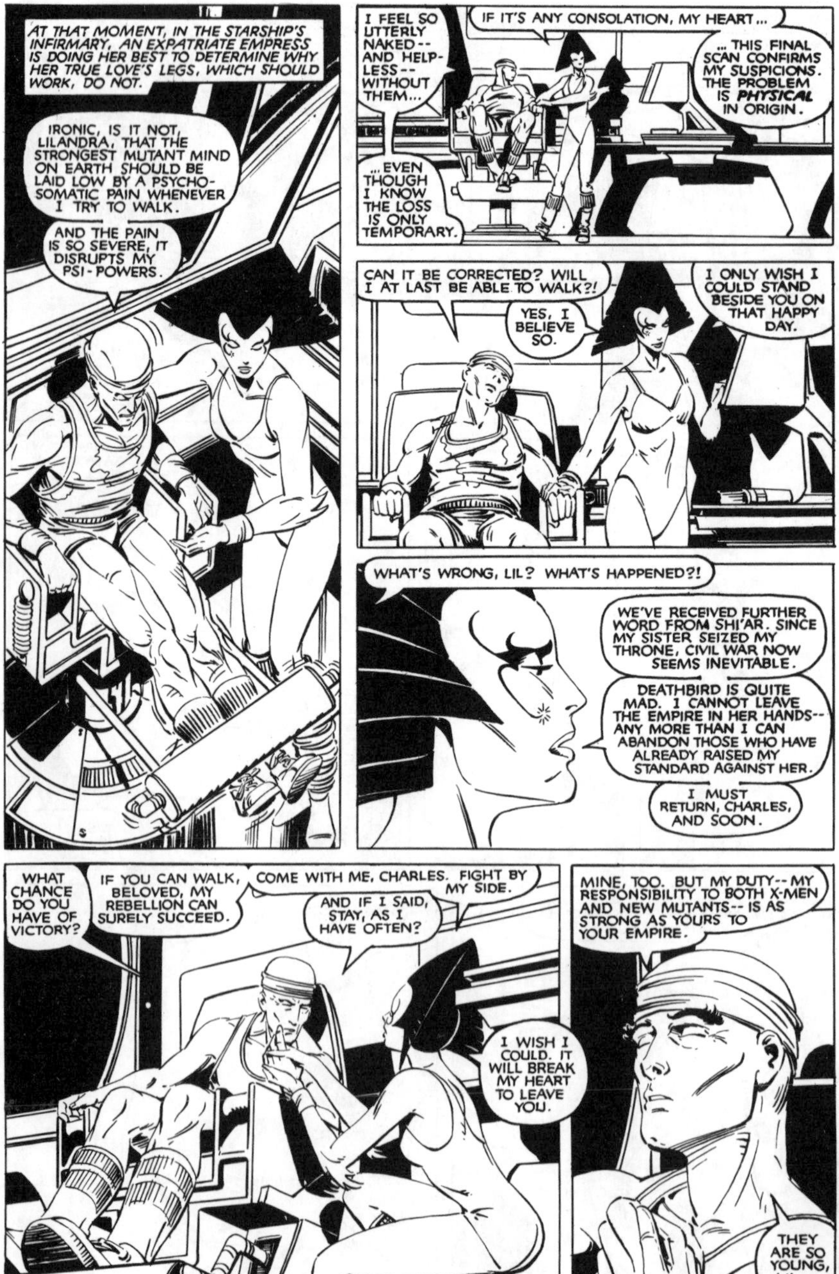
AT THAT MOMENT, IN THE STARSHIP'S INFIRMARY, AN EXPATRIATE EMPRESS IS DOING HER BEST TO DETERMINE WHY HER TRUE LOVE'S LEGS, WHICH SHOULD WORK, DO NOT.
IRONIC, IS IT NOT, LILANDRA, THAT THE STRONGEST MUTANT MIND ON EARTH SHOULD BE LAID LOW BY A PSYCHOSOMATIC PAIN WHENEVER I TRY TO WALK.
AND THE PAIN IS SO SEVERE, IT DISRUPTS MY PSI-POWERS.
I FEEL SO UTTERLY NAKED-- AND HELPLESS-- WITHOUT THEM...
...EVEN THOUGH I KNOW THE LOSS IS ONLY TEMPORARY.
IF IT'S ANY CONSOLATION, MY HEART...
...THIS FINAL SCAN CONFIRMS MY SUSPICIONS. THE PROBLEM IS PHYSICAL IN ORIGIN.
CAN IT BE CORRECTED? WILL I AT LAST BE ABLE TO WALK?!
YES, I BELIEVE SO.
I ONLY WISH I COULD STAND BESIDE YOU ON THAT HAPPY DAY.
WHAT'S WRONG, LIL? WHAT'S HAPPENED?!
WE'VE RECEIVED FURTHER WORD FROM SHI'AR. SINCE MY SISTER SEIZED MY THRONE, CIVIL WAR NOW SEEMS INEVITABLE.
DEATHBIRD IS QUITE MAD. I CANNOT LEAVE THE EMPIRE IN HER HANDS-- ANY MORE THAN I CAN ABANDON THOSE WHO HAVE ALREADY RAISED MY STANDARD AGAINST HER.
I MUST RETURN, CHARLES, AND SOON.
WHAT CHANCE DO YOU HAVE OF VICTORY?
IF YOU CAN WALK, BELOVED, MY REBELLION CAN SURELY SUCCEED.
COME WITH ME, CHARLES. FIGHT BY MY SIDE.
AND IF I SAID, STAY, AS I HAVE OFTEN?
I WISH I COULD. IT WILL BREAK MY HEART TO LEAVE YOU.
MINE, TOO. BUT MY DUTY-- MY RESPONSIBILITY TO BOTH X-MEN AND NEW MUTANTS-- IS AS STRONG AS YOURS TO YOUR EMPIRE.
THEY ARE SO YOUNG, LIL...

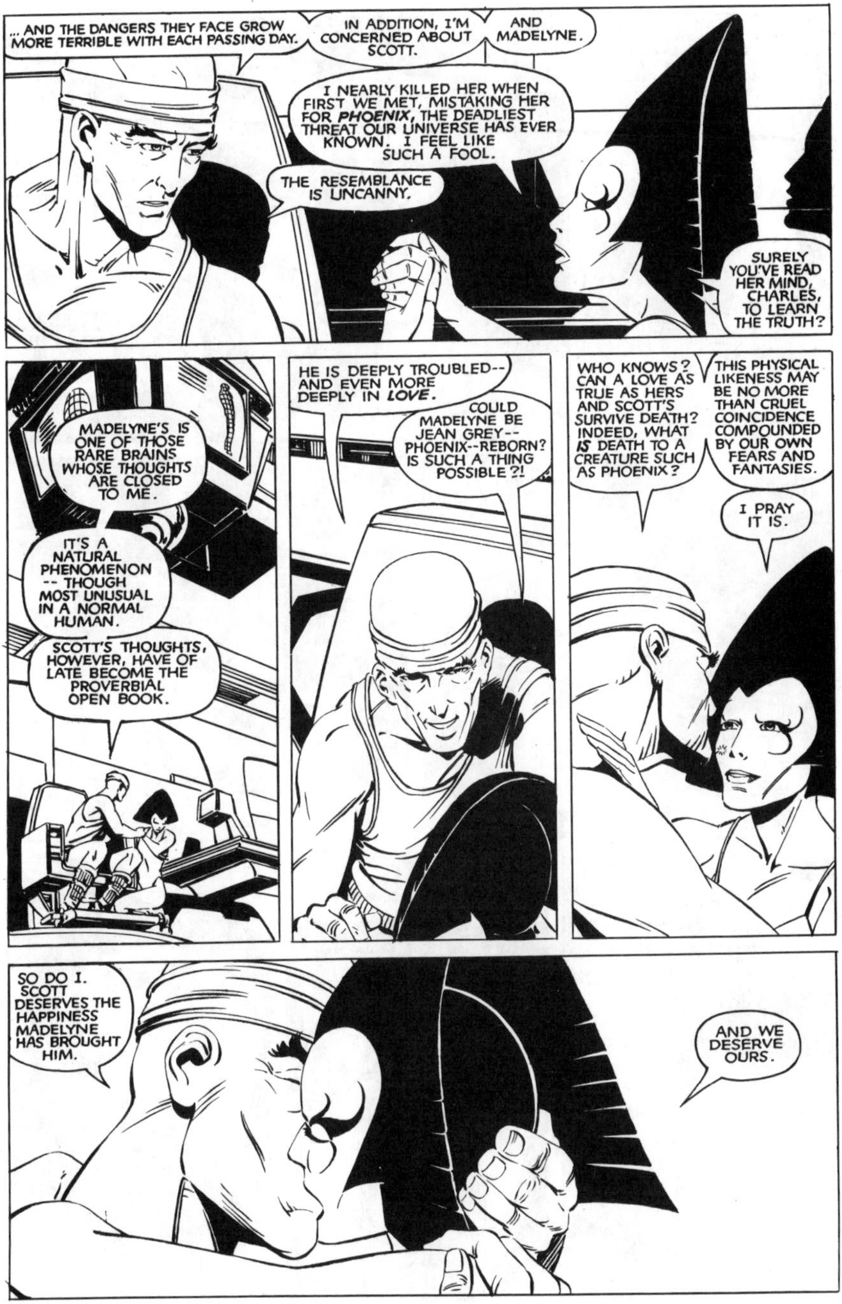
...AND THE DANGERS THEY FACE GROW MORE TERRIBLE WITH EACH PASSING DAY.
IN ADDITION, I'M CONCERNED ABOUT SCOTT.
AND MADELYNE.
I NEARLY KILLED HER WHEN FIRST WE MET, MISTAKING HER FOR PHOENIX, THE DEADLIEST THREAT OUR UNIVERSE HAS EVER KNOWN. I FEEL LIKE SUCH A FOOL.
THE RESEMBLANCE IS UNCANNY.
SURELY YOU'VE READ HER MIND, CHARLES, TO LEARN THE TRUTH?
MADELYNE'S IS ONE OF THOSE RARE BRAINS WHOSE THOUGHTS ARE CLOSED TO ME.
IT'S A NATURAL PHENOMENON -- THOUGH MOST UNUSUAL IN A NORMAL HUMAN.
SCOTT'S THOUGHTS, HOWEVER, HAVE OF LATE BECOME THE PROVERBIAL OPEN BOOK.
HE IS DEEPLY TROUBLED-- AND EVEN MORE DEEPLY IN LOVE.
COULD MADELYNE BE JEAN GREY-- PHOENIX--REBORN? IS SUCH A THING POSSIBLE?!
WHO KNOWS? CAN A LOVE AS TRUE AS HERS AND SCOTT'S SURVIVE DEATH? INDEED, WHAT IS DEATH TO A CREATURE SUCH AS PHOENIX?
THIS PHYSICAL LIKENESS MAY BE NO MORE THAN CRUEL COINCIDENCE COMPOUNDED BY OUR OWN FEARS AND FANTASIES.
I PRAY IT IS.
SO DO I. SCOTT DESERVES THE HAPPINESS MADELYNE HAS BROUGHT HIM.
AND WE DESERVE OURS.

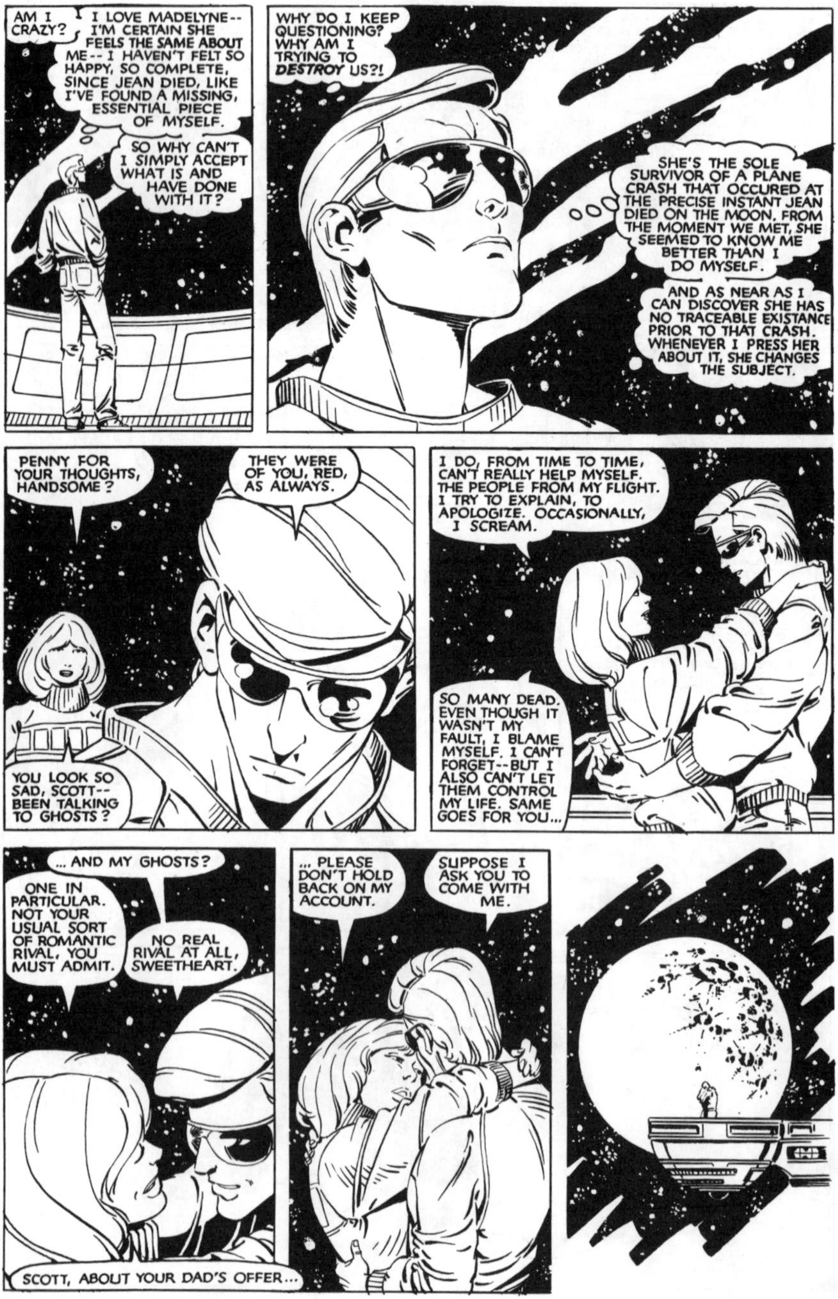
AM I CRAZY?
I LOVE MADELYNE-- I'M CERTAIN SHE FEELS THE SAME ABOUT ME-- I HAVEN'T FELT SO HAPPY, SO COMPLETE, SINCE JEAN DIED, LIKE I'VE FOUND A MISSING, ESSENTIAL PIECE OF MYSELF.
SO WHY CAN'T I SIMPLY ACCEPT WHAT IS AND HAVE DONE WITH IT?
WHY DO I KEEP QUESTIONING? WHY AM I TRYING TO DESTROY US?!
SHE'S THE SOLE SURVIVOR OF A PLANE CRASH THAT OCCURED AT THE PRECISE INSTANT JEAN DIED ON THE MOON. FROM THE MOMENT WE MET, SHE SEEMED TO KNOW ME BETTER THAN I DO MYSELF.
AND AS NEAR AS I CAN DISCOVER SHE HAS NO TRACEABLE EXISTANCE PRIOR TO THAT CRASH. WHENEVER I PRESS HER ABOUT IT, SHE CHANGES THE SUBJECT.
PENNY FOR YOUR THOUGHTS, HANDSOME?
THEY WERE OF YOU, RED, AS ALWAYS.
YOU LOOK SO SAD, SCOTT-- BEEN TALKING TO GHOSTS?
I DO, FROM TIME TO TIME, CAN'T REALLY HELP MYSELF. THE PEOPLE FROM MY FLIGHT. I TRY TO EXPLAIN, TO APOLOGIZE. OCCASIONALLY, I SCREAM.
SO MANY DEAD. EVEN THOUGH IT WASN'T MY FAULT, I BLAME MYSELF. I CAN'T FORGET--BUT I ALSO CAN'T LET THEM CONTROL MY LIFE. SAME GOES FOR YOU...
... AND MY GHOSTS?
ONE IN PARTICULAR. NOT YOUR USUAL SORT OF ROMANTIC RIVAL, YOU MUST ADMIT.
NO REAL RIVAL AT ALL, SWEETHEART.
SCOTT, ABOUT YOUR DAD'S OFFER...
... PLEASE DON'T HOLD BACK ON MY ACCOUNT.
SUPPOSE I ASK YOU TO COME WITH ME.

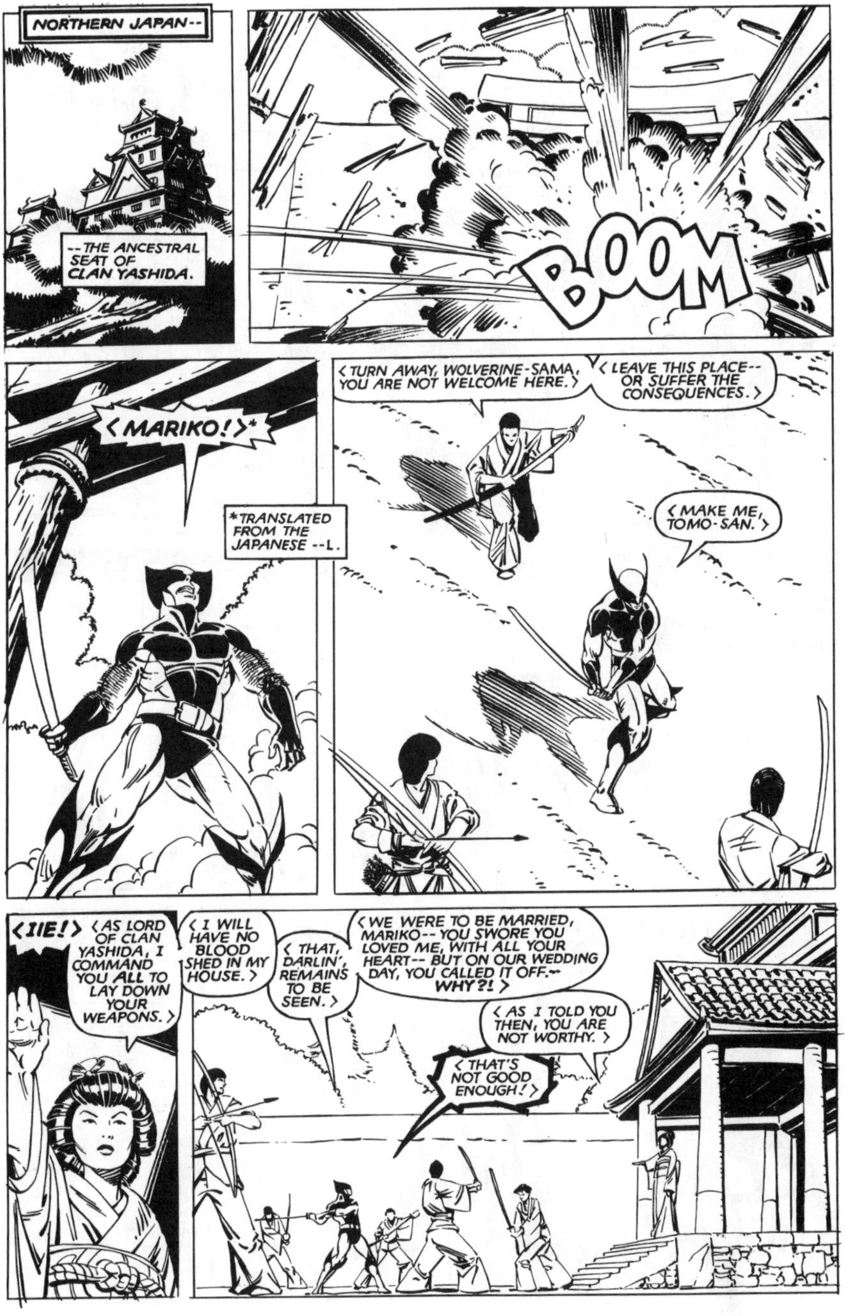

NORTHERN JAPAN--
--THE ANCESTRAL SEAT OF CLAN YASHIDA.
BOOM
<MARIKO!>*
*TRANSLATED FROM THE JAPANESE --L.
<TURN AWAY, WOLVERINE-SAMA, YOU ARE NOT WELCOME HERE.>
<LEAVE THIS PLACE-- OR SUFFER THE CONSEQUENCES.>
<MAKE ME, TOMO-SAN.>
<IIE!>
<AS LORD OF CLAN YASHIDA, I COMMAND YOU ALL TO LAY DOWN YOUR WEAPONS.>
<I WILL HAVE NO BLOOD SHED IN MY HOUSE.>
<THAT, DARLIN', REMAINS TO BE SEEN.>
<WE WERE TO BE MARRIED, MARIKO-- YOU SWORE YOU LOVED ME, WITH ALL YOUR HEART-- BUT ON OUR WEDDING DAY, YOU CALLED IT OFF.-- WHY?!>
<AS I TOLD YOU THEN, YOU ARE NOT WORTHY.>
<THAT'S NOT GOOD ENOUGH!>

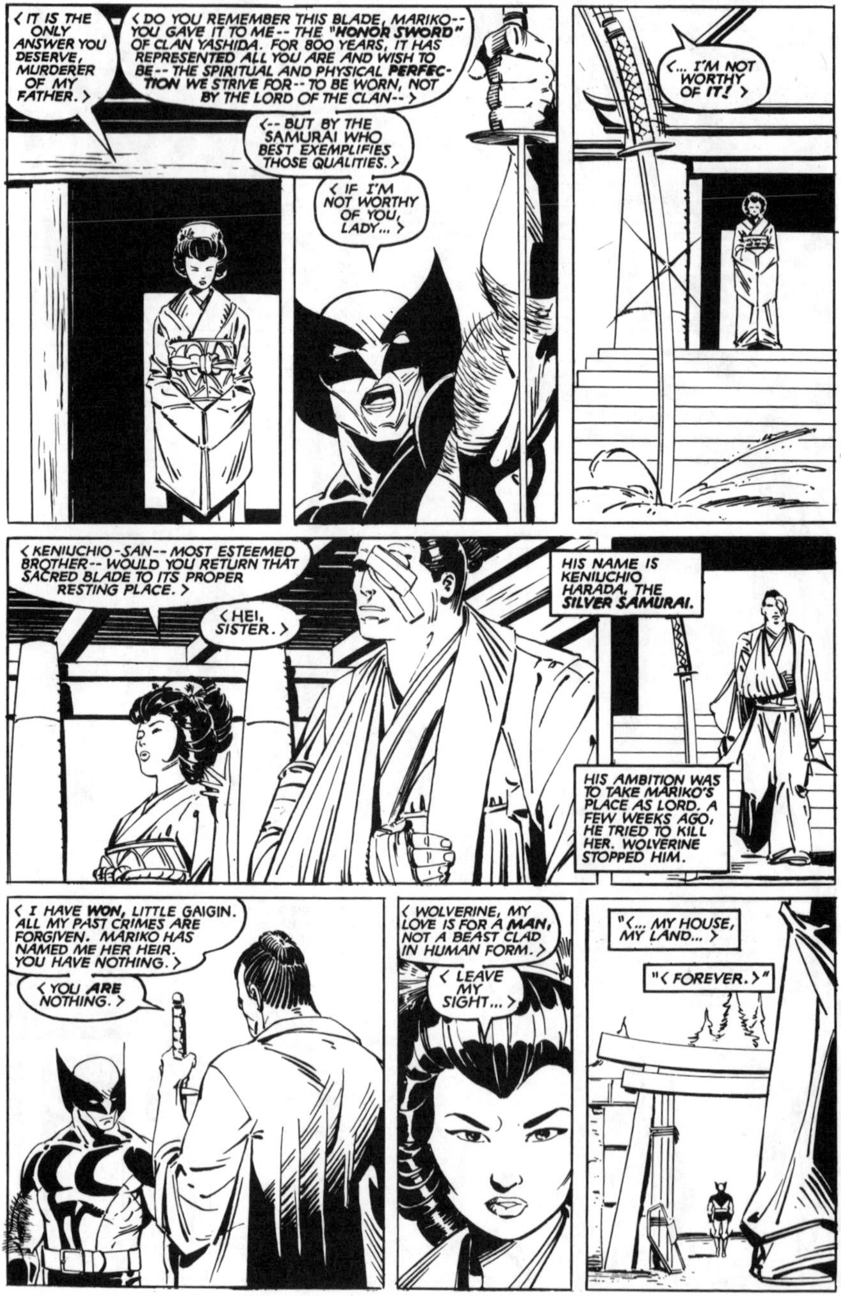

< IT IS THE ONLY ANSWER YOU DESERVE, MURDERER OF MY FATHER. >
< DO YOU REMEMBER THIS BLADE, MARIKO-- YOU GAVE IT TO ME-- THE "HONOR SWORD" OF CLAN YASHIDA. FOR 800 YEARS, IT HAS REPRESENTED ALL YOU ARE AND WISH TO BE-- THE SPIRITUAL AND PHYSICAL PERFECTION WE STRIVE FOR-- TO BE WORN, NOT BY THE LORD OF THE CLAN-- >
<-- BUT BY THE SAMURAI WHO BEST EXEMPLIFIES THOSE QUALITIES. >
< IF I'M NOT WORTHY OF YOU, LADY... >
<... I'M NOT WORTHY OF IT! >
< KENIUCHIO-SAN-- MOST ESTEEMED BROTHER-- WOULD YOU RETURN THAT SACRED BLADE TO ITS PROPER RESTING PLACE. >
< HEI, SISTER. >
HIS NAME IS KENIUCHIO HARADA, THE SILVER SAMURAI.
HIS AMBITION WAS TO TAKE MARIKO'S PLACE AS LORD. A FEW WEEKS AGO, HE TRIED TO KILL HER. WOLVERINE STOPPED HIM.
< I HAVE WON, LITTLE GAIGIN. ALL MY PAST CRIMES ARE FORGIVEN. MARIKO HAS NAMED ME HER HEIR. YOU HAVE NOTHING. >
< YOU ARE NOTHING. >
< WOLVERINE, MY LOVE IS FOR A MAN, NOT A BEAST CLAD IN HUMAN FORM. >
< LEAVE MY SIGHT... >
"<... MY HOUSE, MY LAND... >
"< FOREVER. >"

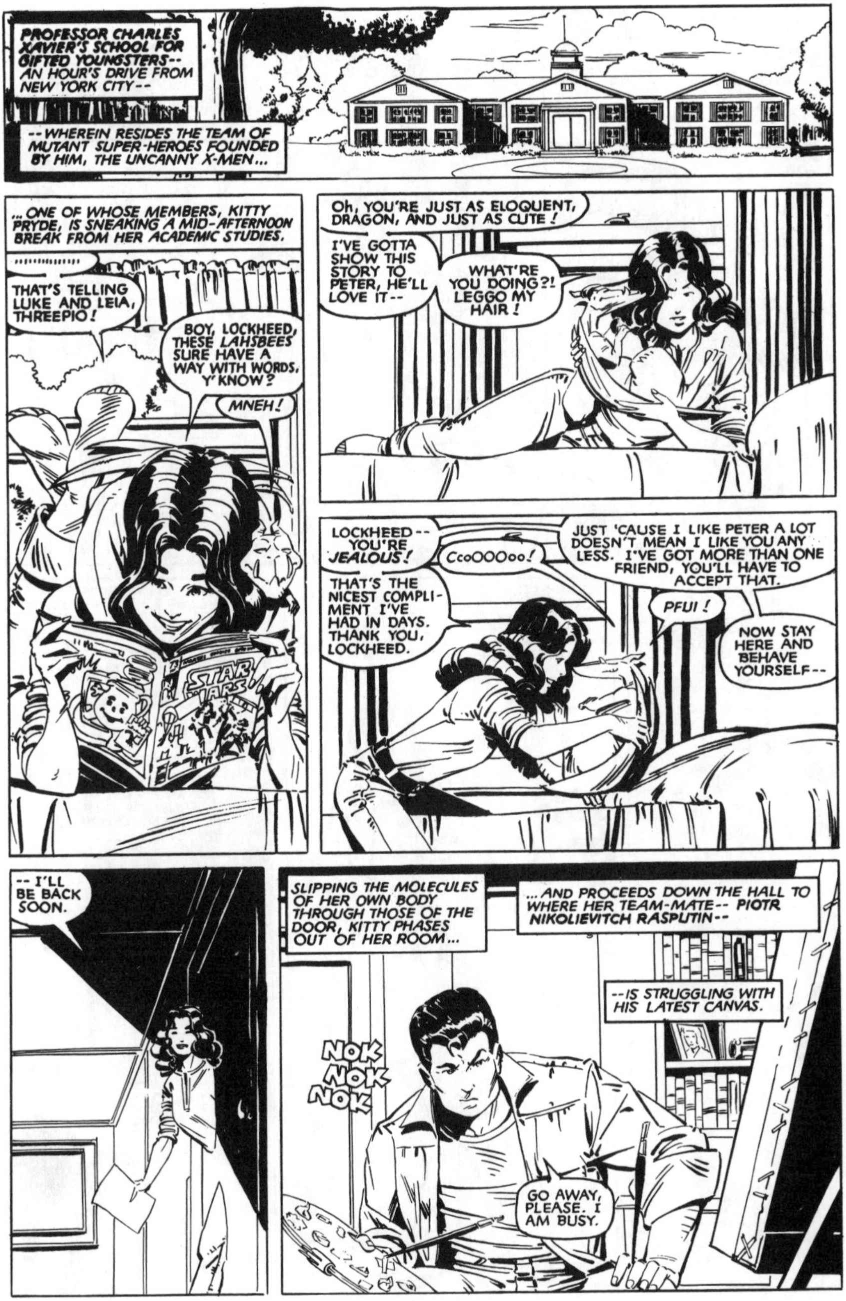

PROFESSOR CHARLES XAVIER'S SCHOOL FOR GIFTED YOUNGSTERS-- AN HOUR'S DRIVE FROM NEW YORK CITY--
--WHEREIN RESIDES THE TEAM OF MUTANT SUPER-HEROES FOUNDED BY HIM, THE UNCANNY X-MEN...
...ONE OF WHOSE MEMBERS, KITTY PRYDE, IS SNEAKING A MID-AFTERNOON BREAK FROM HER ACADEMIC STUDIES.
....
THAT'S TELLING LUKE AND LEIA, THREEPIO!
BOY, LOCKHEED, THESE LAHSBEES SURE HAVE A WAY WITH WORDS, Y'KNOW?
MNEH!
STAR WARS
Oh, YOU'RE JUST AS ELOQUENT, DRAGON, AND JUST AS CUTE!
I'VE GOTTA SHOW THIS STORY TO PETER, HE'LL LOVE IT--
WHAT'RE YOU DOING?! LEGGO MY HAIR!
LOCKHEED-- YOU'RE JEALOUS!
CcoOOOoo!
THAT'S THE NICEST COMPLIMENT I'VE HAD IN DAYS. THANK YOU, LOCKHEED.
JUST 'CAUSE I LIKE PETER A LOT DOESN'T MEAN I LIKE YOU ANY LESS. I'VE GOT MORE THAN ONE FRIEND, YOU'LL HAVE TO ACCEPT THAT.
PFUI!
NOW STAY HERE AND BEHAVE YOURSELF--
-- I'LL BE BACK SOON.
SLIPPING THE MOLECULES OF HER OWN BODY THROUGH THOSE OF THE DOOR, KITTY PHASES OUT OF HER ROOM...
...AND PROCEEDS DOWN THE HALL TO WHERE HER TEAM-MATE-- PIOTR NIKOLIEVITCH RASPUTIN--
--IS STRUGGLING WITH HIS LATEST CANVAS.
NOK NOK NOK
GO AWAY, PLEASE. I AM BUSY.

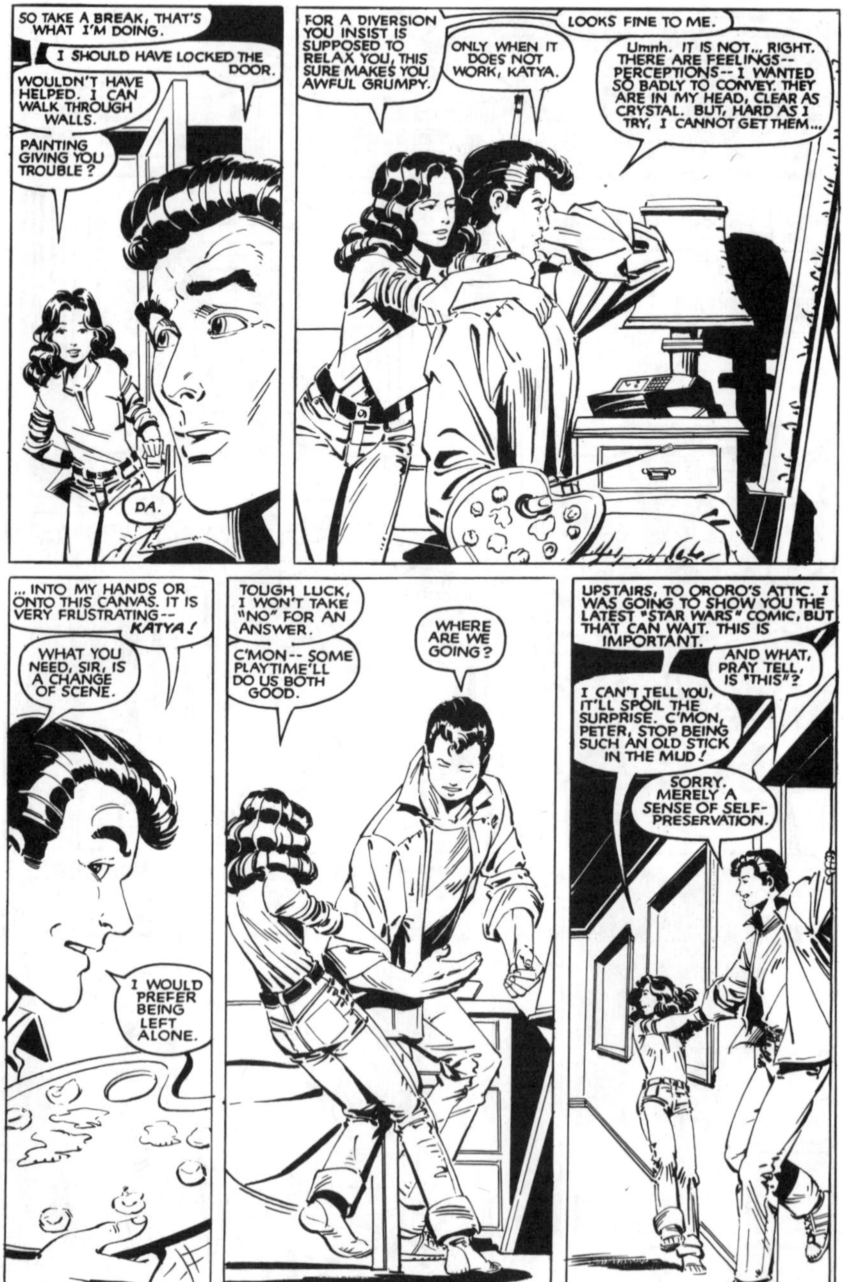
SO TAKE A BREAK, THAT'S WHAT I'M DOING.
I SHOULD HAVE LOCKED THE DOOR.
WOULDN'T HAVE HELPED. I CAN WALK THROUGH WALLS.
PAINTING GIVING YOU TROUBLE?
DA.
FOR A DIVERSION YOU INSIST IS SUPPOSED TO RELAX YOU, THIS SURE MAKES YOU AWFUL GRUMPY.
ONLY WHEN IT DOES NOT WORK, KATYA.
LOOKS FINE TO ME.
Umnh. IT IS NOT... RIGHT. THERE ARE FEELINGS-- PERCEPTIONS-- I WANTED SO BADLY TO CONVEY. THEY ARE IN MY HEAD, CLEAR AS CRYSTAL. BUT, HARD AS I TRY, I CANNOT GET THEM...
... INTO MY HANDS OR ONTO THIS CANVAS. IT IS VERY FRUSTRATING-- KATYA!
WHAT YOU NEED, SIR, IS A CHANGE OF SCENE.
I WOULD PREFER BEING LEFT ALONE.
TOUGH LUCK, I WON'T TAKE "NO" FOR AN ANSWER.
C'MON-- SOME PLAYTIME'LL DO US BOTH GOOD.
WHERE ARE WE GOING?
UPSTAIRS, TO ORORO'S ATTIC. I WAS GOING TO SHOW YOU THE LATEST "STAR WARS" COMIC, BUT THAT CAN WAIT. THIS IS IMPORTANT.
AND WHAT, PRAY TELL, IS "THIS"?
I CAN'T TELL YOU, IT'LL SPOIL THE SURPRISE. C'MON, PETER, STOP BEING SUCH AN OLD STICK IN THE MUD!
SORRY. MERELY A SENSE OF SELF-PRESERVATION.

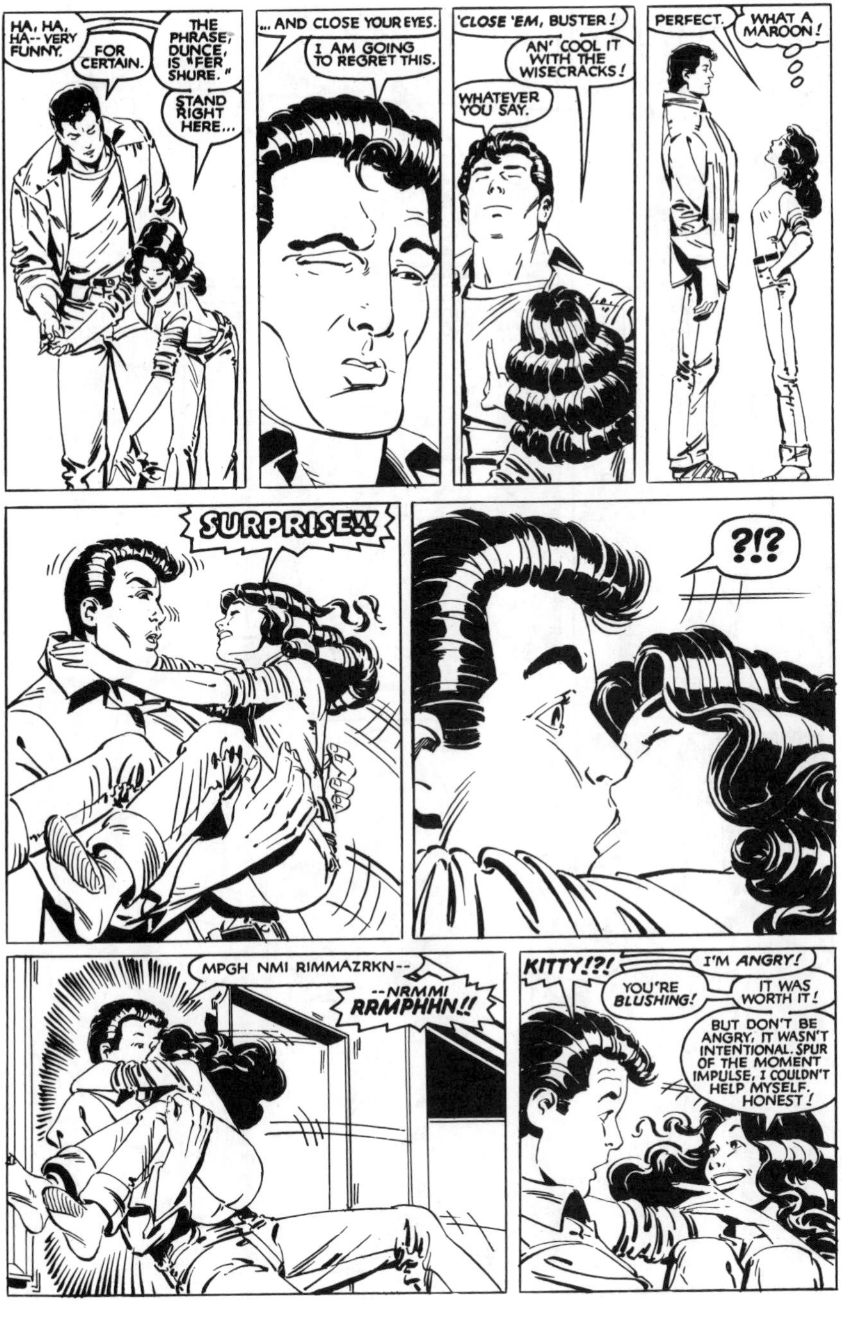
HA, HA, HA-- VERY FUNNY.
FOR CERTAIN.
THE PHRASE, DUNCE, IS "FER SHURE."
STAND RIGHT HERE...
... AND CLOSE YOUR EYES.
I AM GOING TO REGRET THIS.
'CLOSE 'EM, BUSTER!
AN' COOL IT WITH THE WISECRACKS!
WHATEVER YOU SAY.
PERFECT.
WHAT A MAROON!
SURPRISE!!
?!?
MPGH NMI RIMMAZRKN--
--NRMMI RRMPHHN!!
KITTY!?!
I'M ANGRY!
YOU'RE BLUSHING!
IT WAS WORTH IT!
BUT DON'T BE ANGRY, IT WASN'T INTENTIONAL. SPUR OF THE MOMENT IMPULSE, I COULDN'T HELP MYSELF. HONEST!

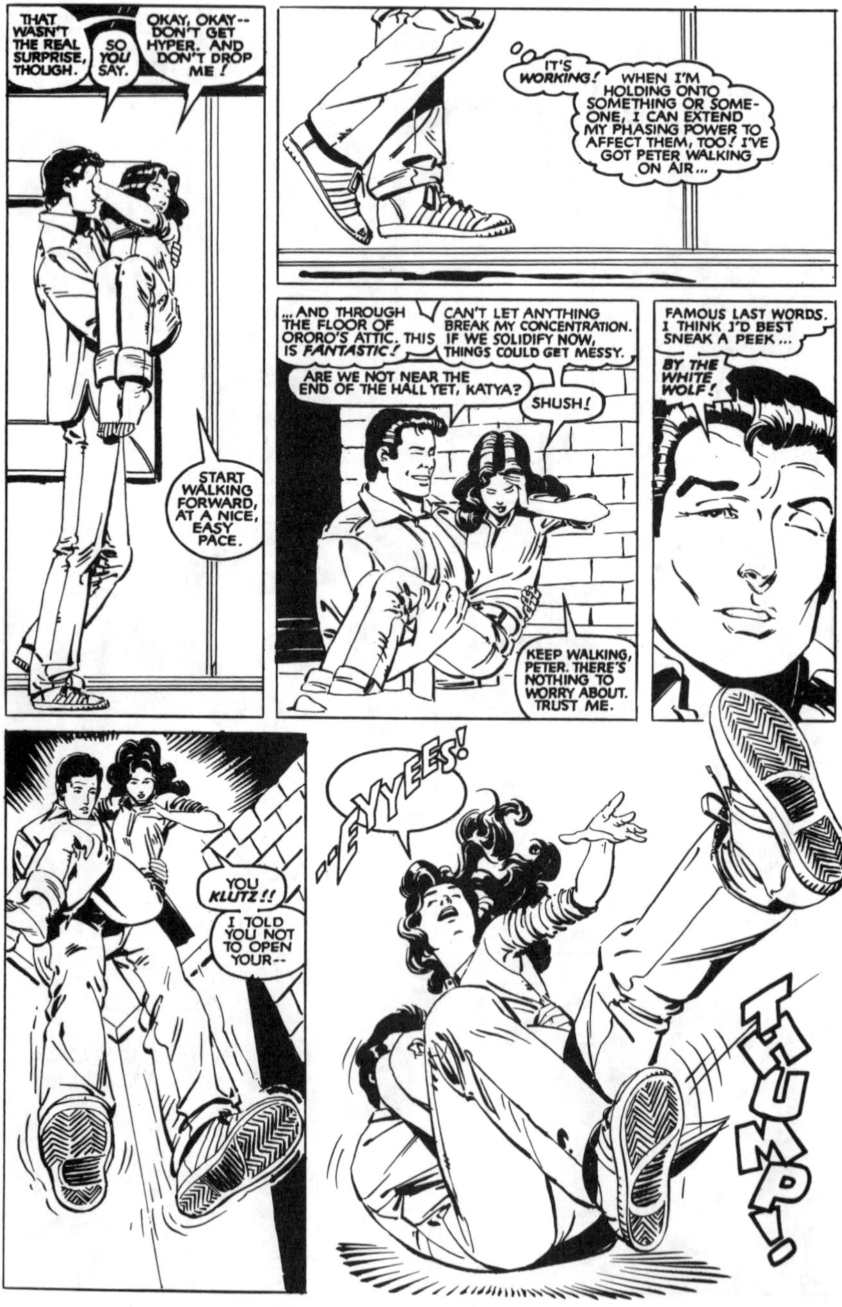
THAT WASN'T THE REAL SURPRISE, THOUGH.
SO YOU SAY.
OKAY, OKAY-- DON'T GET HYPER. AND DON'T DROP ME!
START WALKING FORWARD, AT A NICE, EASY PACE.
IT'S WORKING! WHEN I'M HOLDING ONTO SOMETHING OR SOME-ONE, I CAN EXTEND MY PHASING POWER TO AFFECT THEM, TOO! I'VE GOT PETER WALKING ON AIR...
...AND THROUGH THE FLOOR OF ORORO'S ATTIC. THIS IS FANTASTIC!
CAN'T LET ANYTHING BREAK MY CONCENTRATION. IF WE SOLIDIFY NOW, THINGS COULD GET MESSY.
ARE WE NOT NEAR THE END OF THE HALL YET, KATYA?
SHUSH!
KEEP WALKING, PETER. THERE'S NOTHING TO WORRY ABOUT. TRUST ME.
FAMOUS LAST WORDS. I THINK I'D BEST SNEAK A PEEK...
BY THE WHITE WOLF!
YOU KLUTZ!!
I TOLD YOU NOT TO OPEN YOUR--
--EYYEES!
THUMP!

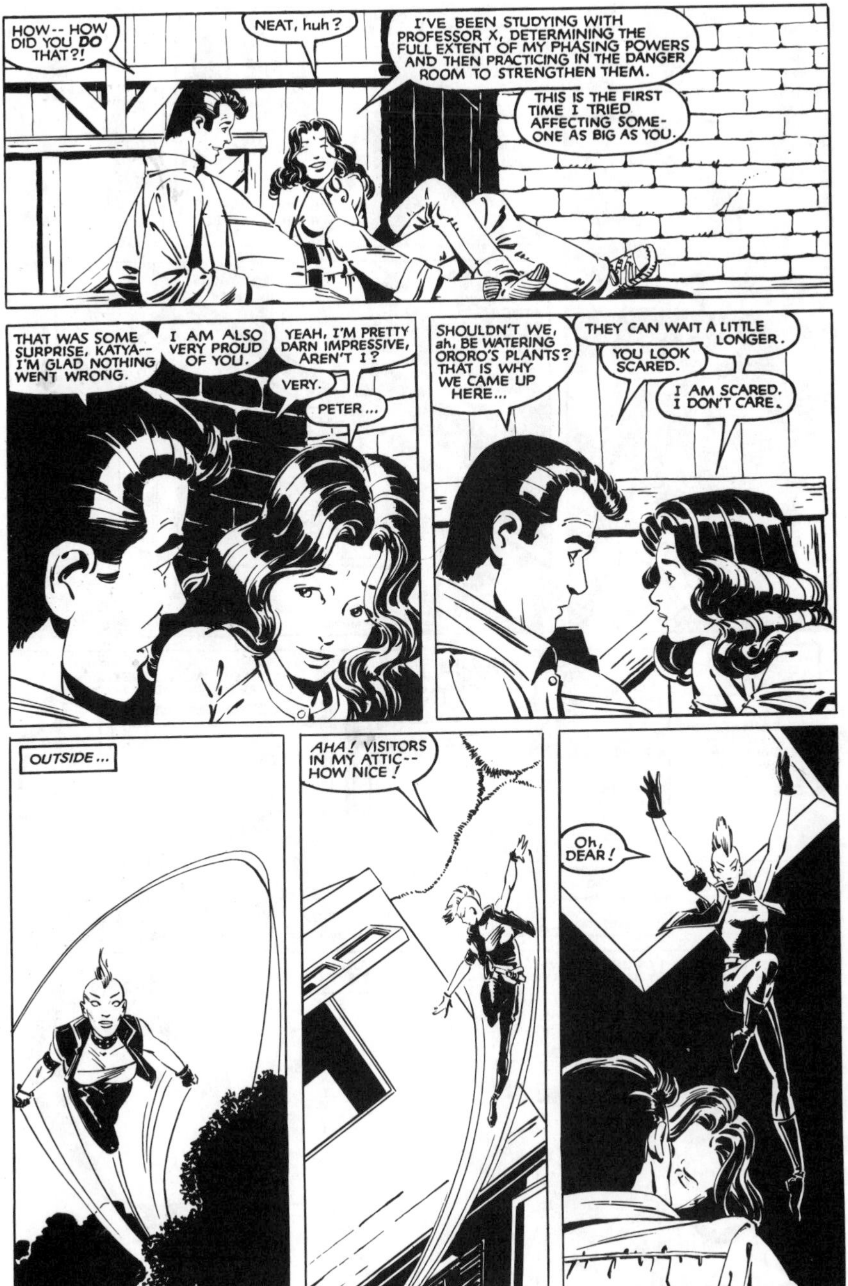
HOW-- HOW DID YOU DO THAT?!
NEAT, huh?
I'VE BEEN STUDYING WITH PROFESSOR X, DETERMINING THE FULL EXTENT OF MY PHASING POWERS AND THEN PRACTICING IN THE DANGER ROOM TO STRENGTHEN THEM.
THIS IS THE FIRST TIME I TRIED AFFECTING SOMEONE AS BIG AS YOU.
THAT WAS SOME SURPRISE, KATYA-- I'M GLAD NOTHING WENT WRONG.
I AM ALSO VERY PROUD OF YOU.
YEAH, I'M PRETTY DARN IMPRESSIVE, AREN'T I?
VERY.
PETER...
SHOULDN'T WE, ah, BE WATERING ORORO'S PLANTS? THAT IS WHY WE CAME UP HERE...
THEY CAN WAIT A LITTLE LONGER.
YOU LOOK SCARED.
I AM SCARED. I DON'T CARE.
OUTSIDE...
AHA! VISITORS IN MY ATTIC-- HOW NICE!
Oh, DEAR!

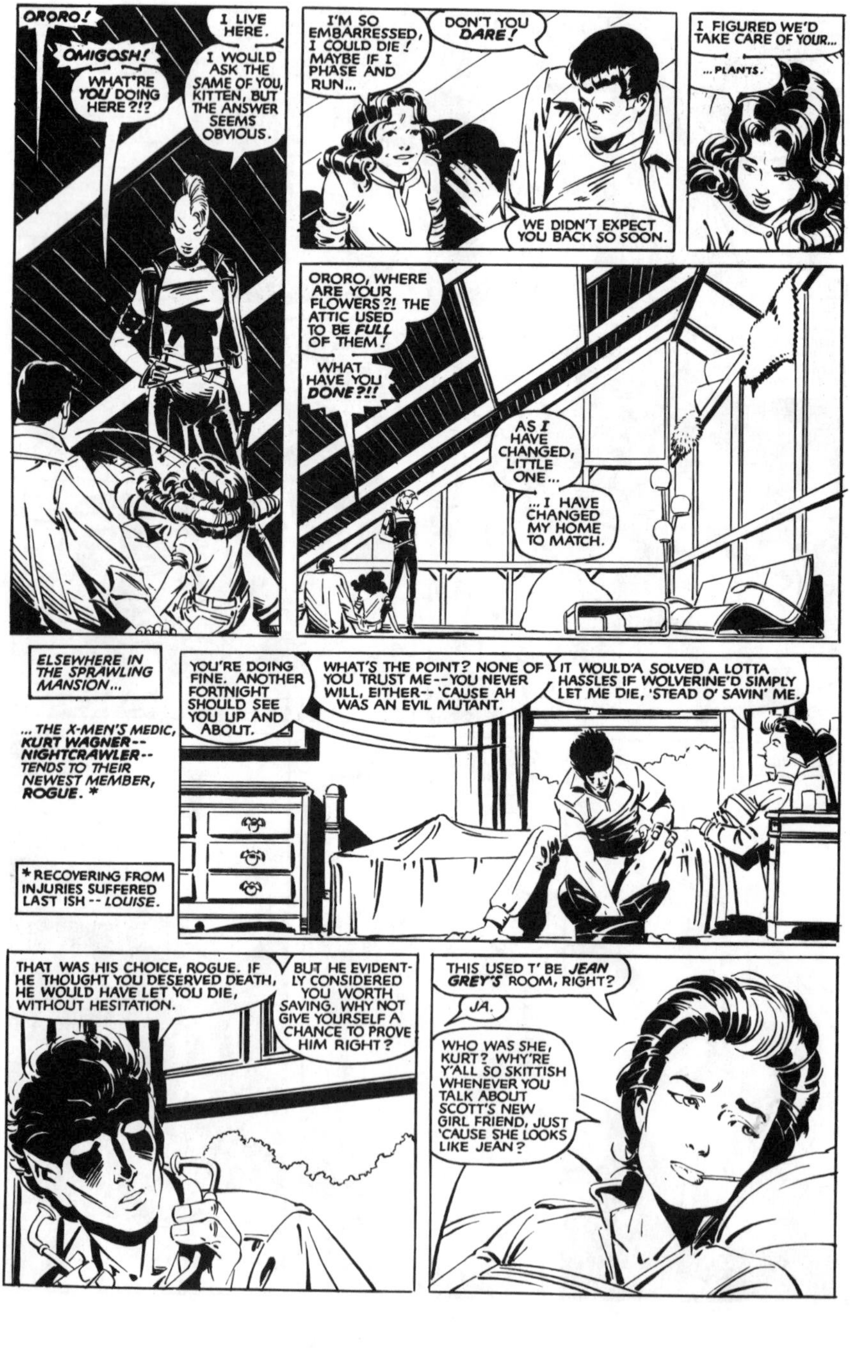
ORORO!
OMIGOSH!
WHAT'RE YOU DOING HERE?!?
I LIVE HERE.
I WOULD ASK THE SAME OF YOU, KITTEN, BUT THE ANSWER SEEMS OBVIOUS.
I'M SO EMBARRESSED, I COULD DIE! MAYBE IF I PHASE AND RUN...
DON'T YOU DARE!
WE DIDN'T EXPECT YOU BACK SO SOON.
I FIGURED WE'D TAKE CARE OF YOUR...
...PLANTS.
ORORO, WHERE ARE YOUR FLOWERS?! THE ATTIC USED TO BE FULL OF THEM!
WHAT HAVE YOU DONE?!!
AS I HAVE CHANGED, LITTLE ONE...
...I HAVE CHANGED MY HOME TO MATCH.
ELSEWHERE IN THE SPRAWLING MANSION...
...THE X-MEN'S MEDIC, KURT WAGNER--NIGHTCRAWLER--TENDS TO THEIR NEWEST MEMBER, ROGUE. *
* RECOVERING FROM INJURIES SUFFERED LAST ISH -- LOUISE.
YOU'RE DOING FINE. ANOTHER FORTNIGHT SHOULD SEE YOU UP AND ABOUT.
WHAT'S THE POINT? NONE OF YOU TRUST ME--YOU NEVER WILL, EITHER--'CAUSE AH WAS AN EVIL MUTANT.
IT WOULD'A SOLVED A LOTTA HASSLES IF WOLVERINE'D SIMPLY LET ME DIE, 'STEAD O' SAVIN' ME.
THAT WAS HIS CHOICE, ROGUE. IF HE THOUGHT YOU DESERVED DEATH, HE WOULD HAVE LET YOU DIE, WITHOUT HESITATION.
BUT HE EVIDENTLY CONSIDERED YOU WORTH SAVING. WHY NOT GIVE YOURSELF A CHANCE TO PROVE HIM RIGHT?
THIS USED T' BE JEAN GREY'S ROOM, RIGHT?
JA.
WHO WAS SHE, KURT? WHY'RE Y'ALL SO SKITTISH WHENEVER YOU TALK ABOUT SCOTT'S NEW GIRL FRIEND, JUST 'CAUSE SHE LOOKS LIKE JEAN?

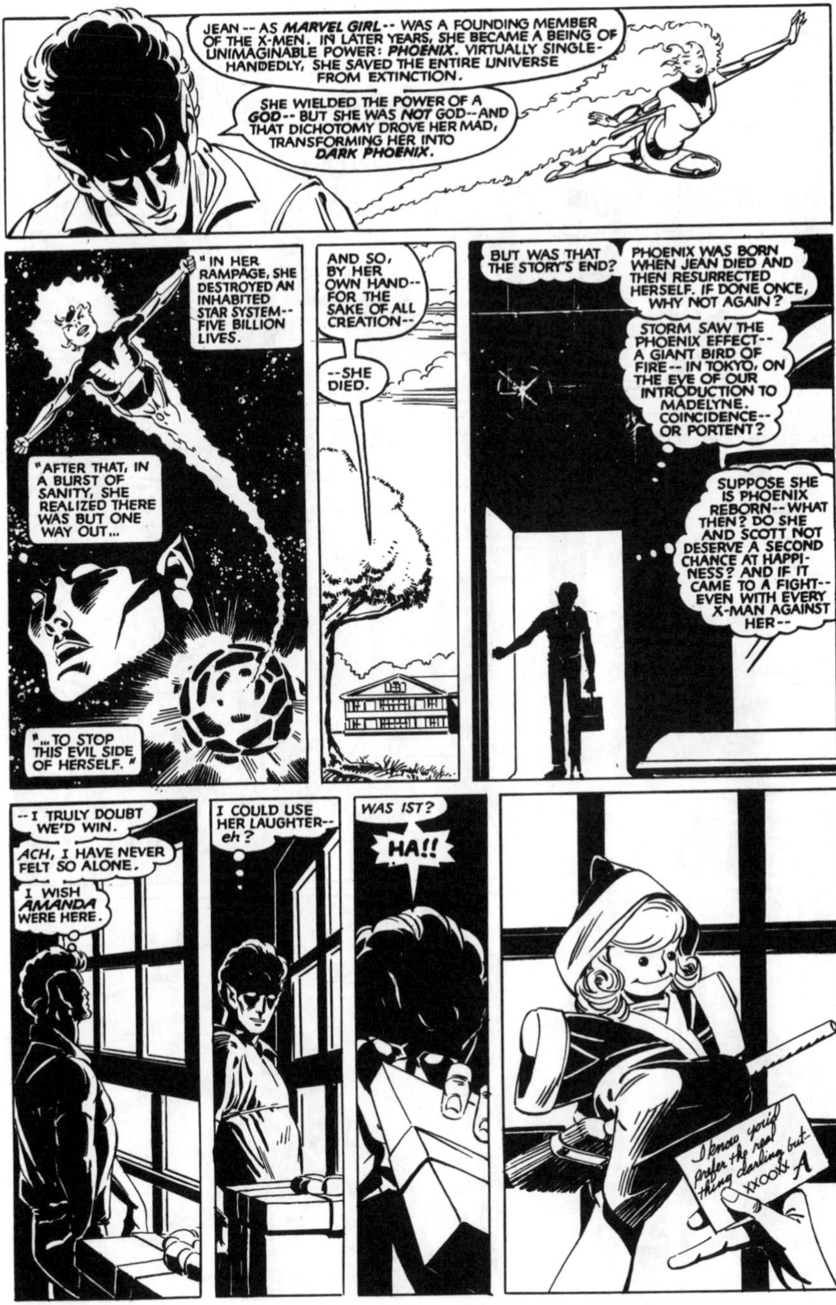
JEAN -- AS MARVEL GIRL -- WAS A FOUNDING MEMBER OF THE X-MEN. IN LATER YEARS, SHE BECAME A BEING OF UNIMAGINABLE POWER: PHOENIX. VIRTUALLY SINGLE-HANDEDLY, SHE SAVED THE ENTIRE UNIVERSE FROM EXTINCTION.
SHE WIELDED THE POWER OF A GOD -- BUT SHE WAS NOT GOD -- AND THAT DICHOTOMY DROVE HER MAD, TRANSFORMING HER INTO DARK PHOENIX.
"IN HER RAMPAGE, SHE DESTROYED AN INHABITED STAR SYSTEM -- FIVE BILLION LIVES.
"AFTER THAT, IN A BURST OF SANITY, SHE REALIZED THERE WAS BUT ONE WAY OUT...
"...TO STOP THIS EVIL SIDE OF HERSELF."
AND SO, BY HER OWN HAND -- FOR THE SAKE OF ALL CREATION --
-- SHE DIED.
BUT WAS THAT THE STORY'S END?
PHOENIX WAS BORN WHEN JEAN DIED AND THEN RESURRECTED HERSELF. IF DONE ONCE, WHY NOT AGAIN?
STORM SAW THE PHOENIX EFFECT -- A GIANT BIRD OF FIRE -- IN TOKYO, ON THE EVE OF OUR INTRODUCTION TO MADELYNE. COINCIDENCE -- OR PORTENT?
SUPPOSE SHE IS PHOENIX REBORN -- WHAT THEN? DO SHE AND SCOTT NOT DESERVE A SECOND CHANCE AT HAPPINESS? AND IF IT CAME TO A FIGHT -- EVEN WITH EVERY X-MAN AGAINST HER --
-- I TRULY DOUBT WE'D WIN.
ACH, I HAVE NEVER FELT SO ALONE.
I WISH AMANDA WERE HERE.
I COULD USE HER LAUGHTER -- eh?
WAS IST?
HA!!
I know you'd prefer the real thing darling but... XXOOXX A

...ABOARD A NORTHSTAR AIRWAYS FLIGHT, BOUND FOR ANCHORAGE...

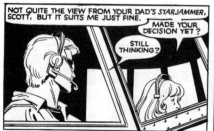

NOT QUITE THE VIEW FROM YOUR DAD'S *STARJAMMER,* SCOTT, BUT IT SUITS ME JUST FINE.

MADE YOUR DECISION YET?

STILL THINKING?

I GUESS THIS RING COMPLICATES MATTERS.

WHATEVER HAPPENS, I WANTED YOU TO KNOW HOW I FELT.

IT'S MUTUAL, SWEETHEART-- 'TIL DEATH DO US PART.

THAT'S THE IDEA.

HOLD THE FORT, RED. I'LL CHECK ON THE PASSENGERS.

RIGHT TO THE END, I WAS POSITIVE I'D CHICKEN OUT-- BUT I DID IT, I ACTUALLY PROPOSED.

AND MADELYNE ACCEPTED.

I DON'T KNOW THE TRUTH ABOUT HER--

--PERHAPS I NEVER WILL-- BUT THAT DOESN'T REALLY MATTER. I'LL LOVE HER JUST THE SAME.

WE'LL BE LANDING SOON, GENTS. PLEASE FASTEN YOUR SEATBELTS...

...AND MAKE SURE YOUR PERSONAL GEAR IS SAFELY STOWED.

YOUNG MAN? PILOT!

YESSIR?

SORRY T' BOTHER YE, LAD, BUT I B'LIEVE YE DROPPED THIS AS YE PASSED.

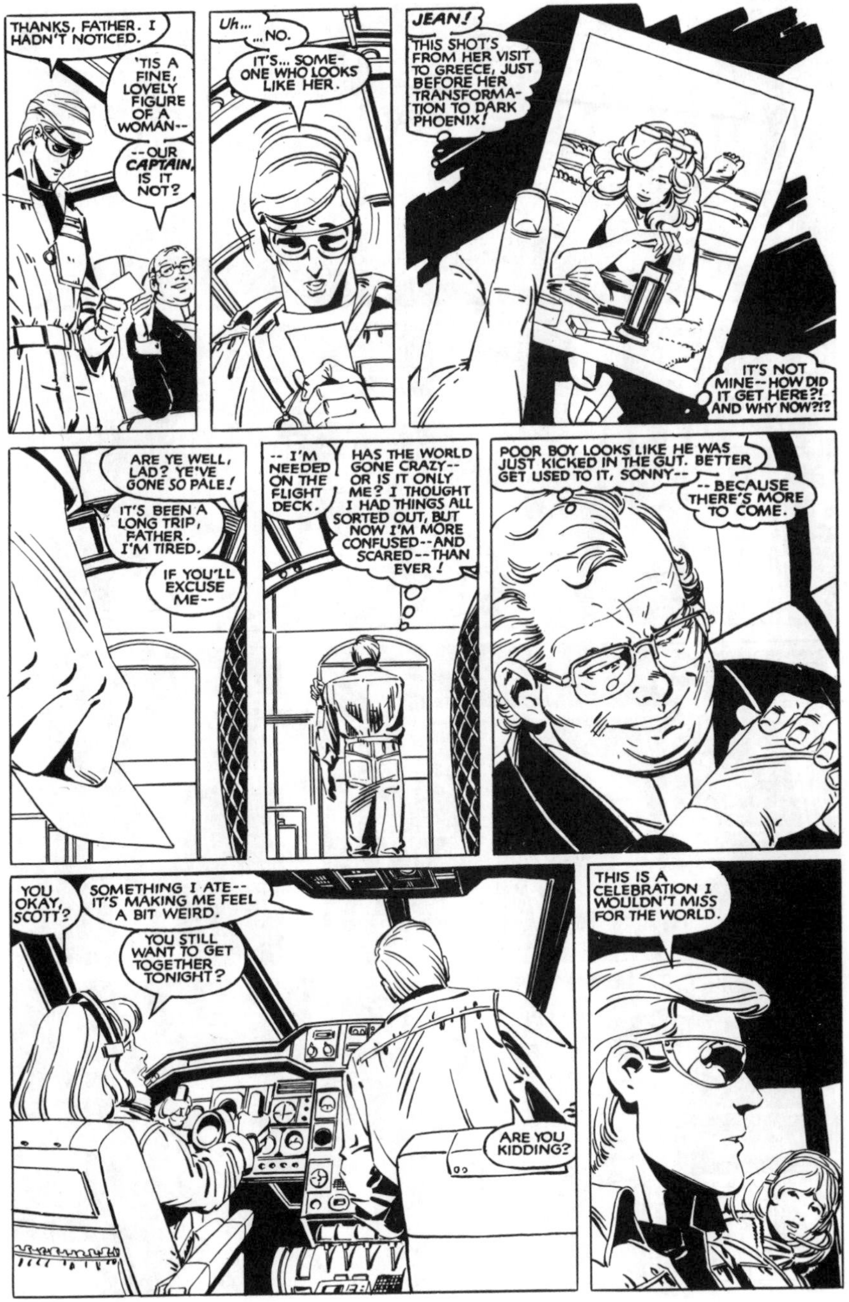
THANKS, FATHER. I HADN'T NOTICED.
'TIS A FINE, LOVELY FIGURE OF A WOMAN--
--OUR CAPTAIN, IS IT NOT?
Uh...
...NO.
IT'S... SOME-ONE WHO LOOKS LIKE HER.
JEAN!
THIS SHOT'S FROM HER VISIT TO GREECE, JUST BEFORE HER TRANSFORMA-TION TO DARK PHOENIX!
IT'S NOT MINE--HOW DID IT GET HERE?! AND WHY NOW?!?
ARE YE WELL, LAD? YE'VE GONE SO PALE!
IT'S BEEN A LONG TRIP, FATHER. I'M TIRED.
IF YOU'LL EXCUSE ME--
-- I'M NEEDED ON THE FLIGHT DECK.
HAS THE WORLD GONE CRAZY-- OR IS IT ONLY ME? I THOUGHT I HAD THINGS ALL SORTED OUT, BUT NOW I'M MORE CONFUSED--AND SCARED--THAN EVER!
POOR BOY LOOKS LIKE HE WAS JUST KICKED IN THE GUT. BETTER GET USED TO IT, SONNY--
-- BECAUSE THERE'S MORE TO COME.
YOU OKAY, SCOTT?
SOMETHING I ATE-- IT'S MAKING ME FEEL A BIT WEIRD.
YOU STILL WANT TO GET TOGETHER TONIGHT?
ARE YOU KIDDING?
THIS IS A CELEBRATION I WOULDN'T MISS FOR THE WORLD.

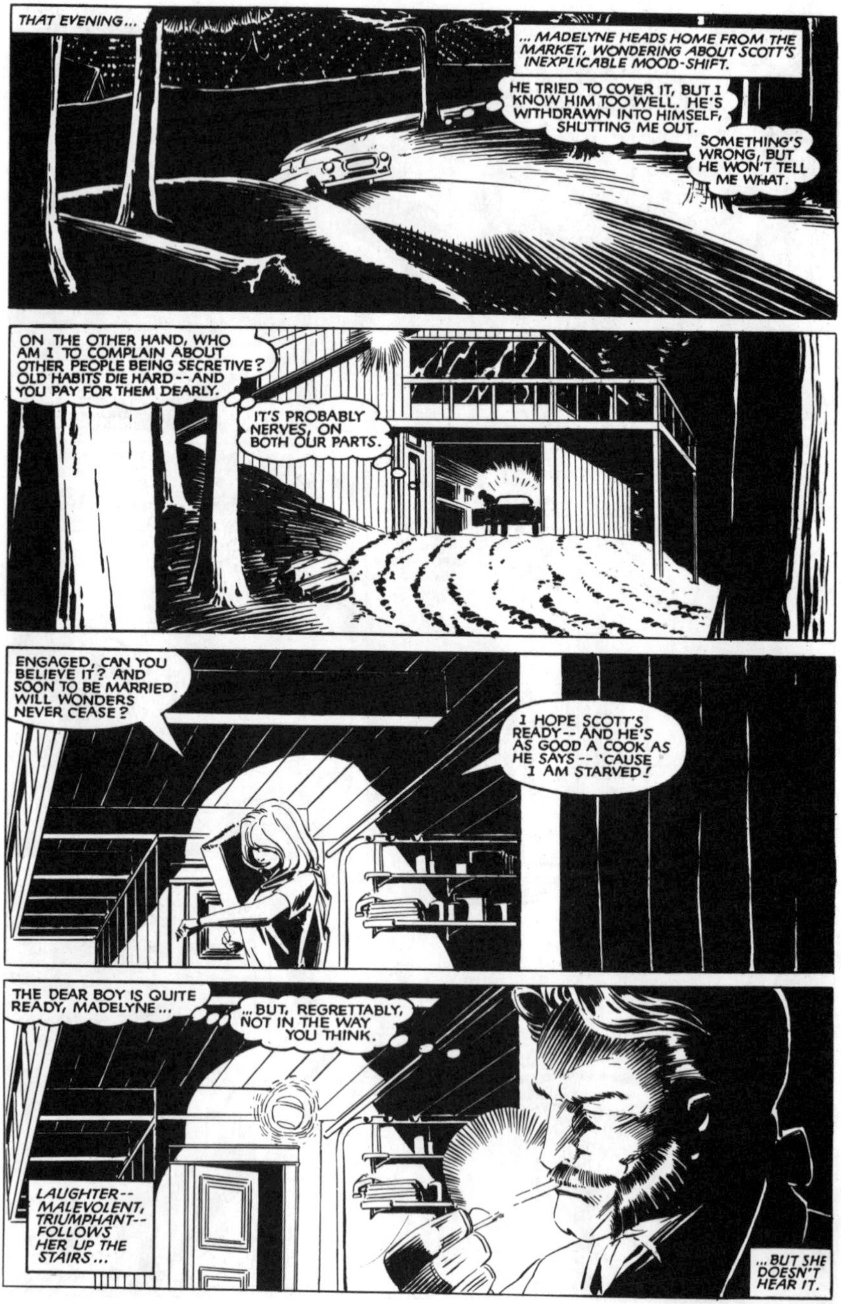

THAT EVENING...
...MADELYNE HEADS HOME FROM THE MARKET, WONDERING ABOUT SCOTT'S INEXPLICABLE MOOD-SHIFT.
HE TRIED TO COVER IT, BUT I KNOW HIM TOO WELL. HE'S WITHDRAWN INTO HIMSELF, SHUTTING ME OUT.
SOMETHING'S WRONG, BUT HE WON'T TELL ME WHAT.
ON THE OTHER HAND, WHO AM I TO COMPLAIN ABOUT OTHER PEOPLE BEING SECRETIVE? OLD HABITS DIE HARD-- AND YOU PAY FOR THEM DEARLY.
IT'S PROBABLY NERVES, ON BOTH OUR PARTS.
ENGAGED, CAN YOU BELIEVE IT? AND SOON TO BE MARRIED. WILL WONDERS NEVER CEASE?
I HOPE SCOTT'S READY-- AND HE'S AS GOOD A COOK AS HE SAYS-- 'CAUSE I AM STARVED!
THE DEAR BOY IS QUITE READY, MADELYNE...
...BUT, REGRETTABLY, NOT IN THE WAY YOU THINK.
LAUGHTER-- MALEVOLENT, TRIUMPHANT-- FOLLOWS HER UP THE STAIRS...
...BUT SHE DOESN'T HEAR IT.

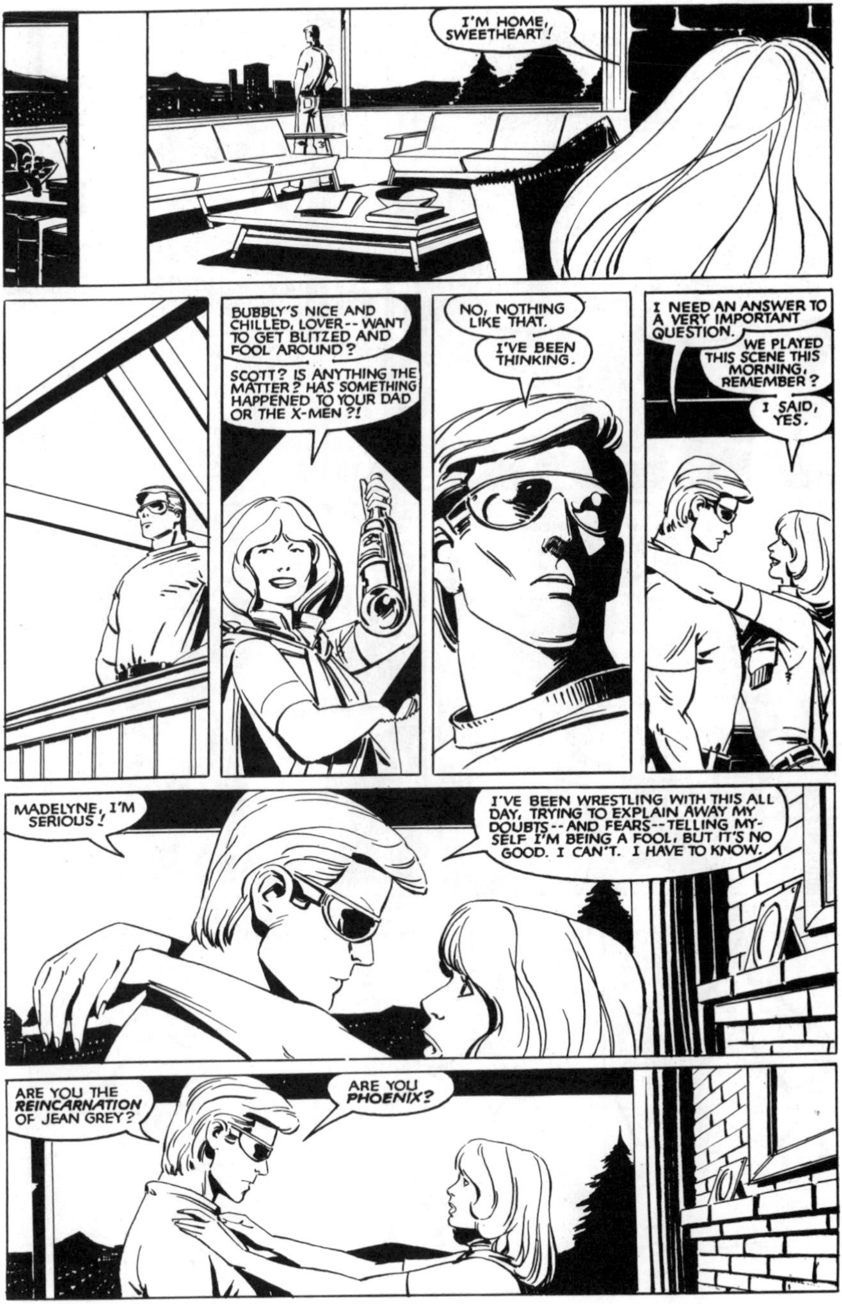
I'M HOME, SWEETHEART!
BUBBLY'S NICE AND CHILLED, LOVER-- WANT TO GET BLITZED AND FOOL AROUND?
SCOTT? IS ANYTHING THE MATTER? HAS SOMETHING HAPPENED TO YOUR DAD OR THE X-MEN?!
NO, NOTHING LIKE THAT.
I'VE BEEN THINKING.
I NEED AN ANSWER TO A VERY IMPORTANT QUESTION.
WE PLAYED THIS SCENE THIS MORNING, REMEMBER?
I SAID, YES.
MADELYNE, I'M SERIOUS!
I'VE BEEN WRESTLING WITH THIS ALL DAY, TRYING TO EXPLAIN AWAY MY DOUBTS--AND FEARS--TELLING MYSELF I'M BEING A FOOL, BUT IT'S NO GOOD. I CAN'T. I HAVE TO KNOW.
ARE YOU THE *REINCARNATION* OF JEAN GREY?
ARE YOU *PHOENIX*?

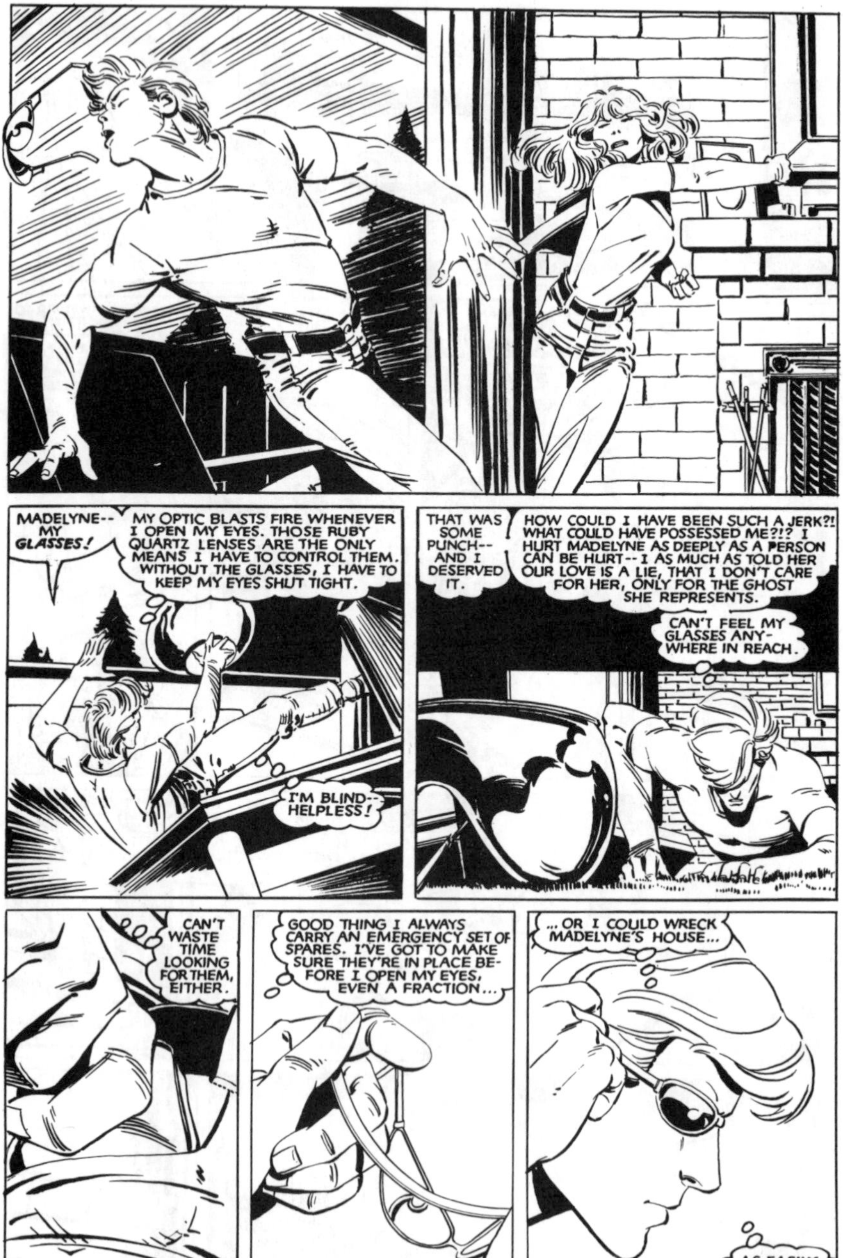
MADELYNE-- MY GLASSES!
MY OPTIC BLASTS FIRE WHENEVER I OPEN MY EYES. THOSE RUBY QUARTZ LENSES ARE THE ONLY MEANS I HAVE TO CONTROL THEM. WITHOUT THE GLASSES, I HAVE TO KEEP MY EYES SHUT TIGHT.
I'M BLIND-- HELPLESS!
THAT WAS SOME PUNCH-- AND I DESERVED IT.
HOW COULD I HAVE BEEN SUCH A JERK?! WHAT COULD HAVE POSSESSED ME?!? I HURT MADELYNE AS DEEPLY AS A PERSON CAN BE HURT-- I AS MUCH AS TOLD HER OUR LOVE IS A LIE, THAT I DON'T CARE FOR HER, ONLY FOR THE GHOST SHE REPRESENTS.
CAN'T FEEL MY GLASSES ANY-WHERE IN REACH.
CAN'T WASTE TIME LOOKING FOR THEM, EITHER.
GOOD THING I ALWAYS CARRY AN EMERGENCY SET OF SPARES. I'VE GOT TO MAKE SURE THEY'RE IN PLACE BE-FORE I OPEN MY EYES, EVEN A FRACTION...
...OR I COULD WRECK MADELYNE'S HOUSE...
...AS EASILY AS I HAVE HER LIFE.

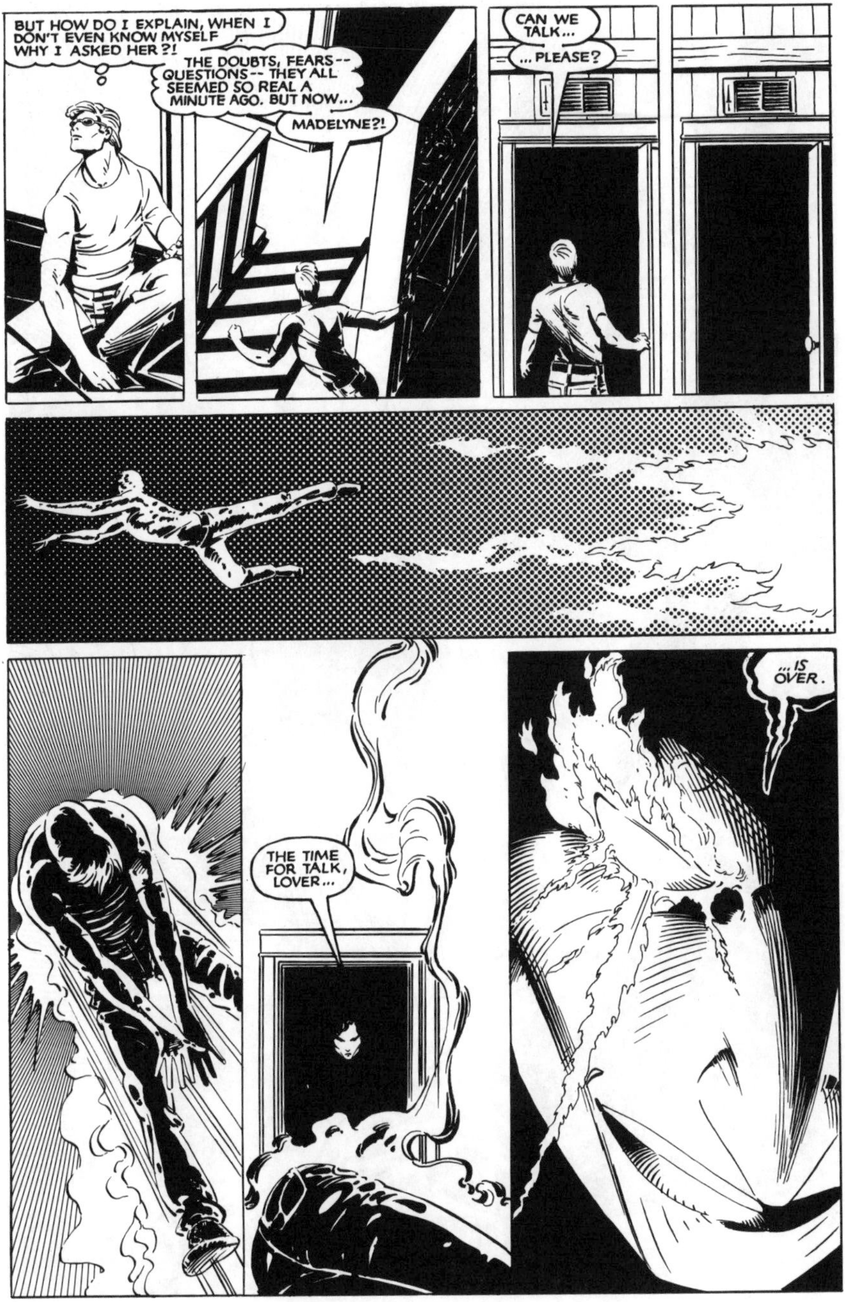
BUT HOW DO I EXPLAIN, WHEN I DON'T EVEN KNOW MYSELF WHY I ASKED HER?!
THE DOUBTS, FEARS-- QUESTIONS-- THEY ALL SEEMED SO REAL A MINUTE AGO. BUT NOW...
MADELYNE?!
CAN WE TALK...
...PLEASE?
THE TIME FOR TALK, LOVER...
...IS OVER.

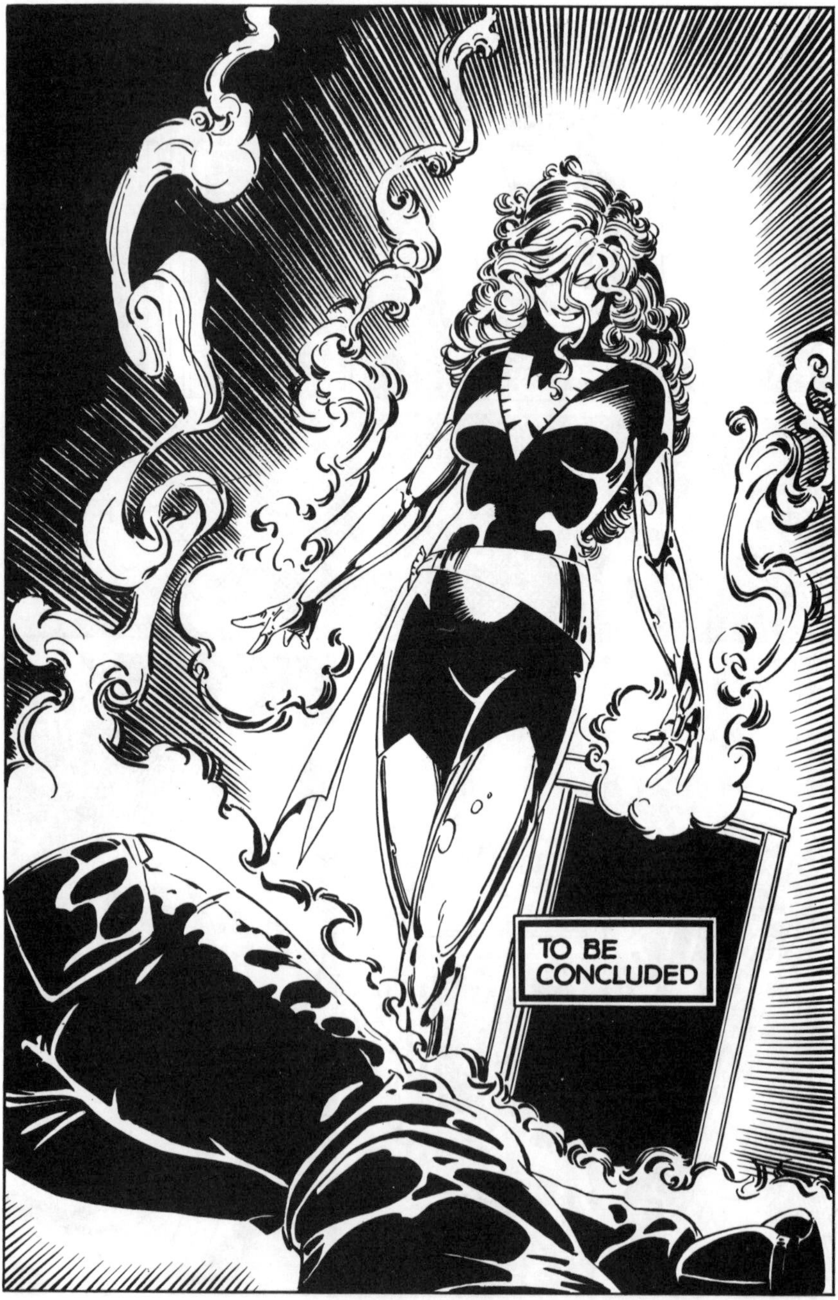
TO BE
CONCLUDED

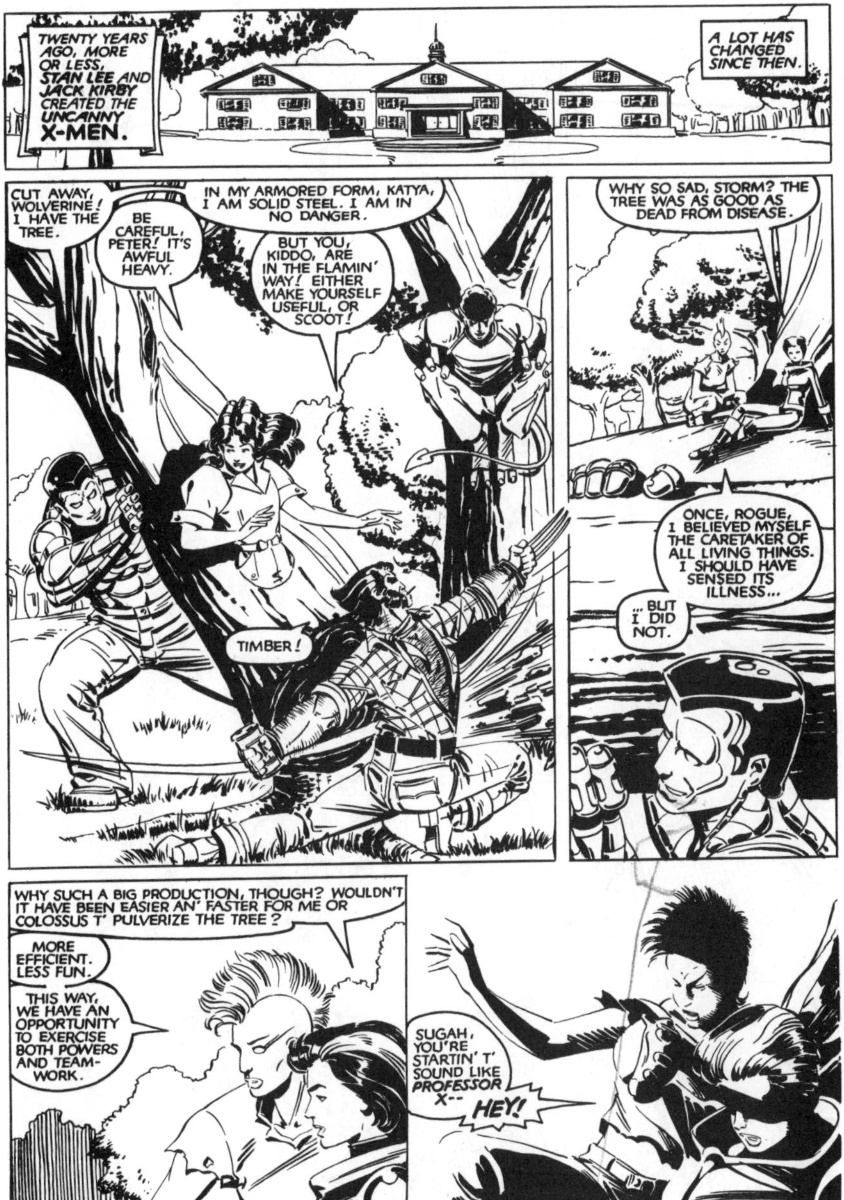
TWENTY YEARS AGO, MORE OR LESS, STAN LEE AND JACK KIRBY CREATED THE UNCANNY X-MEN.
A LOT HAS CHANGED SINCE THEN.
CUT AWAY, WOLVERINE! I HAVE THE TREE.
BE CAREFUL, PETER! IT'S AWFUL HEAVY.
IN MY ARMORED FORM, KATYA, I AM SOLID STEEL. I AM IN NO DANGER.
BUT YOU, KIDDO, ARE IN THE FLAMIN' WAY! EITHER MAKE YOURSELF USEFUL, OR SCOOT!
TIMBER!
WHY SO SAD, STORM? THE TREE WAS AS GOOD AS DEAD FROM DISEASE.
ONCE, ROGUE, I BELIEVED MYSELF THE CARETAKER OF ALL LIVING THINGS. I SHOULD HAVE SENSED ITS ILLNESS...
...BUT I DID NOT.
WHY SUCH A BIG PRODUCTION, THOUGH? WOULDN'T IT HAVE BEEN EASIER AN' FASTER FOR ME OR COLOSSUS T' PULVERIZE THE TREE?
MORE EFFICIENT. LESS FUN.
THIS WAY, WE HAVE AN OPPORTUNITY TO EXERCISE BOTH POWERS AND TEAM-WORK.
SUGAH, YOU'RE STARTIN' T' SOUND LIKE PROFESSOR X--
HEY!

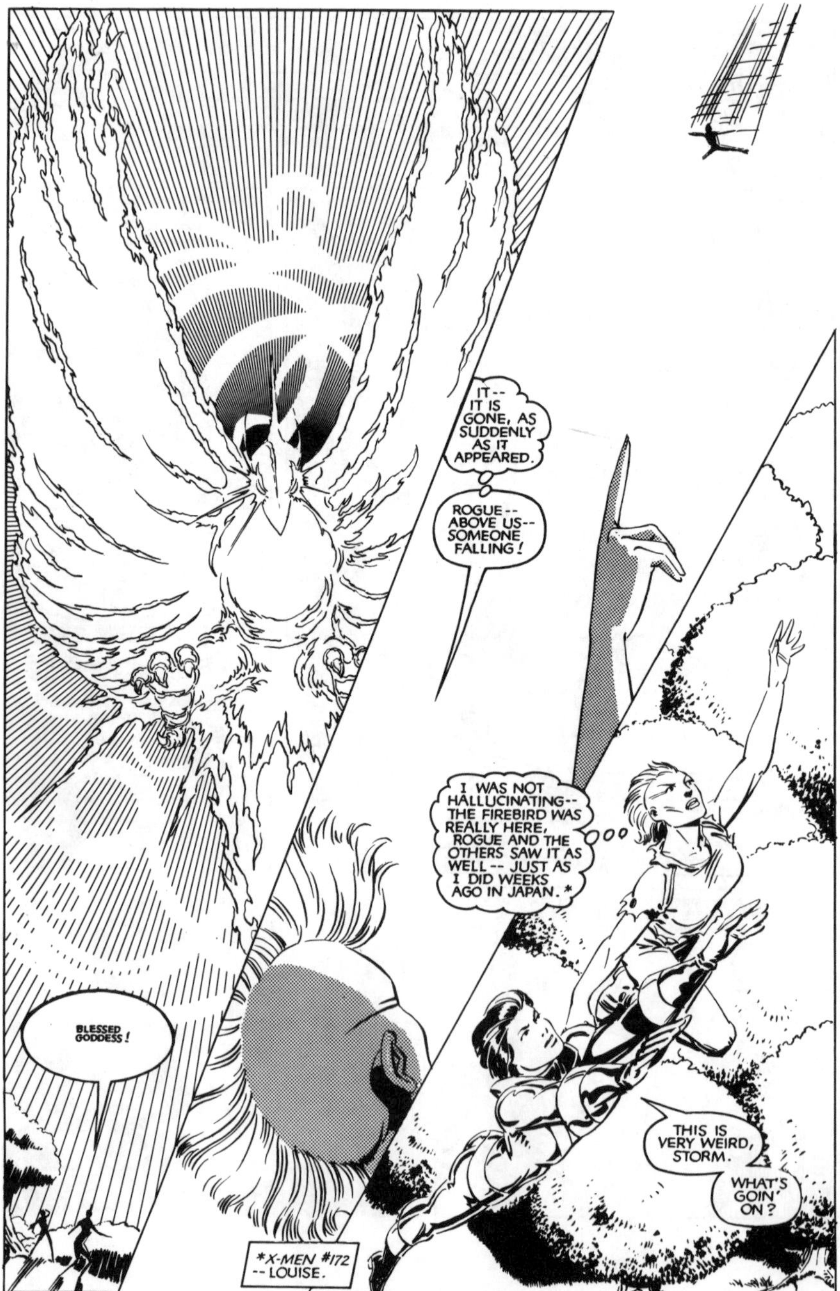
BLESSED GODDESS!
IT-- IT IS GONE, AS SUDDENLY AS IT APPEARED.
ROGUE-- ABOVE US-- SOMEONE FALLING!
I WAS NOT HALLUCINATING-- THE FIREBIRD WAS REALLY HERE, ROGUE AND THE OTHERS SAW IT AS WELL -- JUST AS I DID WEEKS AGO IN JAPAN.*
*X-MEN #172 -- LOUISE.
THIS IS VERY WEIRD, STORM.
WHAT'S GOIN' ON?

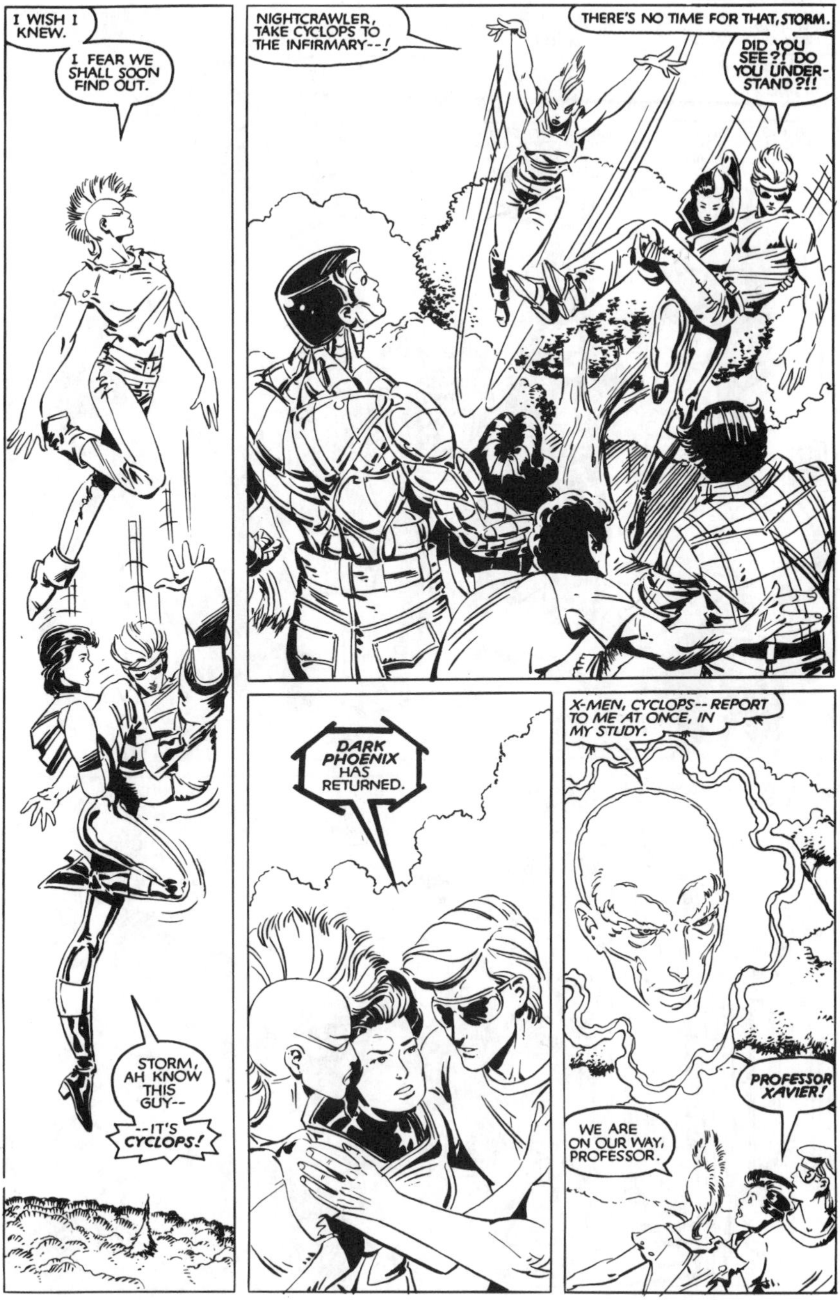
I WISH I KNEW.
I FEAR WE SHALL SOON FIND OUT.
STORM, AH KNOW THIS GUY--
--IT'S CYCLOPS!
NIGHTCRAWLER, TAKE CYCLOPS TO THE INFIRMARY--!
THERE'S NO TIME FOR THAT, STORM.
DID YOU SEE?! DO YOU UNDERSTAND?!!
DARK PHOENIX HAS RETURNED.
X-MEN, CYCLOPS-- REPORT TO ME AT ONCE, IN MY STUDY.
PROFESSOR XAVIER!
WE ARE ON OUR WAY, PROFESSOR.

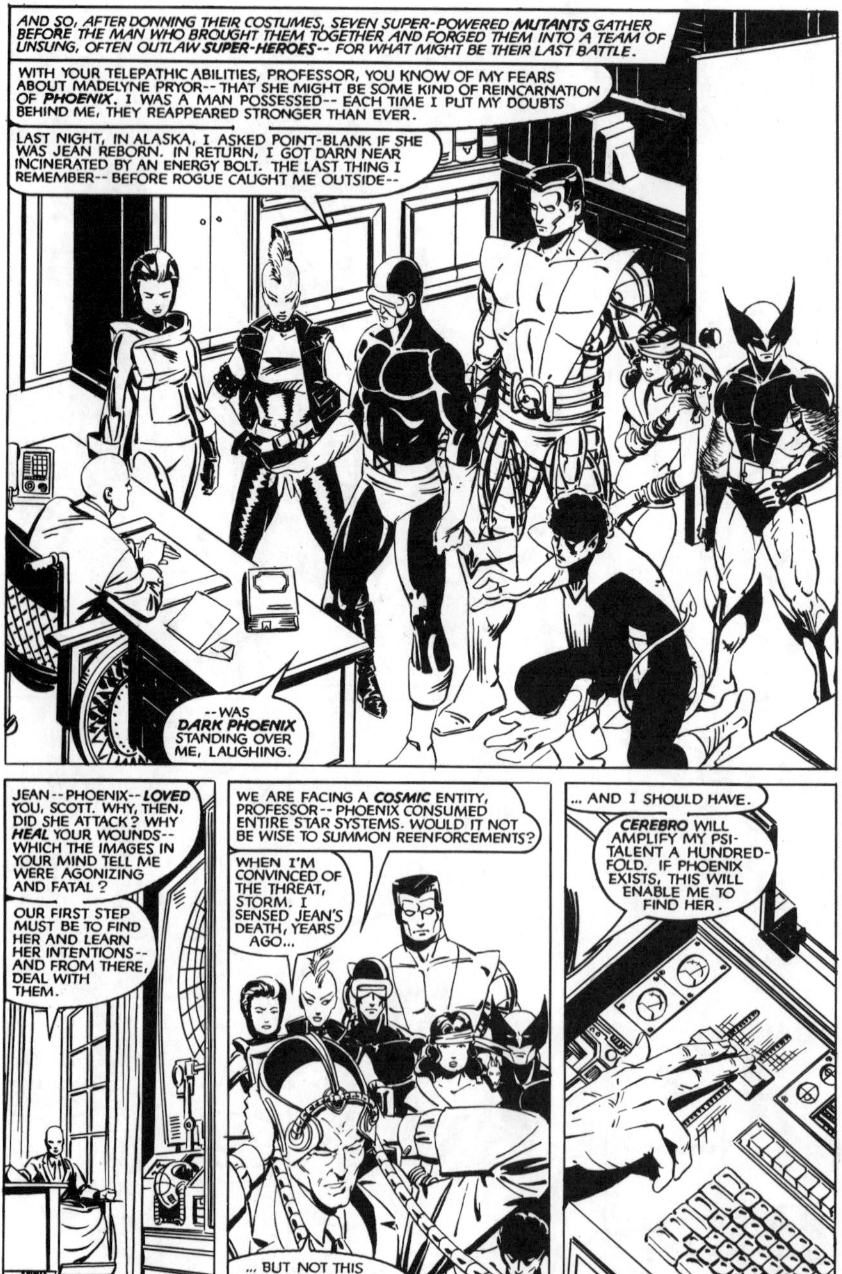

AND SO, AFTER DONNING THEIR COSTUMES, SEVEN SUPER-POWERED MUTANTS GATHER BEFORE THE MAN WHO BROUGHT THEM TOGETHER AND FORGED THEM INTO A TEAM OF UNSUNG, OFTEN OUTLAW SUPER-HEROES-- FOR WHAT MIGHT BE THEIR LAST BATTLE.
WITH YOUR TELEPATHIC ABILITIES, PROFESSOR, YOU KNOW OF MY FEARS ABOUT MADELYNE PRYOR-- THAT SHE MIGHT BE SOME KIND OF REINCARNATION OF PHOENIX. I WAS A MAN POSSESSED-- EACH TIME I PUT MY DOUBTS BEHIND ME, THEY REAPPEARED STRONGER THAN EVER.
LAST NIGHT, IN ALASKA, I ASKED POINT-BLANK IF SHE WAS JEAN REBORN. IN RETURN, I GOT DARN NEAR INCINERATED BY AN ENERGY BOLT. THE LAST THING I REMEMBER-- BEFORE ROGUE CAUGHT ME OUTSIDE--
--WAS DARK PHOENIX STANDING OVER ME, LAUGHING.
JEAN--PHOENIX--LOVED YOU, SCOTT. WHY, THEN, DID SHE ATTACK? WHY HEAL YOUR WOUNDS-- WHICH THE IMAGES IN YOUR MIND TELL ME WERE AGONIZING AND FATAL?
OUR FIRST STEP MUST BE TO FIND HER AND LEARN HER INTENTIONS-- AND FROM THERE, DEAL WITH THEM.
WE ARE FACING A COSMIC ENTITY, PROFESSOR-- PHOENIX CONSUMED ENTIRE STAR SYSTEMS. WOULD IT NOT BE WISE TO SUMMON REENFORCEMENTS?
WHEN I'M CONVINCED OF THE THREAT, STORM. I SENSED JEAN'S DEATH, YEARS AGO...
... BUT NOT THIS MIRACULOUS REBIRTH...
... AND I SHOULD HAVE.
CEREBRO WILL AMPLIFY MY PSI-TALENT A HUNDRED-FOLD. IF PHOENIX EXISTS, THIS WILL ENABLE ME TO FIND HER.

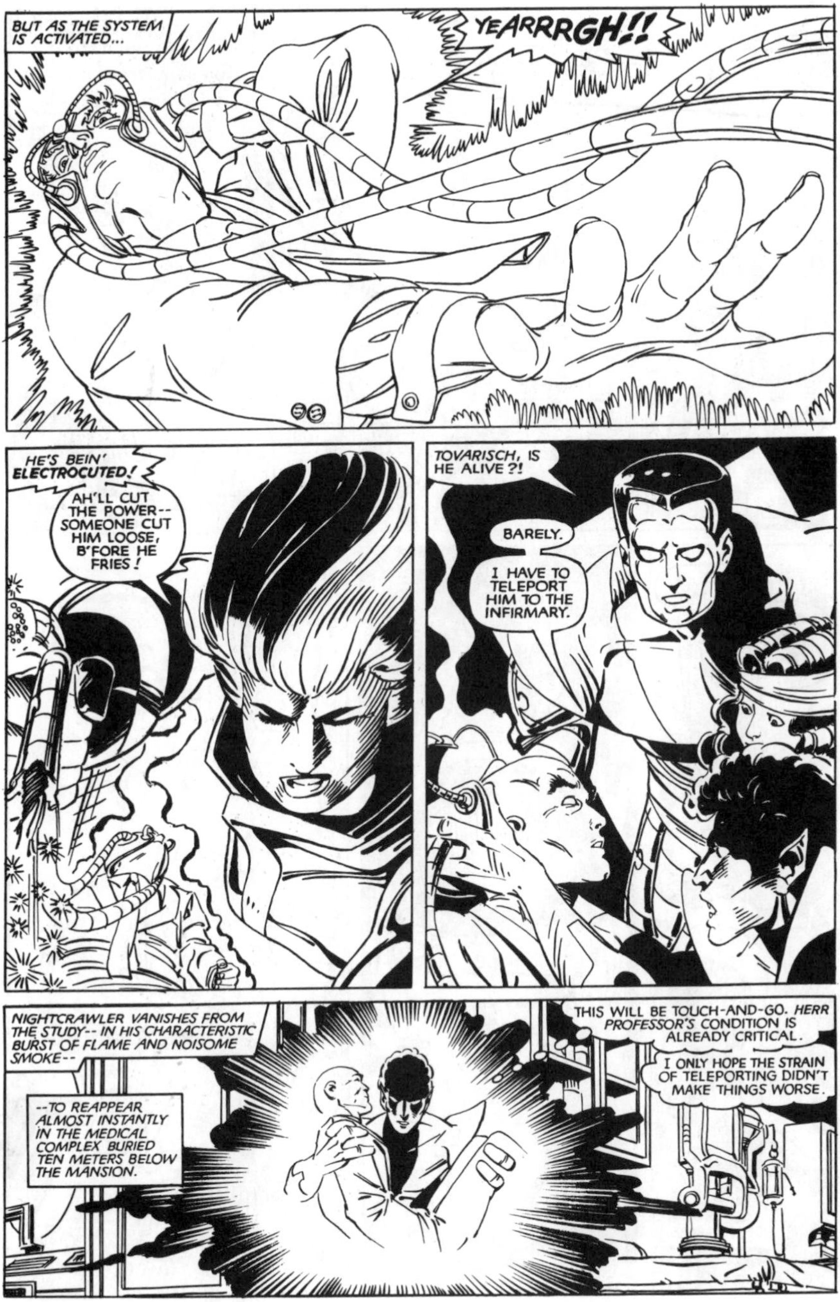
BUT AS THE SYSTEM IS ACTIVATED...
YEARRRGH!!
HE'S BEIN' ELECTROCUTED!
AH'LL CUT THE POWER-- SOMEONE CUT HIM LOOSE, B'FORE HE FRIES!
TOVARISCH, IS HE ALIVE?!
BARELY.
I HAVE TO TELEPORT HIM TO THE INFIRMARY.
NIGHTCRAWLER VANISHES FROM THE STUDY-- IN HIS CHARACTERISTIC BURST OF FLAME AND NOISOME SMOKE--
--TO REAPPEAR ALMOST INSTANTLY IN THE MEDICAL COMPLEX BURIED TEN METERS BELOW THE MANSION.
THIS WILL BE TOUCH-AND-GO. HERR PROFESSOR'S CONDITION IS ALREADY CRITICAL.
I ONLY HOPE THE STRAIN OF TELEPORTING DIDN'T MAKE THINGS WORSE.

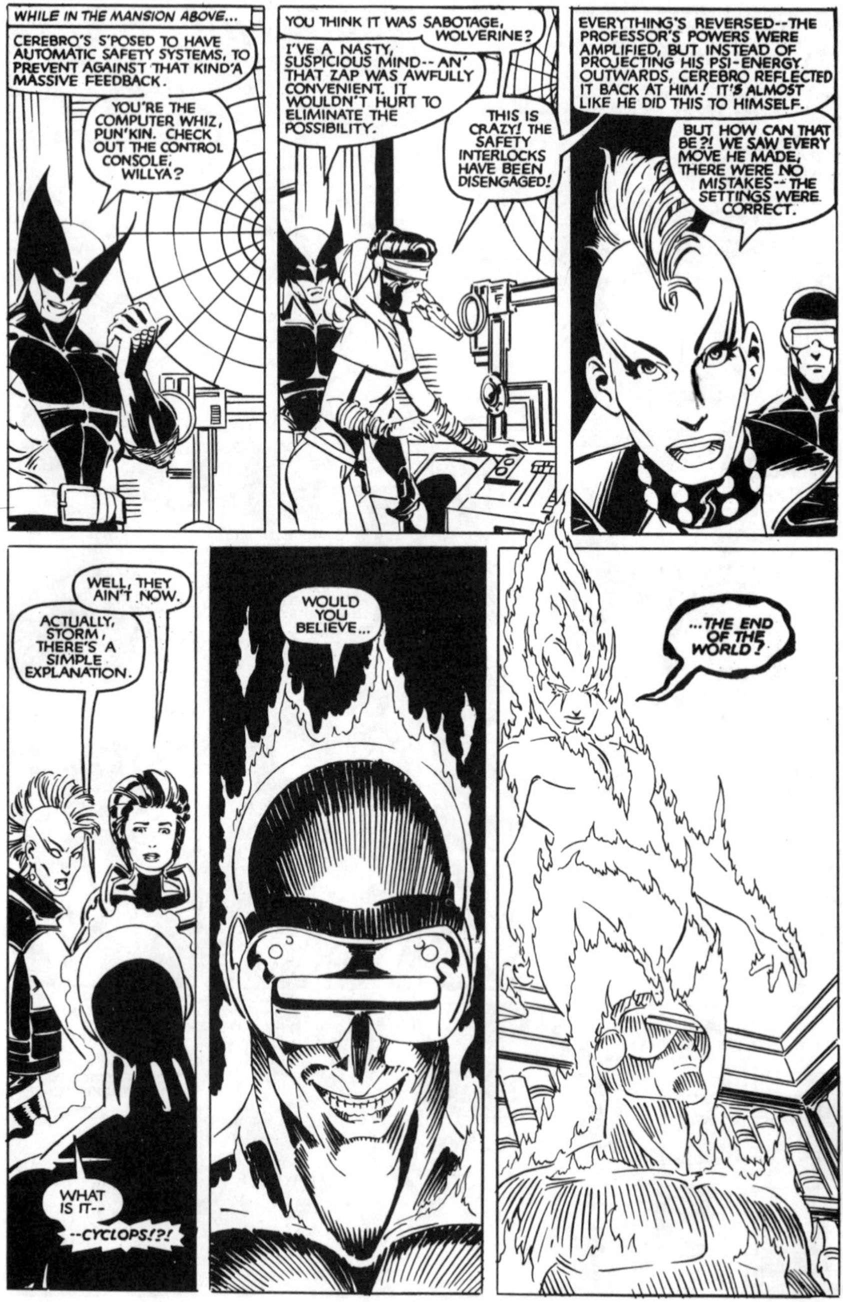
WHILE IN THE MANSION ABOVE...
CEREBRO'S S'POSED TO HAVE AUTOMATIC SAFETY SYSTEMS, TO PREVENT AGAINST THAT KIND'A MASSIVE FEEDBACK.
YOU'RE THE COMPUTER WHIZ, PUN'KIN. CHECK OUT THE CONTROL CONSOLE, WILLYA?
YOU THINK IT WAS SABOTAGE, WOLVERINE?
I'VE A NASTY, SUSPICIOUS MIND-- AN' THAT ZAP WAS AWFULLY CONVENIENT. IT WOULDN'T HURT TO ELIMINATE THE POSSIBILITY.
THIS IS CRAZY! THE SAFETY INTERLOCKS HAVE BEEN DISENGAGED!
EVERYTHING'S REVERSED--THE PROFESSOR'S POWERS WERE AMPLIFIED, BUT INSTEAD OF PROJECTING HIS PSI-ENERGY OUTWARDS, CEREBRO REFLECTED IT BACK AT HIM! IT'S ALMOST LIKE HE DID THIS TO HIMSELF.
BUT HOW CAN THAT BE?! WE SAW EVERY MOVE HE MADE, THERE WERE NO MISTAKES-- THE SETTINGS WERE CORRECT.
WELL, THEY AIN'T NOW.
ACTUALLY, STORM, THERE'S A SIMPLE EXPLANATION.
WHAT IS IT--
--CYCLOPS!?!
WOULD YOU BELIEVE...
...THE END OF THE WORLD?

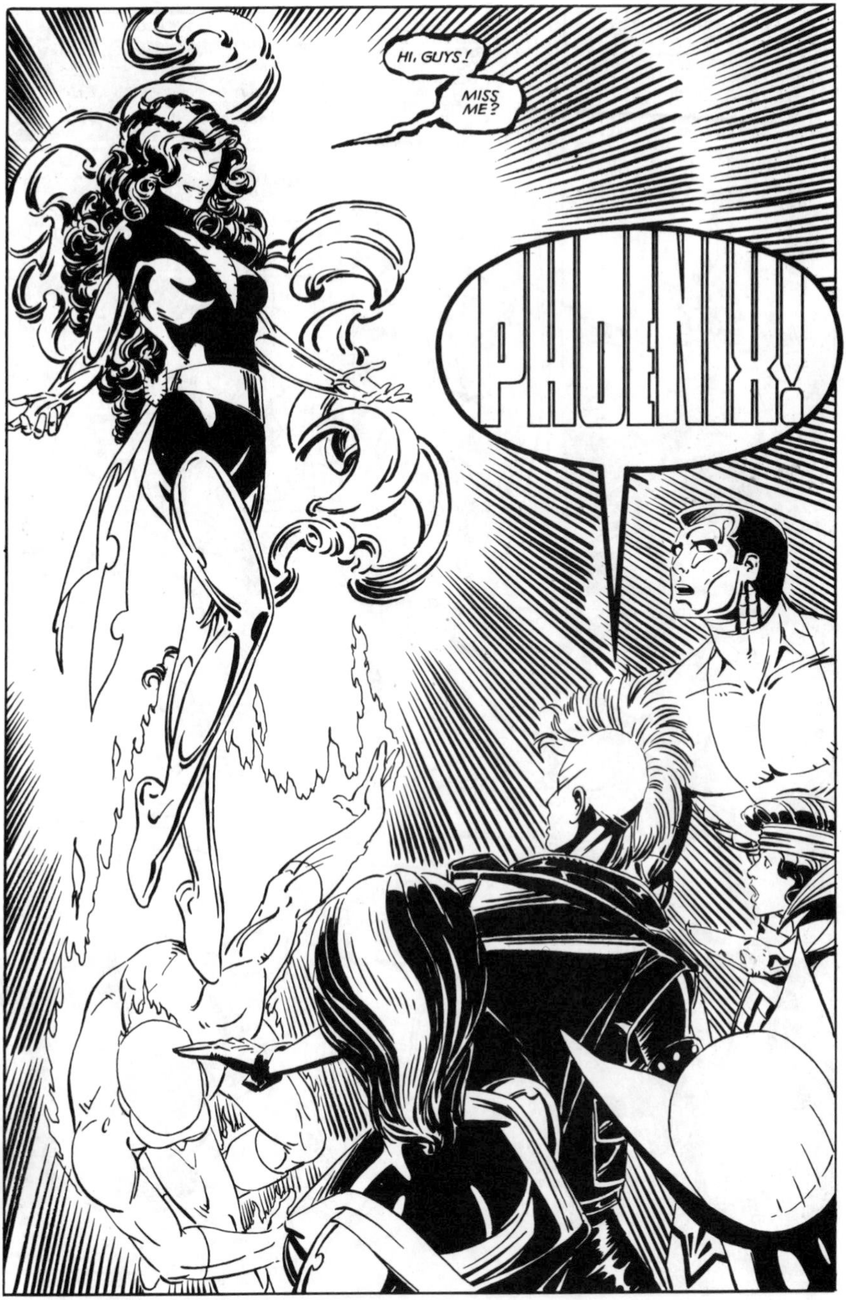
HI, GUYS!
MISS ME?
PHOENIX!

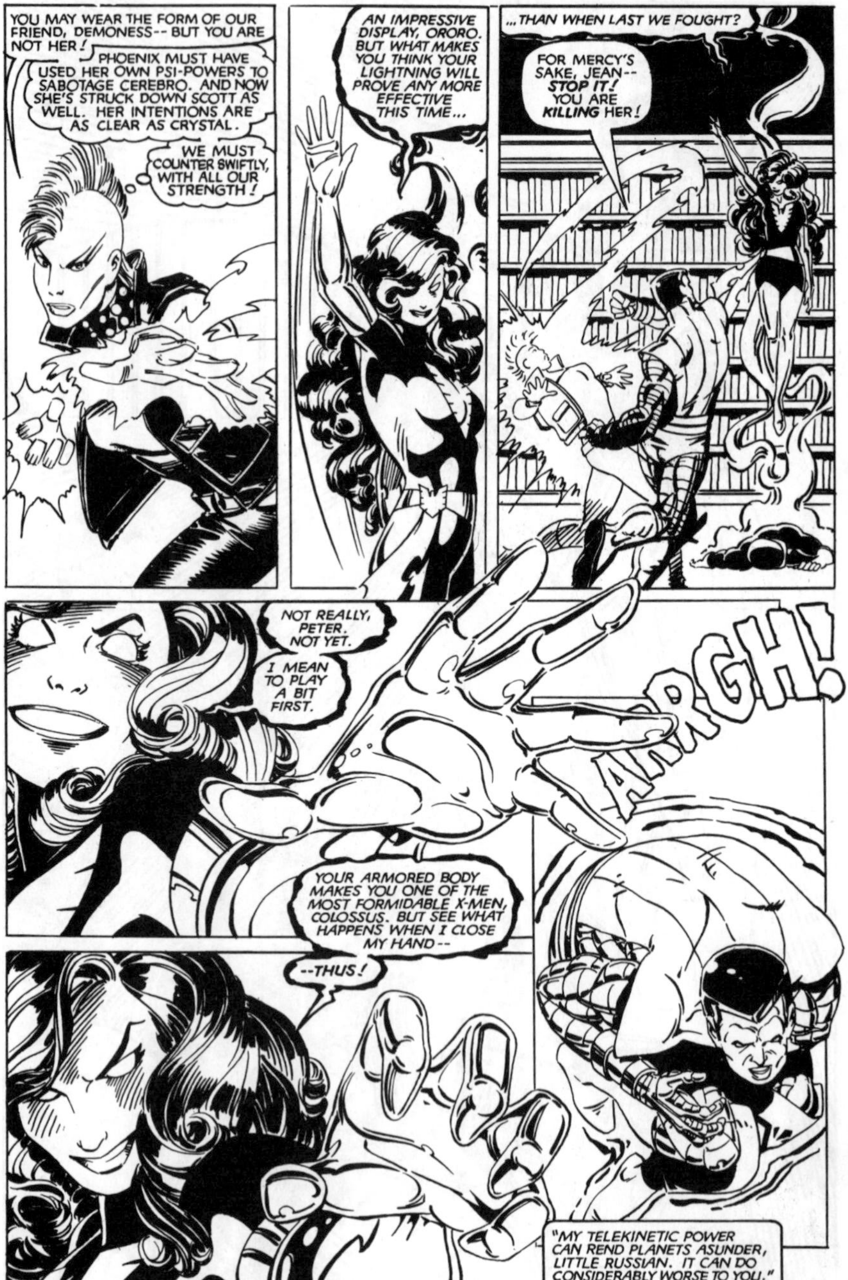
YOU MAY WEAR THE FORM OF OUR FRIEND, DEMONESS-- BUT YOU ARE NOT HER!
PHOENIX MUST HAVE USED HER OWN PSI-POWERS TO SABOTAGE CEREBRO. AND NOW SHE'S STRUCK DOWN SCOTT AS WELL. HER INTENTIONS ARE AS CLEAR AS CRYSTAL.
WE MUST COUNTER SWIFTLY, WITH ALL OUR STRENGTH!
AN IMPRESSIVE DISPLAY, ORORO. BUT WHAT MAKES YOU THINK YOUR LIGHTNING WILL PROVE ANY MORE EFFECTIVE THIS TIME...
...THAN WHEN LAST WE FOUGHT?
FOR MERCY'S SAKE, JEAN-- STOP IT! YOU ARE KILLING HER!
NOT REALLY, PETER. NOT YET.
I MEAN TO PLAY A BIT FIRST.
AARRGH!
YOUR ARMORED BODY MAKES YOU ONE OF THE MOST FORMIDABLE X-MEN, COLOSSUS. BUT SEE WHAT HAPPENS WHEN I CLOSE MY HAND --
--THUS!
"MY TELEKINETIC POWER CAN REND PLANETS ASUNDER, LITTLE RUSSIAN. IT CAN DO CONSIDERABLY WORSE TO YOU."

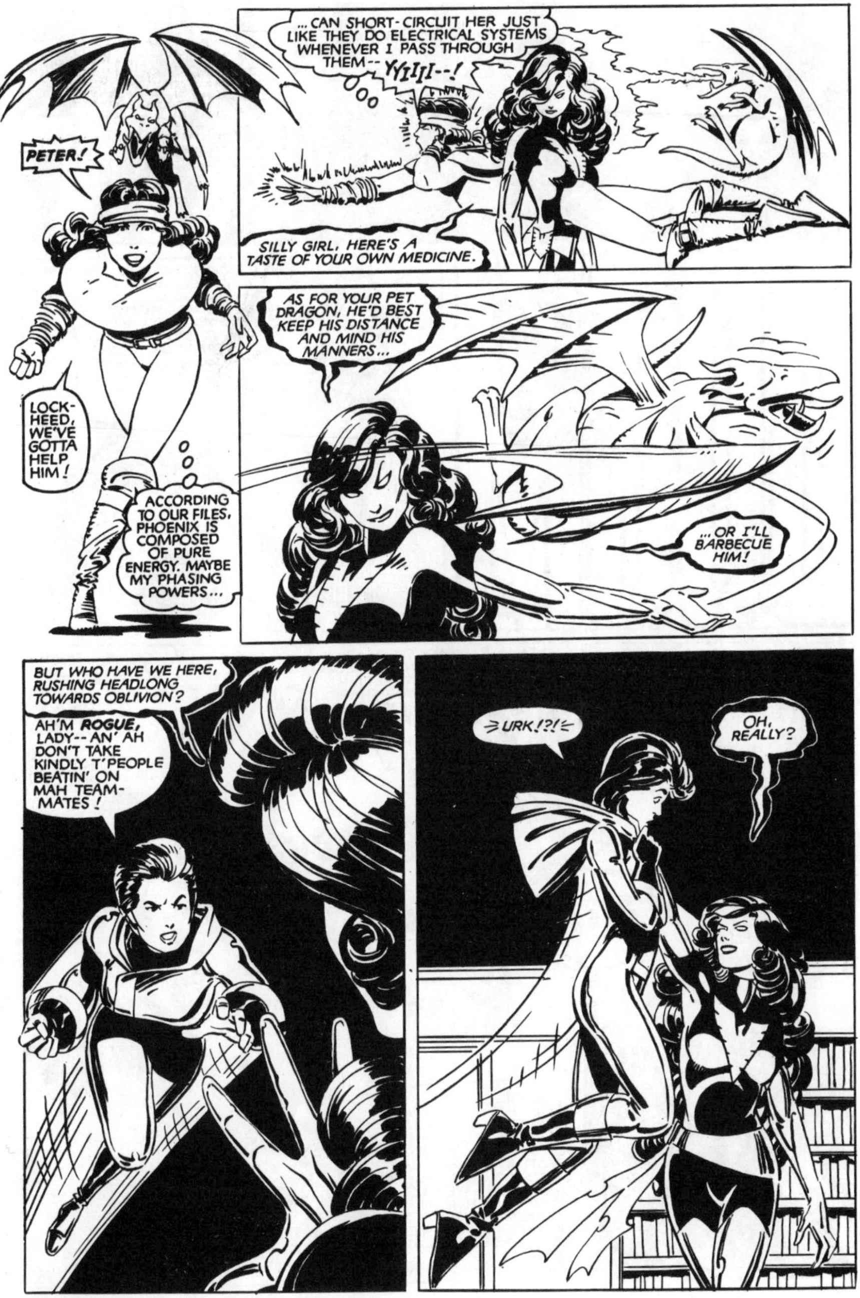
PETER!
...CAN SHORT-CIRCUIT HER JUST LIKE THEY DO ELECTRICAL SYSTEMS WHENEVER I PASS THROUGH THEM-- YYIIII--!
SILLY GIRL, HERE'S A TASTE OF YOUR OWN MEDICINE.
LOCK-HEED, WE'VE GOTTA HELP HIM!
ACCORDING TO OUR FILES, PHOENIX IS COMPOSED OF PURE ENERGY. MAYBE MY PHASING POWERS...
AS FOR YOUR PET DRAGON, HE'D BEST KEEP HIS DISTANCE AND MIND HIS MANNERS...
...OR I'LL BARBECUE HIM!
BUT WHO HAVE WE HERE, RUSHING HEADLONG TOWARDS OBLIVION?
AH'M ROGUE, LADY-- AN' AH DON'T TAKE KINDLY T'PEOPLE BEATIN' ON MAH TEAM-MATES!
URK!?!
OH, REALLY?

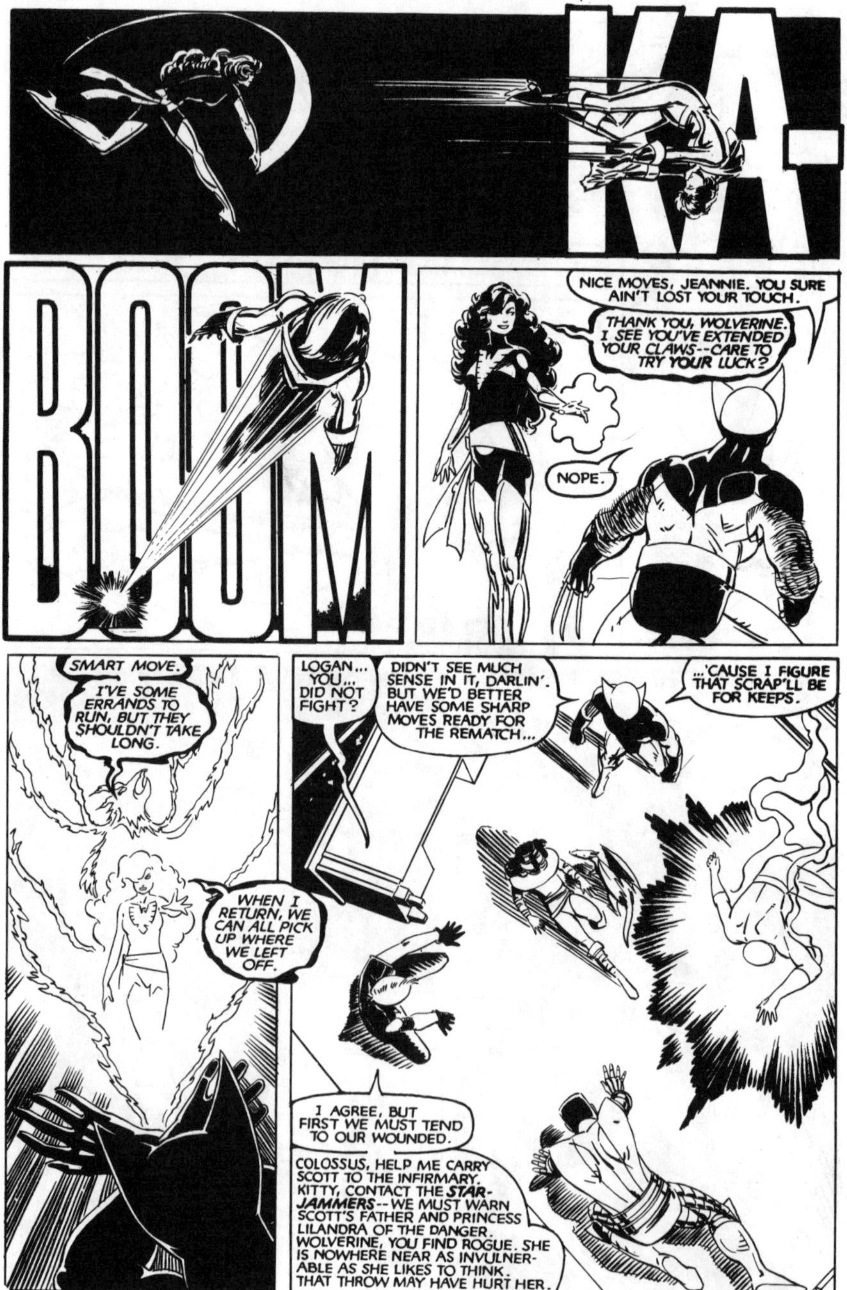
KA-
BOOM
NICE MOVES, JEANNIE. YOU SURE AIN'T LOST YOUR TOUCH.
THANK YOU, WOLVERINE. I SEE YOU'VE EXTENDED YOUR CLAWS--CARE TO TRY YOUR LUCK?
NOPE.
SMART MOVE.
I'VE SOME ERRANDS TO RUN, BUT THEY SHOULDN'T TAKE LONG.
WHEN I RETURN, WE CAN ALL PICK UP WHERE WE LEFT OFF.
LOGAN... YOU... DID NOT FIGHT?
DIDN'T SEE MUCH SENSE IN IT, DARLIN'. BUT WE'D BETTER HAVE SOME SHARP MOVES READY FOR THE REMATCH...
...'CAUSE I FIGURE THAT SCRAP'LL BE FOR KEEPS.
I AGREE, BUT FIRST WE MUST TEND TO OUR WOUNDED.
COLOSSUS, HELP ME CARRY SCOTT TO THE INFIRMARY. KITTY, CONTACT THE STAR-JAMMERS--WE MUST WARN SCOTT'S FATHER AND PRINCESS LILANDRA OF THE DANGER. WOLVERINE, YOU FIND ROGUE. SHE IS NOWHERE NEAR AS INVULNERABLE AS SHE LIKES TO THINK. THAT THROW MAY HAVE HURT HER.

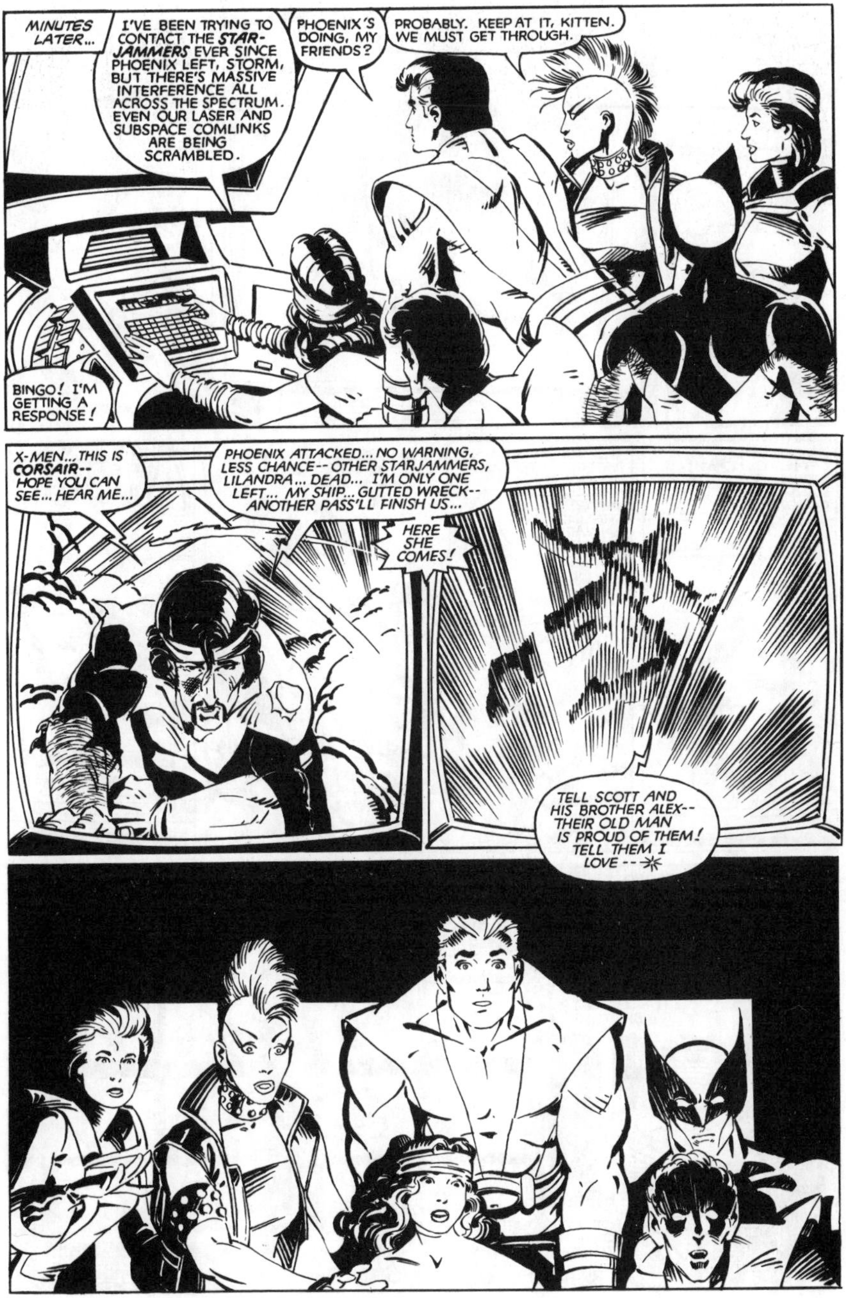
MINUTES LATER...
I'VE BEEN TRYING TO CONTACT THE STAR-JAMMERS EVER SINCE PHOENIX LEFT, STORM, BUT THERE'S MASSIVE INTERFERENCE ALL ACROSS THE SPECTRUM. EVEN OUR LASER AND SUBSPACE COMLINKS ARE BEING SCRAMBLED.
PHOENIX'S DOING, MY FRIENDS?
PROBABLY. KEEP AT IT, KITTEN. WE MUST GET THROUGH.
BINGO! I'M GETTING A RESPONSE!
X-MEN... THIS IS CORSAIR-- HOPE YOU CAN SEE... HEAR ME...
PHOENIX ATTACKED... NO WARNING, LESS CHANCE-- OTHER STARJAMMERS, LILANDRA... DEAD... I'M ONLY ONE LEFT... MY SHIP... GUTTED WRECK-- ANOTHER PASS'LL FINISH US...
HERE SHE COMES!
TELL SCOTT AND HIS BROTHER ALEX-- THEIR OLD MAN IS PROUD OF THEM! TELL THEM I LOVE --

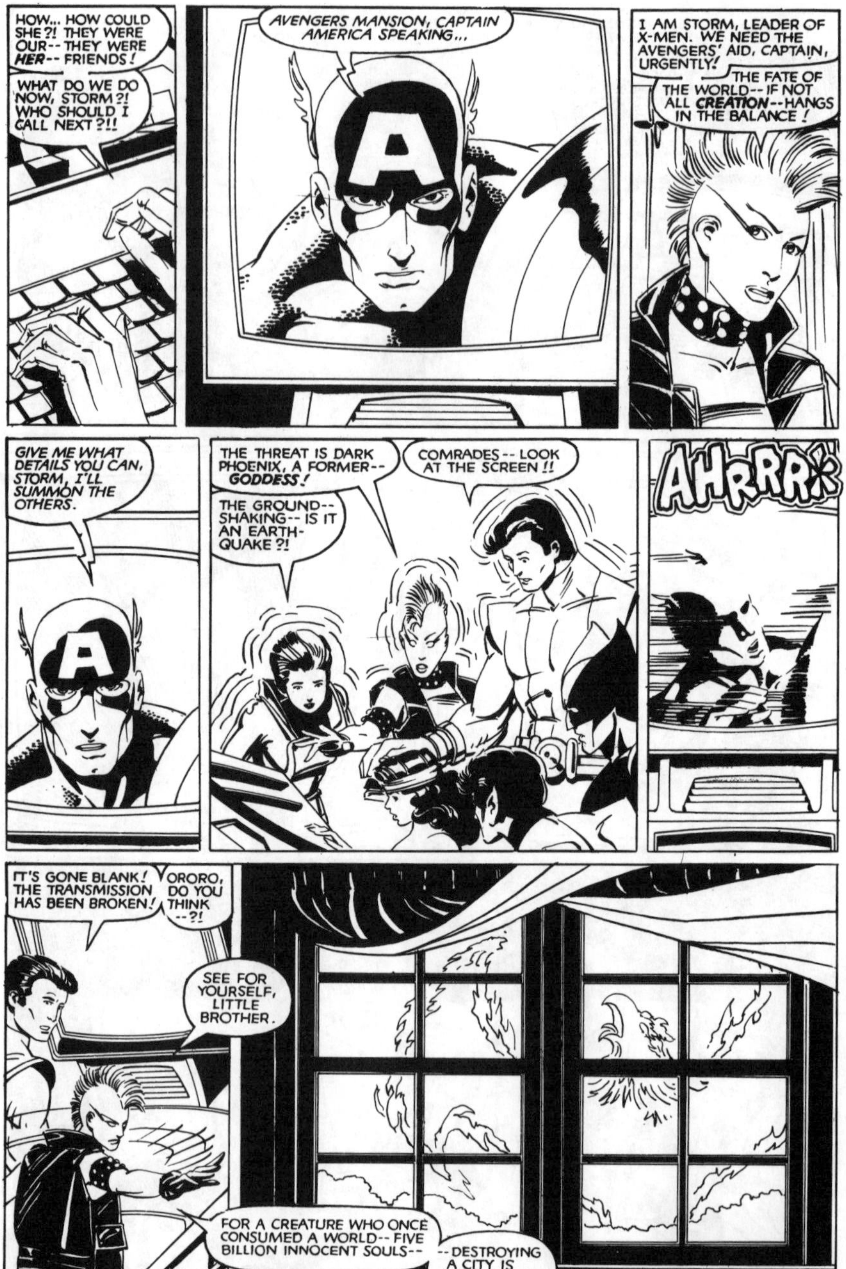
HOW... HOW COULD SHE?! THEY WERE OUR-- THEY WERE HER-- FRIENDS!
WHAT DO WE DO NOW, STORM?! WHO SHOULD I CALL NEXT?!!
AVENGERS MANSION, CAPTAIN AMERICA SPEAKING...
I AM STORM, LEADER OF X-MEN. WE NEED THE AVENGERS' AID, CAPTAIN, URGENTLY!
THE FATE OF THE WORLD-- IF NOT ALL CREATION--HANGS IN THE BALANCE!
GIVE ME WHAT DETAILS YOU CAN, STORM, I'LL SUMMON THE OTHERS.
THE THREAT IS DARK PHOENIX, A FORMER-- GODDESS!
THE GROUND-- SHAKING-- IS IT AN EARTH-QUAKE?!
COMRADES-- LOOK AT THE SCREEN!!
AHRRR
IT'S GONE BLANK! THE TRANSMISSION HAS BEEN BROKEN!
ORORO, DO YOU THINK --?!
SEE FOR YOURSELF, LITTLE BROTHER.
FOR A CREATURE WHO ONCE CONSUMED A WORLD-- FIVE BILLION INNOCENT SOULS--
--DESTROYING A CITY IS CHILD'S PLAY.

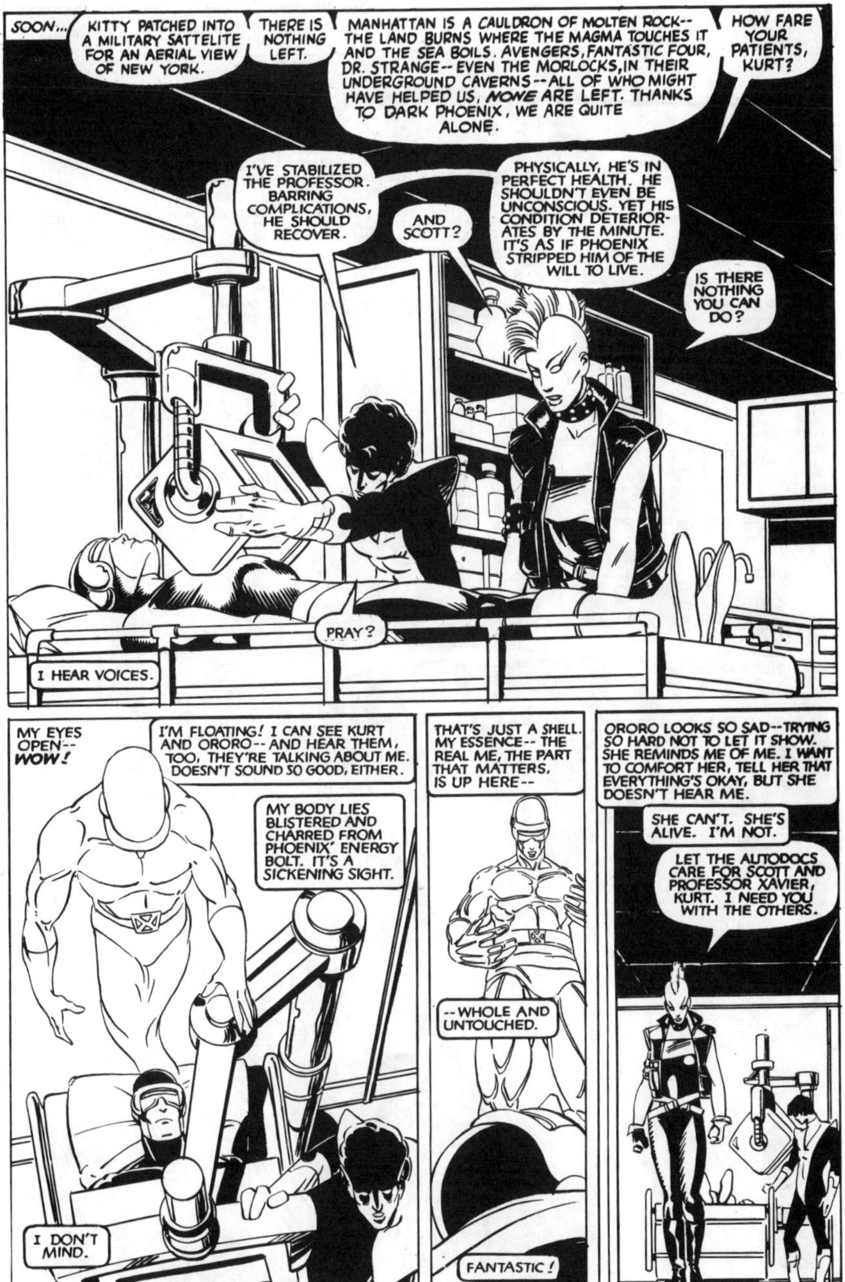

SOON...
KITTY PATCHED INTO A MILITARY SATTELITE FOR AN AERIAL VIEW OF NEW YORK.
THERE IS NOTHING LEFT.
MANHATTAN IS A CAULDRON OF MOLTEN ROCK-- THE LAND BURNS WHERE THE MAGMA TOUCHES IT AND THE SEA BOILS. AVENGERS, FANTASTIC FOUR, DR. STRANGE-- EVEN THE MORLOCKS, IN THEIR UNDERGROUND CAVERNS-- ALL OF WHO MIGHT HAVE HELPED US, NONE ARE LEFT. THANKS TO DARK PHOENIX, WE ARE QUITE ALONE.
HOW FARE YOUR PATIENTS, KURT?
I'VE STABILIZED THE PROFESSOR. BARRING COMPLICATIONS, HE SHOULD RECOVER.
AND SCOTT?
PHYSICALLY, HE'S IN PERFECT HEALTH. HE SHOULDN'T EVEN BE UNCONSCIOUS. YET HIS CONDITION DETERIORATES BY THE MINUTE. IT'S AS IF PHOENIX STRIPPED HIM OF THE WILL TO LIVE.
IS THERE NOTHING YOU CAN DO?
PRAY?
I HEAR VOICES.
MY EYES OPEN-- WOW!
I'M FLOATING! I CAN SEE KURT AND ORORO-- AND HEAR THEM, TOO. THEY'RE TALKING ABOUT ME. DOESN'T SOUND SO GOOD, EITHER.
MY BODY LIES BLISTERED AND CHARRED FROM PHOENIX' ENERGY BOLT. IT'S A SICKENING SIGHT.
I DON'T MIND.
THAT'S JUST A SHELL. MY ESSENCE-- THE REAL ME, THE PART THAT MATTERS, IS UP HERE--
--WHOLE AND UNTOUCHED.
FANTASTIC!
ORORO LOOKS SO SAD--TRYING SO HARD NOT TO LET IT SHOW. SHE REMINDS ME OF ME. I WANT TO COMFORT HER, TELL HER THAT EVERYTHING'S OKAY, BUT SHE DOESN'T HEAR ME.
SHE CAN'T. SHE'S ALIVE. I'M NOT.
LET THE AUTODOCS CARE FOR SCOTT AND PROFESSOR XAVIER, KURT. I NEED YOU WITH THE OTHERS.

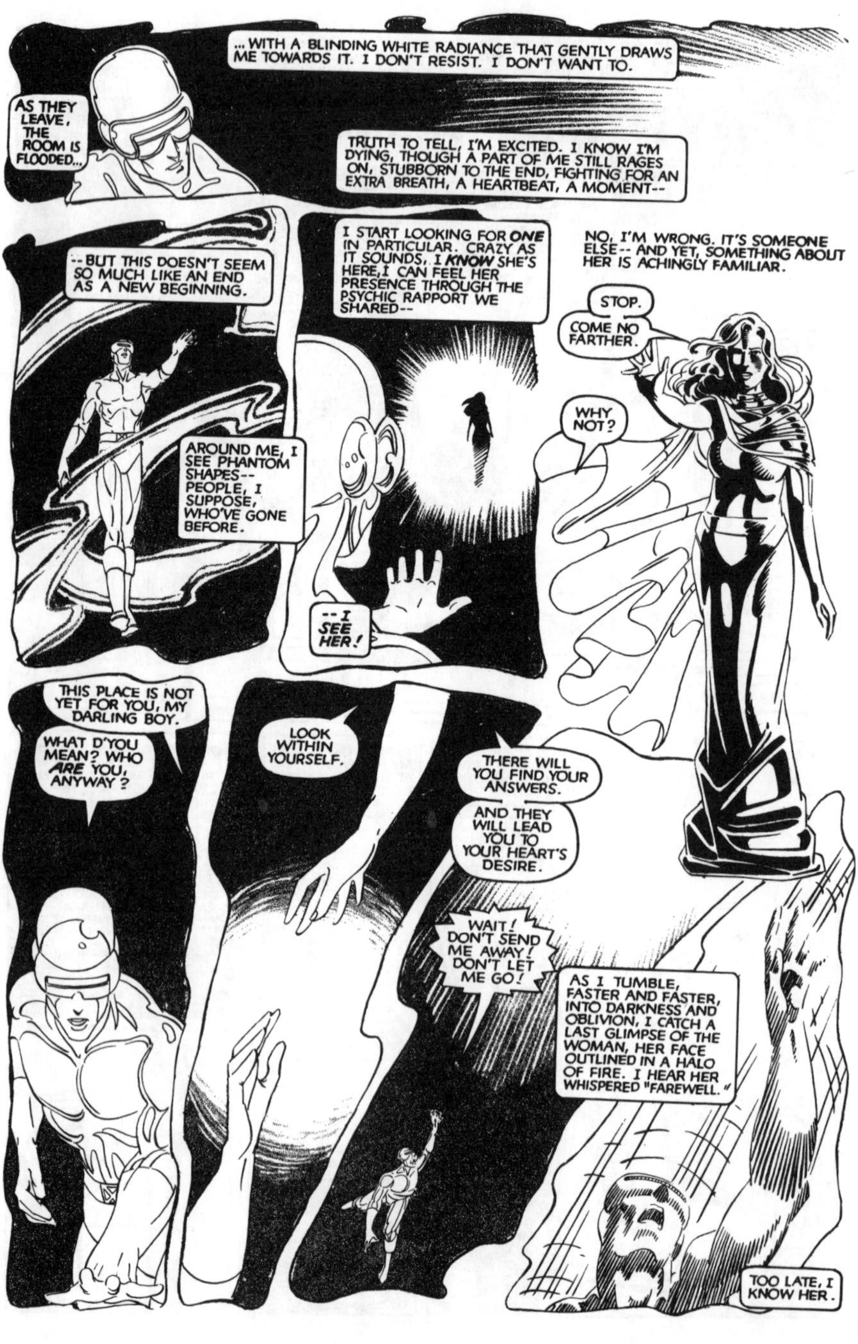

AS THEY LEAVE, THE ROOM IS FLOODED...
...WITH A BLINDING WHITE RADIANCE THAT GENTLY DRAWS ME TOWARDS IT. I DON'T RESIST. I DON'T WANT TO.
TRUTH TO TELL, I'M EXCITED. I KNOW I'M DYING, THOUGH A PART OF ME STILL RAGES ON, STUBBORN TO THE END, FIGHTING FOR AN EXTRA BREATH, A HEARTBEAT, A MOMENT--
--BUT THIS DOESN'T SEEM SO MUCH LIKE AN END AS A NEW BEGINNING.
AROUND ME, I SEE PHANTOM SHAPES-- PEOPLE, I SUPPOSE, WHO'VE GONE BEFORE.
I START LOOKING FOR *ONE* IN PARTICULAR. CRAZY AS IT SOUNDS, I *KNOW* SHE'S HERE, I CAN FEEL HER PRESENCE THROUGH THE PSYCHIC RAPPORT WE SHARED--
--I *SEE HER!*
NO, I'M WRONG. IT'S SOMEONE ELSE-- AND YET, SOMETHING ABOUT HER IS ACHINGLY FAMILIAR.
STOP.
COME NO FARTHER.
WHY NOT?
THIS PLACE IS NOT YET FOR YOU, MY DARLING BOY.
WHAT D'YOU MEAN? WHO *ARE* YOU, ANYWAY?
LOOK WITHIN YOURSELF.
THERE WILL YOU FIND YOUR ANSWERS.
AND THEY WILL LEAD YOU TO YOUR HEART'S DESIRE.
WAIT! DON'T SEND ME AWAY! DON'T LET ME GO!
AS I TUMBLE, FASTER AND FASTER, INTO DARKNESS AND OBLIVION, I CATCH A LAST GLIMPSE OF THE WOMAN, HER FACE OUTLINED IN A HALO OF FIRE. I HEAR HER WHISPERED "FAREWELL."
TOO LATE, I KNOW HER.

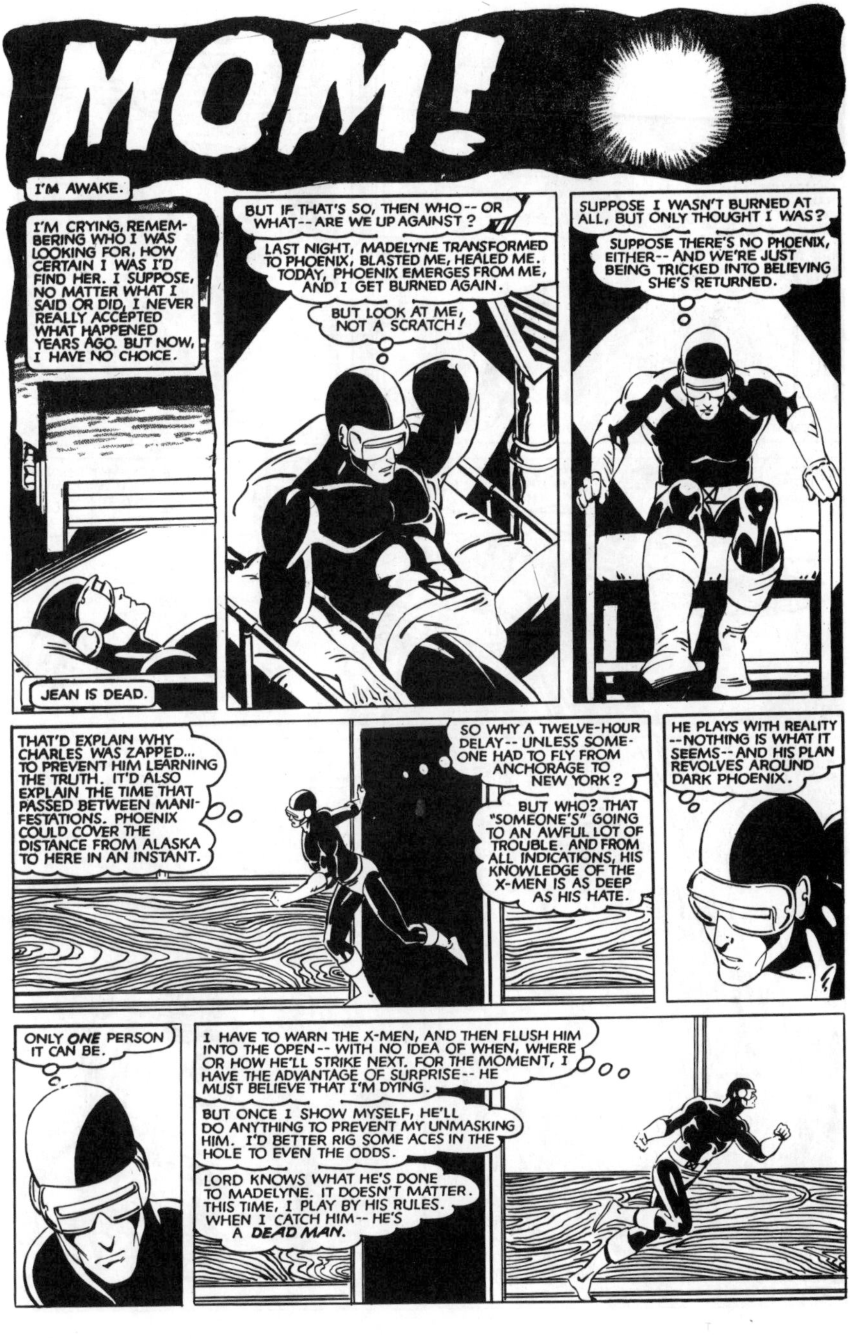
MOM!
I'M AWAKE.
I'M CRYING, REMEMBERING WHO I WAS LOOKING FOR, HOW CERTAIN I WAS I'D FIND HER. I SUPPOSE, NO MATTER WHAT I SAID OR DID, I NEVER REALLY ACCEPTED WHAT HAPPENED YEARS AGO. BUT NOW, I HAVE NO CHOICE.
JEAN IS DEAD.
BUT IF THAT'S SO, THEN WHO -- OR WHAT -- ARE WE UP AGAINST?
LAST NIGHT, MADELYNE TRANSFORMED TO PHOENIX, BLASTED ME, HEALED ME. TODAY, PHOENIX EMERGES FROM ME, AND I GET BURNED AGAIN.
BUT LOOK AT ME, NOT A SCRATCH!
SUPPOSE I WASN'T BURNED AT ALL, BUT ONLY THOUGHT I WAS?
SUPPOSE THERE'S NO PHOENIX, EITHER -- AND WE'RE JUST BEING TRICKED INTO BELIEVING SHE'S RETURNED.
THAT'D EXPLAIN WHY CHARLES WAS ZAPPED... TO PREVENT HIM LEARNING THE TRUTH. IT'D ALSO EXPLAIN THE TIME THAT PASSED BETWEEN MANIFESTATIONS. PHOENIX COULD COVER THE DISTANCE FROM ALASKA TO HERE IN AN INSTANT.
SO WHY A TWELVE-HOUR DELAY -- UNLESS SOMEONE HAD TO FLY FROM ANCHORAGE TO NEW YORK?
BUT WHO? THAT "SOMEONE'S" GOING TO AN AWFUL LOT OF TROUBLE. AND FROM ALL INDICATIONS, HIS KNOWLEDGE OF THE X-MEN IS AS DEEP AS HIS HATE.
HE PLAYS WITH REALITY -- NOTHING IS WHAT IT SEEMS -- AND HIS PLAN REVOLVES AROUND DARK PHOENIX.
ONLY ONE PERSON IT CAN BE.
I HAVE TO WARN THE X-MEN, AND THEN FLUSH HIM INTO THE OPEN -- WITH NO IDEA OF WHEN, WHERE OR HOW HE'LL STRIKE NEXT. FOR THE MOMENT, I HAVE THE ADVANTAGE OF SURPRISE -- HE MUST BELIEVE THAT I'M DYING.
BUT ONCE I SHOW MYSELF, HE'LL DO ANYTHING TO PREVENT MY UNMASKING HIM. I'D BETTER RIG SOME ACES IN THE HOLE TO EVEN THE ODDS.
LORD KNOWS WHAT HE'S DONE TO MADELYNE. IT DOESN'T MATTER. THIS TIME, I PLAY BY HIS RULES. WHEN I CATCH HIM -- HE'S A DEAD MAN.

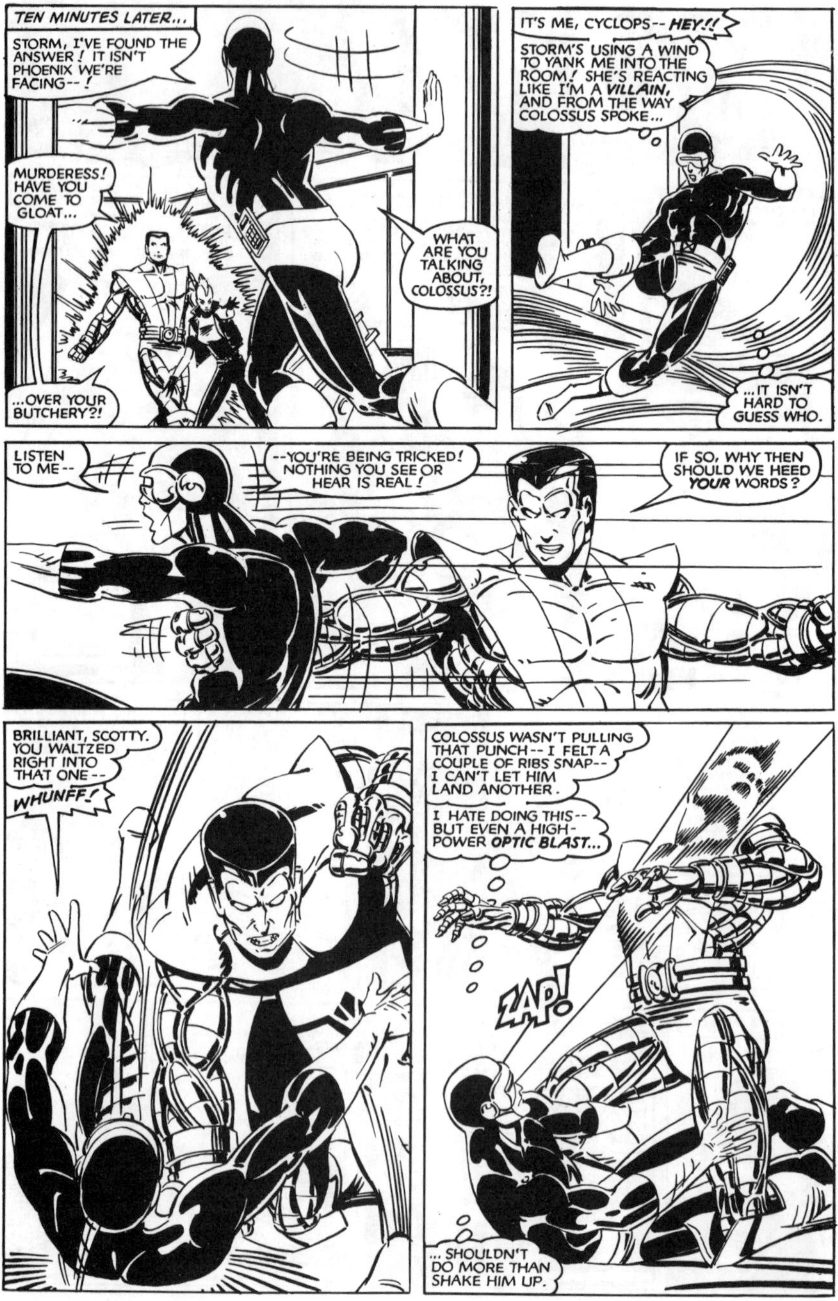
TEN MINUTES LATER...
STORM, I'VE FOUND THE ANSWER! IT ISN'T PHOENIX WE'RE FACING--!
MURDERESS! HAVE YOU COME TO GLOAT...
WHAT ARE YOU TALKING ABOUT, COLOSSUS?!
...OVER YOUR BUTCHERY?!
IT'S ME, CYCLOPS-- HEY!!
STORM'S USING A WIND TO YANK ME INTO THE ROOM! SHE'S REACTING LIKE I'M A VILLAIN, AND FROM THE WAY COLOSSUS SPOKE...
...IT ISN'T HARD TO GUESS WHO.
LISTEN TO ME--
--YOU'RE BEING TRICKED! NOTHING YOU SEE OR HEAR IS REAL!
IF SO, WHY THEN SHOULD WE HEED YOUR WORDS?
BRILLIANT, SCOTTY. YOU WALTZED RIGHT INTO THAT ONE--
WHUNFF!
COLOSSUS WASN'T PULLING THAT PUNCH-- I FELT A COUPLE OF RIBS SNAP-- I CAN'T LET HIM LAND ANOTHER.
I HATE DOING THIS-- BUT EVEN A HIGH-POWER OPTIC BLAST...
ZAP!
...SHOULDN'T DO MORE THAN SHAKE HIM UP.

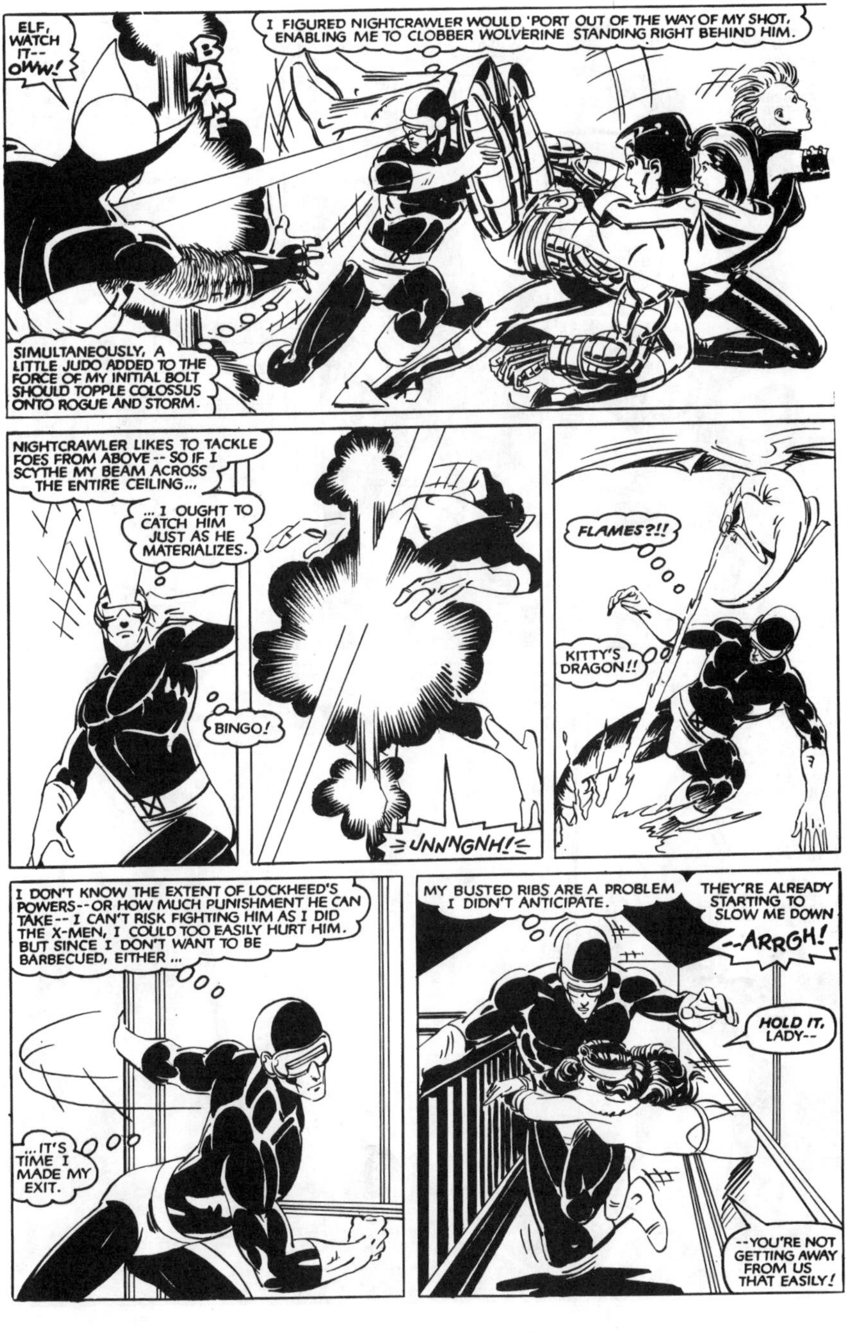
ELF, WATCH IT-- OWW!
BAMF
I FIGURED NIGHTCRAWLER WOULD 'PORT OUT OF THE WAY OF MY SHOT, ENABLING ME TO CLOBBER WOLVERINE STANDING RIGHT BEHIND HIM.
SIMULTANEOUSLY, A LITTLE JUDO ADDED TO THE FORCE OF MY INITIAL BOLT SHOULD TOPPLE COLOSSUS ONTO ROGUE AND STORM.
NIGHTCRAWLER LIKES TO TACKLE FOES FROM ABOVE -- SO IF I SCYTHE MY BEAM ACROSS THE ENTIRE CEILING...
...I OUGHT TO CATCH HIM JUST AS HE MATERIALIZES.
BINGO!
UNNNGNH!
FLAMES?!!
KITTY'S DRAGON!!
I DON'T KNOW THE EXTENT OF LOCKHEED'S POWERS -- OR HOW MUCH PUNISHMENT HE CAN TAKE -- I CAN'T RISK FIGHTING HIM AS I DID THE X-MEN, I COULD TOO EASILY HURT HIM. BUT SINCE I DON'T WANT TO BE BARBECUED, EITHER ...
...IT'S TIME I MADE MY EXIT.
MY BUSTED RIBS ARE A PROBLEM I DIDN'T ANTICIPATE.
THEY'RE ALREADY STARTING TO SLOW ME DOWN
--ARRGH!
HOLD IT, LADY--
--YOU'RE NOT GETTING AWAY FROM US THAT EASILY!

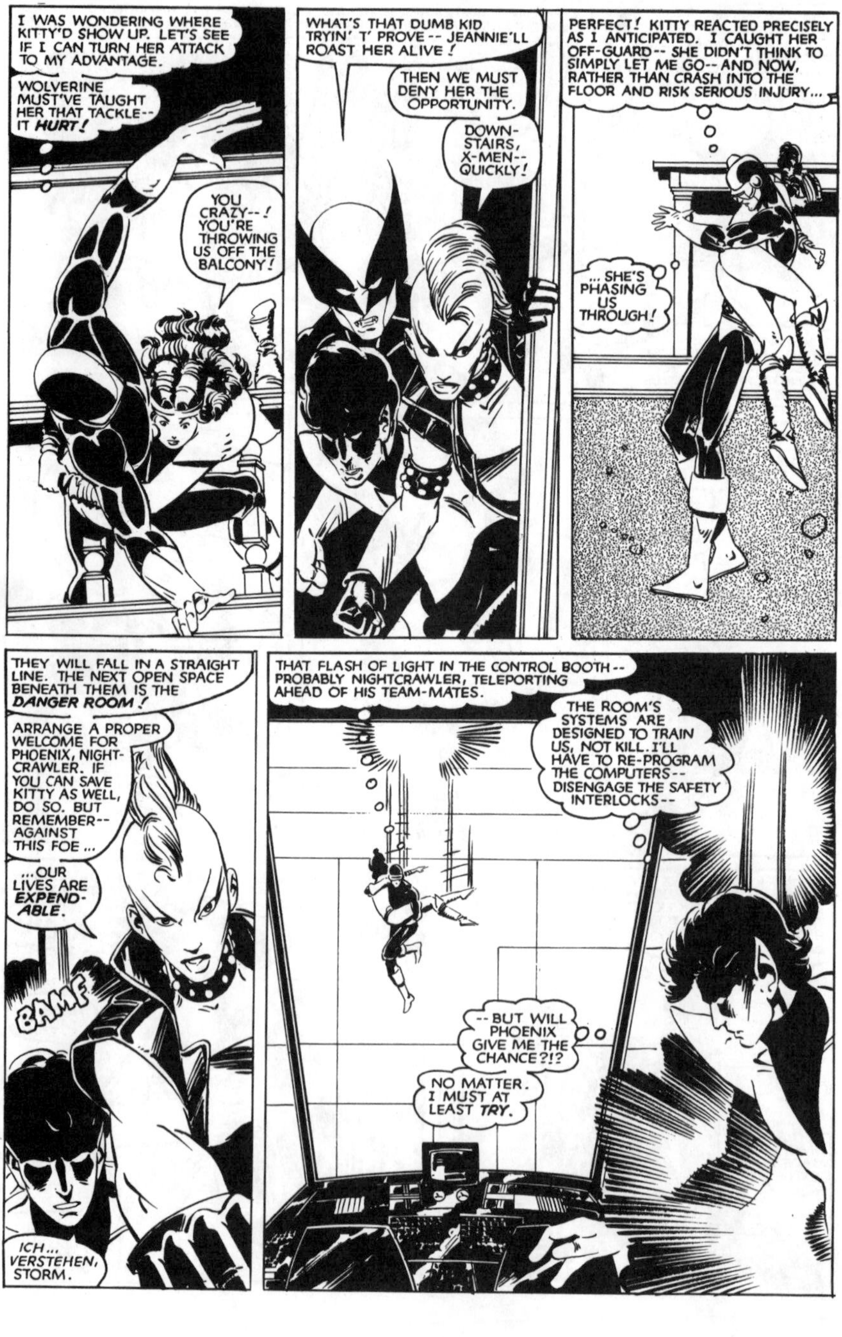
I WAS WONDERING WHERE KITTY'D SHOW UP. LET'S SEE IF I CAN TURN HER ATTACK TO MY ADVANTAGE.
WOLVERINE MUST'VE TAUGHT HER THAT TACKLE-- IT HURT!
YOU CRAZY--! YOU'RE THROWING US OFF THE BALCONY!
WHAT'S THAT DUMB KID TRYIN' T' PROVE -- JEANNIE'LL ROAST HER ALIVE!
THEN WE MUST DENY HER THE OPPORTUNITY.
DOWN-STAIRS, X-MEN-- QUICKLY!
PERFECT! KITTY REACTED PRECISELY AS I ANTICIPATED. I CAUGHT HER OFF-GUARD-- SHE DIDN'T THINK TO SIMPLY LET ME GO-- AND NOW, RATHER THAN CRASH INTO THE FLOOR AND RISK SERIOUS INJURY...
...SHE'S PHASING US THROUGH!
THEY WILL FALL IN A STRAIGHT LINE. THE NEXT OPEN SPACE BENEATH THEM IS THE DANGER ROOM!
ARRANGE A PROPER WELCOME FOR PHOENIX, NIGHT-CRAWLER. IF YOU CAN SAVE KITTY AS WELL, DO SO. BUT REMEMBER-- AGAINST THIS FOE ...
...OUR LIVES ARE EXPEND-ABLE.
BAMF
ICH... VERSTEHEN, STORM.
THAT FLASH OF LIGHT IN THE CONTROL BOOTH-- PROBABLY NIGHTCRAWLER, TELEPORTING AHEAD OF HIS TEAM-MATES.
THE ROOM'S SYSTEMS ARE DESIGNED TO TRAIN US, NOT KILL. I'LL HAVE TO RE-PROGRAM THE COMPUTERS-- DISENGAGE THE SAFETY INTERLOCKS--
--BUT WILL PHOENIX GIVE ME THE CHANCE?!?
NO MATTER. I MUST AT LEAST TRY.

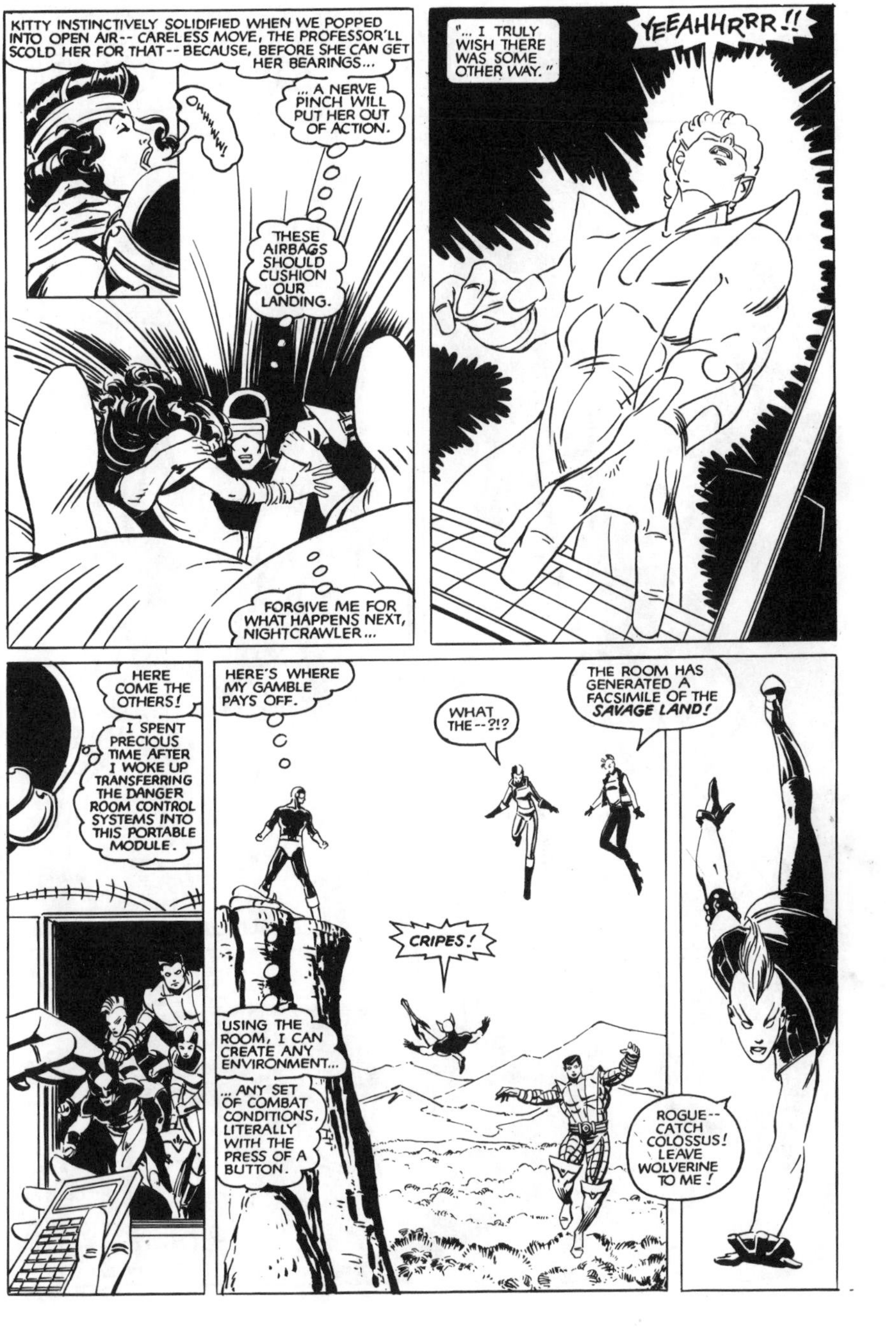
KITTY INSTINCTIVELY SOLIDIFIED WHEN WE POPPED INTO OPEN AIR-- CARELESS MOVE, THE PROFESSOR'LL SCOLD HER FOR THAT-- BECAUSE, BEFORE SHE CAN GET HER BEARINGS...
OHHHWW!
... A NERVE PINCH WILL PUT HER OUT OF ACTION.
THESE AIRBAGS SHOULD CUSHION OUR LANDING.
FORGIVE ME FOR WHAT HAPPENS NEXT, NIGHTCRAWLER...
"... I TRULY WISH THERE WAS SOME OTHER WAY."
YEEAHHRRR!!
HERE COME THE OTHERS!
I SPENT PRECIOUS TIME AFTER I WOKE UP TRANSFERRING THE DANGER ROOM CONTROL SYSTEMS INTO THIS PORTABLE MODULE.
HERE'S WHERE MY GAMBLE PAYS OFF.
WHAT THE--?!?
THE ROOM HAS GENERATED A FACSIMILE OF THE SAVAGE LAND!
CRIPES!
USING THE ROOM, I CAN CREATE ANY ENVIRONMENT...
... ANY SET OF COMBAT CONDITIONS, LITERALLY WITH THE PRESS OF A BUTTON.
ROGUE-- CATCH COLOSSUS! LEAVE WOLVERINE TO ME!

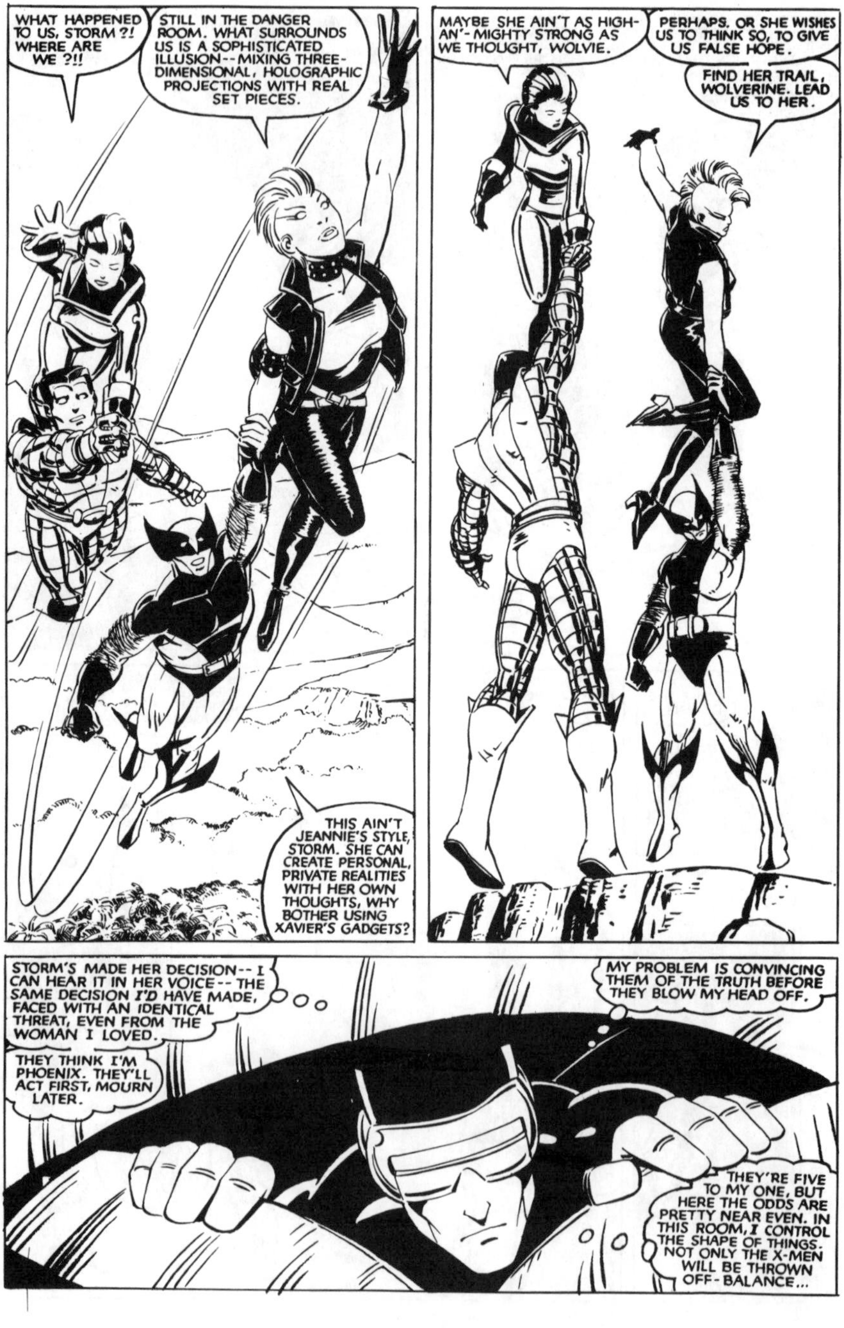
WHAT HAPPENED TO US, STORM ?! WHERE ARE WE ?!!
STILL IN THE DANGER ROOM. WHAT SURROUNDS US IS A SOPHISTICATED ILLUSION--MIXING THREE-DIMENSIONAL, HOLOGRAPHIC PROJECTIONS WITH REAL SET PIECES.
THIS AIN'T JEANNIE'S STYLE, STORM. SHE CAN CREATE PERSONAL, PRIVATE REALITIES WITH HER OWN THOUGHTS, WHY BOTHER USING XAVIER'S GADGETS?
MAYBE SHE AIN'T AS HIGH-AN'-MIGHTY STRONG AS WE THOUGHT, WOLVIE.
PERHAPS. OR SHE WISHES US TO THINK SO, TO GIVE US FALSE HOPE.
FIND HER TRAIL, WOLVERINE. LEAD US TO HER.
STORM'S MADE HER DECISION-- I CAN HEAR IT IN HER VOICE-- THE SAME DECISION I'D HAVE MADE, FACED WITH AN IDENTICAL THREAT, EVEN FROM THE WOMAN I LOVED.
THEY THINK I'M PHOENIX. THEY'LL ACT FIRST, MOURN LATER.
MY PROBLEM IS CONVINCING THEM OF THE TRUTH BEFORE THEY BLOW MY HEAD OFF.
THEY'RE FIVE TO MY ONE, BUT HERE THE ODDS ARE PRETTY NEAR EVEN. IN THIS ROOM, I CONTROL THE SHAPE OF THINGS. NOT ONLY THE X-MEN WILL BE THROWN OFF-BALANCE...

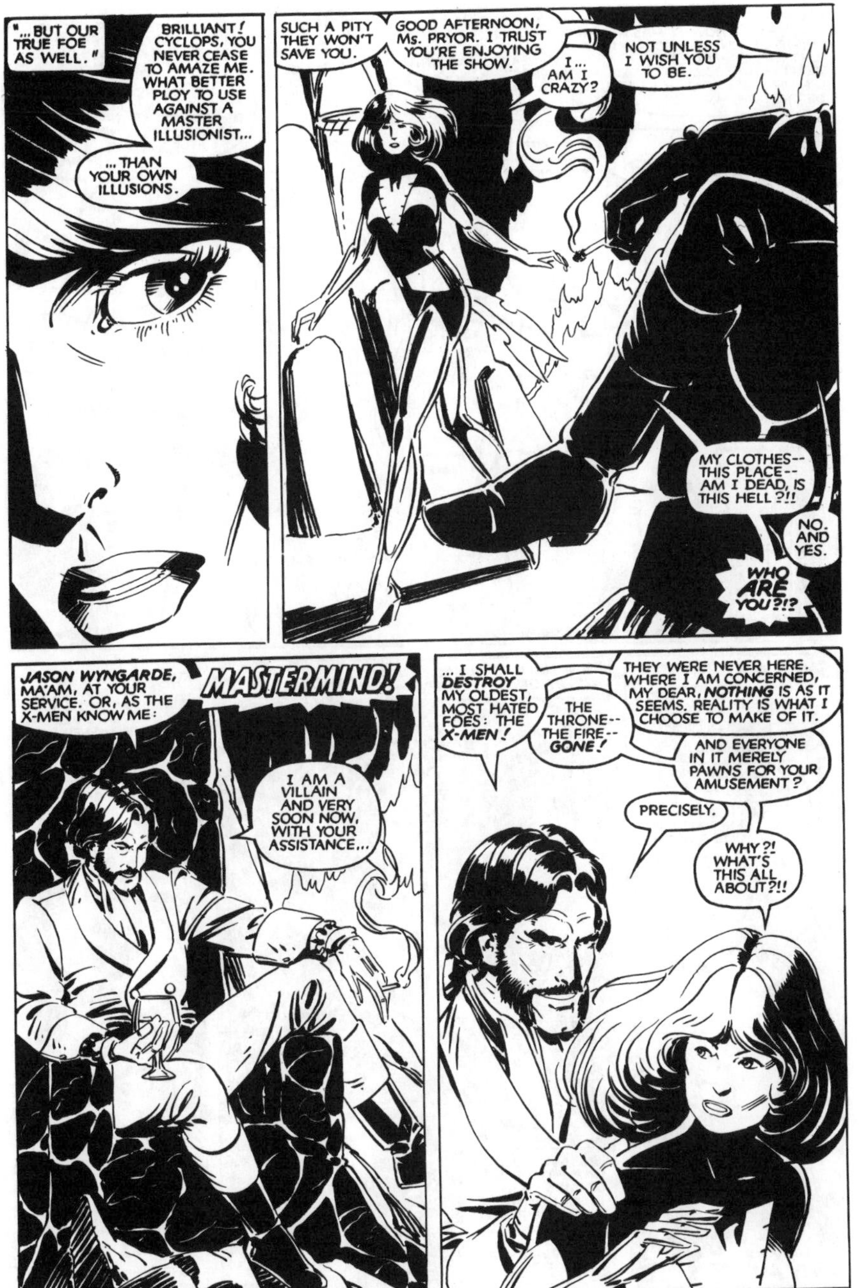
"...BUT OUR TRUE FOE AS WELL."
BRILLIANT! CYCLOPS, YOU NEVER CEASE TO AMAZE ME. WHAT BETTER PLOY TO USE AGAINST A MASTER ILLUSIONIST...
...THAN YOUR OWN ILLUSIONS.
SUCH A PITY THEY WON'T SAVE YOU.
GOOD AFTERNOON, Ms. PRYOR. I TRUST YOU'RE ENJOYING THE SHOW.
I... AM I CRAZY?
NOT UNLESS I WISH YOU TO BE.
MY CLOTHES-- THIS PLACE-- AM I DEAD, IS THIS HELL?!!
NO. AND YES.
WHO ARE YOU?!?
JASON WYNGARDE, MA'AM, AT YOUR SERVICE. OR, AS THE X-MEN KNOW ME:
MASTERMIND!
I AM A VILLAIN AND VERY SOON NOW, WITH YOUR ASSISTANCE...
...I SHALL DESTROY MY OLDEST, MOST HATED FOES: THE X-MEN!
THE THRONE-- THE FIRE-- GONE!
THEY WERE NEVER HERE. WHERE I AM CONCERNED, MY DEAR, NOTHING IS AS IT SEEMS. REALITY IS WHAT I CHOOSE TO MAKE OF IT.
AND EVERYONE IN IT MERELY PAWNS FOR YOUR AMUSEMENT?
PRECISELY.
WHY?! WHAT'S THIS ALL ABOUT?!!

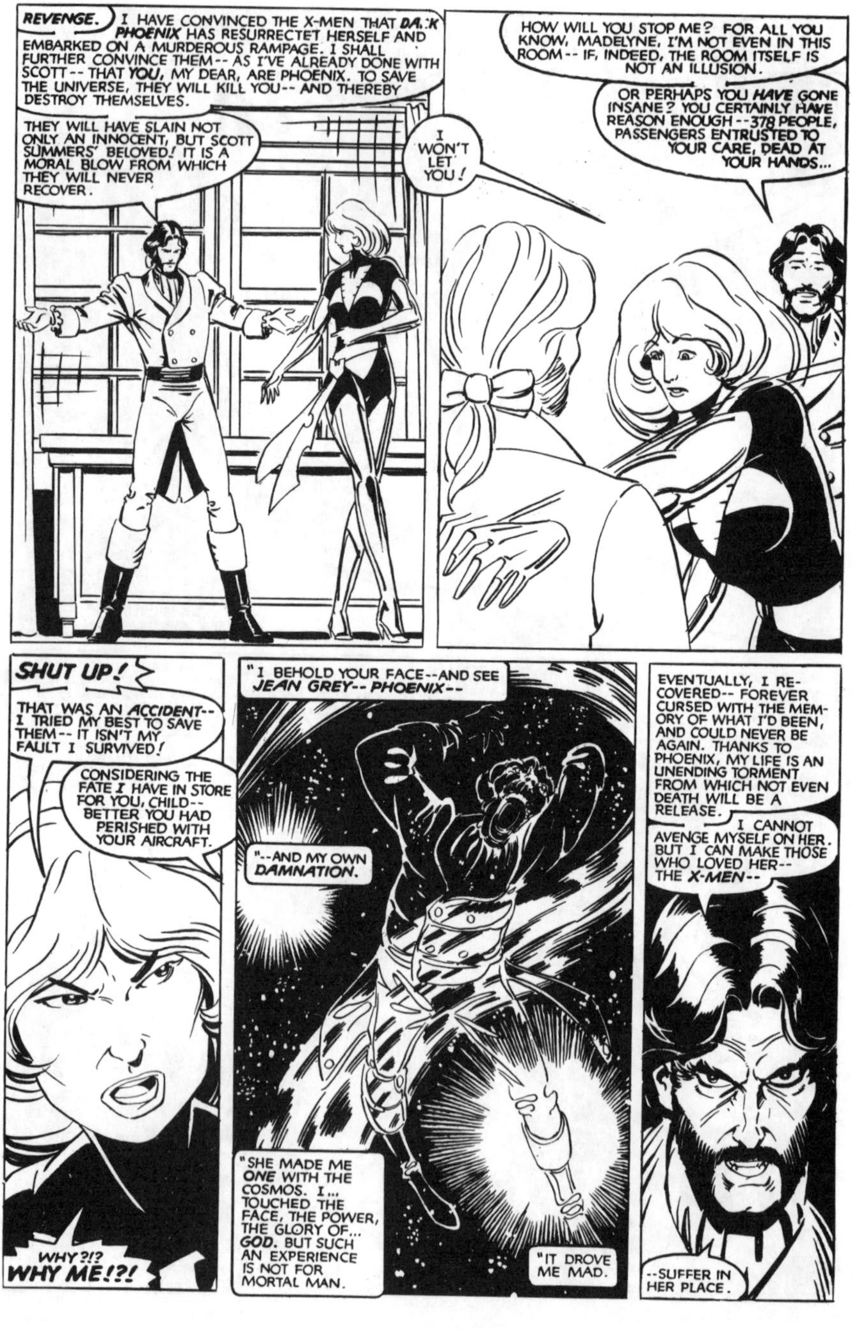
REVENGE.
I HAVE CONVINCED THE X-MEN THAT DA.K PHOENIX HAS RESURRECTET HERSELF AND EMBARKED ON A MURDEROUS RAMPAGE. I SHALL FURTHER CONVINCE THEM-- AS I'VE ALREADY DONE WITH SCOTT-- THAT YOU, MY DEAR, ARE PHOENIX. TO SAVE THE UNIVERSE, THEY WILL KILL YOU-- AND THEREBY DESTROY THEMSELVES.
THEY WILL HAVE SLAIN NOT ONLY AN INNOCENT, BUT SCOTT SUMMERS' BELOVED! IT IS A MORAL BLOW FROM WHICH THEY WILL NEVER RECOVER.
I WON'T LET YOU!
HOW WILL YOU STOP ME? FOR ALL YOU KNOW, MADELYNE, I'M NOT EVEN IN THIS ROOM-- IF, INDEED, THE ROOM ITSELF IS NOT AN ILLUSION.
OR PERHAPS YOU HAVE GONE INSANE? YOU CERTAINLY HAVE REASON ENOUGH--378 PEOPLE, PASSENGERS ENTRUSTED TO YOUR CARE, DEAD AT YOUR HANDS...
SHUT UP!
THAT WAS AN ACCIDENT-- I TRIED MY BEST TO SAVE THEM-- IT ISN'T MY FAULT I SURVIVED!
CONSIDERING THE FATE I HAVE IN STORE FOR YOU, CHILD-- BETTER YOU HAD PERISHED WITH YOUR AIRCRAFT.
WHY?!? WHY ME!?!
"I BEHOLD YOUR FACE--AND SEE JEAN GREY-- PHOENIX--
"--AND MY OWN DAMNATION.
"SHE MADE ME ONE WITH THE COSMOS. I... TOUCHED THE FACE, THE POWER, THE GLORY OF... GOD. BUT SUCH AN EXPERIENCE IS NOT FOR MORTAL MAN.
"IT DROVE ME MAD.
EVENTUALLY, I RE-COVERED-- FOREVER CURSED WITH THE MEM-ORY OF WHAT I'D BEEN, AND COULD NEVER BE AGAIN. THANKS TO PHOENIX, MY LIFE IS AN UNENDING TORMENT FROM WHICH NOT EVEN DEATH WILL BE A RELEASE.
I CANNOT AVENGE MYSELF ON HER. BUT I CAN MAKE THOSE WHO LOVED HER-- THE X-MEN--
--SUFFER IN HER PLACE.

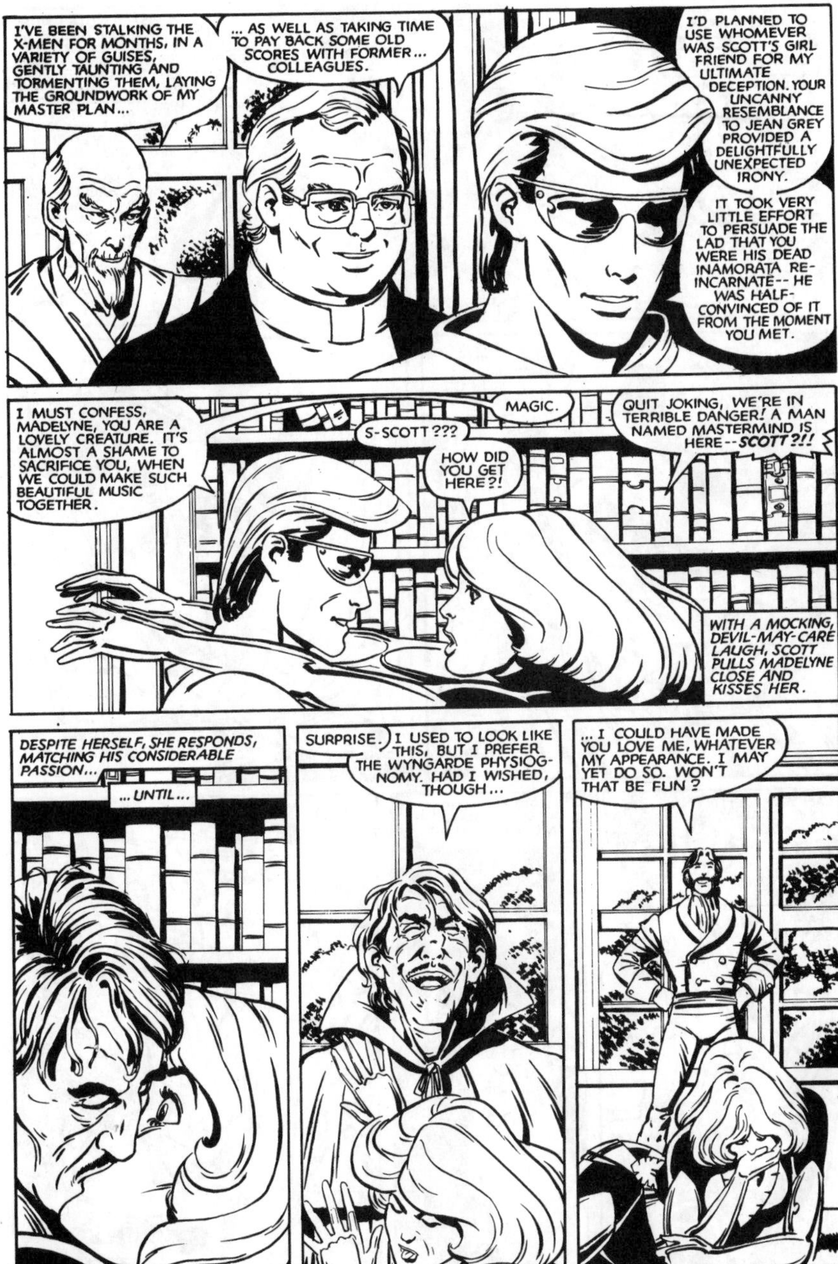
I'VE BEEN STALKING THE X-MEN FOR MONTHS, IN A VARIETY OF GUISES, GENTLY TAUNTING AND TORMENTING THEM, LAYING THE GROUNDWORK OF MY MASTER PLAN...
... AS WELL AS TAKING TIME TO PAY BACK SOME OLD SCORES WITH FORMER... COLLEAGUES.
I'D PLANNED TO USE WHOMEVER WAS SCOTT'S GIRL FRIEND FOR MY ULTIMATE DECEPTION. YOUR UNCANNY RESEMBLANCE TO JEAN GREY PROVIDED A DELIGHTFULLY UNEXPECTED IRONY.
IT TOOK VERY LITTLE EFFORT TO PERSUADE THE LAD THAT YOU WERE HIS DEAD INAMORATA RE-INCARNATE-- HE WAS HALF-CONVINCED OF IT FROM THE MOMENT YOU MET.
I MUST CONFESS, MADELYNE, YOU ARE A LOVELY CREATURE. IT'S ALMOST A SHAME TO SACRIFICE YOU, WHEN WE COULD MAKE SUCH BEAUTIFUL MUSIC TOGETHER.
MAGIC.
S-SCOTT???
HOW DID YOU GET HERE?!
QUIT JOKING, WE'RE IN TERRIBLE DANGER! A MAN NAMED MASTERMIND IS HERE--SCOTT?!!
WITH A MOCKING, DEVIL-MAY-CARE LAUGH, SCOTT PULLS MADELYNE CLOSE AND KISSES HER.
DESPITE HERSELF, SHE RESPONDS, MATCHING HIS CONSIDERABLE PASSION...
...UNTIL...
SURPRISE.
I USED TO LOOK LIKE THIS, BUT I PREFER THE WYNGARDE PHYSIOGNOMY. HAD I WISHED, THOUGH...
...I COULD HAVE MADE YOU LOVE ME, WHATEVER MY APPEARANCE. I MAY YET DO SO. WON'T THAT BE FUN?

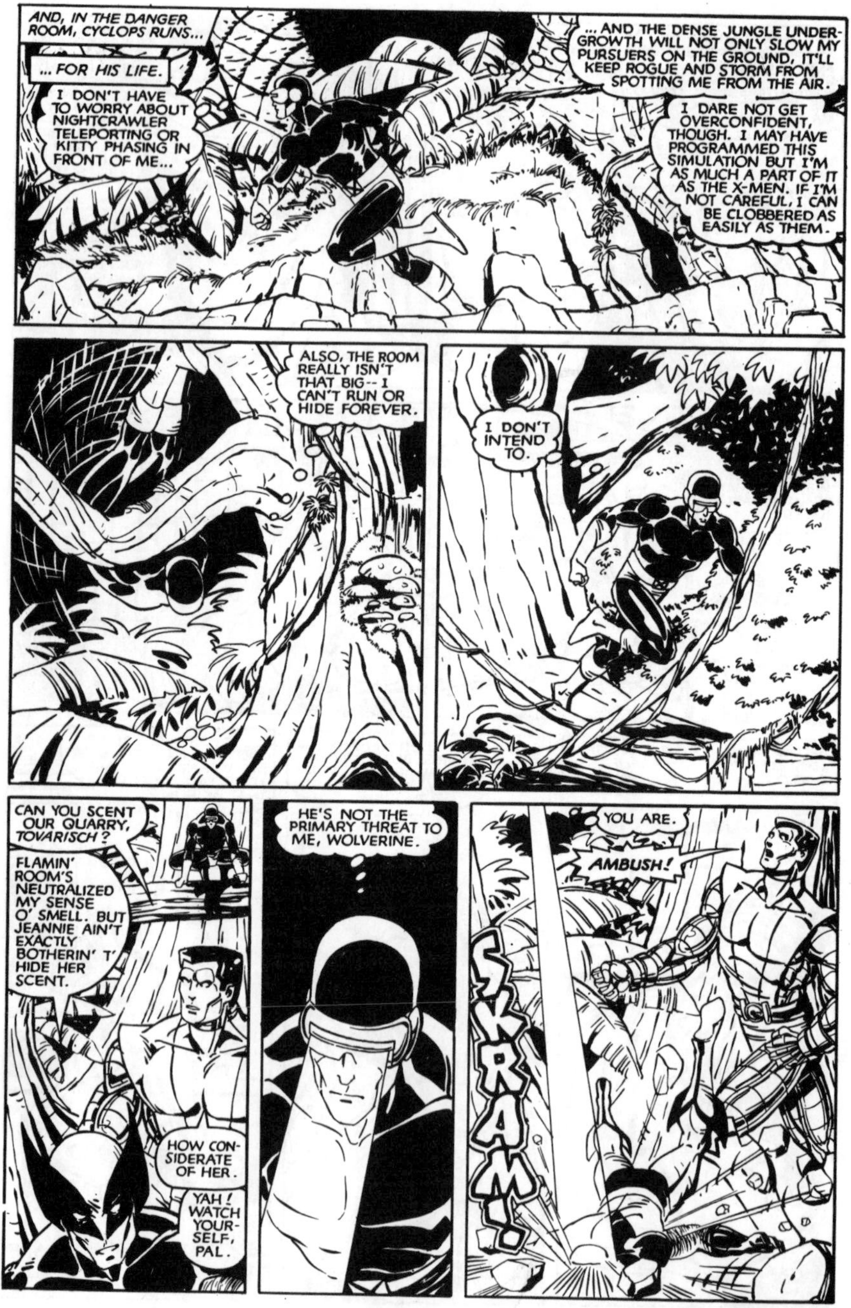
AND, IN THE DANGER ROOM, CYCLOPS RUNS...
... FOR HIS LIFE.
I DON'T HAVE TO WORRY ABOUT NIGHTCRAWLER TELEPORTING OR KITTY PHASING IN FRONT OF ME...
... AND THE DENSE JUNGLE UNDERGROWTH WILL NOT ONLY SLOW MY PURSUERS ON THE GROUND, IT'LL KEEP ROGUE AND STORM FROM SPOTTING ME FROM THE AIR.
I DARE NOT GET OVERCONFIDENT, THOUGH. I MAY HAVE PROGRAMMED THIS SIMULATION BUT I'M AS MUCH A PART OF IT AS THE X-MEN. IF I'M NOT CAREFUL, I CAN BE CLOBBERED AS EASILY AS THEM.
ALSO, THE ROOM REALLY ISN'T THAT BIG-- I CAN'T RUN OR HIDE FOREVER.
I DON'T INTEND TO.
CAN YOU SCENT OUR QUARRY, *TOVARISCH*?
FLAMIN' ROOM'S NEUTRALIZED MY SENSE O' SMELL. BUT JEANNIE AIN'T EXACTLY BOTHERIN' T' HIDE HER SCENT.
HOW CONSIDERATE OF HER.
YAH! WATCH YOURSELF, PAL.
HE'S NOT THE PRIMARY THREAT TO ME, WOLVERINE.
YOU ARE.
AMBUSH!
SKRAM!

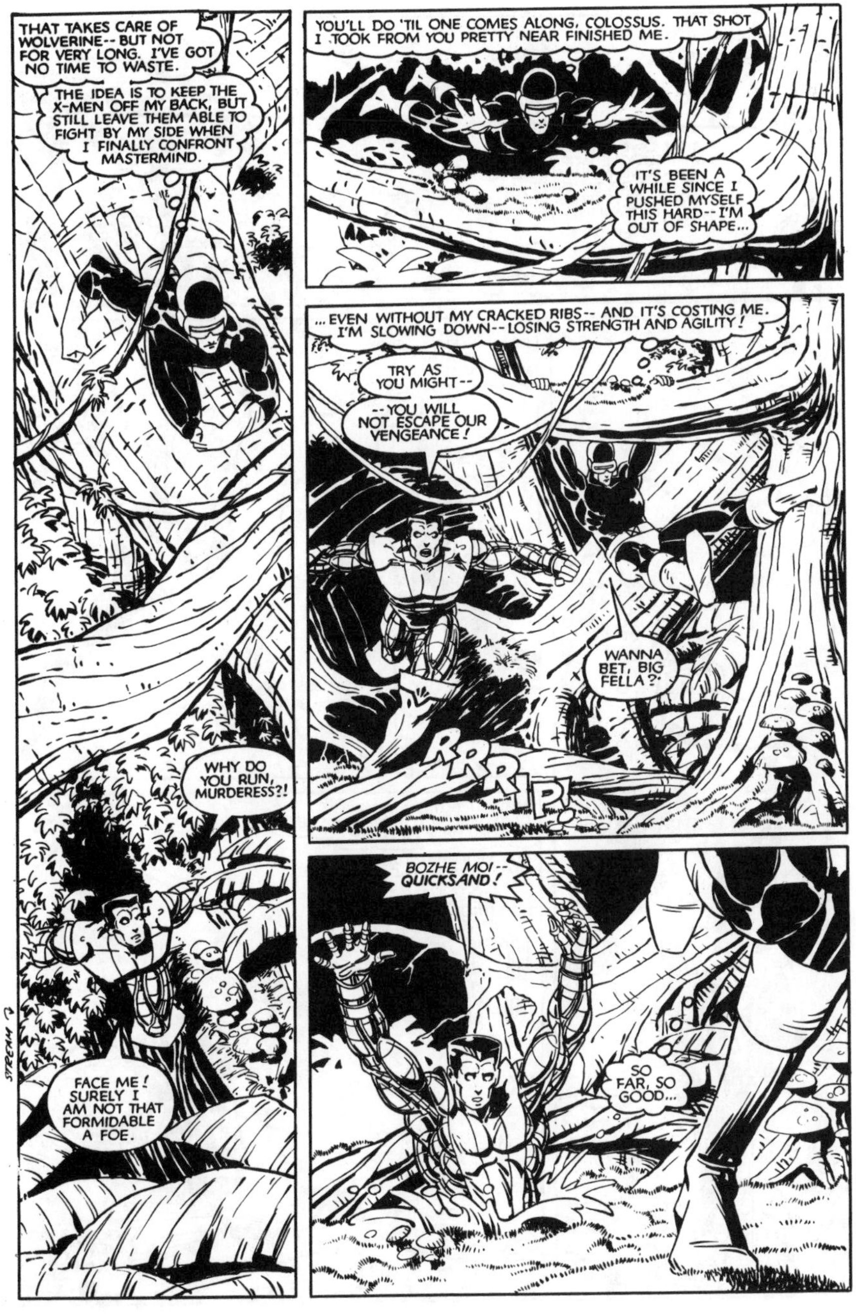
THAT TAKES CARE OF WOLVERINE-- BUT NOT FOR VERY LONG. I'VE GOT NO TIME TO WASTE.
THE IDEA IS TO KEEP THE X-MEN OFF MY BACK, BUT STILL LEAVE THEM ABLE TO FIGHT BY MY SIDE WHEN I FINALLY CONFRONT MASTERMIND.
WHY DO YOU RUN, MURDERESS?!
FACE ME! SURELY I AM NOT THAT FORMIDABLE A FOE.
YOU'LL DO 'TIL ONE COMES ALONG, COLOSSUS. THAT SHOT I TOOK FROM YOU PRETTY NEAR FINISHED ME.
IT'S BEEN A WHILE SINCE I PUSHED MYSELF THIS HARD-- I'M OUT OF SHAPE...
... EVEN WITHOUT MY CRACKED RIBS-- AND IT'S COSTING ME. I'M SLOWING DOWN-- LOSING STRENGTH AND AGILITY!
TRY AS YOU MIGHT--
--YOU WILL NOT ESCAPE OUR VENGEANCE!
WANNA BET, BIG FELLA?
RRRIP!
BOZHE MOI-- QUICKSAND!
SO FAR, SO GOOD...

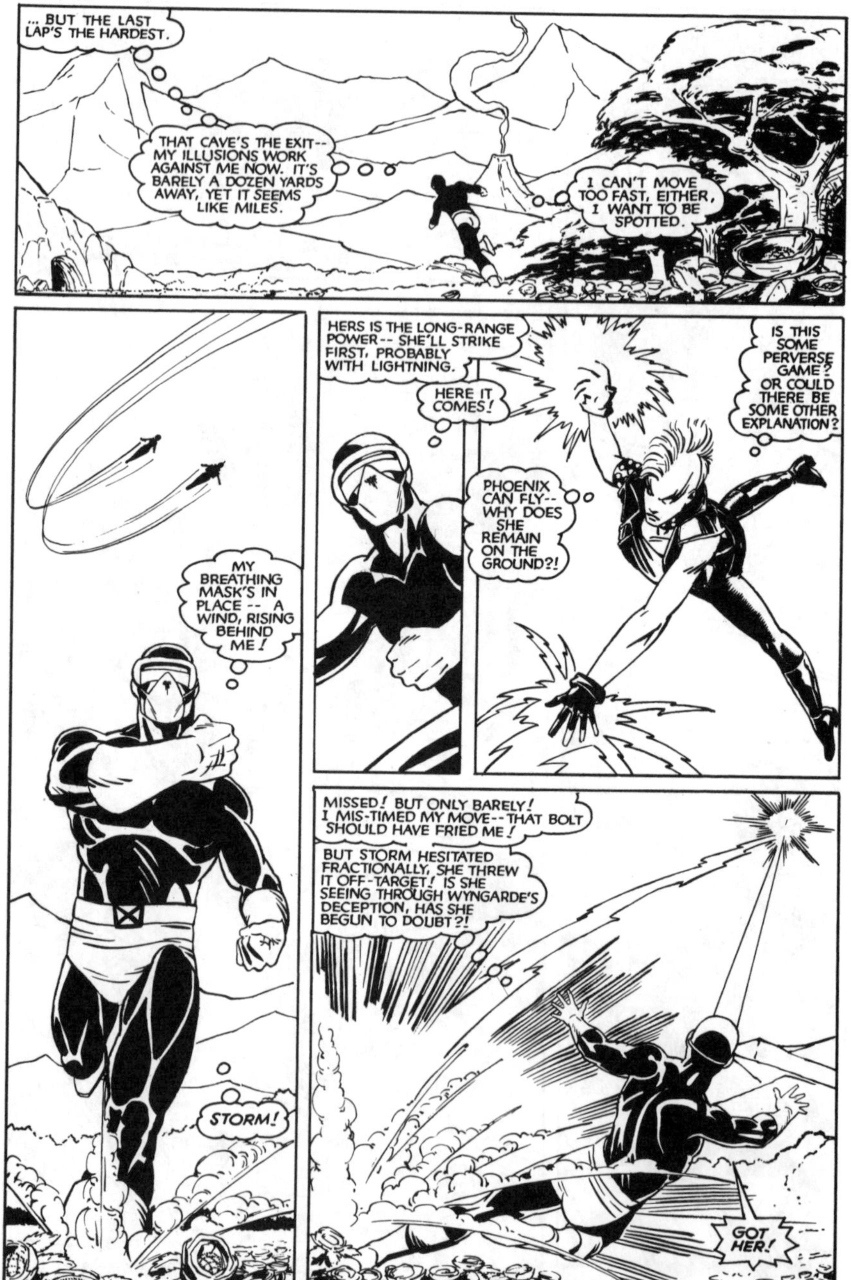
... BUT THE LAST LAP'S THE HARDEST.
THAT CAVE'S THE EXIT-- MY ILLUSIONS WORK AGAINST ME NOW. IT'S BARELY A DOZEN YARDS AWAY, YET IT SEEMS LIKE MILES.
I CAN'T MOVE TOO FAST, EITHER, I WANT TO BE SPOTTED.
MY BREATHING MASK'S IN PLACE -- A WIND, RISING BEHIND ME!
STORM!
HERS IS THE LONG-RANGE POWER-- SHE'LL STRIKE FIRST, PROBABLY WITH LIGHTNING.
HERE IT COMES!
IS THIS SOME PERVERSE GAME? OR COULD THERE BE SOME OTHER EXPLANATION?
PHOENIX CAN FLY-- WHY DOES SHE REMAIN ON THE GROUND?!
MISSED! BUT ONLY BARELY! I MIS-TIMED MY MOVE--THAT BOLT SHOULD HAVE FRIED ME!
BUT STORM HESITATED FRACTIONALLY, SHE THREW IT OFF-TARGET! IS SHE SEEING THROUGH WYNGARDE'S DECEPTION, HAS SHE BEGUN TO DOUBT?!
GOT HER!

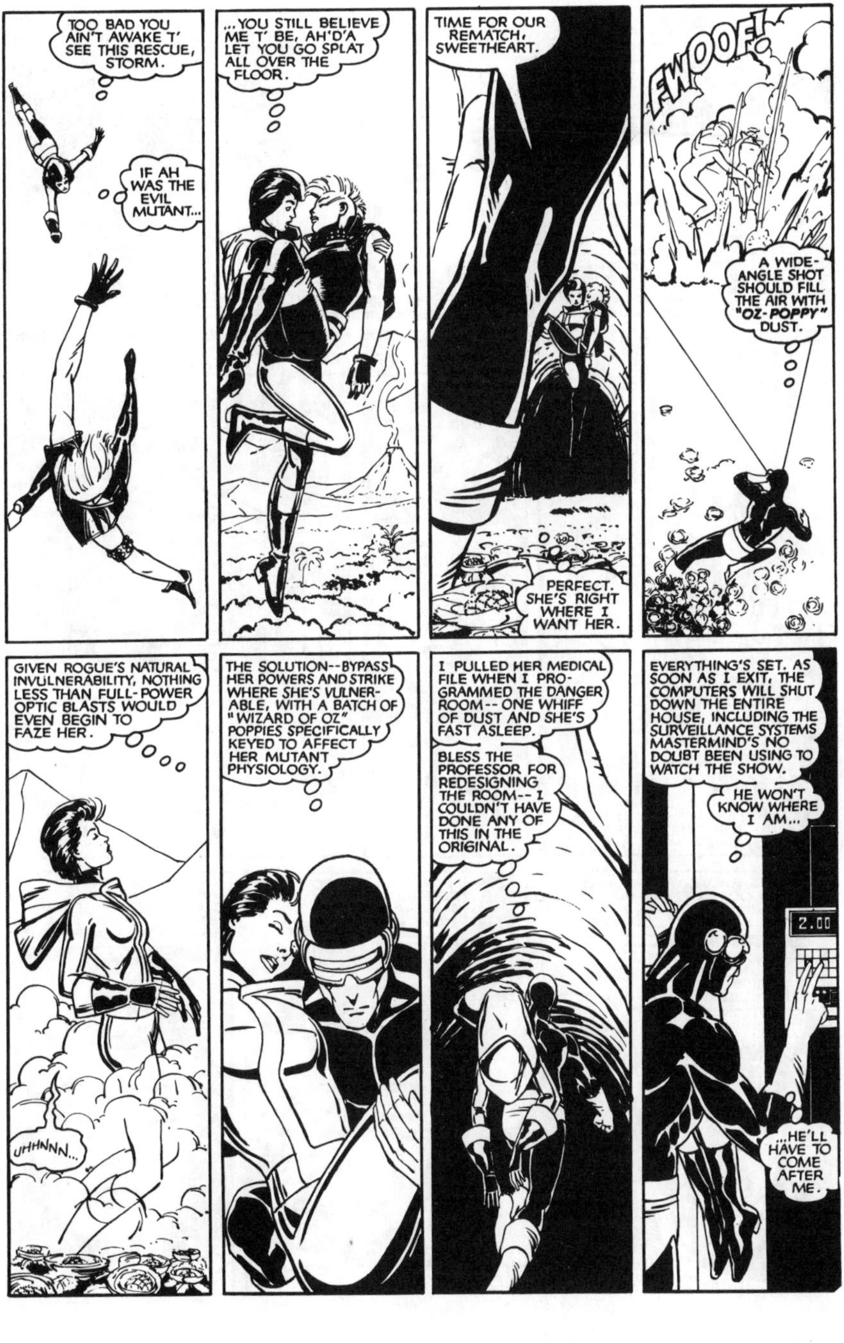
TOO BAD YOU AIN'T AWAKE T' SEE THIS RESCUE, STORM.
IF AH WAS THE EVIL MUTANT...
...YOU STILL BELIEVE ME T' BE, AH'D'A LET YOU GO SPLAT ALL OVER THE FLOOR.
TIME FOR OUR REMATCH, SWEETHEART.
PERFECT. SHE'S RIGHT WHERE I WANT HER.
FWOOF!
A WIDE-ANGLE SHOT SHOULD FILL THE AIR WITH "OZ-POPPY" DUST.
GIVEN ROGUE'S NATURAL INVULNERABILITY, NOTHING LESS THAN FULL-POWER OPTIC BLASTS WOULD EVEN BEGIN TO FAZE HER.
UHHNNN...
THE SOLUTION--BYPASS HER POWERS AND STRIKE WHERE SHE'S VULNERABLE, WITH A BATCH OF "WIZARD OF OZ" POPPIES SPECIFICALLY KEYED TO AFFECT HER MUTANT PHYSIOLOGY.
I PULLED HER MEDICAL FILE WHEN I PROGRAMMED THE DANGER ROOM-- ONE WHIFF OF DUST AND SHE'S FAST ASLEEP.
BLESS THE PROFESSOR FOR REDESIGNING THE ROOM-- I COULDN'T HAVE DONE ANY OF THIS IN THE ORIGINAL.
EVERYTHING'S SET. AS SOON AS I EXIT, THE COMPUTERS WILL SHUT DOWN THE ENTIRE HOUSE, INCLUDING THE SURVEILLANCE SYSTEMS MASTERMIND'S NO DOUBT BEEN USING TO WATCH THE SHOW.
HE WON'T KNOW WHERE I AM...
2.00
...HE'LL HAVE TO COME AFTER ME.

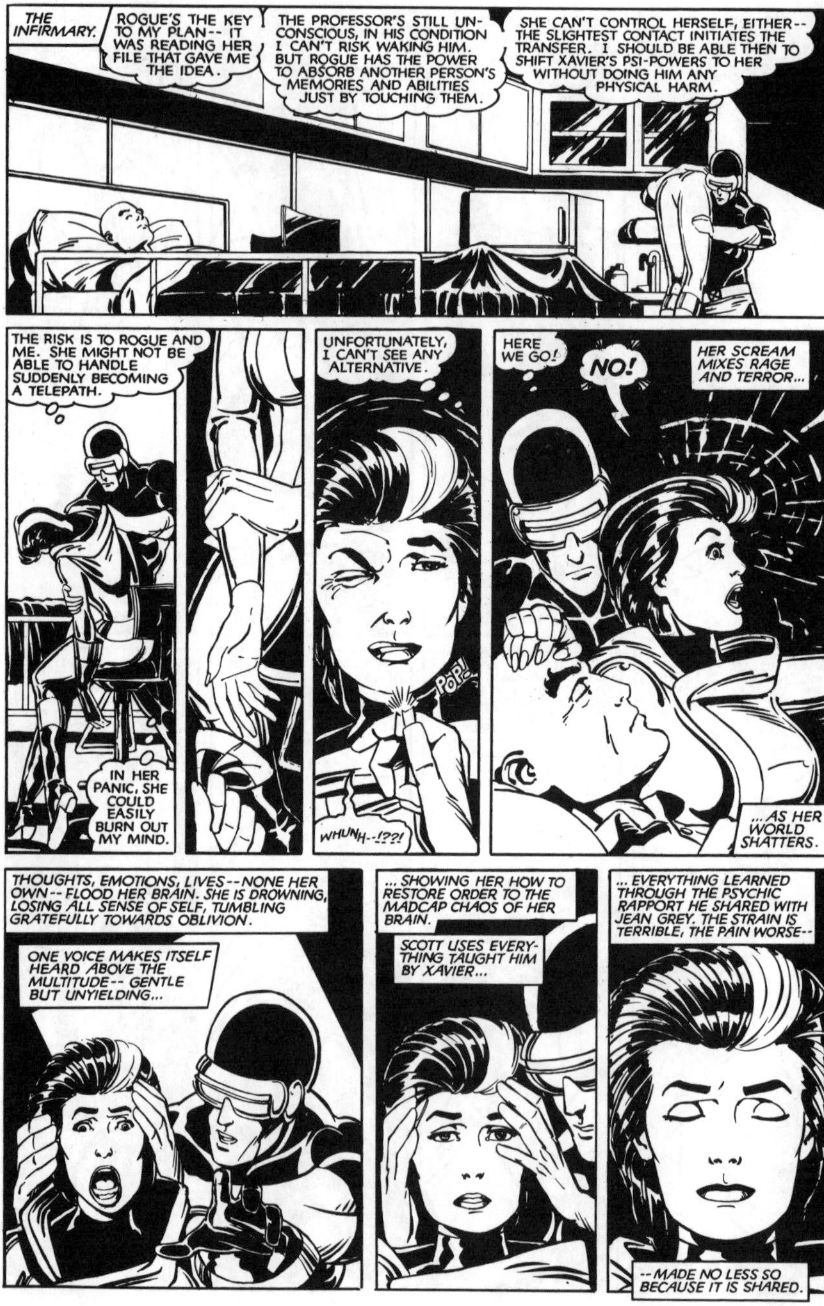
THE INFIRMARY.
ROGUE'S THE KEY TO MY PLAN-- IT WAS READING HER FILE THAT GAVE ME THE IDEA.
THE PROFESSOR'S STILL UNCONSCIOUS, IN HIS CONDITION I CAN'T RISK WAKING HIM. BUT ROGUE HAS THE POWER TO ABSORB ANOTHER PERSON'S MEMORIES AND ABILITIES JUST BY TOUCHING THEM.
SHE CAN'T CONTROL HERSELF, EITHER-- THE SLIGHTEST CONTACT INITIATES THE TRANSFER. I SHOULD BE ABLE THEN TO SHIFT XAVIER'S PSI-POWERS TO HER WITHOUT DOING HIM ANY PHYSICAL HARM.
THE RISK IS TO ROGUE AND ME. SHE MIGHT NOT BE ABLE TO HANDLE SUDDENLY BECOMING A TELEPATH.
IN HER PANIC, SHE COULD EASILY BURN OUT MY MIND.
UNFORTUNATELY, I CAN'T SEE ANY ALTERNATIVE.
POP!
WHUNH--!??!
HERE WE GO!
NO!
HER SCREAM MIXES RAGE AND TERROR...
...AS HER WORLD SHATTERS.
THOUGHTS, EMOTIONS, LIVES--NONE HER OWN--FLOOD HER BRAIN. SHE IS DROWNING, LOSING ALL SENSE OF SELF, TUMBLING GRATEFULLY TOWARDS OBLIVION.
ONE VOICE MAKES ITSELF HEARD ABOVE THE MULTITUDE-- GENTLE BUT UNYIELDING...
...SHOWING HER HOW TO RESTORE ORDER TO THE MADCAP CHAOS OF HER BRAIN.
SCOTT USES EVERYTHING TAUGHT HIM BY XAVIER...
...EVERYTHING LEARNED THROUGH THE PSYCHIC RAPPORT HE SHARED WITH JEAN GREY. THE STRAIN IS TERRIBLE, THE PAIN WORSE--
--MADE NO LESS SO BECAUSE IT IS SHARED.

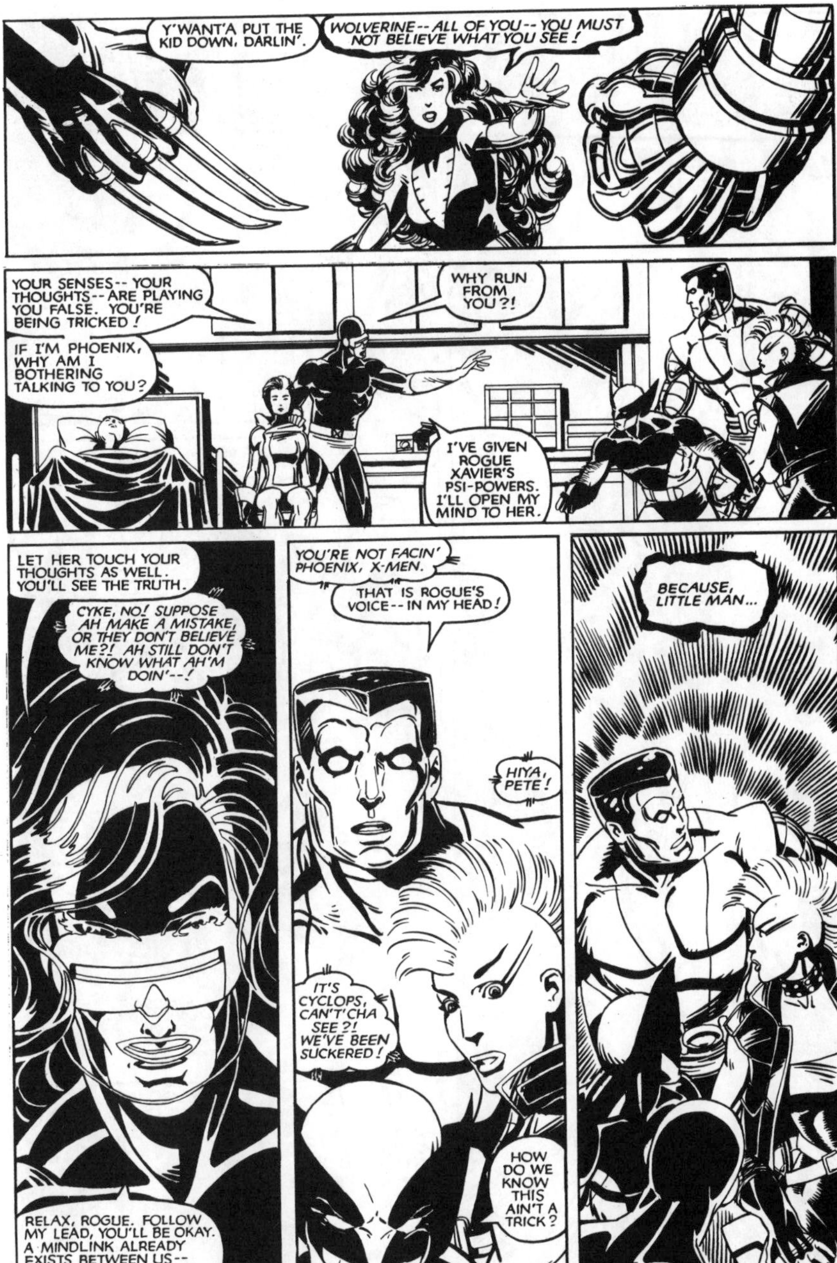
Y'WANT'A PUT THE KID DOWN, DARLIN'.
WOLVERINE-- ALL OF YOU-- YOU MUST NOT BELIEVE WHAT YOU SEE!
YOUR SENSES-- YOUR THOUGHTS-- ARE PLAYING YOU FALSE. YOU'RE BEING TRICKED!
WHY RUN FROM YOU?!
IF I'M PHOENIX, WHY AM I BOTHERING TALKING TO YOU?
I'VE GIVEN ROGUE XAVIER'S PSI-POWERS. I'LL OPEN MY MIND TO HER.
LET HER TOUCH YOUR THOUGHTS AS WELL. YOU'LL SEE THE TRUTH.
CYKE, NO! SUPPOSE AH MAKE A MISTAKE, OR THEY DON'T BELIEVE ME?! AH STILL DON'T KNOW WHAT AH'M DOIN'--!
RELAX, ROGUE. FOLLOW MY LEAD, YOU'LL BE OKAY. A MINDLINK ALREADY EXISTS BETWEEN US-- SIMPLY EXPAND IT TO INCLUDE THE OTHERS...
YOU'RE NOT FACIN' PHOENIX, X-MEN.
THAT IS ROGUE'S VOICE-- IN MY HEAD!
HIYA, PETE!
IT'S CYCLOPS, CAN'T'CHA SEE?! WE'VE BEEN SUCKERED!
HOW DO WE KNOW THIS AIN'T A TRICK?
BECAUSE, LITTLE MAN...

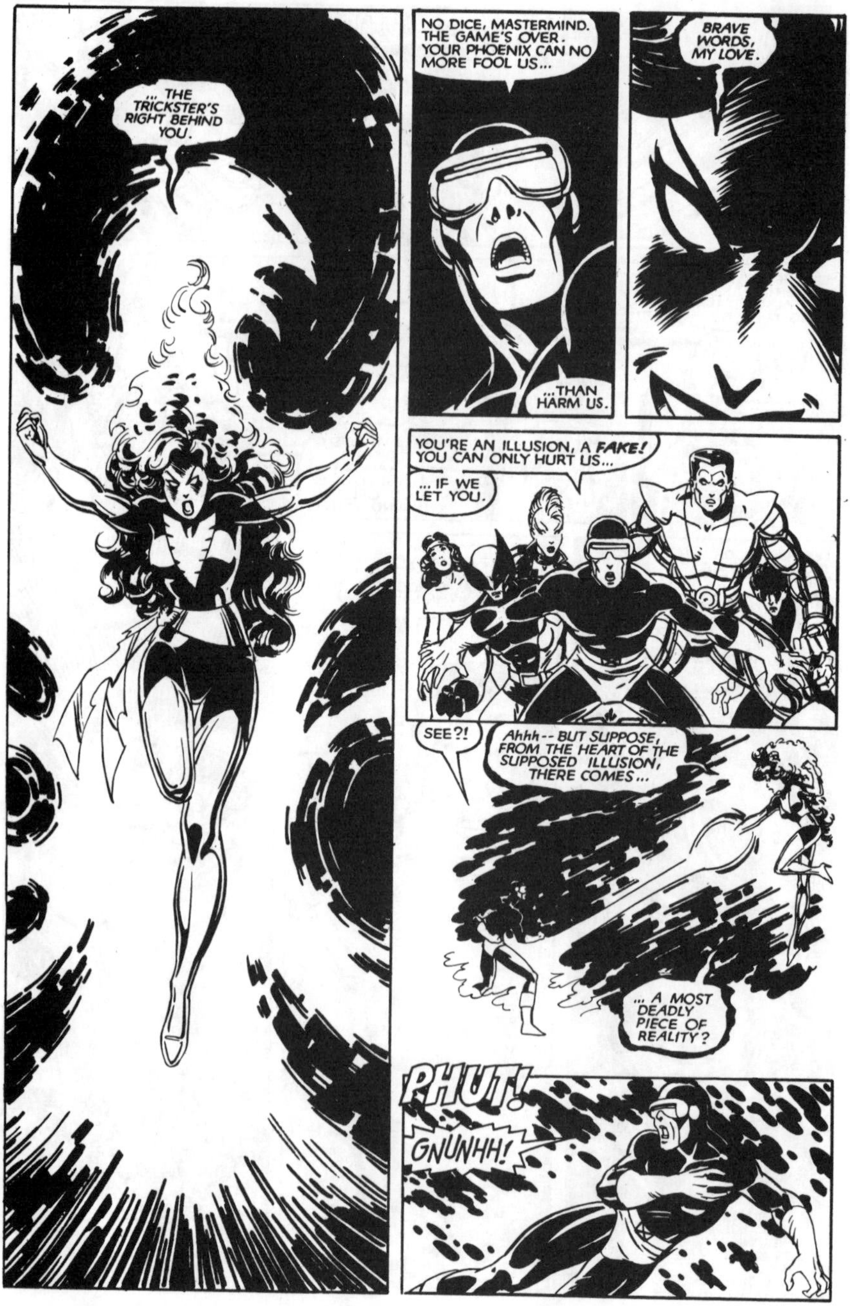
... THE TRICKSTER'S RIGHT BEHIND YOU.
NO DICE, MASTERMIND. THE GAME'S OVER. YOUR PHOENIX CAN NO MORE FOOL US...
...THAN HARM US.
BRAVE WORDS, MY LOVE.
YOU'RE AN ILLUSION, A FAKE! YOU CAN ONLY HURT US...
... IF WE LET YOU.
SEE?!
Ahhh-- BUT SUPPOSE, FROM THE HEART OF THE SUPPOSED ILLUSION, THERE COMES...
... A MOST DEADLY PIECE OF REALITY?
PHUT!
GNUNHH!

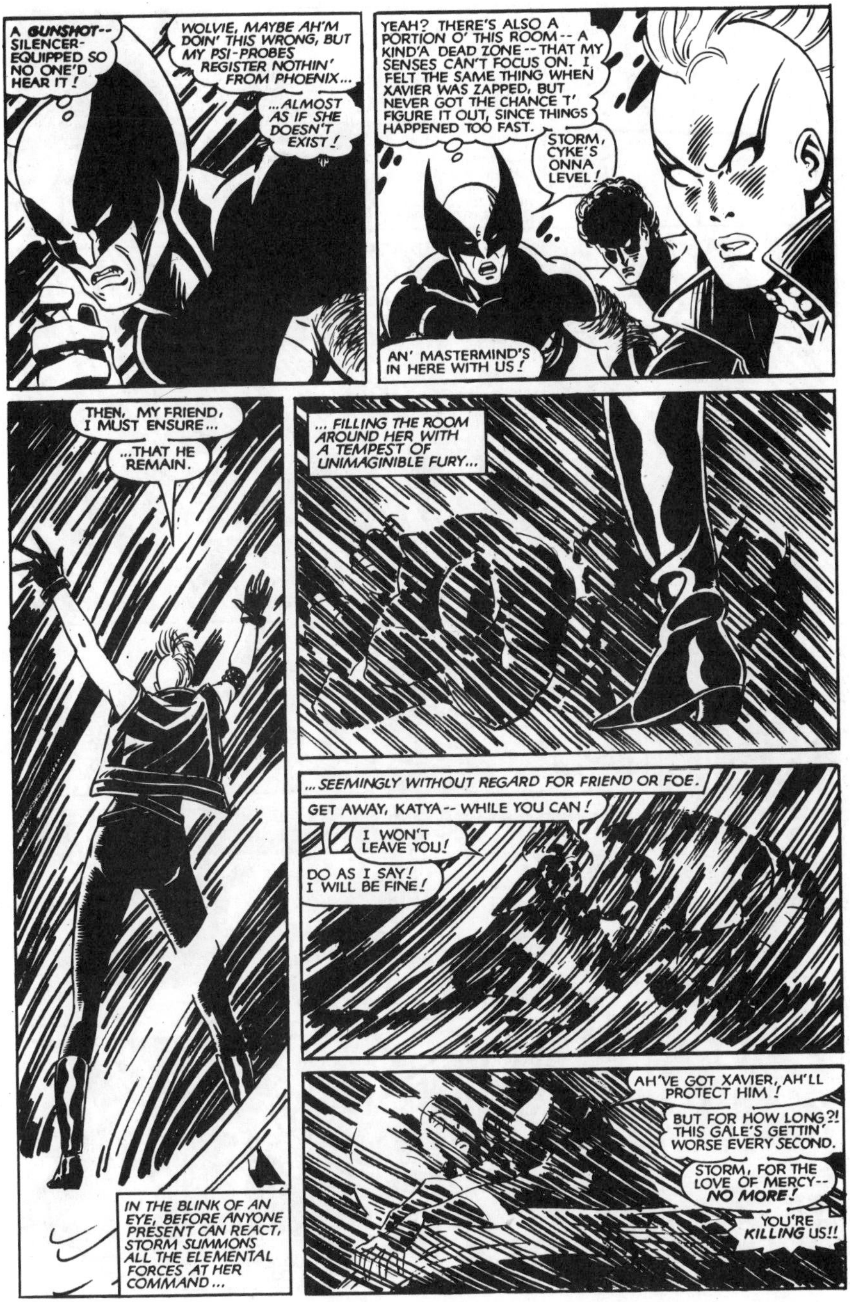
A GUNSHOT-- SILENCER-EQUIPPED SO NO ONE'D HEAR IT!
WOLVIE, MAYBE AH'M DOIN' THIS WRONG, BUT MY PSI-PROBES REGISTER NOTHIN' FROM PHOENIX...
...ALMOST AS IF SHE DOESN'T EXIST!
YEAH? THERE'S ALSO A PORTION O' THIS ROOM-- A KIND'A DEAD ZONE-- THAT MY SENSES CAN'T FOCUS ON. I FELT THE SAME THING WHEN XAVIER WAS ZAPPED, BUT NEVER GOT THE CHANCE T' FIGURE IT OUT, SINCE THINGS HAPPENED TOO FAST.
STORM, CYKE'S ONNA LEVEL!
AN' MASTERMIND'S IN HERE WITH US!
THEN, MY FRIEND, I MUST ENSURE...
...THAT HE REMAIN.
IN THE BLINK OF AN EYE, BEFORE ANYONE PRESENT CAN REACT, STORM SUMMONS ALL THE ELEMENTAL FORCES AT HER COMMAND...
...FILLING THE ROOM AROUND HER WITH A TEMPEST OF UNIMAGINIBLE FURY...
...SEEMINGLY WITHOUT REGARD FOR FRIEND OR FOE.
GET AWAY, KATYA-- WHILE YOU CAN!
I WON'T LEAVE YOU!
DO AS I SAY! I WILL BE FINE!
AH'VE GOT XAVIER, AH'LL PROTECT HIM!
BUT FOR HOW LONG?! THIS GALE'S GETTIN' WORSE EVERY SECOND.
STORM, FOR THE LOVE OF MERCY-- NO MORE!
YOU'RE KILLING US!!

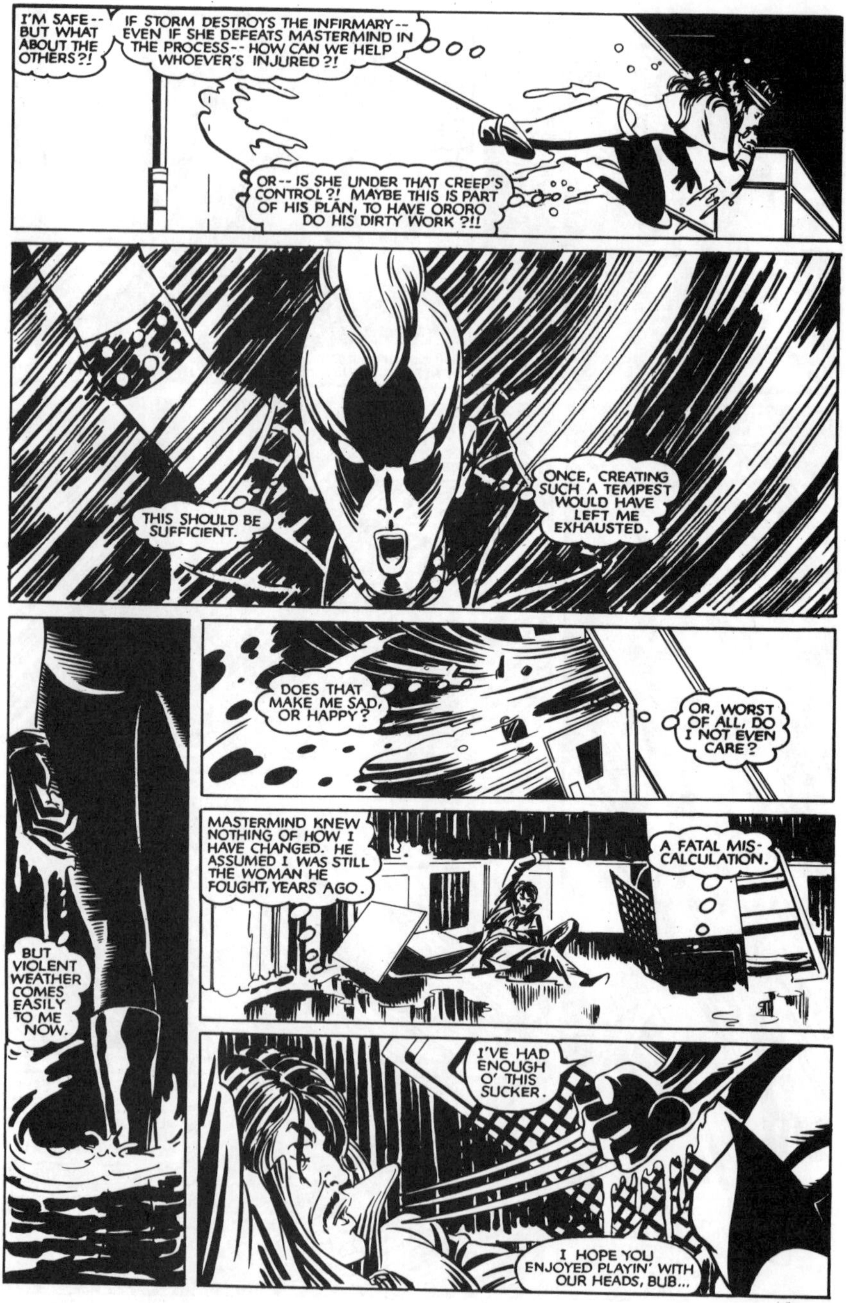
I'M SAFE -- BUT WHAT ABOUT THE OTHERS?!
IF STORM DESTROYS THE INFIRMARY -- EVEN IF SHE DEFEATS MASTERMIND IN THE PROCESS -- HOW CAN WE HELP WHOEVER'S INJURED?!
OR -- IS SHE UNDER THAT CREEP'S CONTROL?! MAYBE THIS IS PART OF HIS PLAN, TO HAVE ORORO DO HIS DIRTY WORK?!!
THIS SHOULD BE SUFFICIENT.
ONCE, CREATING SUCH A TEMPEST WOULD HAVE LEFT ME EXHAUSTED.
BUT VIOLENT WEATHER COMES EASILY TO ME NOW.
DOES THAT MAKE ME SAD, OR HAPPY?
OR, WORST OF ALL, DO I NOT EVEN CARE?
MASTERMIND KNEW NOTHING OF HOW I HAVE CHANGED. HE ASSUMED I WAS STILL THE WOMAN HE FOUGHT, YEARS AGO.
A FATAL MIS-CALCULATION.
I'VE HAD ENOUGH O' THIS SUCKER.
I HOPE YOU ENJOYED PLAYIN' WITH OUR HEADS, BUB...

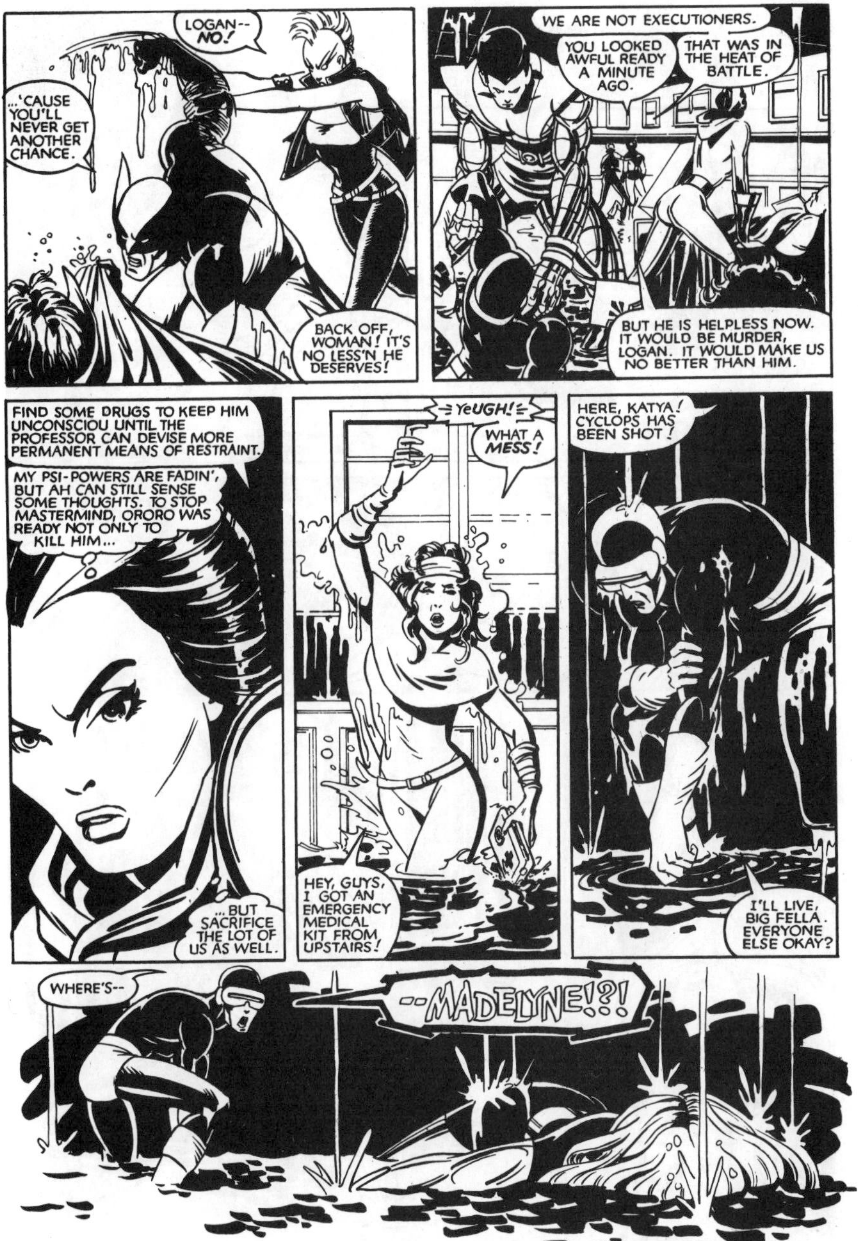
LOGAN-- NO!
...'CAUSE YOU'LL NEVER GET ANOTHER CHANCE.
BACK OFF, WOMAN! IT'S NO LESS'N HE DESERVES!
WE ARE NOT EXECUTIONERS.
YOU LOOKED AWFUL READY A MINUTE AGO.
THAT WAS IN THE HEAT OF BATTLE.
BUT HE IS HELPLESS NOW. IT WOULD BE MURDER, LOGAN. IT WOULD MAKE US NO BETTER THAN HIM.
FIND SOME DRUGS TO KEEP HIM UNCONSCIOU UNTIL THE PROFESSOR CAN DEVISE MORE PERMANENT MEANS OF RESTRAINT.
MY PSI-POWERS ARE FADIN', BUT AH CAN STILL SENSE SOME THOUGHTS. TO STOP MASTERMIND, ORORO WAS READY NOT ONLY TO KILL HIM...
...BUT SACRIFICE THE LOT OF US AS WELL.
YeUGH!
WHAT A MESS!
HEY, GUYS, I GOT AN EMERGENCY MEDICAL KIT FROM UPSTAIRS!
HERE, KATYA! CYCLOPS HAS BEEN SHOT!
I'LL LIVE, BIG FELLA. EVERYONE ELSE OKAY?
WHERE'S--
--MADELYNE!?!

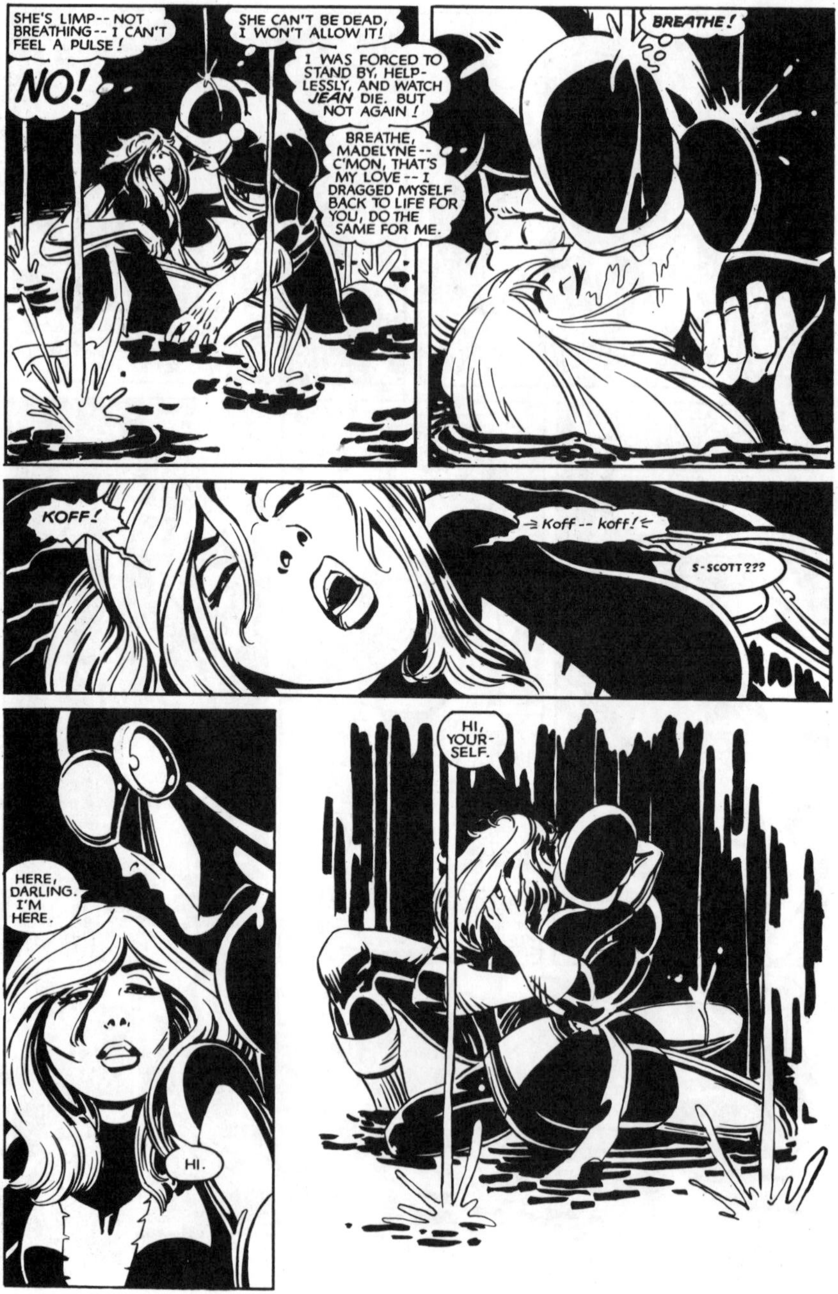
SHE'S LIMP-- NOT BREATHING-- I CAN'T FEEL A PULSE!
NO!
SHE CAN'T BE DEAD, I WON'T ALLOW IT!
I WAS FORCED TO STAND BY, HELPLESSLY, AND WATCH JEAN DIE. BUT NOT AGAIN!
BREATHE, MADELYNE-- C'MON, THAT'S MY LOVE-- I DRAGGED MYSELF BACK TO LIFE FOR YOU, DO THE SAME FOR ME.
BREATHE!
KOFF!
Koff -- koff!
S-SCOTT???
HERE, DARLING. I'M HERE.
HI.
HI, YOURSELF.

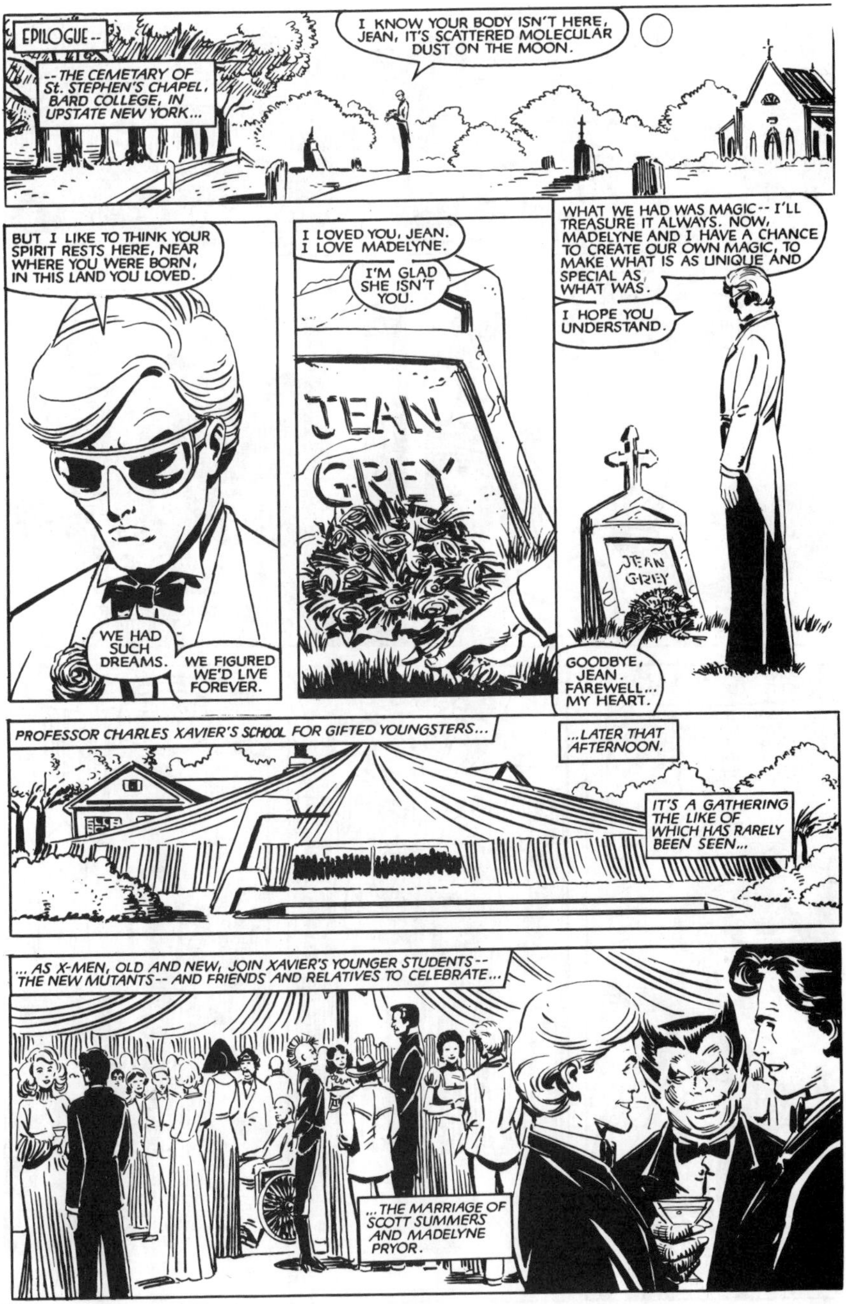
EPILOGUE--
--THE CEMETARY OF St. STEPHEN'S CHAPEL, BARD COLLEGE, IN UPSTATE NEW YORK...
I KNOW YOUR BODY ISN'T HERE, JEAN, IT'S SCATTERED MOLECULAR DUST ON THE MOON.
BUT I LIKE TO THINK YOUR SPIRIT RESTS HERE, NEAR WHERE YOU WERE BORN, IN THIS LAND YOU LOVED.
WE HAD SUCH DREAMS.
WE FIGURED WE'D LIVE FOREVER.
I LOVED YOU, JEAN. I LOVE MADELYNE.
I'M GLAD SHE ISN'T YOU.
JEAN GREY
WHAT WE HAD WAS MAGIC-- I'LL TREASURE IT ALWAYS. NOW, MADELYNE AND I HAVE A CHANCE TO CREATE OUR OWN MAGIC, TO MAKE WHAT IS AS UNIQUE AND SPECIAL AS WHAT WAS.
I HOPE YOU UNDERSTAND.
JEAN GREY
GOODBYE, JEAN. FAREWELL... MY HEART.
PROFESSOR CHARLES XAVIER'S SCHOOL FOR GIFTED YOUNGSTERS...
...LATER THAT AFTERNOON.
IT'S A GATHERING THE LIKE OF WHICH HAS RARELY BEEN SEEN...
...AS X-MEN, OLD AND NEW, JOIN XAVIER'S YOUNGER STUDENTS-- THE NEW MUTANTS-- AND FRIENDS AND RELATIVES TO CELEBRATE...
...THE MARRIAGE OF SCOTT SUMMERS AND MADELYNE PRYOR.

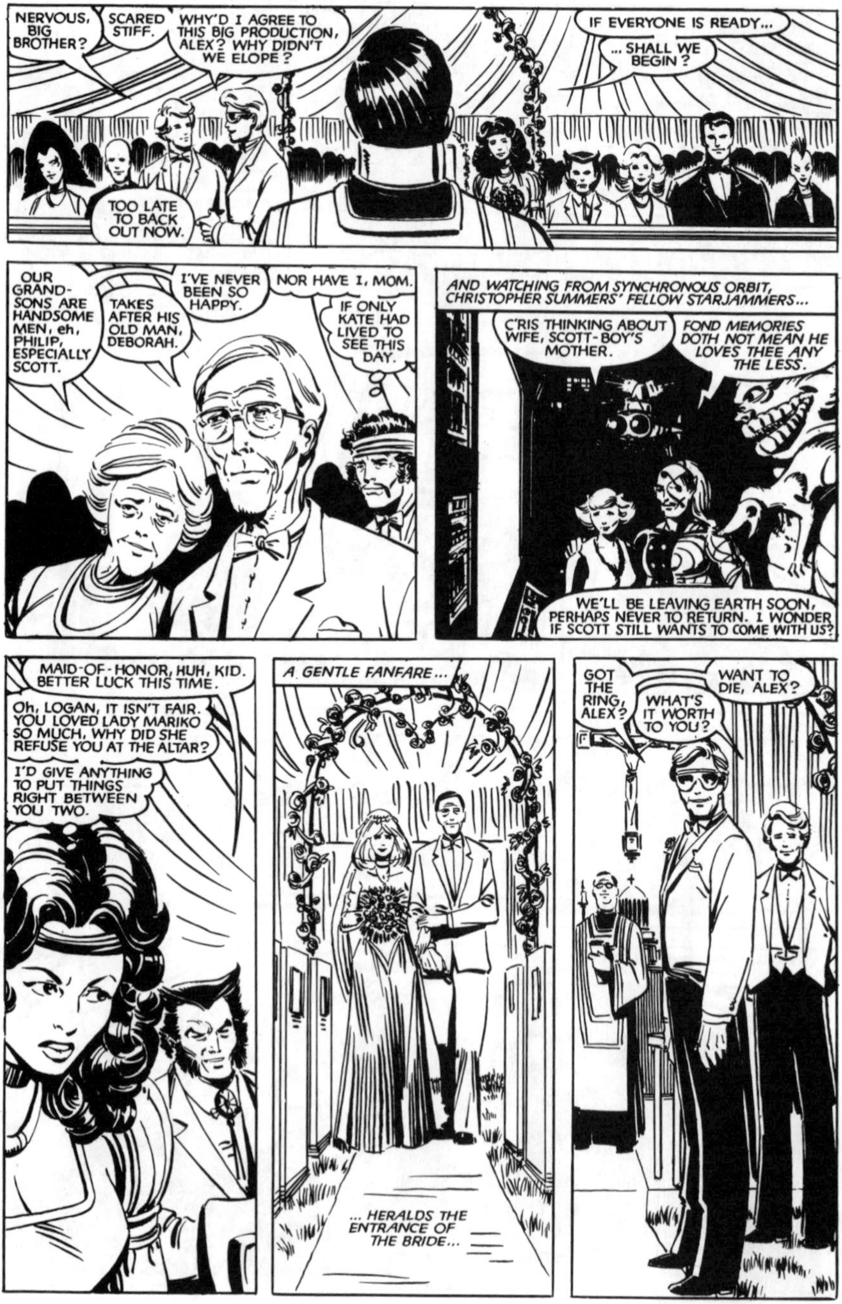
NERVOUS, BIG BROTHER?
SCARED STIFF.
WHY'D I AGREE TO THIS BIG PRODUCTION, ALEX? WHY DIDN'T WE ELOPE?
TOO LATE TO BACK OUT NOW.
IF EVERYONE IS READY...
...SHALL WE BEGIN?
OUR GRANDSONS ARE HANDSOME MEN, eh, PHILIP, ESPECIALLY SCOTT.
TAKES AFTER HIS OLD MAN, DEBORAH.
I'VE NEVER BEEN SO HAPPY.
NOR HAVE I, MOM.
IF ONLY KATE HAD LIVED TO SEE THIS DAY.
AND WATCHING FROM SYNCHRONOUS ORBIT, CHRISTOPHER SUMMERS' FELLOW STARJAMMERS...
C'RIS THINKING ABOUT WIFE, SCOTT-BOY'S MOTHER.
FOND MEMORIES DOTH NOT MEAN HE LOVES THEE ANY THE LESS.
WE'LL BE LEAVING EARTH SOON, PERHAPS NEVER TO RETURN. I WONDER IF SCOTT STILL WANTS TO COME WITH US?
MAID-OF-HONOR, HUH, KID. BETTER LUCK THIS TIME.
Oh, LOGAN, IT ISN'T FAIR. YOU LOVED LADY MARIKO SO MUCH, WHY DID SHE REFUSE YOU AT THE ALTAR?
I'D GIVE ANYTHING TO PUT THINGS RIGHT BETWEEN YOU TWO.
A GENTLE FANFARE...
...HERALDS THE ENTRANCE OF THE BRIDE...
GOT THE RING, ALEX?
WHAT'S IT WORTH TO YOU?
WANT TO DIE, ALEX?

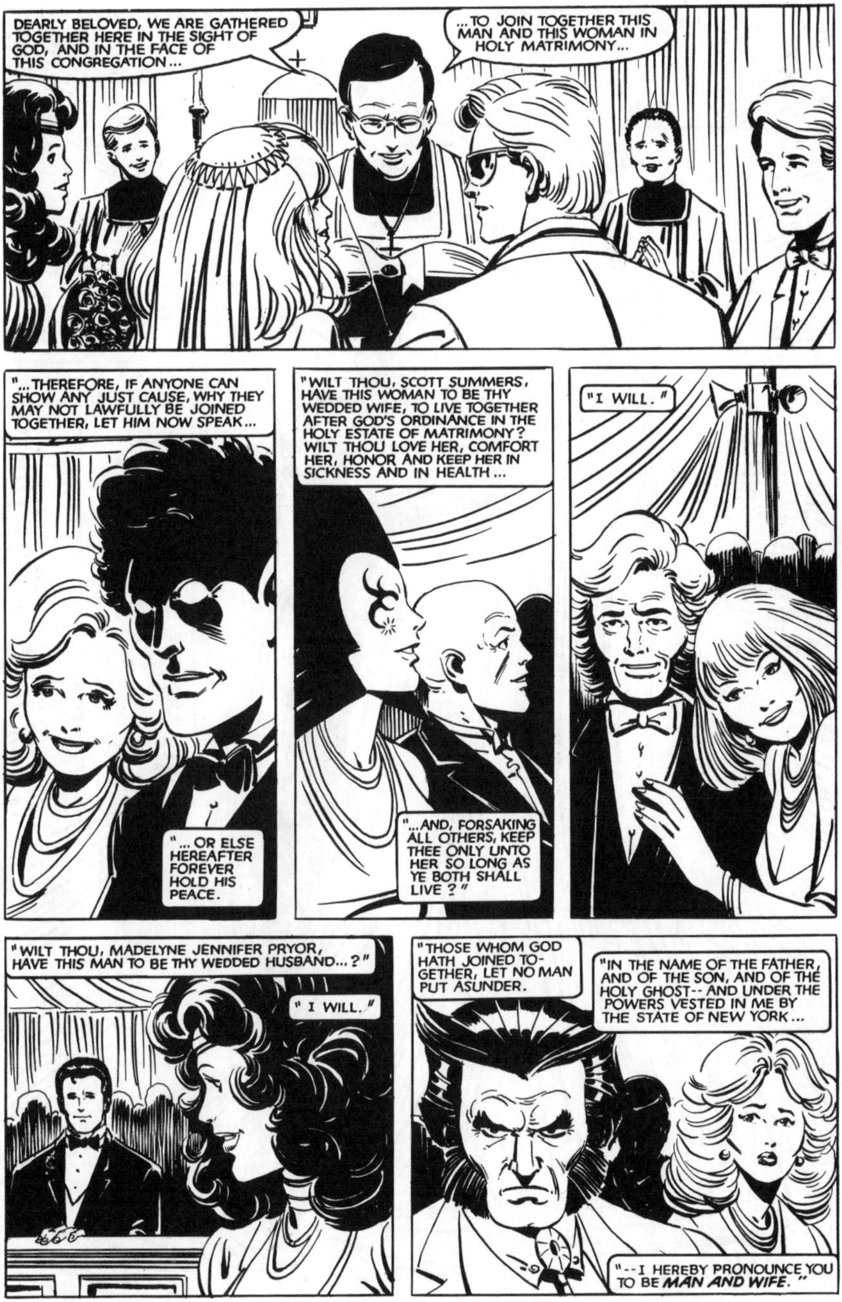
DEARLY BELOVED, WE ARE GATHERED TOGETHER HERE IN THE SIGHT OF GOD, AND IN THE FACE OF THIS CONGREGATION...
...TO JOIN TOGETHER THIS MAN AND THIS WOMAN IN HOLY MATRIMONY...
"...THEREFORE, IF ANYONE CAN SHOW ANY JUST CAUSE, WHY THEY MAY NOT LAWFULLY BE JOINED TOGETHER, LET HIM NOW SPEAK...
"...OR ELSE HEREAFTER FOREVER HOLD HIS PEACE.
"WILT THOU, SCOTT SUMMERS, HAVE THIS WOMAN TO BE THY WEDDED WIFE, TO LIVE TOGETHER AFTER GOD'S ORDINANCE IN THE HOLY ESTATE OF MATRIMONY? WILT THOU LOVE HER, COMFORT HER, HONOR AND KEEP HER IN SICKNESS AND IN HEALTH...
"...AND, FORSAKING ALL OTHERS, KEEP THEE ONLY UNTO HER SO LONG AS YE BOTH SHALL LIVE?"
"I WILL."
"WILT THOU, MADELYNE JENNIFER PRYOR, HAVE THIS MAN TO BE THY WEDDED HUSBAND...?"
"I WILL."
"THOSE WHOM GOD HATH JOINED TOGETHER, LET NO MAN PUT ASUNDER.
"IN THE NAME OF THE FATHER, AND OF THE SON, AND OF THE HOLY GHOST-- AND UNDER THE POWERS VESTED IN ME BY THE STATE OF NEW YORK...
"--I HEREBY PRONOUNCE YOU TO BE MAN AND WIFE."

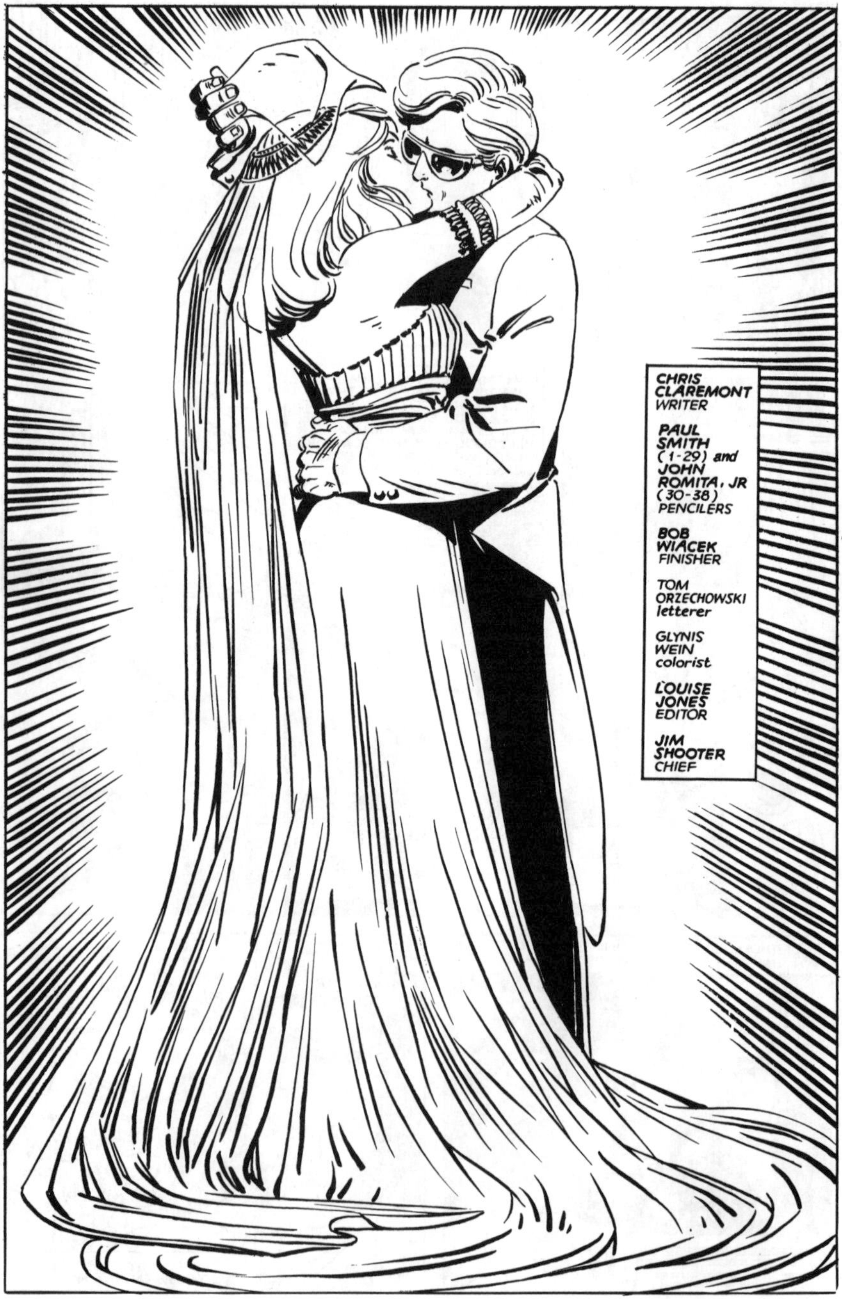
CHRIS CLAREMONT WRITER
PAUL SMITH (1-29) and JOHN ROMITA, JR (30-38) PENCILERS
BOB WIACEK FINISHER
TOM ORZECHOWSKI letterer
GLYNIS WEIN colorist
LOUISE JONES EDITOR
JIM SHOOTER CHIEF

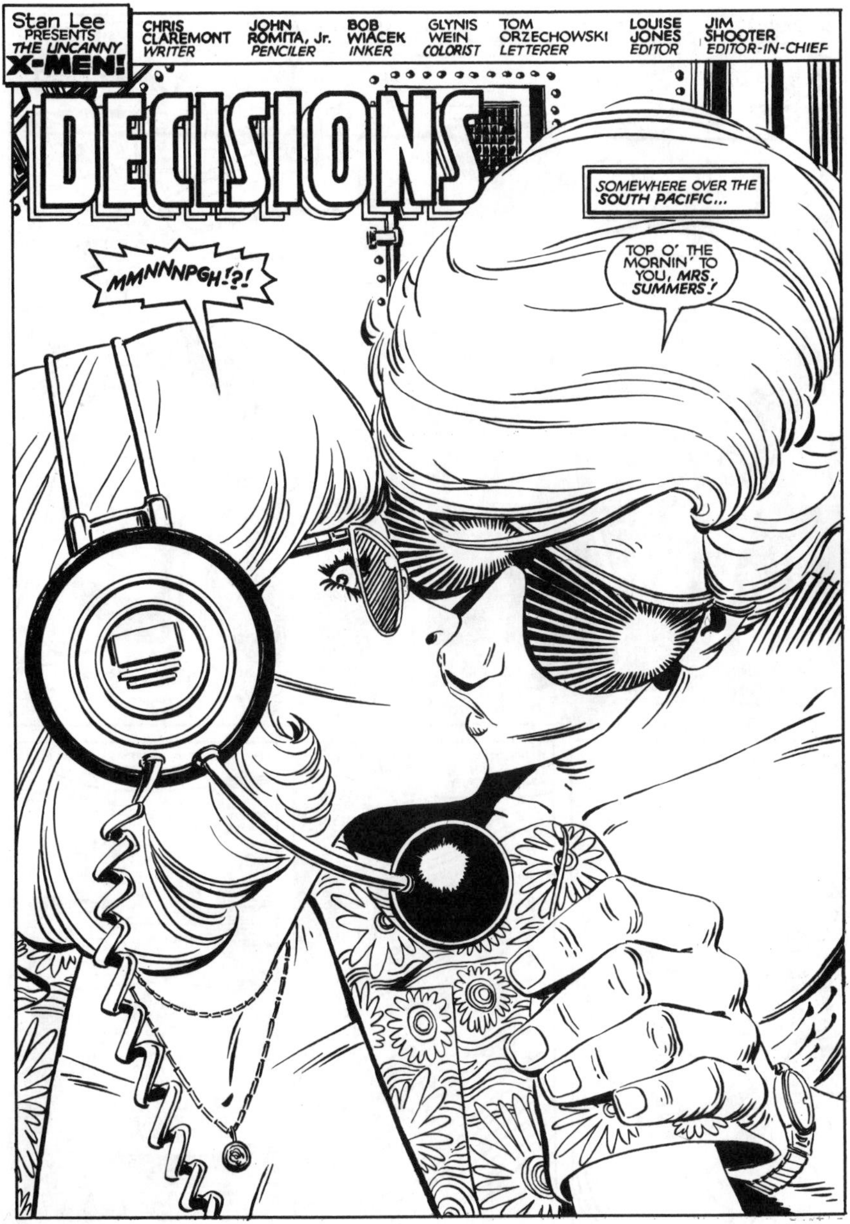
Stan Lee PRESENTS THE UNCANNY X-MEN!
CHRIS CLAREMONT WRITER
JOHN ROMITA, Jr. PENCILER
BOB WIACEK INKER
GLYNIS WEIN COLORIST
TOM ORZECHOWSKI LETTERER
LOUISE JONES EDITOR
JIM SHOOTER EDITOR-IN-CHIEF
DECISIONS
SOMEWHERE OVER THE SOUTH PACIFIC...
TOP O' THE MORNIN' TO YOU, MRS. SUMMERS!
MMNNNPGH!?!

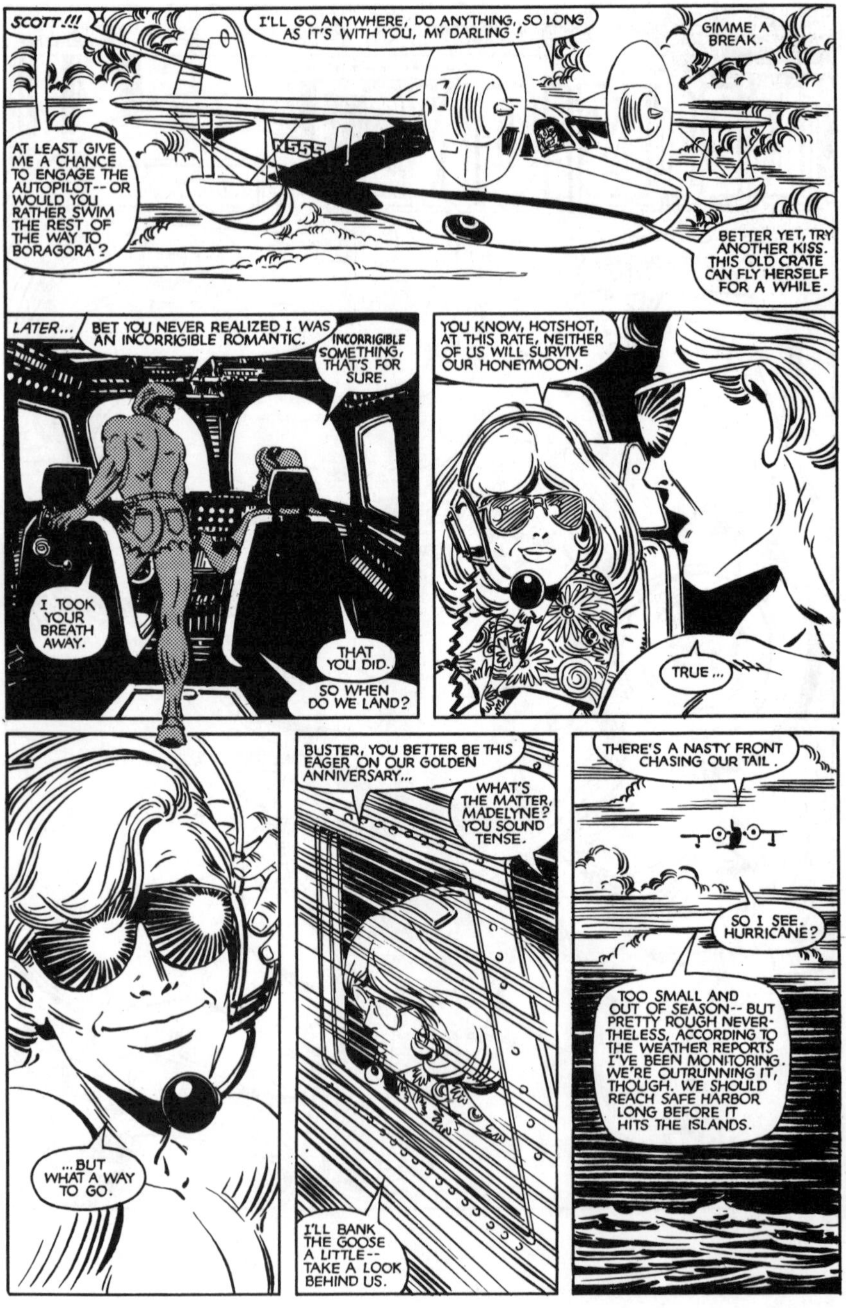
SCOTT!!!
I'LL GO ANYWHERE, DO ANYTHING, SO LONG AS IT'S WITH YOU, MY DARLING!
GIMME A BREAK.
AT LEAST GIVE ME A CHANCE TO ENGAGE THE AUTOPILOT-- OR WOULD YOU RATHER SWIM THE REST OF THE WAY TO BORAGORA?
BETTER YET, TRY ANOTHER KISS. THIS OLD CRATE CAN FLY HERSELF FOR A WHILE.
LATER...
BET YOU NEVER REALIZED I WAS AN INCORRIGIBLE ROMANTIC.
INCORRIGIBLE SOMETHING, THAT'S FOR SURE.
I TOOK YOUR BREATH AWAY.
THAT YOU DID.
SO WHEN DO WE LAND?
YOU KNOW, HOTSHOT, AT THIS RATE, NEITHER OF US WILL SURVIVE OUR HONEYMOON.
TRUE...
...BUT WHAT A WAY TO GO.
BUSTER, YOU BETTER BE THIS EAGER ON OUR GOLDEN ANNIVERSARY...
WHAT'S THE MATTER, MADELYNE? YOU SOUND TENSE.
I'LL BANK THE GOOSE A LITTLE-- TAKE A LOOK BEHIND US.
THERE'S A NASTY FRONT CHASING OUR TAIL.
SO I SEE. HURRICANE?
TOO SMALL AND OUT OF SEASON-- BUT PRETTY ROUGH NEVERTHELESS, ACCORDING TO THE WEATHER REPORTS I'VE BEEN MONITORING. WE'RE OUTRUNNING IT, THOUGH. WE SHOULD REACH SAFE HARBOR LONG BEFORE IT HITS THE ISLANDS.

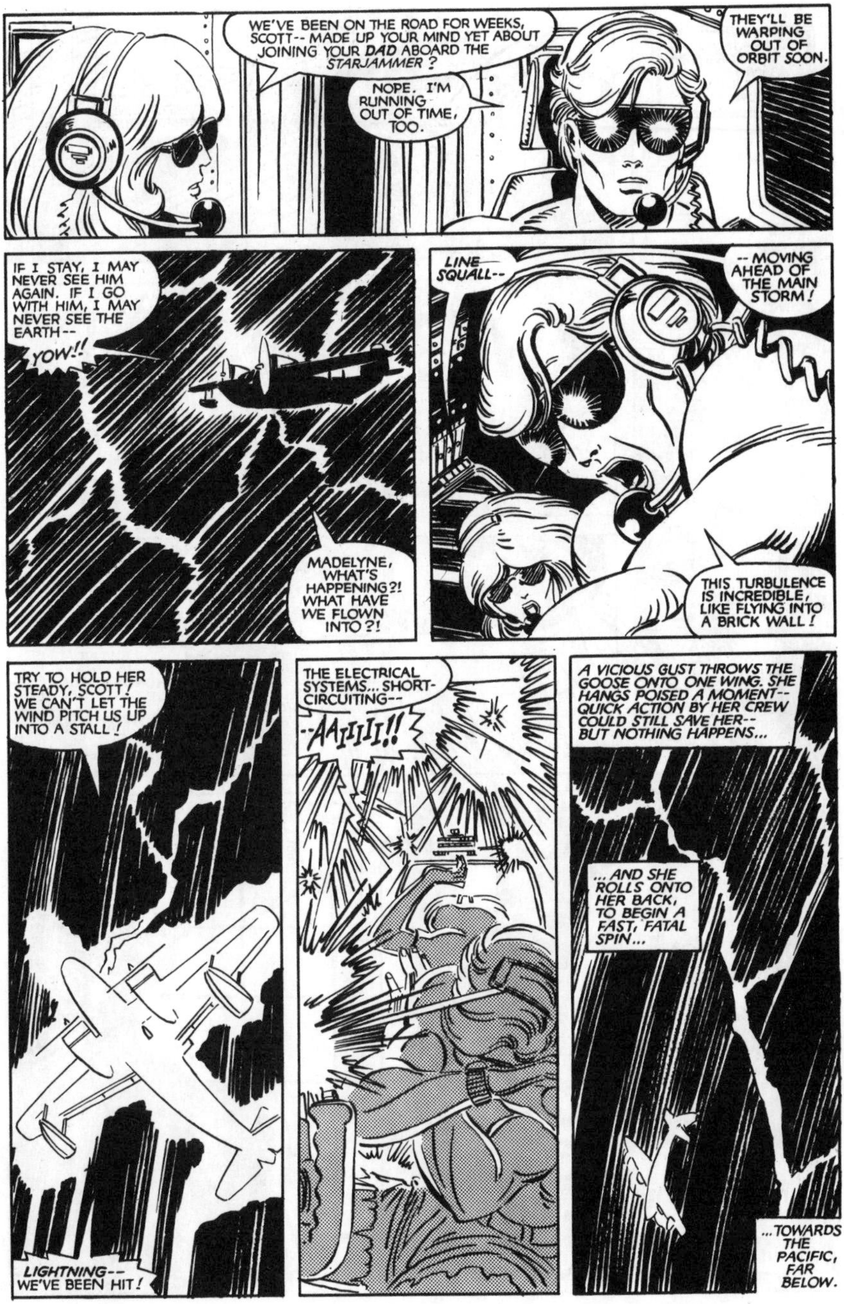
WE'VE BEEN ON THE ROAD FOR WEEKS, SCOTT-- MADE UP YOUR MIND YET ABOUT JOINING YOUR DAD ABOARD THE STARJAMMER?
NOPE. I'M RUNNING OUT OF TIME, TOO.
THEY'LL BE WARPING OUT OF ORBIT SOON.
IF I STAY, I MAY NEVER SEE HIM AGAIN. IF I GO WITH HIM, I MAY NEVER SEE THE EARTH--
YOW!!
MADELYNE, WHAT'S HAPPENING?! WHAT HAVE WE FLOWN INTO?!
LINE SQUALL--
--MOVING AHEAD OF THE MAIN STORM!
THIS TURBULENCE IS INCREDIBLE, LIKE FLYING INTO A BRICK WALL!
TRY TO HOLD HER STEADY, SCOTT! WE CAN'T LET THE WIND PITCH US UP INTO A STALL!
LIGHTNING-- WE'VE BEEN HIT!
THE ELECTRICAL SYSTEMS... SHORT-CIRCUITING--
--AAIIIII!!
A VICIOUS GUST THROWS THE GOOSE ONTO ONE WING. SHE HANGS POISED A MOMENT-- QUICK ACTION BY HER CREW COULD STILL SAVE HER-- BUT NOTHING HAPPENS...
...AND SHE ROLLS ONTO HER BACK, TO BEGIN A FAST, FATAL SPIN...
...TOWARDS THE PACIFIC, FAR BELOW.

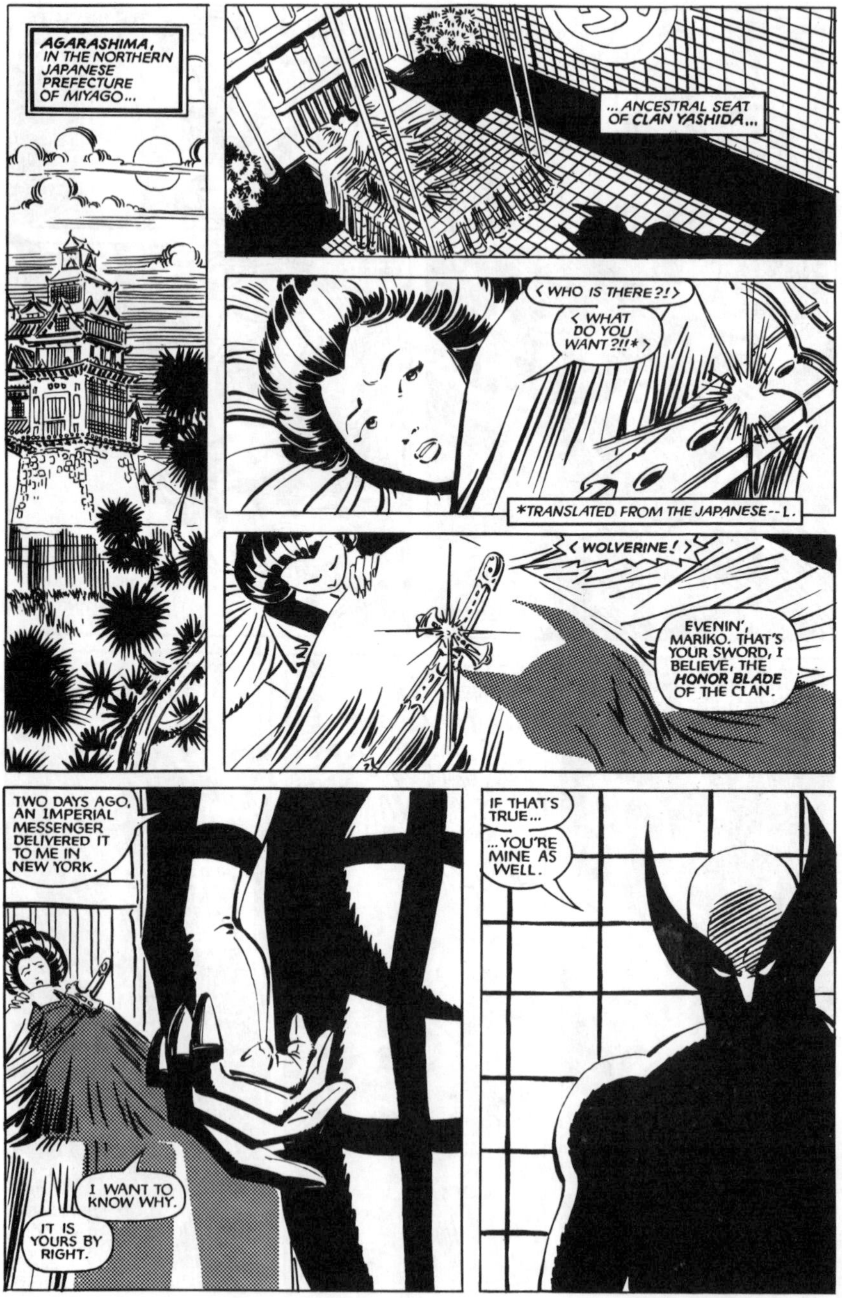
AGARASHIMA, IN THE NORTHERN JAPANESE PREFECTURE OF MIYAGO...
...ANCESTRAL SEAT OF CLAN YASHIDA...
< WHO IS THERE?! >
< WHAT DO YOU WANT?!!* >
*TRANSLATED FROM THE JAPANESE--L.
< WOLVERINE! >
EVENIN', MARIKO. THAT'S YOUR SWORD, I BELIEVE, THE HONOR BLADE OF THE CLAN.
TWO DAYS AGO, AN IMPERIAL MESSENGER DELIVERED IT TO ME IN NEW YORK.
I WANT TO KNOW WHY.
IT IS YOURS BY RIGHT.
IF THAT'S TRUE...
...YOU'RE MINE AS WELL.

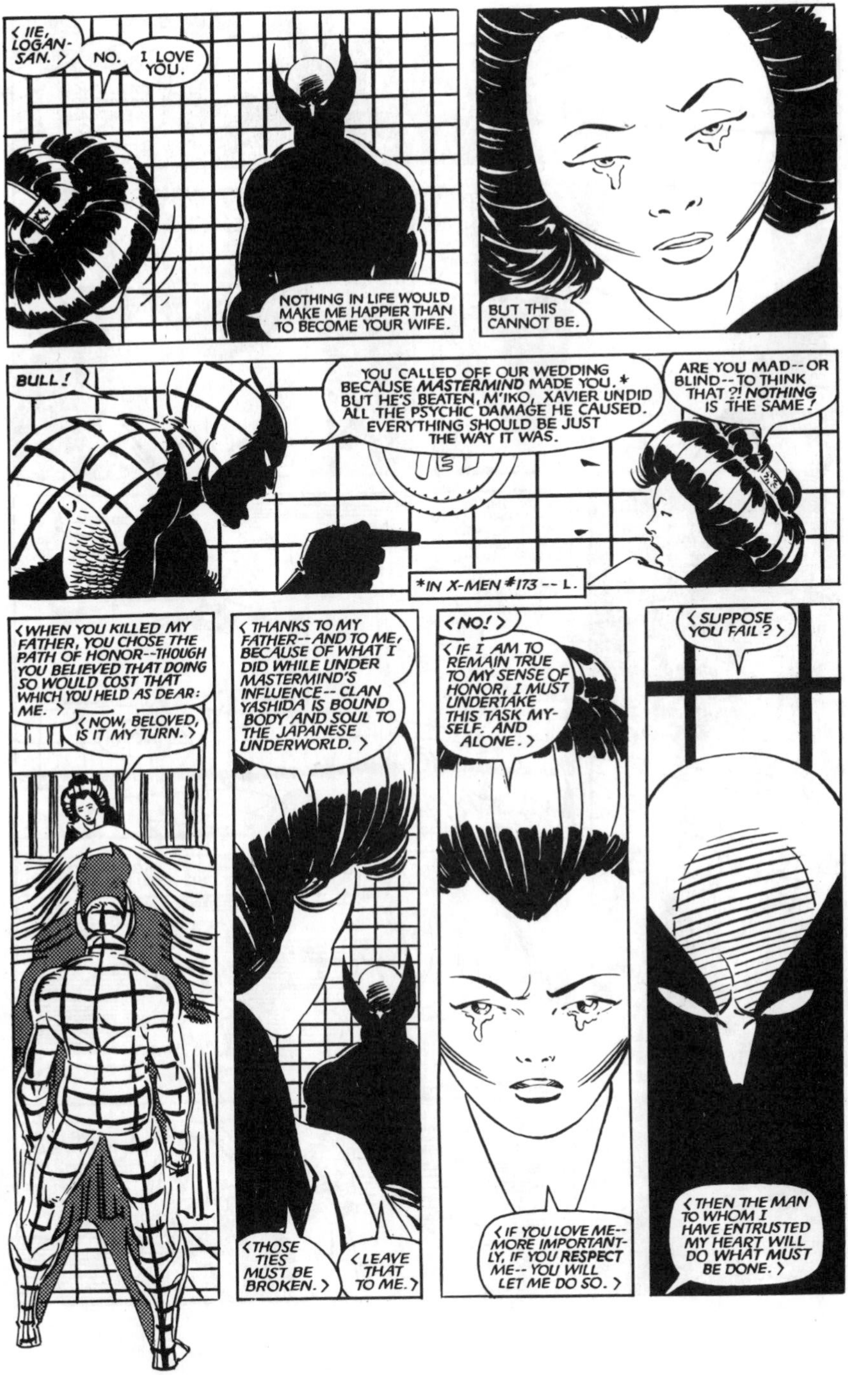

< IIE, LOGAN-SAN. >
NO.
I LOVE YOU.
NOTHING IN LIFE WOULD MAKE ME HAPPIER THAN TO BECOME YOUR WIFE.
BUT THIS CANNOT BE.
BULL!
YOU CALLED OFF OUR WEDDING BECAUSE MASTERMIND MADE YOU.* BUT HE'S BEATEN, M'IKO, XAVIER UNDID ALL THE PSYCHIC DAMAGE HE CAUSED. EVERYTHING SHOULD BE JUST THE WAY IT WAS.
ARE YOU MAD--OR BLIND--TO THINK THAT?! NOTHING IS THE SAME!
*IN X-MEN #173 -- L.
< WHEN YOU KILLED MY FATHER, YOU CHOSE THE PATH OF HONOR--THOUGH YOU BELIEVED THAT DOING SO WOULD COST THAT WHICH YOU HELD AS DEAR: ME. >
< NOW, BELOVED, IS IT MY TURN. >
< THANKS TO MY FATHER--AND TO ME, BECAUSE OF WHAT I DID WHILE UNDER MASTERMIND'S INFLUENCE--CLAN YASHIDA IS BOUND BODY AND SOUL TO THE JAPANESE UNDERWORLD. >
< THOSE TIES MUST BE BROKEN. >
< LEAVE THAT TO ME. >
< NO! >
< IF I AM TO REMAIN TRUE TO MY SENSE OF HONOR, I MUST UNDERTAKE THIS TASK MY-SELF. AND ALONE. >
< IF YOU LOVE ME-- MORE IMPORTANT-LY, IF YOU RESPECT ME-- YOU WILL LET ME DO SO. >
< SUPPOSE YOU FAIL? >
< THEN THE MAN TO WHOM I HAVE ENTRUSTED MY HEART WILL DO WHAT MUST BE DONE. >

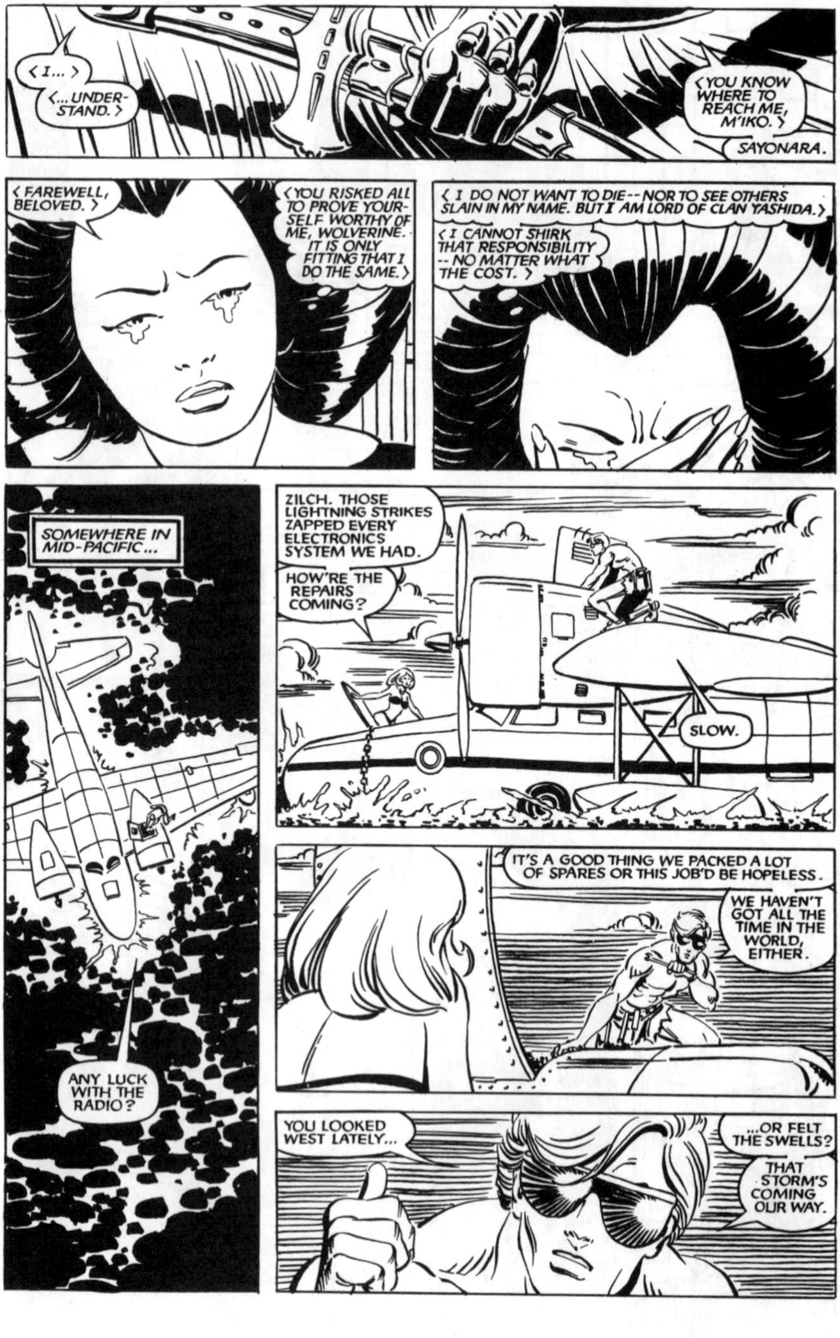

< I... >
< ...UNDER-STAND. >
< YOU KNOW WHERE TO REACH ME, M'IKO. >
SAYONARA.
< FAREWELL, BELOVED. >
< YOU RISKED ALL TO PROVE YOURSELF WORTHY OF ME, WOLVERINE. IT IS ONLY FITTING THAT I DO THE SAME. >
< I DO NOT WANT TO DIE--NOR TO SEE OTHERS SLAIN IN MY NAME. BUT I AM LORD OF CLAN YASHIDA. >
< I CANNOT SHIRK THAT RESPONSIBILITY --NO MATTER WHAT THE COST. >
SOMEWHERE IN MID-PACIFIC...
ANY LUCK WITH THE RADIO?
ZILCH. THOSE LIGHTNING STRIKES ZAPPED EVERY ELECTRONICS SYSTEM WE HAD.
HOW'RE THE REPAIRS COMING?
SLOW.
IT'S A GOOD THING WE PACKED A LOT OF SPARES OR THIS JOB'D BE HOPELESS.
WE HAVEN'T GOT ALL THE TIME IN THE WORLD, EITHER.
YOU LOOKED WEST LATELY...
...OR FELT THE SWELLS?
THAT STORM'S COMING OUR WAY.

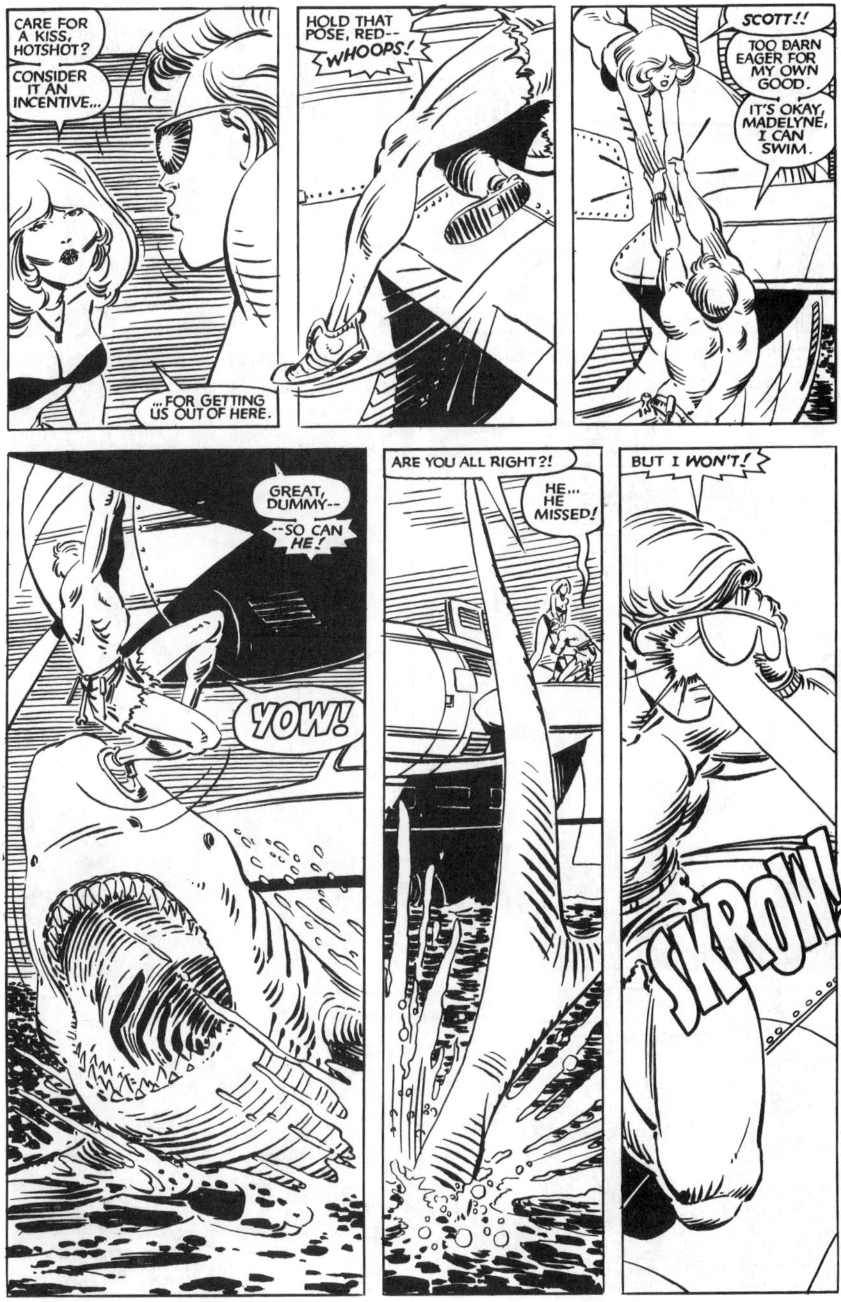
CARE FOR A KISS, HOTSHOT?
CONSIDER IT AN INCENTIVE...
...FOR GETTING US OUT OF HERE.
HOLD THAT POSE, RED--
WHOOPS!
SCOTT!!
TOO DARN EAGER FOR MY OWN GOOD.
IT'S OKAY, MADELYNE, I CAN SWIM.
GREAT, DUMMY--
--SO CAN HE!
YOW!
ARE YOU ALL RIGHT?!
HE... HE MISSED!
BUT I WON'T!
SKROW!

YOU'RE SHAKING!

I'M SCARED!

I MEAN, AFTER ALL I'VE BEEN THROUGH AS AN *X-MAN*...

... TO GET EATEN BY A SHARK ON MY HONEY-MOON IS A BIT MUCH.

SO HOW 'BOUT WE FIX THE ENGINES AND BLOW THIS JOINT...

... BEFORE THE STORM ARRIVES TO GIVE THAT CRITTER ANOTHER CHANCE?

GOOD POINT.

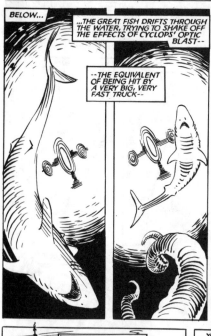

BELOW...

...THE GREAT FISH DRIFTS THROUGH THE WATER, TRYING TO SHAKE OFF THE EFFECTS OF CYCLOPS' OPTIC BLAST--

--THE EQUIVALENT OF BEING HIT BY A VERY BIG, VERY FAST TRUCK--

--UNAWARE UNTIL IT'S TOO LATE THAT IT'S ROLE HAS CHANGED...

... FROM HUNTER TO PREY.

WASHINGTON, D.C...

YOUR IDENTIFICATION, SIR?

HENRY PETER GYRICH, NATIONAL SECURITY COUNCIL. I'M EXPECTED.

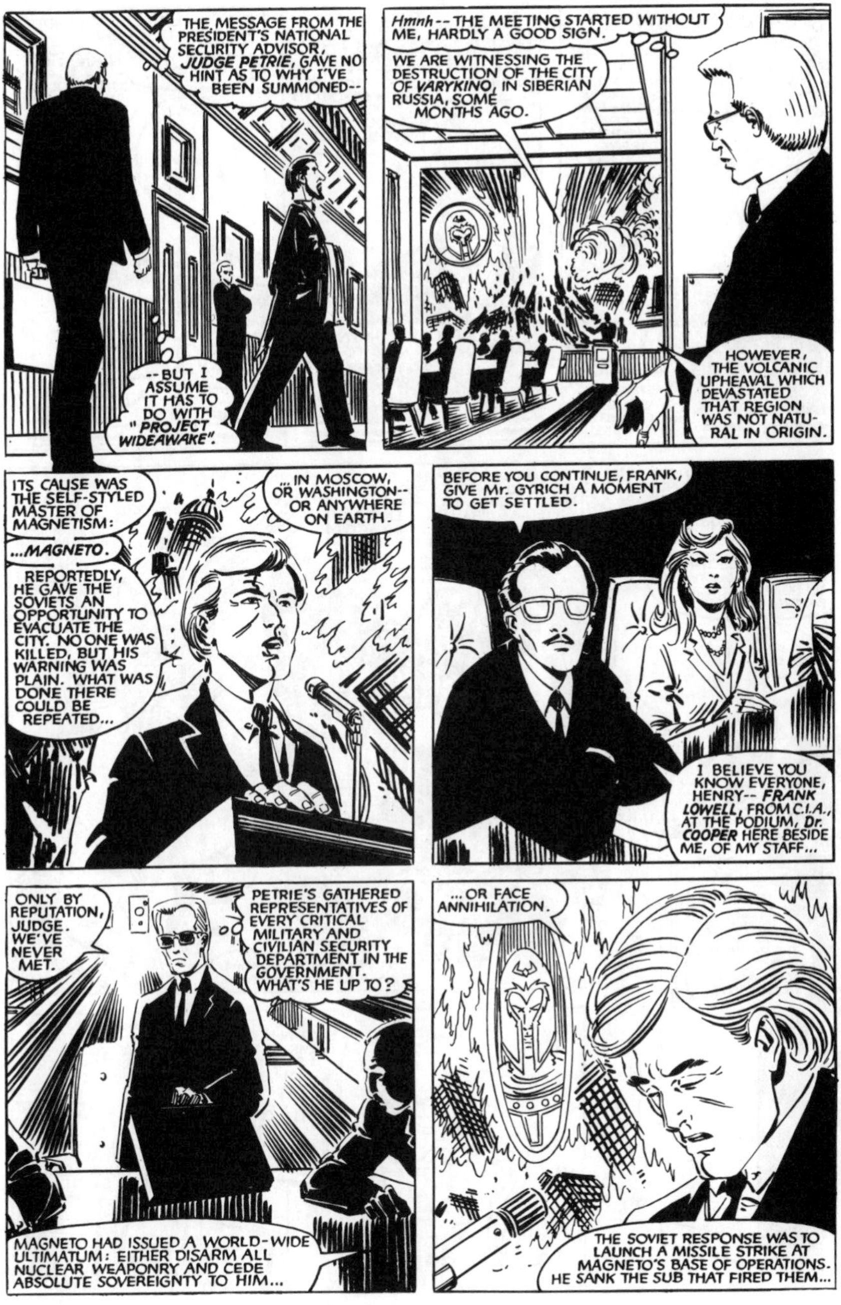
THE MESSAGE FROM THE PRESIDENT'S NATIONAL SECURITY ADVISOR, JUDGE PETRIE, GAVE NO HINT AS TO WHY I'VE BEEN SUMMONED--
--BUT I ASSUME IT HAS TO DO WITH "PROJECT WIDEAWAKE".
Hmnh-- THE MEETING STARTED WITHOUT ME, HARDLY A GOOD SIGN.
WE ARE WITNESSING THE DESTRUCTION OF THE CITY OF VARYKINO, IN SIBERIAN RUSSIA, SOME MONTHS AGO.
HOWEVER, THE VOLCANIC UPHEAVAL WHICH DEVASTATED THAT REGION WAS NOT NATURAL IN ORIGIN.
ITS CAUSE WAS THE SELF-STYLED MASTER OF MAGNETISM:
...MAGNETO.
REPORTEDLY, HE GAVE THE SOVIETS AN OPPORTUNITY TO EVACUATE THE CITY. NO ONE WAS KILLED, BUT HIS WARNING WAS PLAIN. WHAT WAS DONE THERE COULD BE REPEATED...
...IN MOSCOW, OR WASHINGTON-- OR ANYWHERE ON EARTH.
BEFORE YOU CONTINUE, FRANK, GIVE Mr. GYRICH A MOMENT TO GET SETTLED.
I BELIEVE YOU KNOW EVERYONE, HENRY-- FRANK LOWELL, FROM C.I.A., AT THE PODIUM, Dr. COOPER HERE BESIDE ME, OF MY STAFF...
ONLY BY REPUTATION, JUDGE. WE'VE NEVER MET.
PETRIE'S GATHERED REPRESENTATIVES OF EVERY CRITICAL MILITARY AND CIVILIAN SECURITY DEPARTMENT IN THE GOVERNMENT. WHAT'S HE UP TO?
MAGNETO HAD ISSUED A WORLD-WIDE ULTIMATUM: EITHER DISARM ALL NUCLEAR WEAPONRY AND CEDE ABSOLUTE SOVEREIGNTY TO HIM...
...OR FACE ANNIHILATION.
THE SOVIET RESPONSE WAS TO LAUNCH A MISSILE STRIKE AT MAGNETO'S BASE OF OPERATIONS. HE SANK THE SUB THAT FIRED THEM...

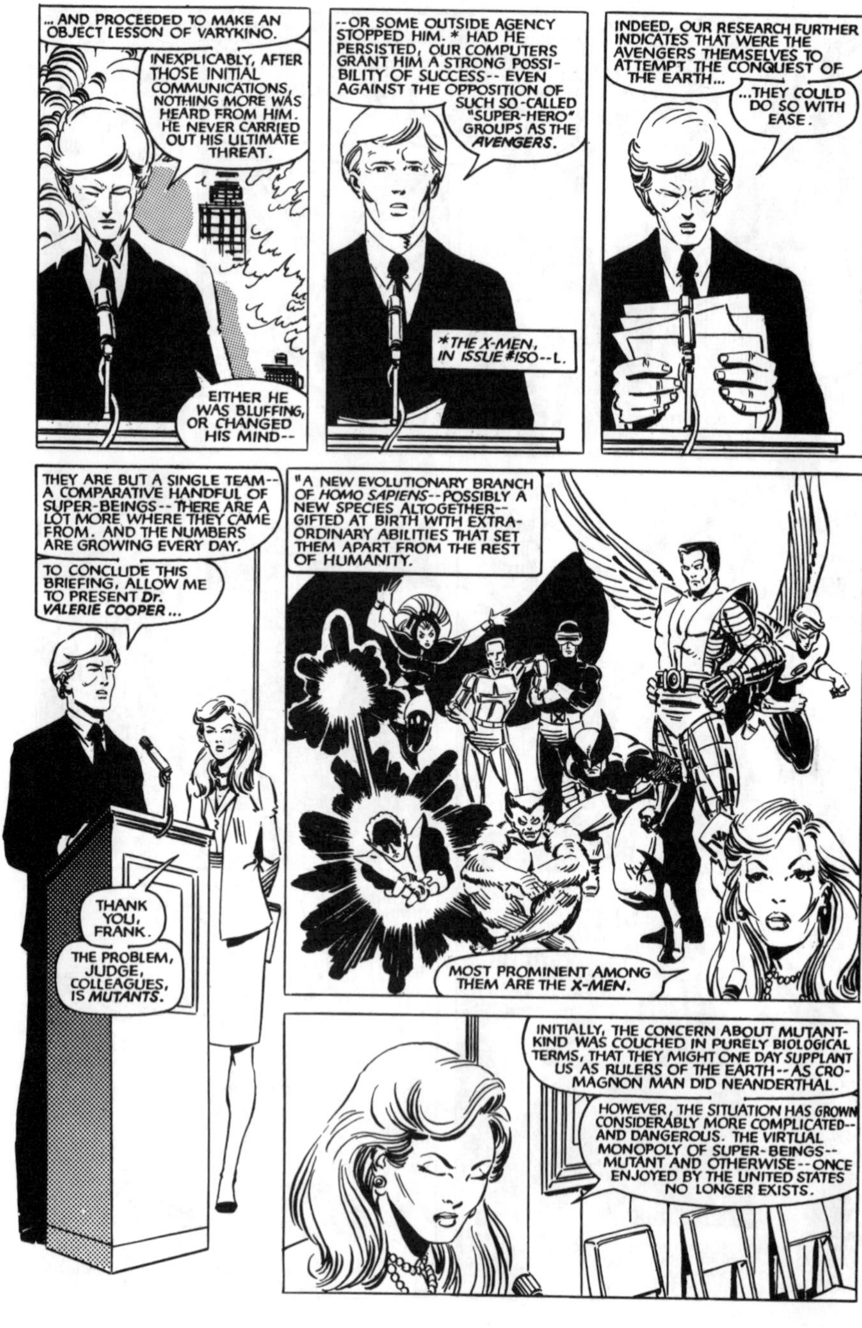
...AND PROCEEDED TO MAKE AN OBJECT LESSON OF VARYKINO.
INEXPLICABLY, AFTER THOSE INITIAL COMMUNICATIONS, NOTHING MORE WAS HEARD FROM HIM. HE NEVER CARRIED OUT HIS ULTIMATE THREAT.
EITHER HE WAS BLUFFING, OR CHANGED HIS MIND--
--OR SOME OUTSIDE AGENCY STOPPED HIM. * HAD HE PERSISTED, OUR COMPUTERS GRANT HIM A STRONG POSSIBILITY OF SUCCESS-- EVEN AGAINST THE OPPOSITION OF SUCH SO-CALLED "SUPER-HERO" GROUPS AS THE AVENGERS.
*THE X-MEN, IN ISSUE #150--L.
INDEED, OUR RESEARCH FURTHER INDICATES THAT WERE THE AVENGERS THEMSELVES TO ATTEMPT THE CONQUEST OF THE EARTH...
...THEY COULD DO SO WITH EASE.
THEY ARE BUT A SINGLE TEAM-- A COMPARATIVE HANDFUL OF SUPER-BEINGS-- THERE ARE A LOT MORE WHERE THEY CAME FROM. AND THE NUMBERS ARE GROWING EVERY DAY.
TO CONCLUDE THIS BRIEFING, ALLOW ME TO PRESENT Dr. VALERIE COOPER...
THANK YOU, FRANK.
THE PROBLEM, JUDGE, COLLEAGUES, IS MUTANTS.
"A NEW EVOLUTIONARY BRANCH OF HOMO SAPIENS--POSSIBLY A NEW SPECIES ALTOGETHER-- GIFTED AT BIRTH WITH EXTRAORDINARY ABILITIES THAT SET THEM APART FROM THE REST OF HUMANITY.
MOST PROMINENT AMONG THEM ARE THE X-MEN.
INITIALLY, THE CONCERN ABOUT MUTANTKIND WAS COUCHED IN PURELY BIOLOGICAL TERMS, THAT THEY MIGHT ONE DAY SUPPLANT US AS RULERS OF THE EARTH--AS CRO-MAGNON MAN DID NEANDERTHAL.
HOWEVER, THE SITUATION HAS GROWN CONSIDERABLY MORE COMPLICATED-- AND DANGEROUS. THE VIRTUAL MONOPOLY OF SUPER-BEINGS-- MUTANT AND OTHERWISE--ONCE ENJOYED BY THE UNITED STATES NO LONGER EXISTS.

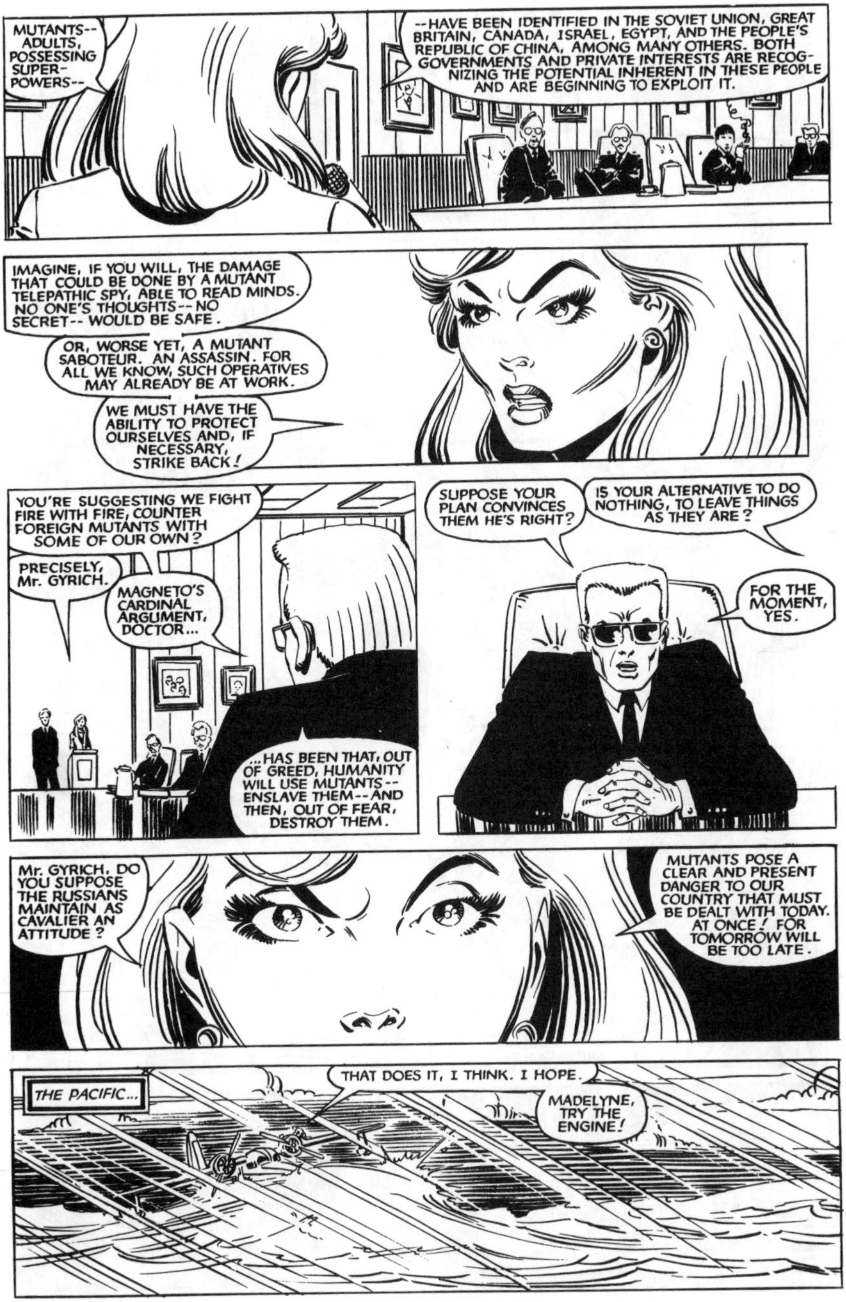

MUTANTS-- ADULTS, POSSESSING SUPER-POWERS--
--HAVE BEEN IDENTIFIED IN THE SOVIET UNION, GREAT BRITAIN, CANADA, ISRAEL, EGYPT, AND THE PEOPLE'S REPUBLIC OF CHINA, AMONG MANY OTHERS. BOTH GOVERNMENTS AND PRIVATE INTERESTS ARE RECOGNIZING THE POTENTIAL INHERENT IN THESE PEOPLE AND ARE BEGINNING TO EXPLOIT IT.
IMAGINE, IF YOU WILL, THE DAMAGE THAT COULD BE DONE BY A MUTANT TELEPATHIC SPY, ABLE TO READ MINDS. NO ONE'S THOUGHTS--NO SECRET--WOULD BE SAFE.
OR, WORSE YET, A MUTANT SABOTEUR. AN ASSASSIN. FOR ALL WE KNOW, SUCH OPERATIVES MAY ALREADY BE AT WORK.
WE MUST HAVE THE ABILITY TO PROTECT OURSELVES AND, IF NECESSARY, STRIKE BACK!
YOU'RE SUGGESTING WE FIGHT FIRE WITH FIRE, COUNTER FOREIGN MUTANTS WITH SOME OF OUR OWN?
PRECISELY, Mr. GYRICH.
MAGNETO'S CARDINAL ARGUMENT, DOCTOR...
...HAS BEEN THAT, OUT OF GREED, HUMANITY WILL USE MUTANTS--ENSLAVE THEM--AND THEN, OUT OF FEAR, DESTROY THEM.
SUPPOSE YOUR PLAN CONVINCES THEM HE'S RIGHT?
IS YOUR ALTERNATIVE TO DO NOTHING, TO LEAVE THINGS AS THEY ARE?
FOR THE MOMENT, YES.
Mr. GYRICH, DO YOU SUPPOSE THE RUSSIANS MAINTAIN AS CAVALIER AN ATTITUDE?
MUTANTS POSE A CLEAR AND PRESENT DANGER TO OUR COUNTRY THAT MUST BE DEALT WITH TODAY. AT ONCE! FOR TOMORROW WILL BE TOO LATE.
THE PACIFIC...
THAT DOES IT, I THINK. I HOPE.
MADELYNE, TRY THE ENGINE!

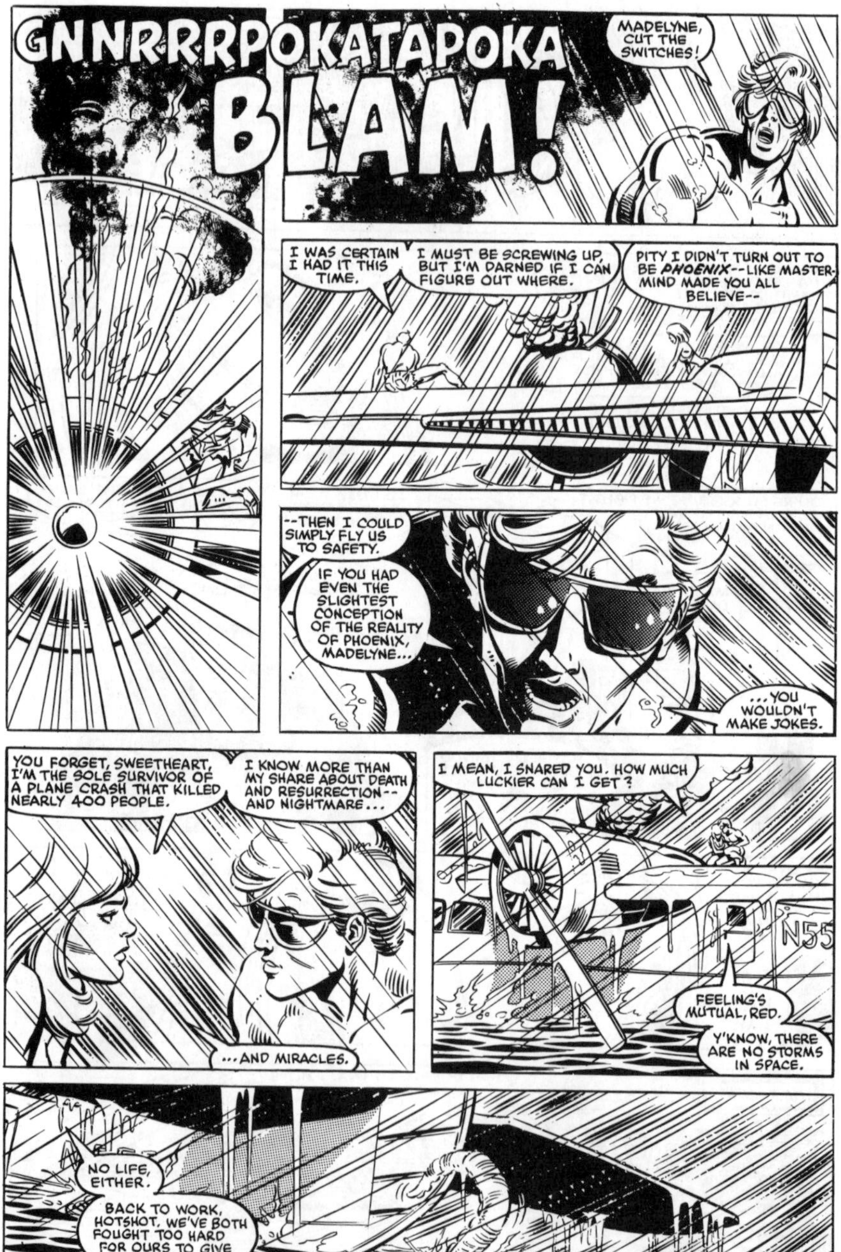
GNNRRRPOKATAPOKA
BLAM!
MADELYNE, CUT THE SWITCHES!
I WAS CERTAIN I HAD IT THIS TIME.
I MUST BE SCREWING UP, BUT I'M DARNED IF I CAN FIGURE OUT WHERE.
PITY I DIDN'T TURN OUT TO BE PHOENIX--LIKE MASTERMIND MADE YOU ALL BELIEVE--
--THEN I COULD SIMPLY FLY US TO SAFETY.
IF YOU HAD EVEN THE SLIGHTEST CONCEPTION OF THE REALITY OF PHOENIX, MADELYNE...
...YOU WOULDN'T MAKE JOKES.
YOU FORGET, SWEETHEART, I'M THE SOLE SURVIVOR OF A PLANE CRASH THAT KILLED NEARLY 400 PEOPLE.
I KNOW MORE THAN MY SHARE ABOUT DEATH AND RESURRECTION--AND NIGHTMARE...
...AND MIRACLES.
I MEAN, I SNARED YOU. HOW MUCH LUCKIER CAN I GET?
N55
FEELING'S MUTUAL, RED.
Y'KNOW, THERE ARE NO STORMS IN SPACE.
NO LIFE, EITHER.
BACK TO WORK, HOTSHOT. WE'VE BOTH FOUGHT TOO HARD FOR OURS TO GIVE UP NOW.

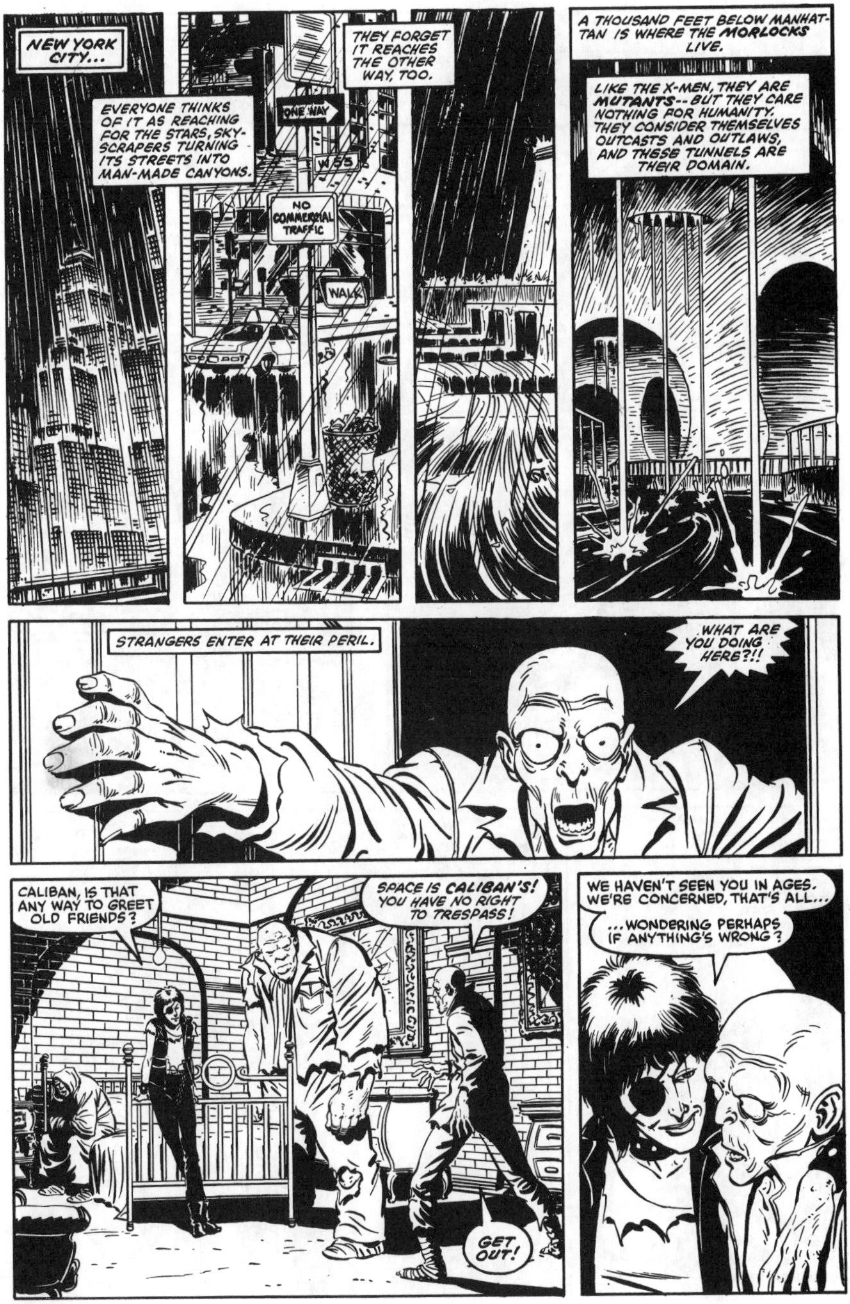
NEW YORK CITY...
EVERYONE THINKS OF IT AS REACHING FOR THE STARS, SKY-SCRAPERS TURNING ITS STREETS INTO MAN-MADE CANYONS.
ONE WAY
NO COMMERCIAL TRAFFIC
WALK
THEY FORGET IT REACHES THE OTHER WAY, TOO.
A THOUSAND FEET BELOW MANHATTAN IS WHERE THE MORLOCKS LIVE.
LIKE THE X-MEN, THEY ARE MUTANTS-- BUT THEY CARE NOTHING FOR HUMANITY. THEY CONSIDER THEMSELVES OUTCASTS AND OUTLAWS, AND THESE TUNNELS ARE THEIR DOMAIN.
STRANGERS ENTER AT THEIR PERIL.
WHAT ARE YOU DOING HERE?!!
CALIBAN, IS THAT ANY WAY TO GREET OLD FRIENDS?
SPACE IS CALIBAN'S! YOU HAVE NO RIGHT TO TRESPASS!
GET OUT!
WE HAVEN'T SEEN YOU IN AGES. WE'RE CONCERNED, THAT'S ALL...
...WONDERING PERHAPS IF ANYTHING'S WRONG?

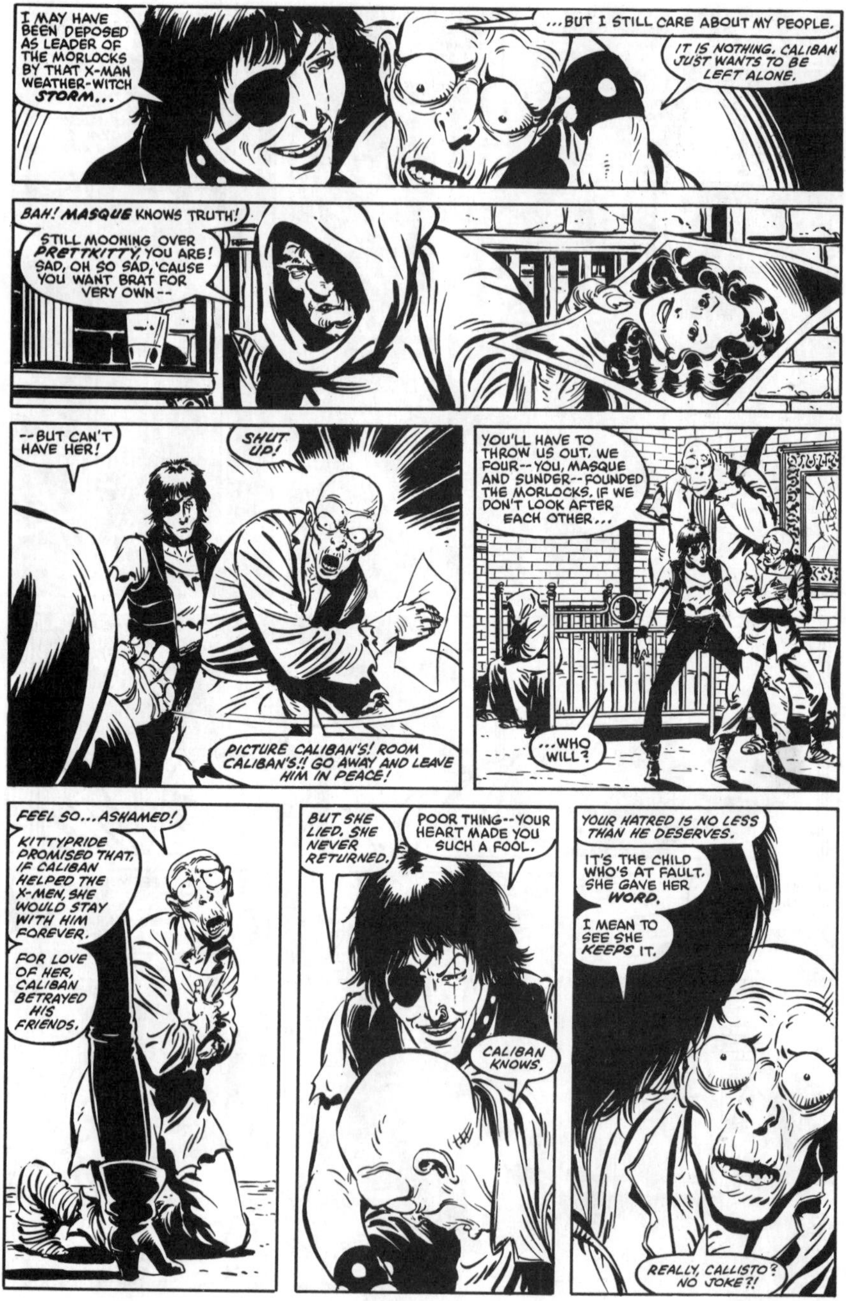
I MAY HAVE BEEN DEPOSED AS LEADER OF THE MORLOCKS BY THAT X-MAN WEATHER-WITCH STORM...
...BUT I STILL CARE ABOUT MY PEOPLE.
IT IS NOTHING. CALIBAN JUST WANTS TO BE LEFT ALONE.
BAH! MASQUE KNOWS TRUTH!
STILL MOONING OVER PRETTKITTY, YOU ARE! SAD, OH SO SAD, 'CAUSE YOU WANT BRAT FOR VERY OWN--
--BUT CAN'T HAVE HER!
SHUT UP!
PICTURE CALIBAN'S! ROOM CALIBAN'S!! GO AWAY AND LEAVE HIM IN PEACE!
YOU'LL HAVE TO THROW US OUT. WE FOUR--YOU, MASQUE AND SUNDER--FOUNDED THE MORLOCKS. IF WE DON'T LOOK AFTER EACH OTHER...
...WHO WILL?
FEEL SO...ASHAMED!
KITTYPRIDE PROMISED THAT, IF CALIBAN HELPED THE X-MEN, SHE WOULD STAY WITH HIM FOREVER.
FOR LOVE OF HER, CALIBAN BETRAYED HIS FRIENDS.
BUT SHE LIED. SHE NEVER RETURNED.
POOR THING--YOUR HEART MADE YOU SUCH A FOOL.
CALIBAN KNOWS.
YOUR HATRED IS NO LESS THAN HE DESERVES.
IT'S THE CHILD WHO'S AT FAULT. SHE GAVE HER WORD.
I MEAN TO SEE SHE KEEPS IT.
REALLY, CALLISTO? NO JOKE?!

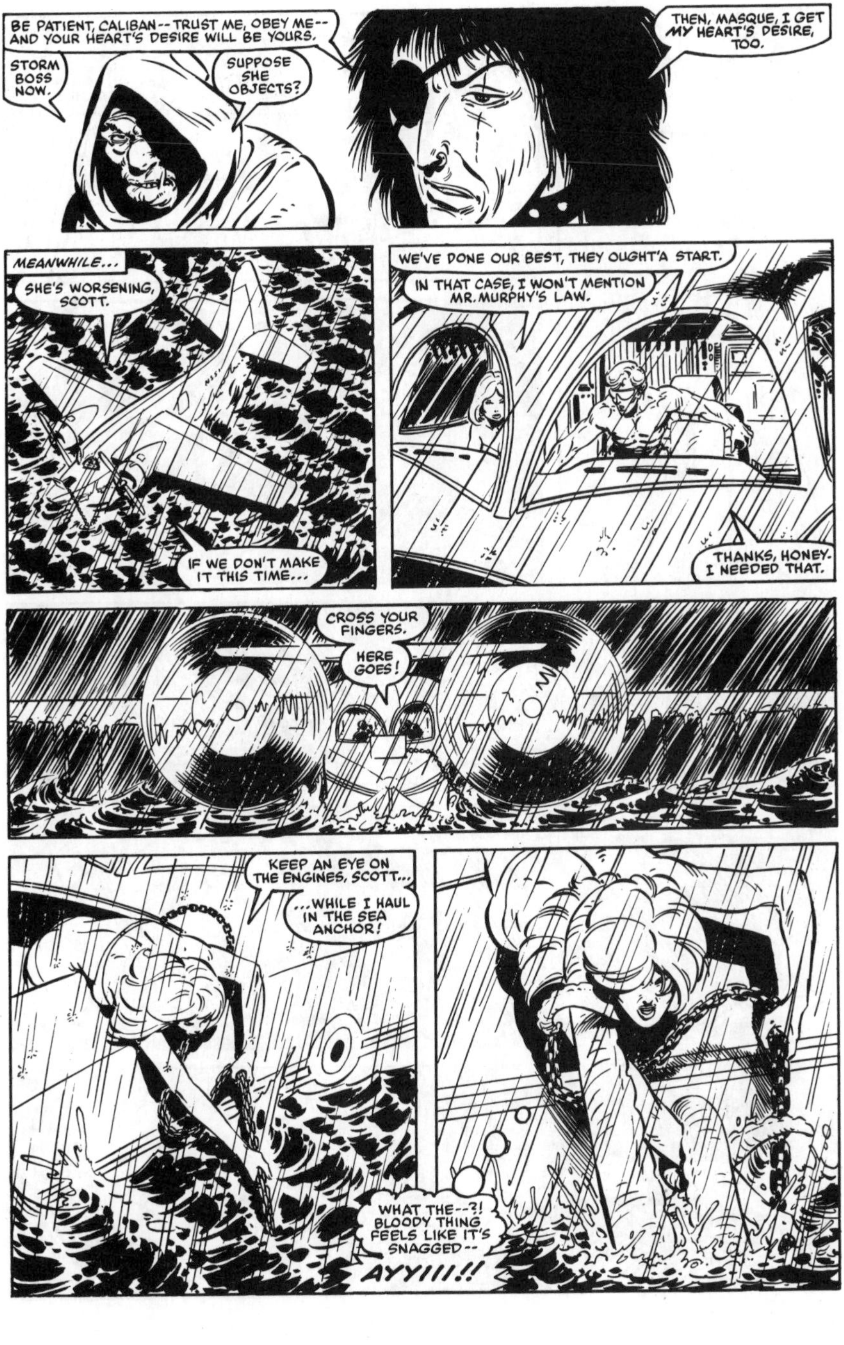
BE PATIENT, CALIBAN-- TRUST ME, OBEY ME-- AND YOUR HEART'S DESIRE WILL BE YOURS.
STORM BOSS NOW.
SUPPOSE SHE OBJECTS?
THEN, MASQUE, I GET MY HEART'S DESIRE, TOO.
MEANWHILE...
SHE'S WORSENING, SCOTT.
IF WE DON'T MAKE IT THIS TIME...
WE'VE DONE OUR BEST, THEY OUGHT'A START.
IN THAT CASE, I WON'T MENTION MR. MURPHY'S LAW.
THANKS, HONEY-I NEEDED THAT.
CROSS YOUR FINGERS.
HERE GOES!
KEEP AN EYE ON THE ENGINES, SCOTT...
...WHILE I HAUL IN THE SEA ANCHOR!
WHAT THE--?! BLOODY THING FEELS LIKE IT'S SNAGGED--
AYYIII!!

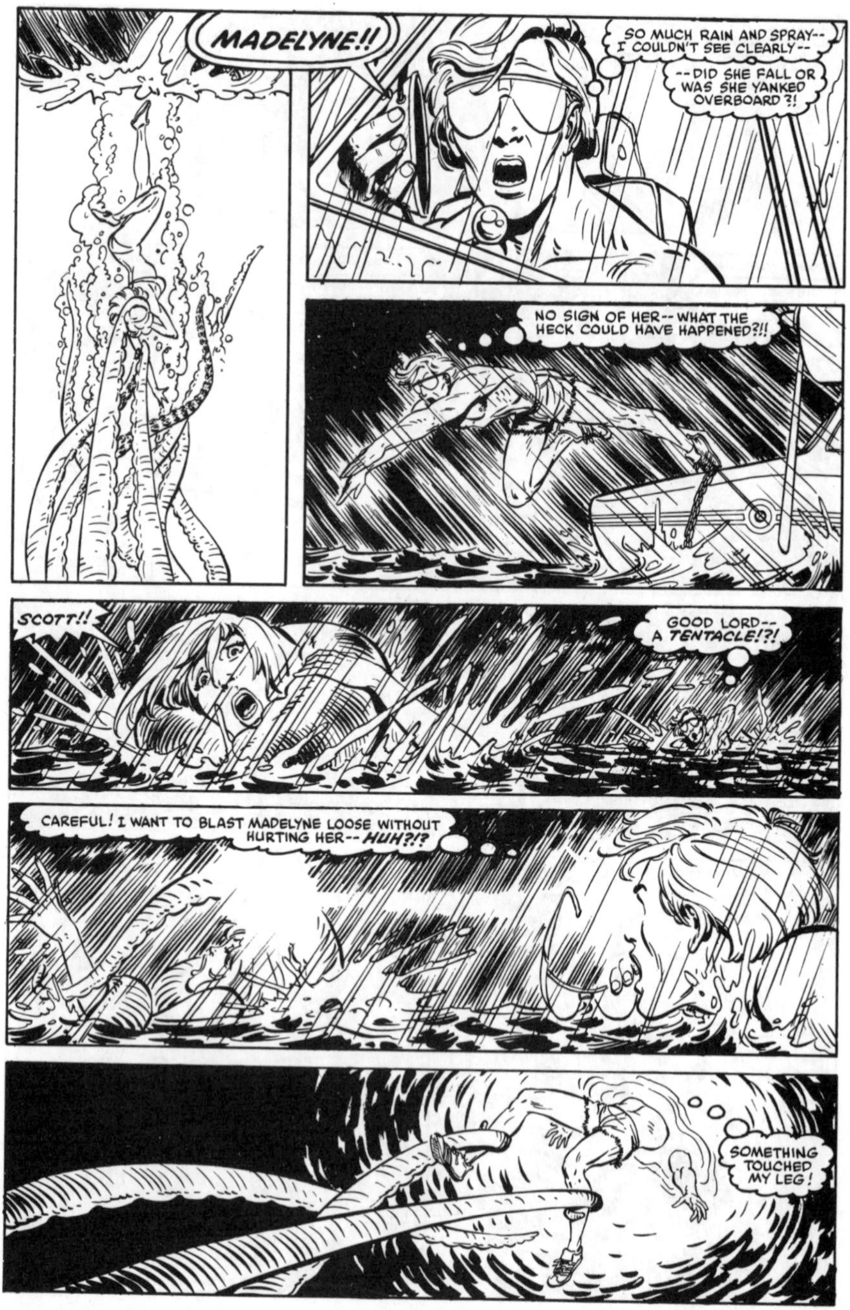
MADELYNE!!
SO MUCH RAIN AND SPRAY-- I COULDN'T SEE CLEARLY--
--DID SHE FALL OR WAS SHE YANKED OVERBOARD ?!
NO SIGN OF HER--WHAT THE HECK COULD HAVE HAPPENED?!!
SCOTT!!
GOOD LORD-- A TENTACLE!?!
CAREFUL! I WANT TO BLAST MADELYNE LOOSE WITHOUT HURTING HER-- HUH?!?
SOMETHING TOUCHED MY LEG!

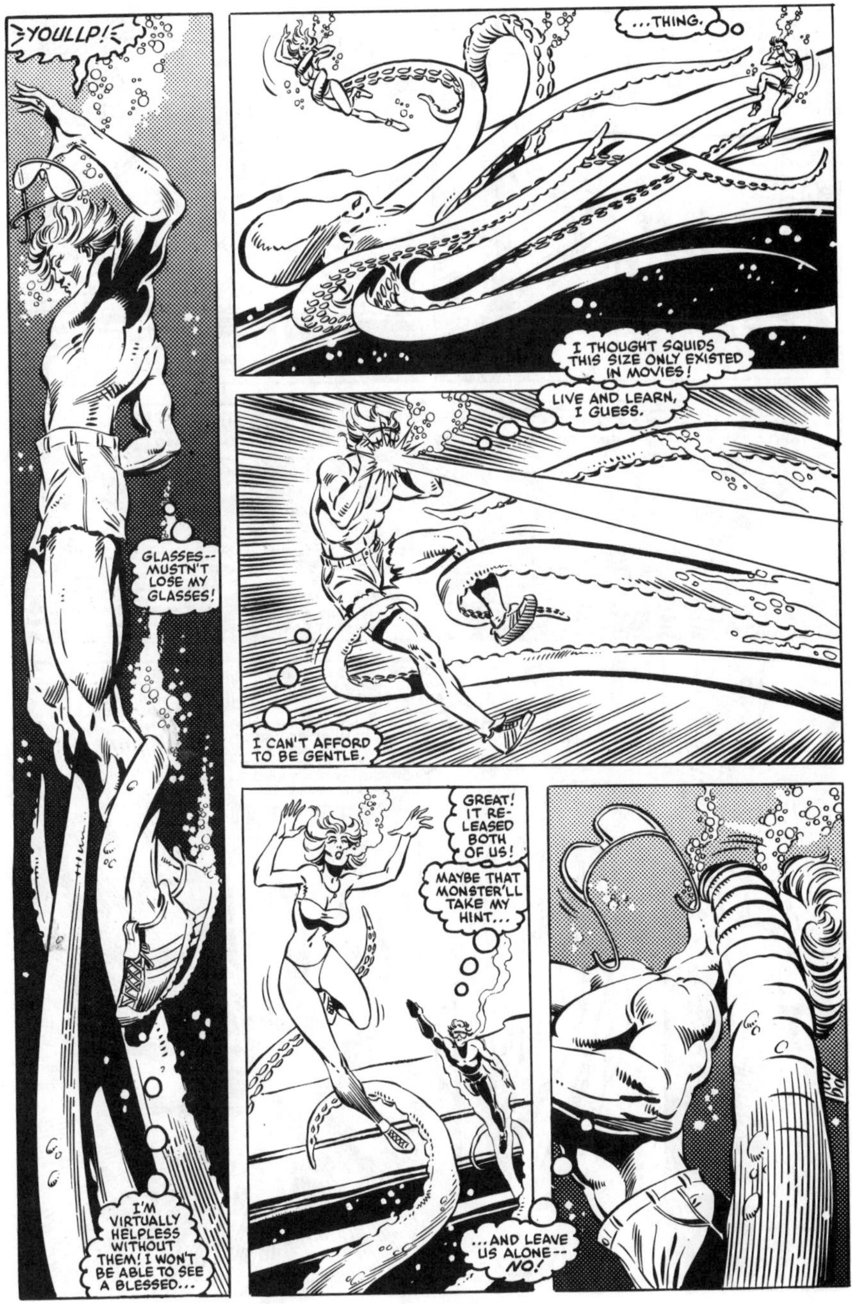
YOULLP!
GLASSES-- MUSTN'T LOSE MY GLASSES!
I'M VIRTUALLY HELPLESS WITHOUT THEM! I WON'T BE ABLE TO SEE A BLESSED...
...THING.
I THOUGHT SQUIDS THIS SIZE ONLY EXISTED IN MOVIES!
LIVE AND LEARN, I GUESS.
I CAN'T AFFORD TO BE GENTLE.
GREAT! IT RE-LEASED BOTH OF US!
MAYBE THAT MONSTER'LL TAKE MY HINT...
...AND LEAVE US ALONE-- NO!

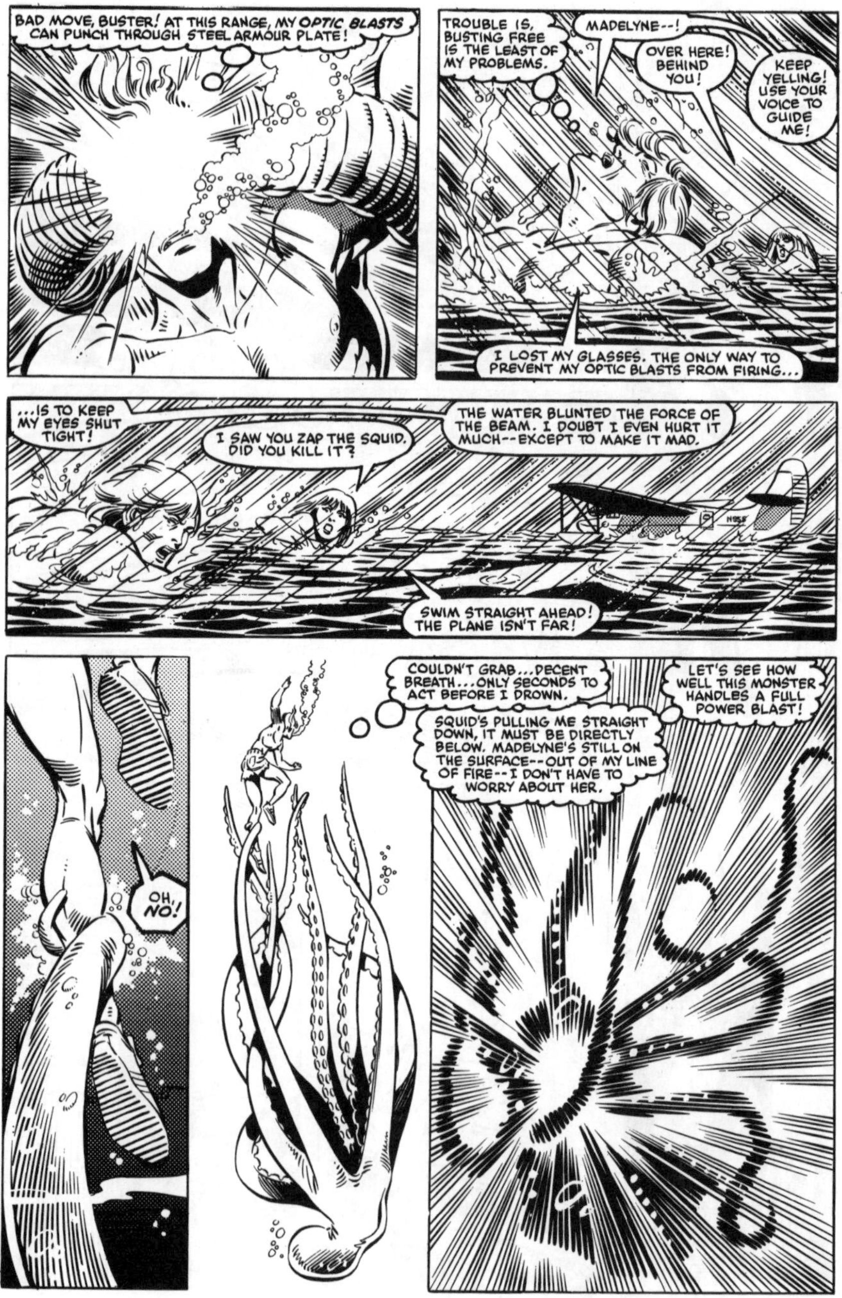
BAD MOVE, BUSTER! AT THIS RANGE, MY OPTIC BLASTS CAN PUNCH THROUGH STEEL ARMOUR PLATE!
TROUBLE IS, BUSTING FREE IS THE LEAST OF MY PROBLEMS.
MADELYNE--!
OVER HERE! BEHIND YOU!
KEEP YELLING! USE YOUR VOICE TO GUIDE ME!
I LOST MY GLASSES. THE ONLY WAY TO PREVENT MY OPTIC BLASTS FROM FIRING...
...IS TO KEEP MY EYES SHUT TIGHT!
I SAW YOU ZAP THE SQUID. DID YOU KILL IT?
THE WATER BLUNTED THE FORCE OF THE BEAM. I DOUBT I EVEN HURT IT MUCH--EXCEPT TO MAKE IT MAD.
SWIM STRAIGHT AHEAD! THE PLANE ISN'T FAR!
OH, NO!
COULDN'T GRAB... DECENT BREATH... ONLY SECONDS TO ACT BEFORE I DROWN.
SQUID'S PULLING ME STRAIGHT DOWN, IT MUST BE DIRECTLY BELOW. MADELYNE'S STILL ON THE SURFACE--OUT OF MY LINE OF FIRE--I DON'T HAVE TO WORRY ABOUT HER.
LET'S SEE HOW WELL THIS MONSTER HANDLES A FULL POWER BLAST!

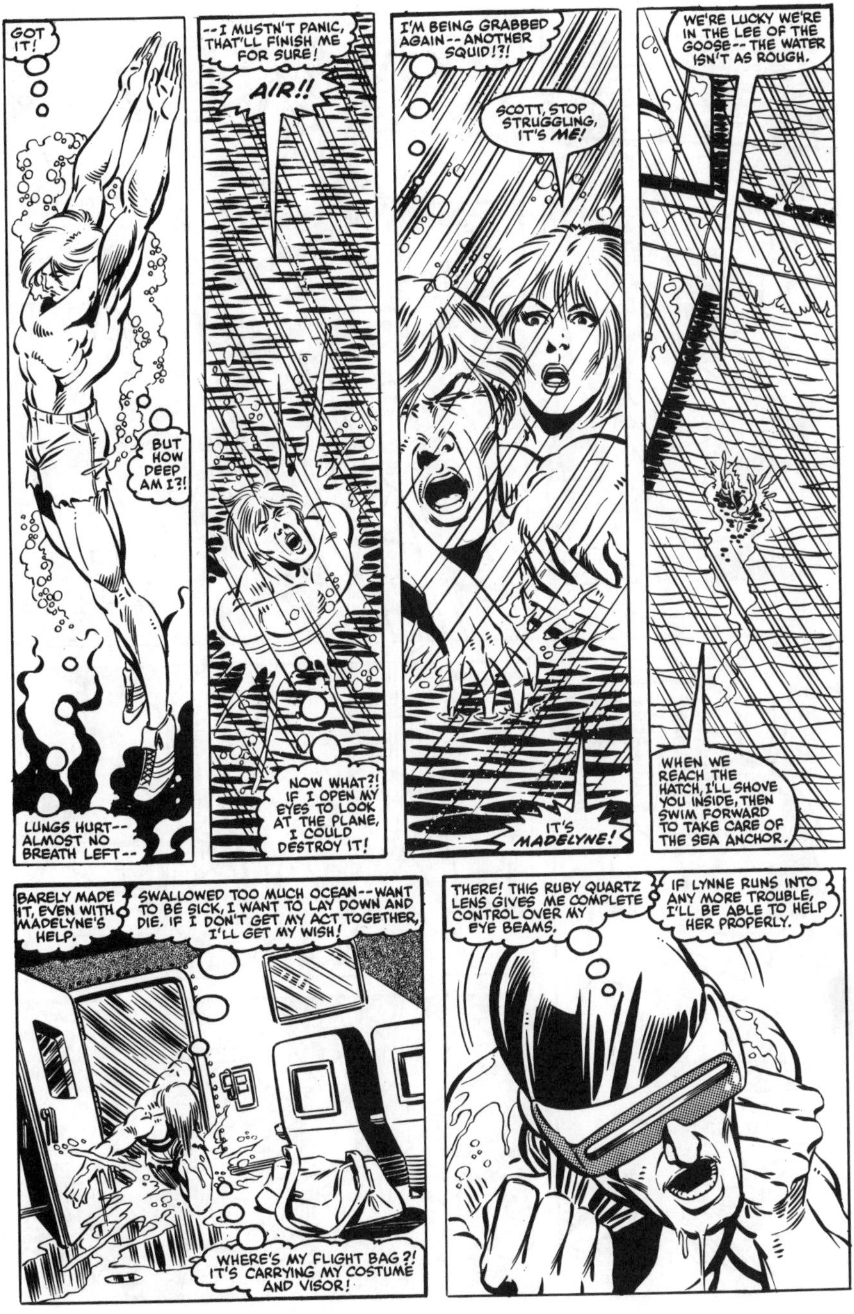

GOT IT!
BUT HOW DEEP AM I?!
LUNGS HURT-- ALMOST NO BREATH LEFT--
--I MUSTN'T PANIC, THAT'LL FINISH ME FOR SURE!
AIR!!
NOW WHAT?! IF I OPEN MY EYES TO LOOK AT THE PLANE, I COULD DESTROY IT!
I'M BEING GRABBED AGAIN--ANOTHER SQUID!?!
SCOTT, STOP STRUGGLING, IT'S ME!
IT'S MADELYNE!
WE'RE LUCKY WE'RE IN THE LEE OF THE GOOSE--THE WATER ISN'T AS ROUGH.
WHEN WE REACH THE HATCH, I'LL SHOVE YOU INSIDE, THEN SWIM FORWARD TO TAKE CARE OF THE SEA ANCHOR.
BARELY MADE IT, EVEN WITH MADELYNE'S HELP.
SWALLOWED TOO MUCH OCEAN--WANT TO BE SICK, I WANT TO LAY DOWN AND DIE. IF I DON'T GET MY ACT TOGETHER, I'LL GET MY WISH!
WHERE'S MY FLIGHT BAG?! IT'S CARRYING MY COSTUME AND VISOR!
THERE! THIS RUBY QUARTZ LENS GIVES ME COMPLETE CONTROL OVER MY EYE BEAMS.
IF LYNNE RUNS INTO ANY MORE TROUBLE, I'LL BE ABLE TO HELP HER PROPERLY.

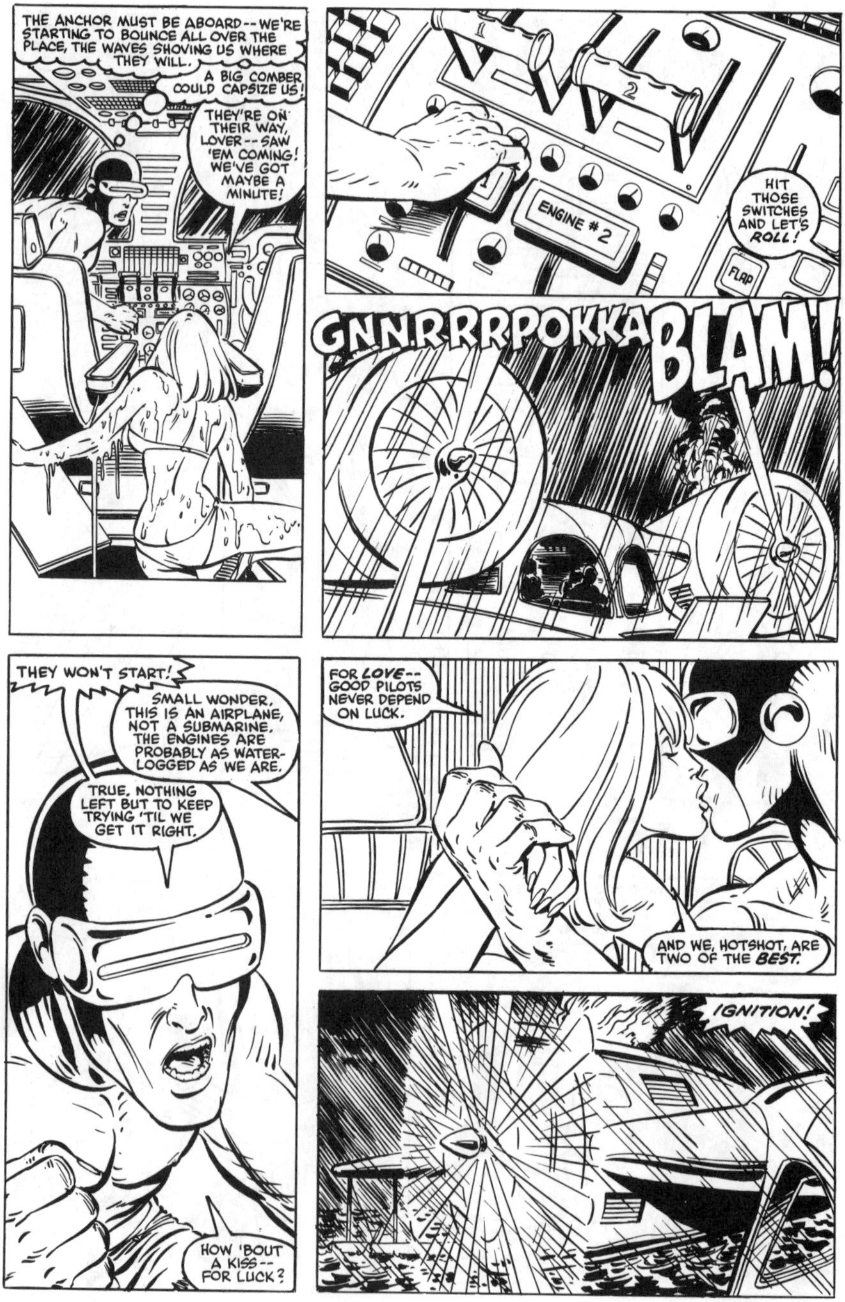
THE ANCHOR MUST BE ABOARD--WE'RE STARTING TO BOUNCE ALL OVER THE PLACE, THE WAVES SHOVING US WHERE THEY WILL.
A BIG COMBER COULD CAPSIZE US!
THEY'RE ON THEIR WAY, LOVER--SAW 'EM COMING! WE'VE GOT MAYBE A MINUTE!
ENGINE #2
FLAP
HIT THOSE SWITCHES AND LET'S ROLL!
GNNRRRPOKKA BLAM!
THEY WON'T START!
SMALL WONDER. THIS IS AN AIRPLANE, NOT A SUBMARINE. THE ENGINES ARE PROBABLY AS WATER-LOGGED AS WE ARE.
TRUE. NOTHING LEFT BUT TO KEEP TRYING 'TIL WE GET IT RIGHT.
HOW 'BOUT A KISS--FOR LUCK?
FOR LOVE--GOOD PILOTS NEVER DEPEND ON LUCK.
AND WE, HOTSHOT, ARE TWO OF THE BEST.
IGNITION!

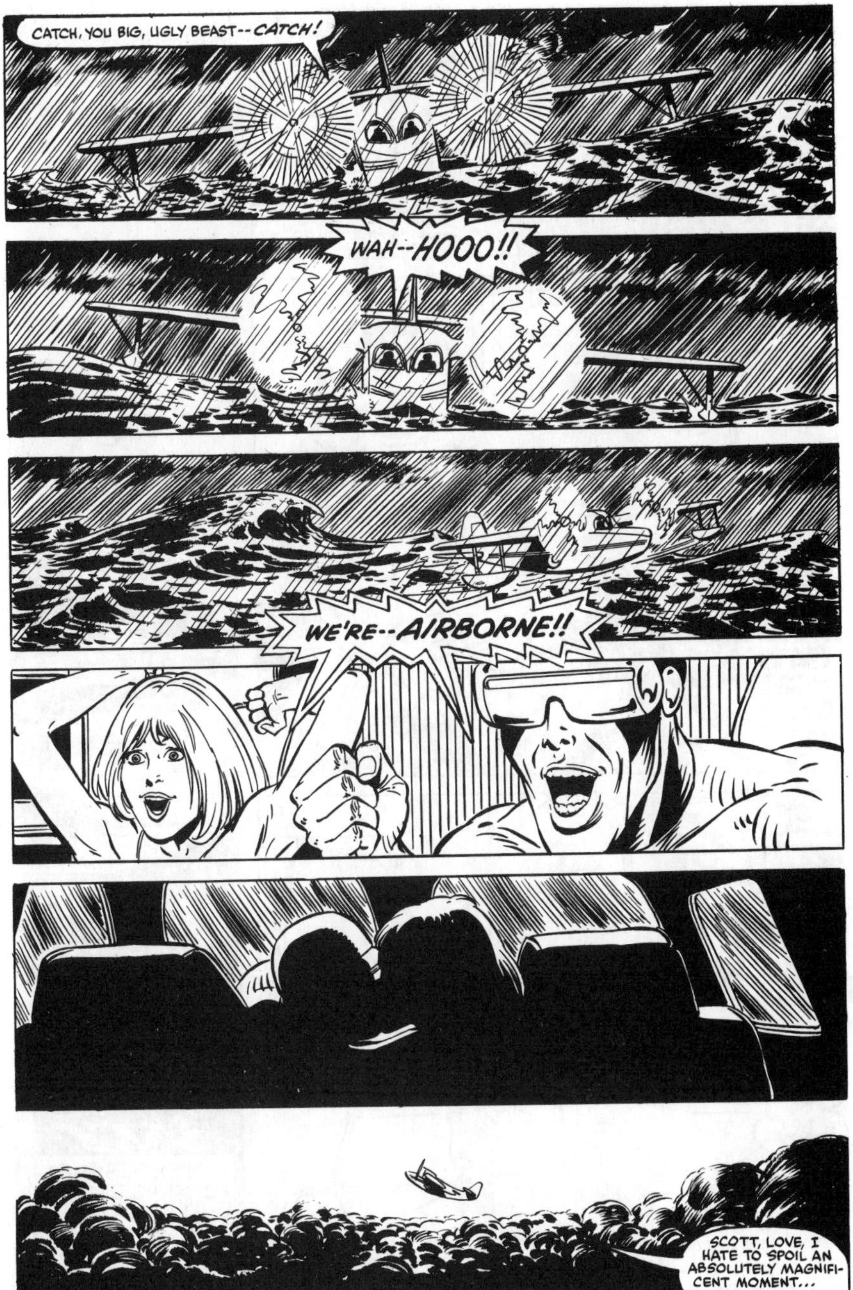
CATCH, YOU BIG, UGLY BEAST--CATCH!
WAH--HOOO!!
WE'RE--AIRBORNE!!
SCOTT, LOVE, I HATE TO SPOIL AN ABSOLUTELY MAGNIFICENT MOMENT...

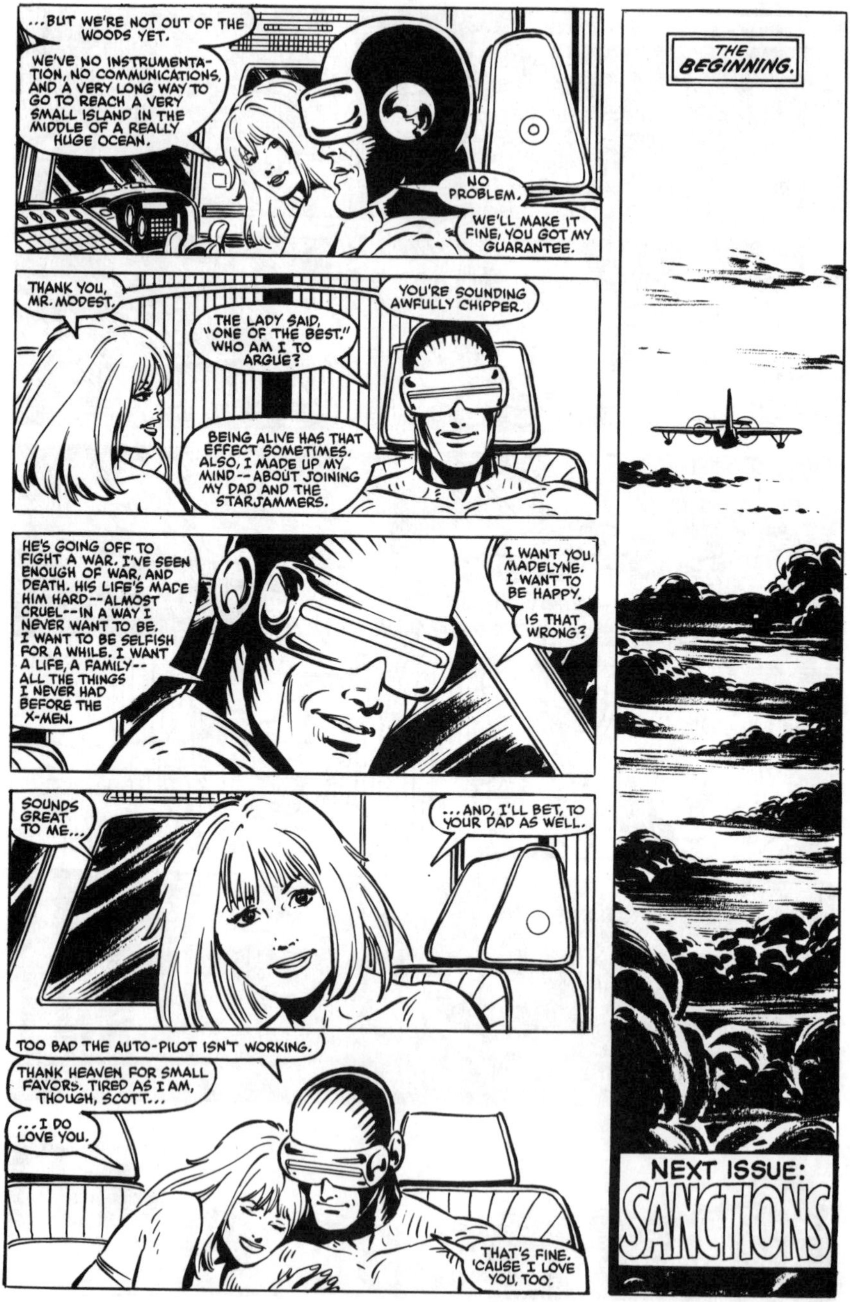
...BUT WE'RE NOT OUT OF THE WOODS YET.
WE'VE NO INSTRUMENTATION, NO COMMUNICATIONS, AND A VERY LONG WAY TO GO TO REACH A VERY SMALL ISLAND IN THE MIDDLE OF A REALLY HUGE OCEAN.
NO PROBLEM.
WE'LL MAKE IT FINE, YOU GOT MY GUARANTEE.
THANK YOU, MR. MODEST.
YOU'RE SOUNDING AWFULLY CHIPPER.
THE LADY SAID, "ONE OF THE BEST." WHO AM I TO ARGUE?
BEING ALIVE HAS THAT EFFECT SOMETIMES. ALSO, I MADE UP MY MIND--ABOUT JOINING MY DAD AND THE STARJAMMERS.
HE'S GOING OFF TO FIGHT A WAR. I'VE SEEN ENOUGH OF WAR, AND DEATH. HIS LIFE'S MADE HIM HARD--ALMOST CRUEL--IN A WAY I NEVER WANT TO BE. I WANT TO BE SELFISH FOR A WHILE. I WANT A LIFE, A FAMILY--ALL THE THINGS I NEVER HAD BEFORE THE X-MEN.
I WANT YOU, MADELYNE. I WANT TO BE HAPPY.
IS THAT WRONG?
SOUNDS GREAT TO ME...
...AND, I'LL BET, TO YOUR DAD AS WELL.
TOO BAD THE AUTO-PILOT ISN'T WORKING.
THANK HEAVEN FOR SMALL FAVORS. TIRED AS I AM, THOUGH, SCOTT...
...I DO LOVE YOU.
THAT'S FINE. 'CAUSE I LOVE YOU, TOO.
THE BEGINNING.
NEXT ISSUE:
SANCTIONS

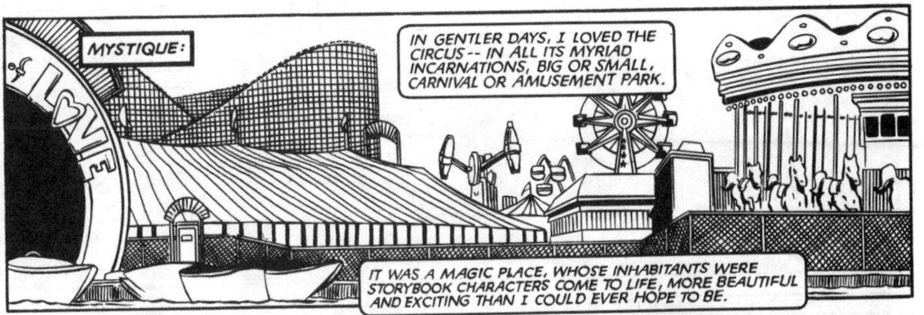
MYSTIQUE:
IN GENTLER DAYS, I LOVED THE CIRCUS-- IN ALL ITS MYRIAD INCARNATIONS, BIG OR SMALL, CARNIVAL OR AMUSEMENT PARK.
LOVE
IT WAS A MAGIC PLACE, WHOSE INHABITANTS WERE STORYBOOK CHARACTERS COME TO LIFE, MORE BEAUTIFUL AND EXCITING THAN I COULD EVER HOPE TO BE.

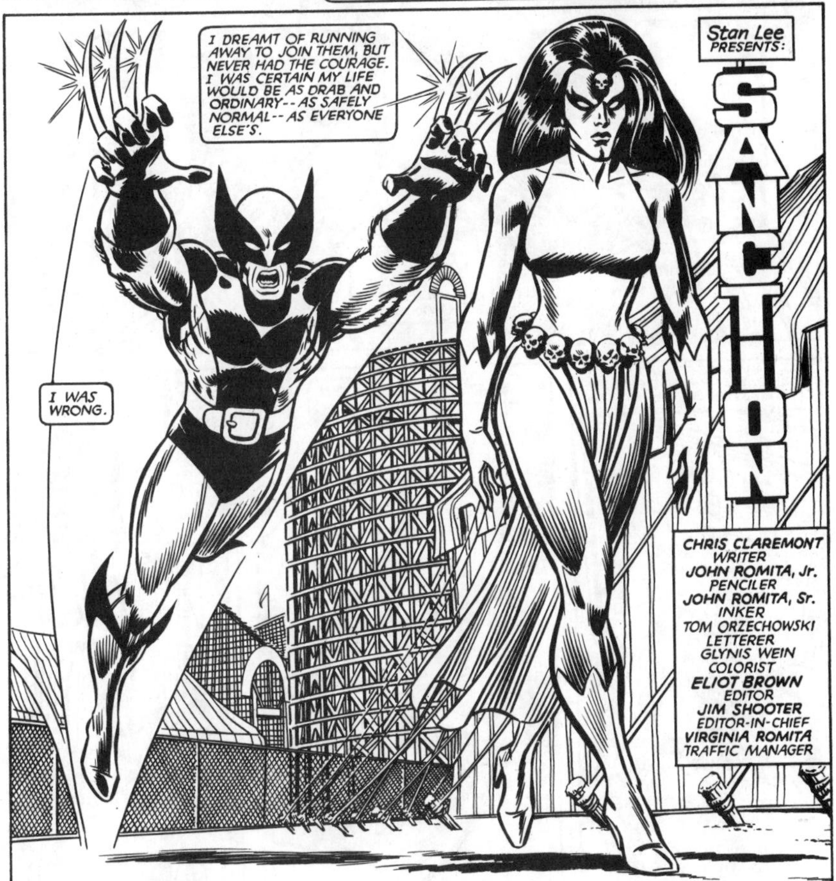
I DREAMT OF RUNNING AWAY TO JOIN THEM, BUT NEVER HAD THE COURAGE. I WAS CERTAIN MY LIFE WOULD BE AS DRAB AND ORDINARY-- AS SAFELY NORMAL-- AS EVERYONE ELSE'S.
Stan Lee PRESENTS:
SANCTION
I WAS WRONG.
CHRIS CLAREMONT WRITER
JOHN ROMITA, Jr. PENCILER
JOHN ROMITA, Sr. INKER
TOM ORZECHOWSKI LETTERER
GLYNIS WEIN COLORIST
ELIOT BROWN EDITOR
JIM SHOOTER EDITOR-IN-CHIEF
VIRGINIA ROMITA TRAFFIC MANAGER

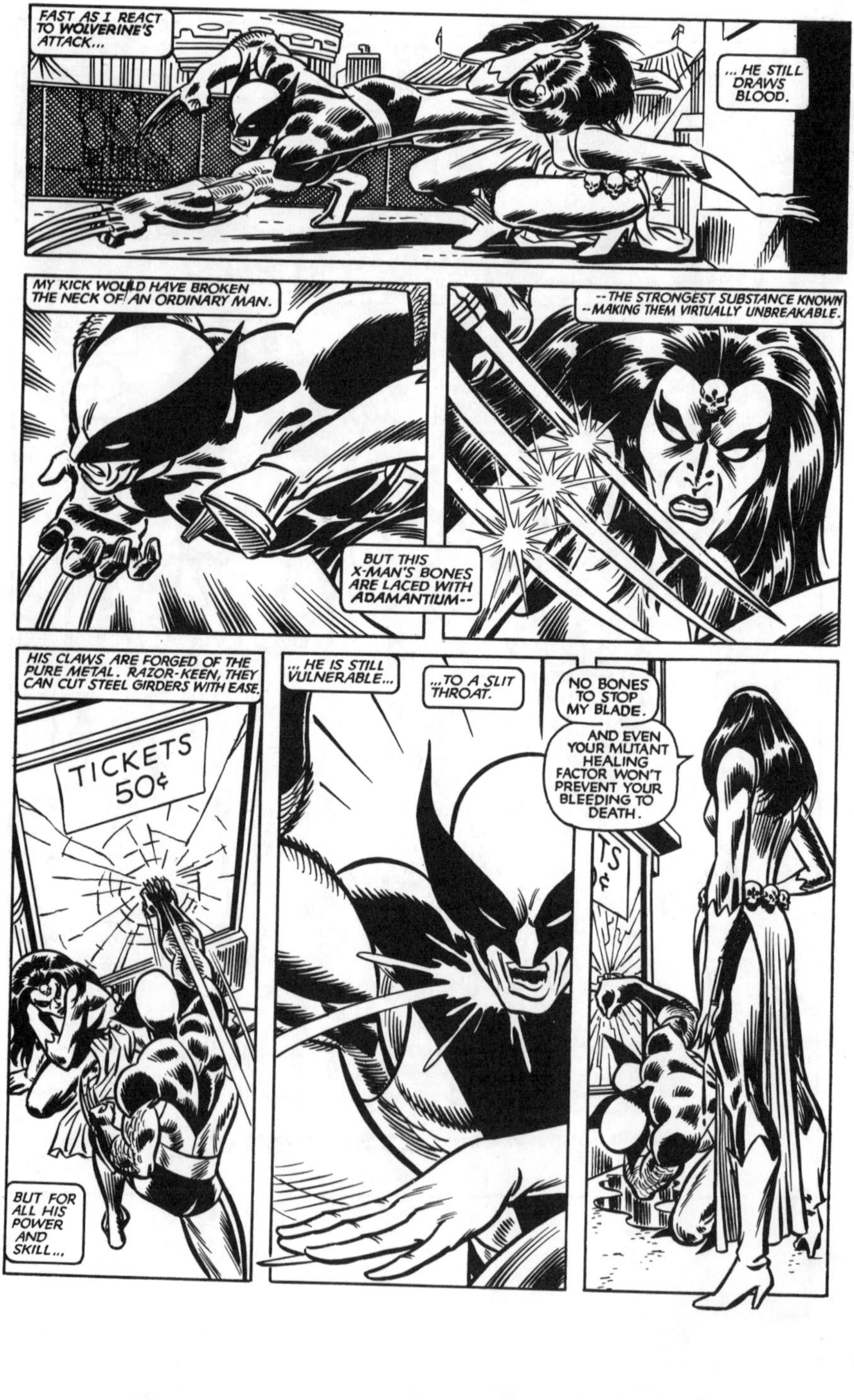

FAST AS I REACT TO WOLVERINE'S ATTACK...
...HE STILL DRAWS BLOOD.
MY KICK WOULD HAVE BROKEN THE NECK OF AN ORDINARY MAN.
BUT THIS X-MAN'S BONES ARE LACED WITH ADAMANTIUM--
--THE STRONGEST SUBSTANCE KNOWN --MAKING THEM VIRTUALLY UNBREAKABLE.
HIS CLAWS ARE FORGED OF THE PURE METAL. RAZOR-KEEN, THEY CAN CUT STEEL GIRDERS WITH EASE.
TICKETS 50¢
BUT FOR ALL HIS POWER AND SKILL...
...HE IS STILL VULNERABLE...
...TO A SLIT THROAT.
NO BONES TO STOP MY BLADE.
AND EVEN YOUR MUTANT HEALING FACTOR WON'T PREVENT YOUR BLEEDING TO DEATH.

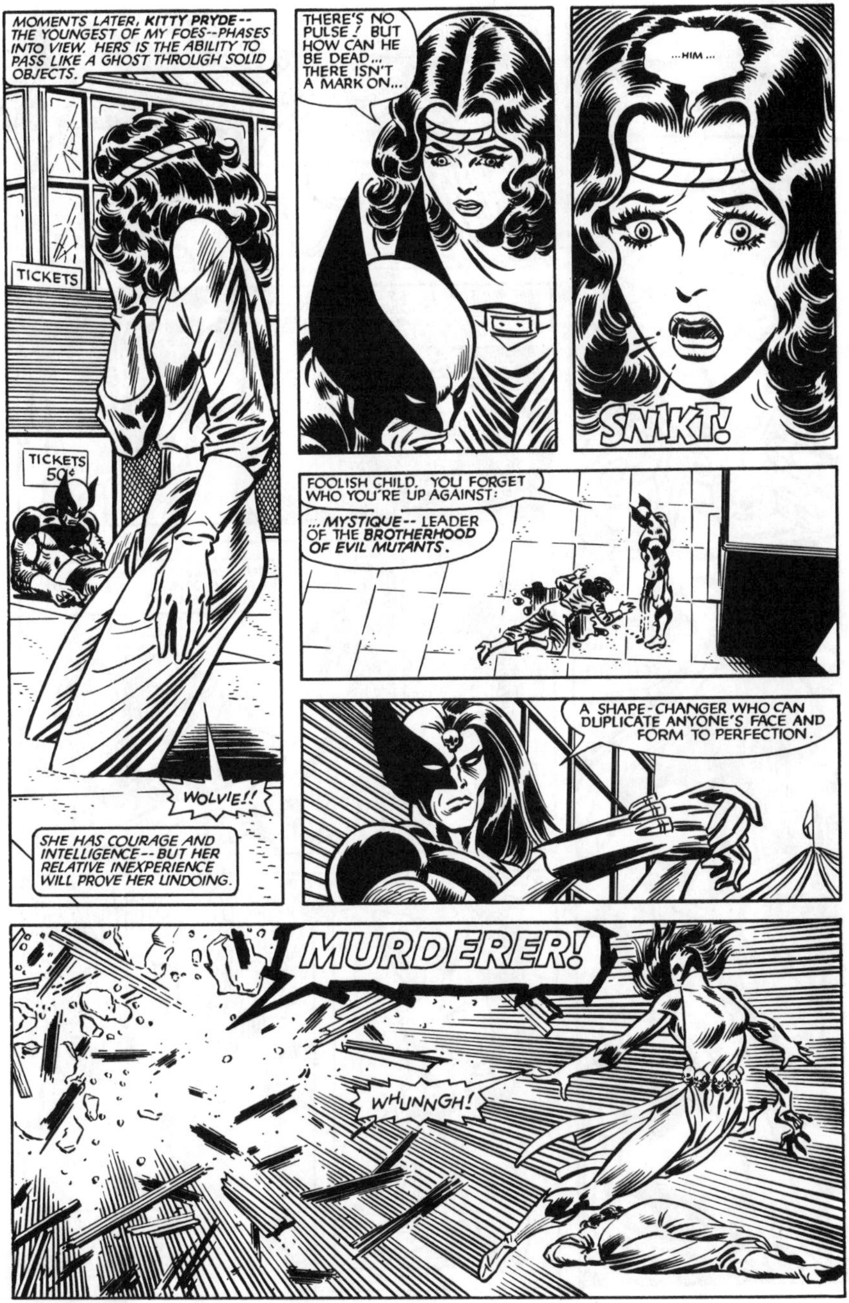

MOMENTS LATER, KITTY PRYDE-- THE YOUNGEST OF MY FOES--PHASES INTO VIEW. HERS IS THE ABILITY TO PASS LIKE A GHOST THROUGH SOLID OBJECTS.
TICKETS
TICKETS 50¢
WOLVIE!!
SHE HAS COURAGE AND INTELLIGENCE--BUT HER RELATIVE INEXPERIENCE WILL PROVE HER UNDOING.
THERE'S NO PULSE! BUT HOW CAN HE BE DEAD... THERE ISN'T A MARK ON...
...HIM ...
SNIKT!
FOOLISH CHILD. YOU FORGET WHO YOU'RE UP AGAINST:
...MYSTIQUE-- LEADER OF THE BROTHERHOOD OF EVIL MUTANTS.
A SHAPE-CHANGER WHO CAN DUPLICATE ANYONE'S FACE AND FORM TO PERFECTION.
MURDERER!
WHUNNGH!

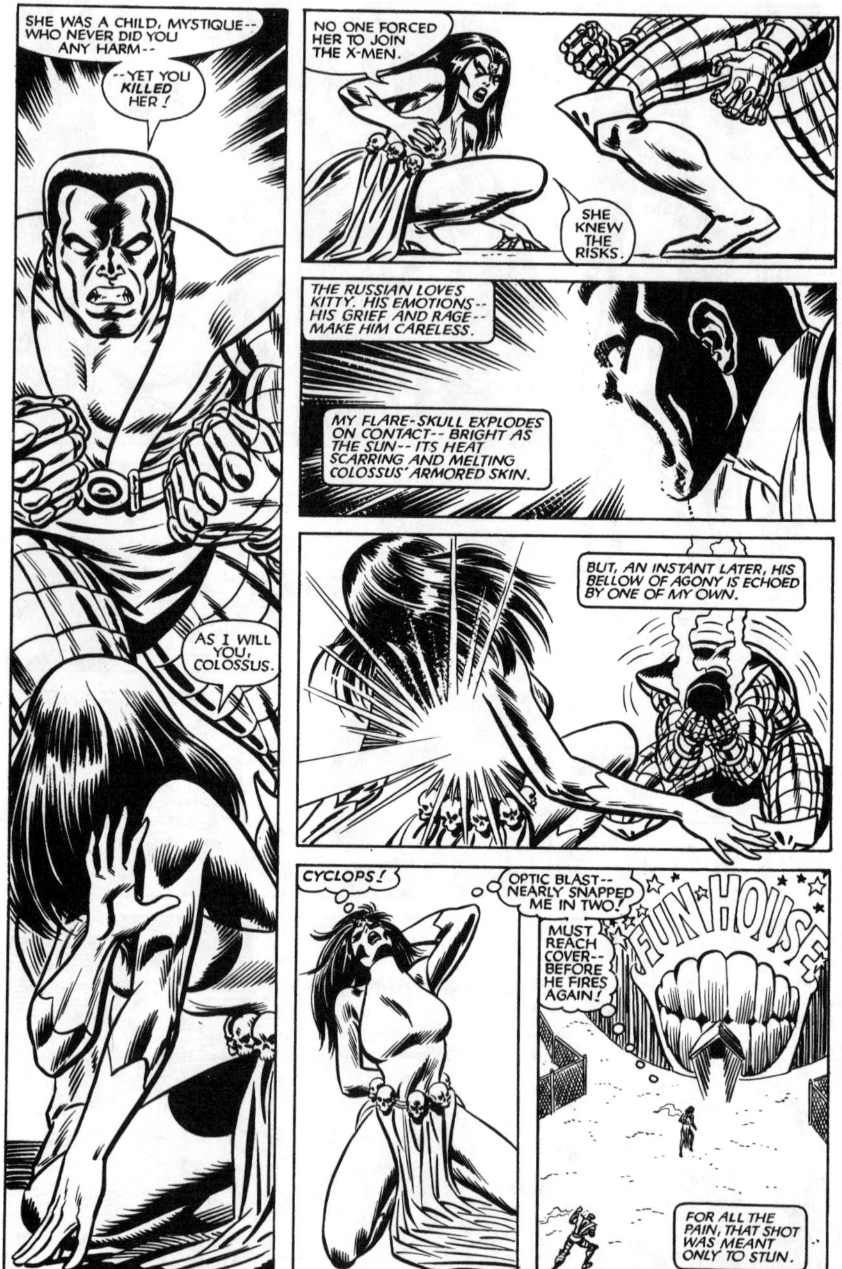
SHE WAS A CHILD, MYSTIQUE-- WHO NEVER DID YOU ANY HARM--
--YET YOU KILLED HER!
AS I WILL YOU, COLOSSUS.
NO ONE FORCED HER TO JOIN THE X-MEN.
SHE KNEW THE RISKS.
THE RUSSIAN LOVES KITTY. HIS EMOTIONS-- HIS GRIEF AND RAGE-- MAKE HIM CARELESS.
MY FLARE-SKULL EXPLODES ON CONTACT-- BRIGHT AS THE SUN-- ITS HEAT SCARRING AND MELTING COLOSSUS' ARMORED SKIN.
BUT, AN INSTANT LATER, HIS BELLOW OF AGONY IS ECHOED BY ONE OF MY OWN.
CYCLOPS!
OPTIC BLAST-- NEARLY SNAPPED ME IN TWO!
MUST REACH COVER-- BEFORE HE FIRES AGAIN!
FUNHOUSE
FOR ALL THE PAIN, THAT SHOT WAS MEANT ONLY TO STUN.

CYCLOPS WAS A FOUNDING MEMBER OF THE X-MEN-- THEIR FIRST, BEST LEADER-- AND HE STILL PLAYS BY THE OLD RULES. EVEN AFTER WHAT'S HAPPENED TONIGHT, HE'LL TRY TO TAKE ME ALIVE.

HIS SCRUPLES GIVE ME MY EDGE.

COLOSSUS, DON'T FOLLOW HER IN THERE! THAT'S WHAT SHE WANTS!

WITHIN THE FUNHOUSE ARE SCORES OF MIRRORS-- AND CYCLOPS HAS NO WAY OF TELLING REFLECTION FROM REALITY.

COLOSSUS STILL SUFFERS FROM THE EFFECTS OF MY FLARE-SKULL, HELPLESS AS HE IS VIRTUALLY BLIND.

I MILK THE MOMENT...

...TAKING SLOW, DELIBERATE AIM.

PETER-- BEHIND YOU!

ZZAP

ANOTHER STUN BEAM...

...THAT PASSES HARMLESSLY THROUGH A HOLOGRAPHIC PROJECTION OF MYSELF, BEFORE BOUNCING OFF THE MIRRORS...

...AND INTO A CAREFULLY-PLACED AMPLIFIER MODULE-- EACH OF WHOSE LENSES AMPLIFIES THE BEAM'S FORCE A HUNDRED-FOLD--

--MAKING IT POWERFUL ENOUGH TO PENETRATE ANYTHING.

EVEN A BODY COMPOSED OF ORGANIC STEEL.

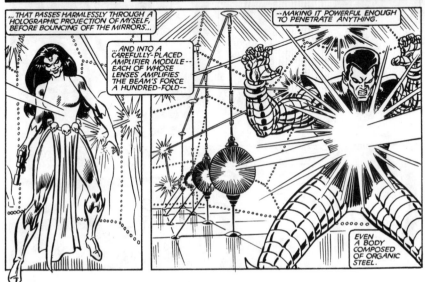

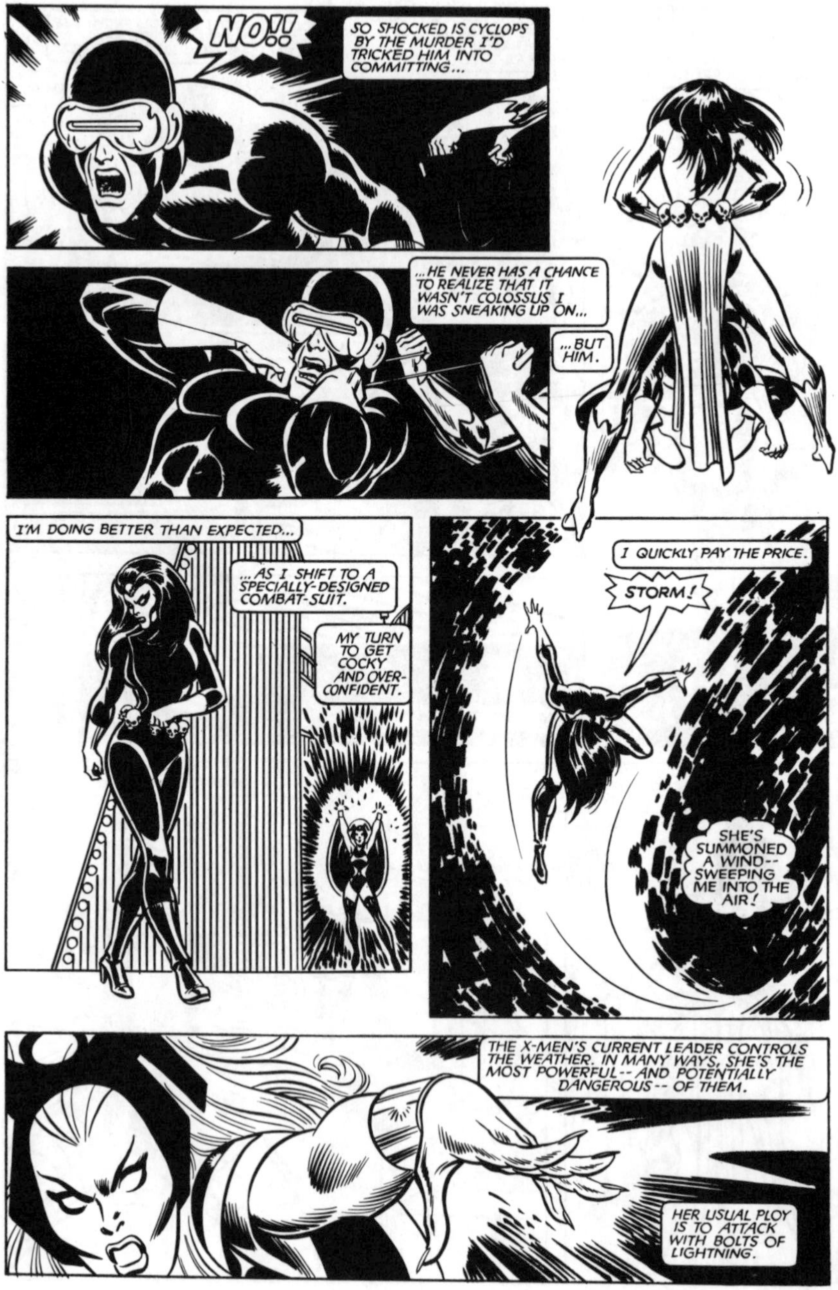
NO!!
SO SHOCKED IS CYCLOPS BY THE MURDER I'D TRICKED HIM INTO COMMITTING...
...HE NEVER HAS A CHANCE TO REALIZE THAT IT WASN'T COLOSSUS I WAS SNEAKING UP ON...
...BUT HIM.
I'M DOING BETTER THAN EXPECTED...
...AS I SHIFT TO A SPECIALLY-DESIGNED COMBAT-SUIT.
MY TURN TO GET COCKY AND OVER-CONFIDENT.
I QUICKLY PAY THE PRICE.
STORM!
SHE'S SUMMONED A WIND--SWEEPING ME INTO THE AIR!
THE X-MEN'S CURRENT LEADER CONTROLS THE WEATHER. IN MANY WAYS, SHE'S THE MOST POWERFUL-- AND POTENTIALLY DANGEROUS-- OF THEM.
HER USUAL PLOY IS TO ATTACK WITH BOLTS OF LIGHTNING.

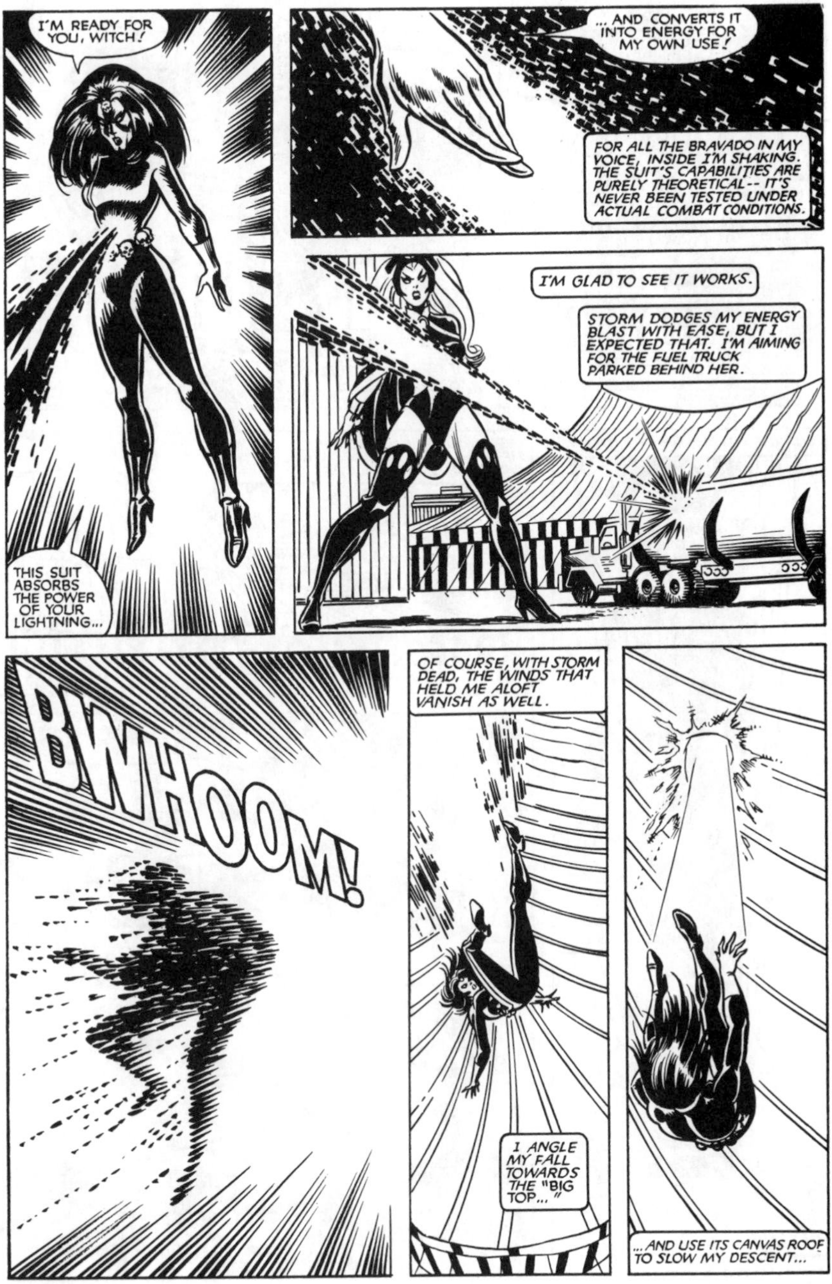
I'M READY FOR YOU, WITCH!
THIS SUIT ABSORBS THE POWER OF YOUR LIGHTNING...
... AND CONVERTS IT INTO ENERGY FOR MY OWN USE!
FOR ALL THE BRAVADO IN MY VOICE, INSIDE I'M SHAKING. THE SUIT'S CAPABILITIES ARE PURELY THEORETICAL-- IT'S NEVER BEEN TESTED UNDER ACTUAL COMBAT CONDITIONS.
I'M GLAD TO SEE IT WORKS.
STORM DODGES MY ENERGY BLAST WITH EASE, BUT I EXPECTED THAT. I'M AIMING FOR THE FUEL TRUCK PARKED BEHIND HER.
BWHOOM!
OF COURSE, WITH STORM DEAD, THE WINDS THAT HELD ME ALOFT VANISH AS WELL.
I ANGLE MY FALL TOWARDS THE "BIG TOP..."
...AND USE ITS CANVAS ROOF TO SLOW MY DESCENT...

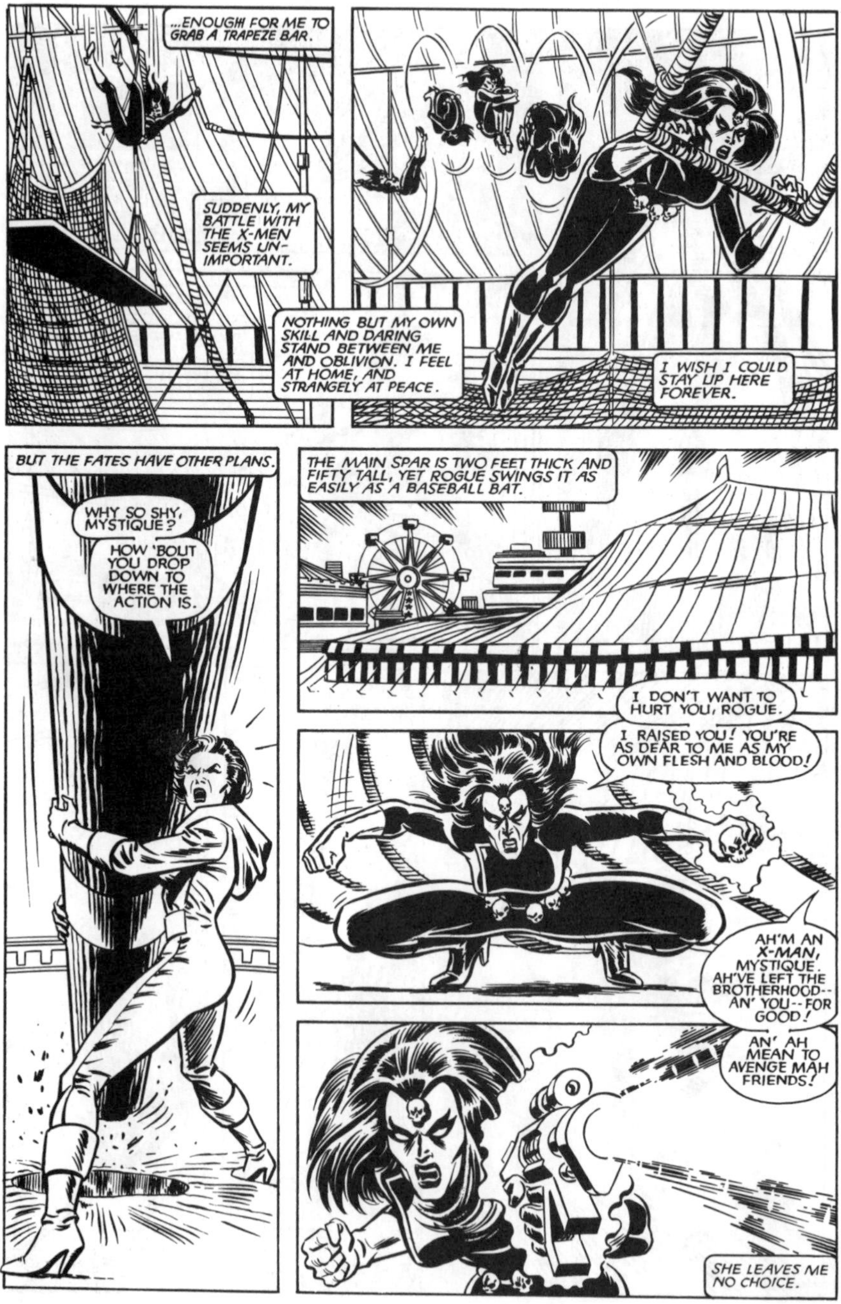
...ENOUGH FOR ME TO GRAB A TRAPEZE BAR.
SUDDENLY, MY BATTLE WITH THE X-MEN SEEMS UN-IMPORTANT.
NOTHING BUT MY OWN SKILL AND DARING STAND BETWEEN ME AND OBLIVION. I FEEL AT HOME, AND STRANGELY AT PEACE.
I WISH I COULD STAY UP HERE FOREVER.
BUT THE FATES HAVE OTHER PLANS.
WHY SO SHY, MYSTIQUE?
HOW 'BOUT YOU DROP DOWN TO WHERE THE ACTION IS.
THE MAIN SPAR IS TWO FEET THICK AND FIFTY TALL, YET ROGUE SWINGS IT AS EASILY AS A BASEBALL BAT.
I DON'T WANT TO HURT YOU, ROGUE.
I RAISED YOU! YOU'RE AS DEAR TO ME AS MY OWN FLESH AND BLOOD!
AH'M AN X-MAN, MYSTIQUE. AH'VE LEFT THE BROTHERHOOD-- AN' YOU--FOR GOOD!
AN' AH MEAN TO AVENGE MAH FRIENDS!
SHE LEAVES ME NO CHOICE.

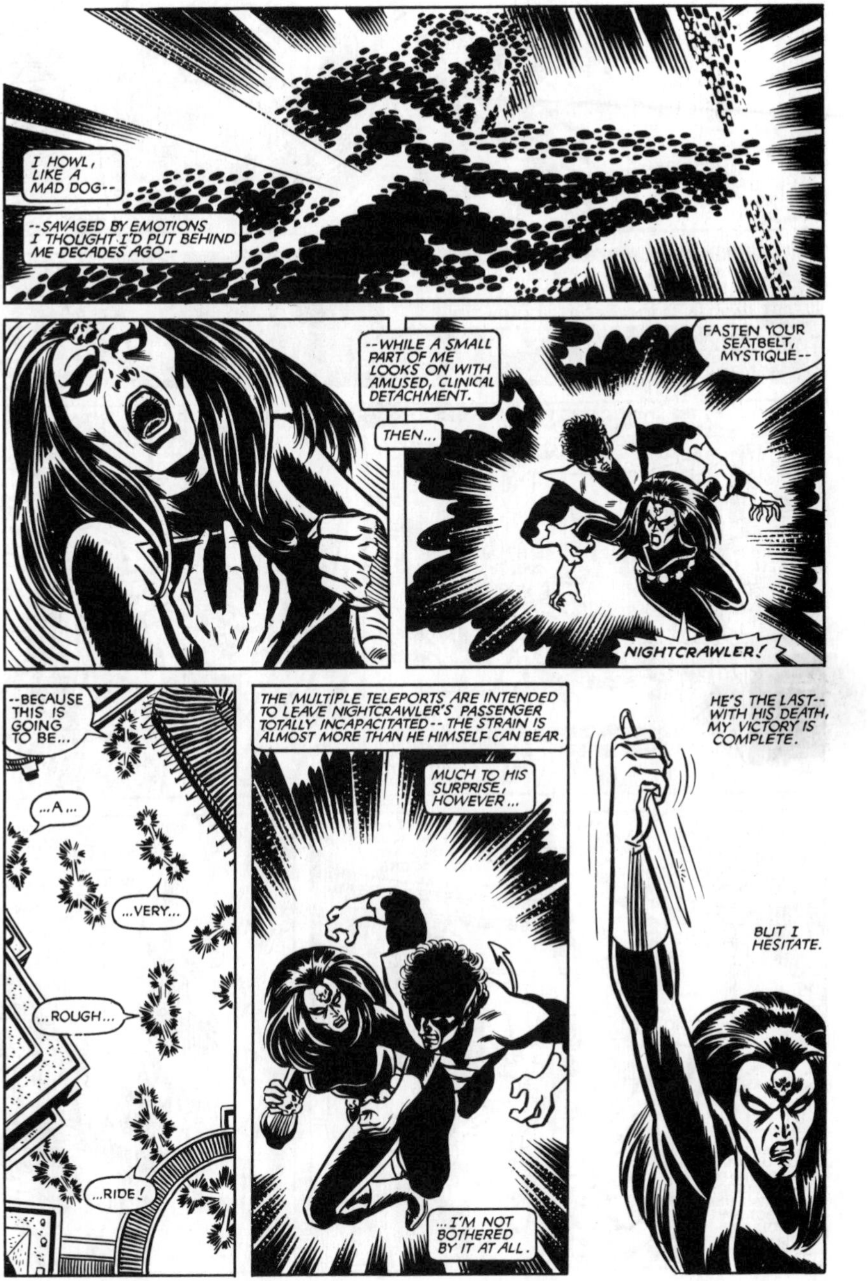
I HOWL, LIKE A MAD DOG--
--SAVAGED BY EMOTIONS I THOUGHT I'D PUT BEHIND ME DECADES AGO--
--WHILE A SMALL PART OF ME LOOKS ON WITH AMUSED, CLINICAL DETACHMENT.
THEN...
FASTEN YOUR SEATBELT, MYSTIQUE--
NIGHTCRAWLER!
--BECAUSE THIS IS GOING TO BE...
...A...
...VERY...
...ROUGH...
...RIDE!
THE MULTIPLE TELEPORTS ARE INTENDED TO LEAVE NIGHTCRAWLER'S PASSENGER TOTALLY INCAPACITATED-- THE STRAIN IS ALMOST MORE THAN HE HIMSELF CAN BEAR.
MUCH TO HIS SURPRISE, HOWEVER...
...I'M NOT BOTHERED BY IT AT ALL.
HE'S THE LAST-- WITH HIS DEATH, MY VICTORY IS COMPLETE.
BUT I HESITATE.

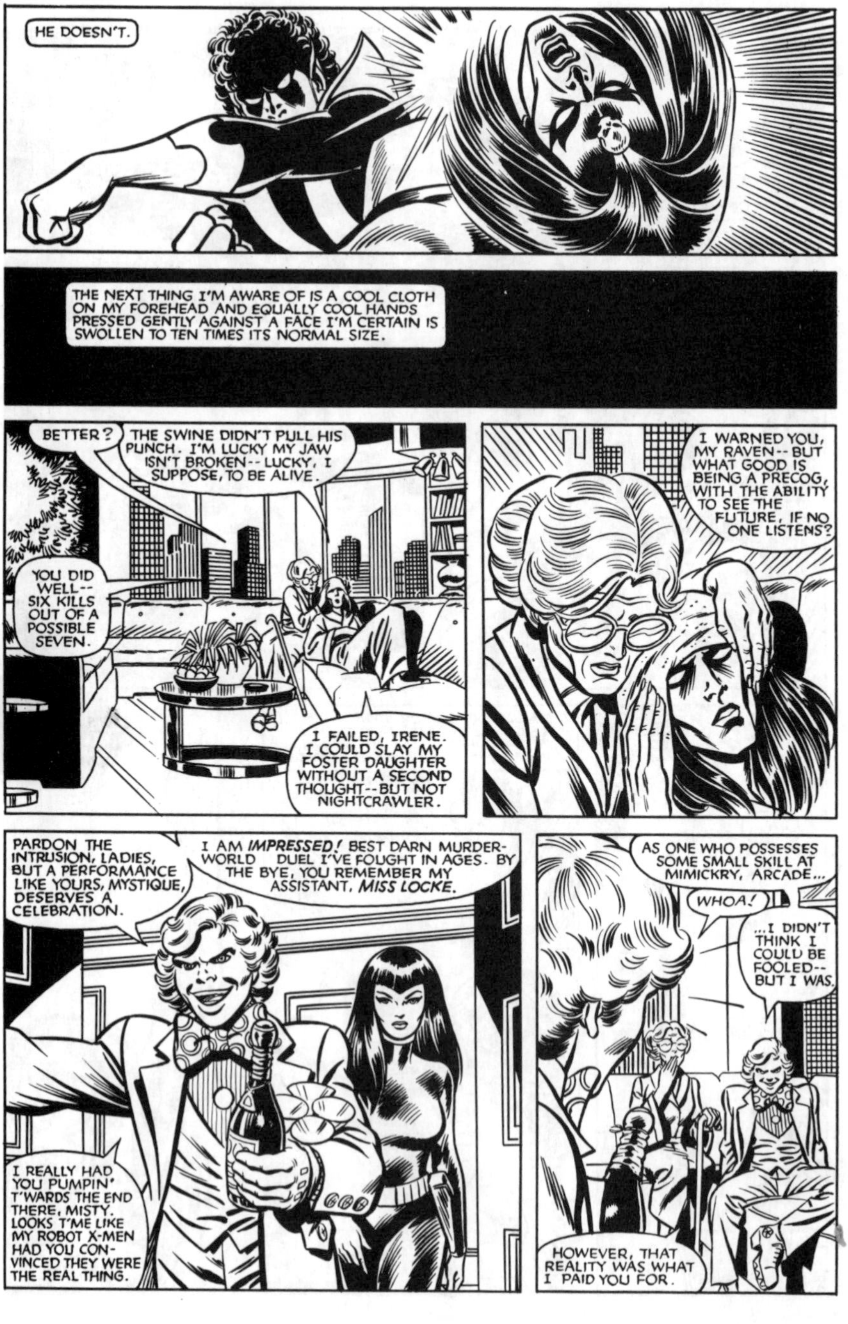
HE DOESN'T.
THE NEXT THING I'M AWARE OF IS A COOL CLOTH ON MY FOREHEAD AND EQUALLY COOL HANDS PRESSED GENTLY AGAINST A FACE I'M CERTAIN IS SWOLLEN TO TEN TIMES ITS NORMAL SIZE.
BETTER?
THE SWINE DIDN'T PULL HIS PUNCH. I'M LUCKY MY JAW ISN'T BROKEN-- LUCKY, I SUPPOSE, TO BE ALIVE.
YOU DID WELL-- SIX KILLS OUT OF A POSSIBLE SEVEN.
I FAILED, IRENE. I COULD SLAY MY FOSTER DAUGHTER WITHOUT A SECOND THOUGHT--BUT NOT NIGHTCRAWLER.
I WARNED YOU, MY RAVEN-- BUT WHAT GOOD IS BEING A PRECOG, WITH THE ABILITY TO SEE THE FUTURE, IF NO ONE LISTENS?
PARDON THE INTRUSION, LADIES, BUT A PERFORMANCE LIKE YOURS, MYSTIQUE, DESERVES A CELEBRATION.
I AM IMPRESSED! BEST DARN MURDER-WORLD DUEL I'VE FOUGHT IN AGES. BY THE BYE, YOU REMEMBER MY ASSISTANT, MISS LOCKE.
I REALLY HAD YOU PUMPIN' T'WARDS THE END THERE, MISTY. LOOKS T'ME LIKE MY ROBOT X-MEN HAD YOU CONVINCED THEY WERE THE REAL THING.
AS ONE WHO POSSESSES SOME SMALL SKILL AT MIMICKRY, ARCADE...
WHOA!
...I DIDN'T THINK I COULD BE FOOLED-- BUT I WAS.
HOWEVER, THAT REALITY WAS WHAT I PAID YOU FOR.

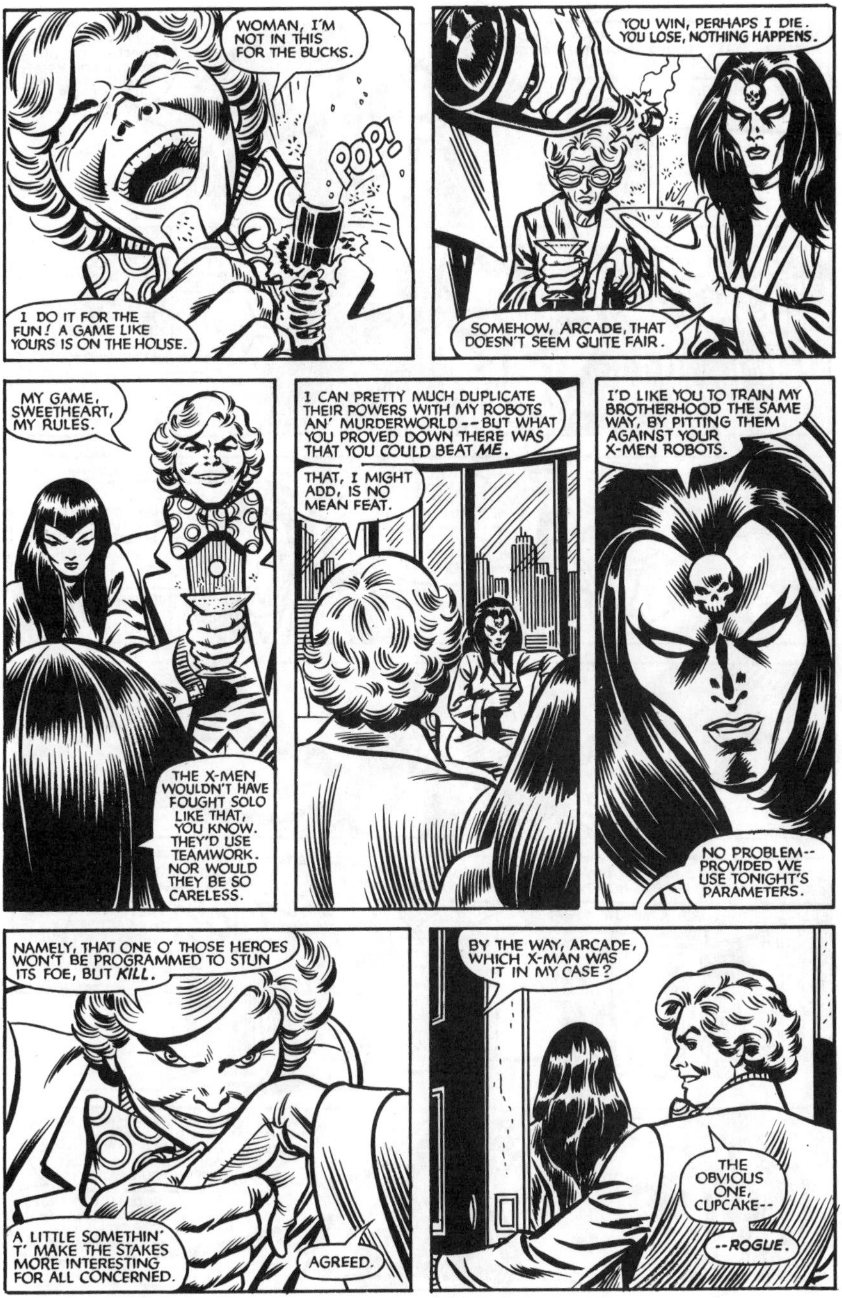
WOMAN, I'M NOT IN THIS FOR THE BUCKS.
POP!
I DO IT FOR THE FUN! A GAME LIKE YOURS IS ON THE HOUSE.
YOU WIN, PERHAPS I DIE. YOU LOSE, NOTHING HAPPENS.
SOMEHOW, ARCADE, THAT DOESN'T SEEM QUITE FAIR.
MY GAME, SWEETHEART, MY RULES.
THE X-MEN WOULDN'T HAVE FOUGHT SOLO LIKE THAT, YOU KNOW. THEY'D USE TEAMWORK. NOR WOULD THEY BE SO CARELESS.
I CAN PRETTY MUCH DUPLICATE THEIR POWERS WITH MY ROBOTS AN' MURDERWORLD -- BUT WHAT YOU PROVED DOWN THERE WAS THAT YOU COULD BEAT ME.
THAT, I MIGHT ADD, IS NO MEAN FEAT.
I'D LIKE YOU TO TRAIN MY BROTHERHOOD THE SAME WAY, BY PITTING THEM AGAINST YOUR X-MEN ROBOTS.
NO PROBLEM-- PROVIDED WE USE TONIGHT'S PARAMETERS.
NAMELY, THAT ONE O' THOSE HEROES WON'T BE PROGRAMMED TO STUN ITS FOE, BUT KILL.
A LITTLE SOMETHIN' T' MAKE THE STAKES MORE INTERESTING FOR ALL CONCERNED.
AGREED.
BY THE WAY, ARCADE, WHICH X-MAN WAS IT IN MY CASE?
THE OBVIOUS ONE, CUPCAKE--
--ROGUE.

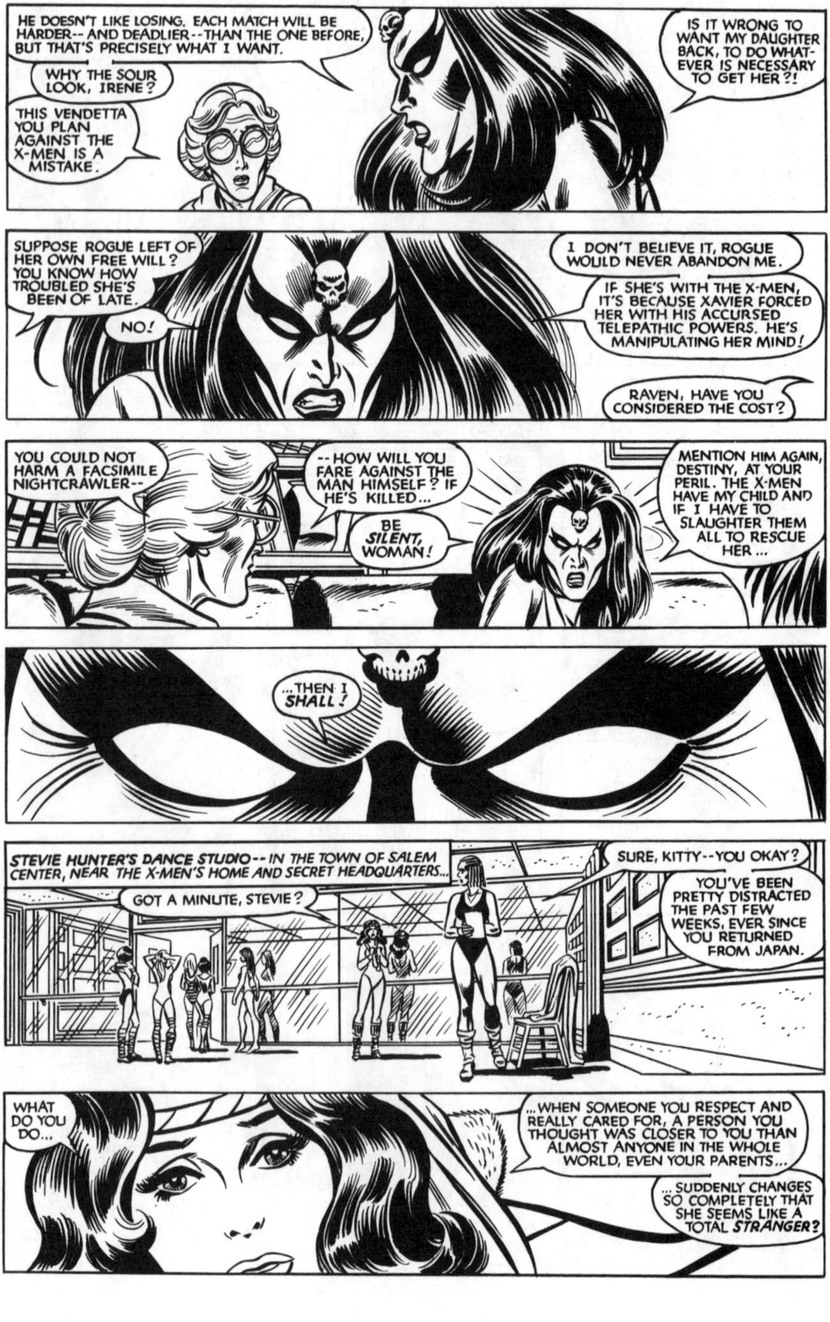

HE DOESN'T LIKE LOSING. EACH MATCH WILL BE HARDER-- AND DEADLIER--THAN THE ONE BEFORE, BUT THAT'S PRECISELY WHAT I WANT.
WHY THE SOUR LOOK, IRENE?
THIS VENDETTA YOU PLAN AGAINST THE X-MEN IS A MISTAKE.
IS IT WRONG TO WANT MY DAUGHTER BACK, TO DO WHATEVER IS NECESSARY TO GET HER?!
SUPPOSE ROGUE LEFT OF HER OWN FREE WILL? YOU KNOW HOW TROUBLED SHE'S BEEN OF LATE.
NO!
I DON'T BELIEVE IT, ROGUE WOULD NEVER ABANDON ME.
IF SHE'S WITH THE X-MEN, IT'S BECAUSE XAVIER FORCED HER WITH HIS ACCURSED TELEPATHIC POWERS. HE'S MANIPULATING HER MIND!
RAVEN, HAVE YOU CONSIDERED THE COST?
YOU COULD NOT HARM A FACSIMILE NIGHTCRAWLER--
--HOW WILL YOU FARE AGAINST THE MAN HIMSELF? IF HE'S KILLED...
BE SILENT, WOMAN!
MENTION HIM AGAIN, DESTINY, AT YOUR PERIL. THE X-MEN HAVE MY CHILD AND IF I HAVE TO SLAUGHTER THEM ALL TO RESCUE HER...
...THEN I SHALL!
STEVIE HUNTER'S DANCE STUDIO--IN THE TOWN OF SALEM CENTER, NEAR THE X-MEN'S HOME AND SECRET HEADQUARTERS...
GOT A MINUTE, STEVIE?
SURE, KITTY--YOU OKAY?
YOU'VE BEEN PRETTY DISTRACTED THE PAST FEW WEEKS, EVER SINCE YOU RETURNED FROM JAPAN.
WHAT DO YOU DO...
...WHEN SOMEONE YOU RESPECT AND REALLY CARED FOR, A PERSON YOU THOUGHT WAS CLOSER TO YOU THAN ALMOST ANYONE IN THE WHOLE WORLD, EVEN YOUR PARENTS...
...SUDDENLY CHANGES SO COMPLETELY THAT SHE SEEMS LIKE A TOTAL STRANGER?

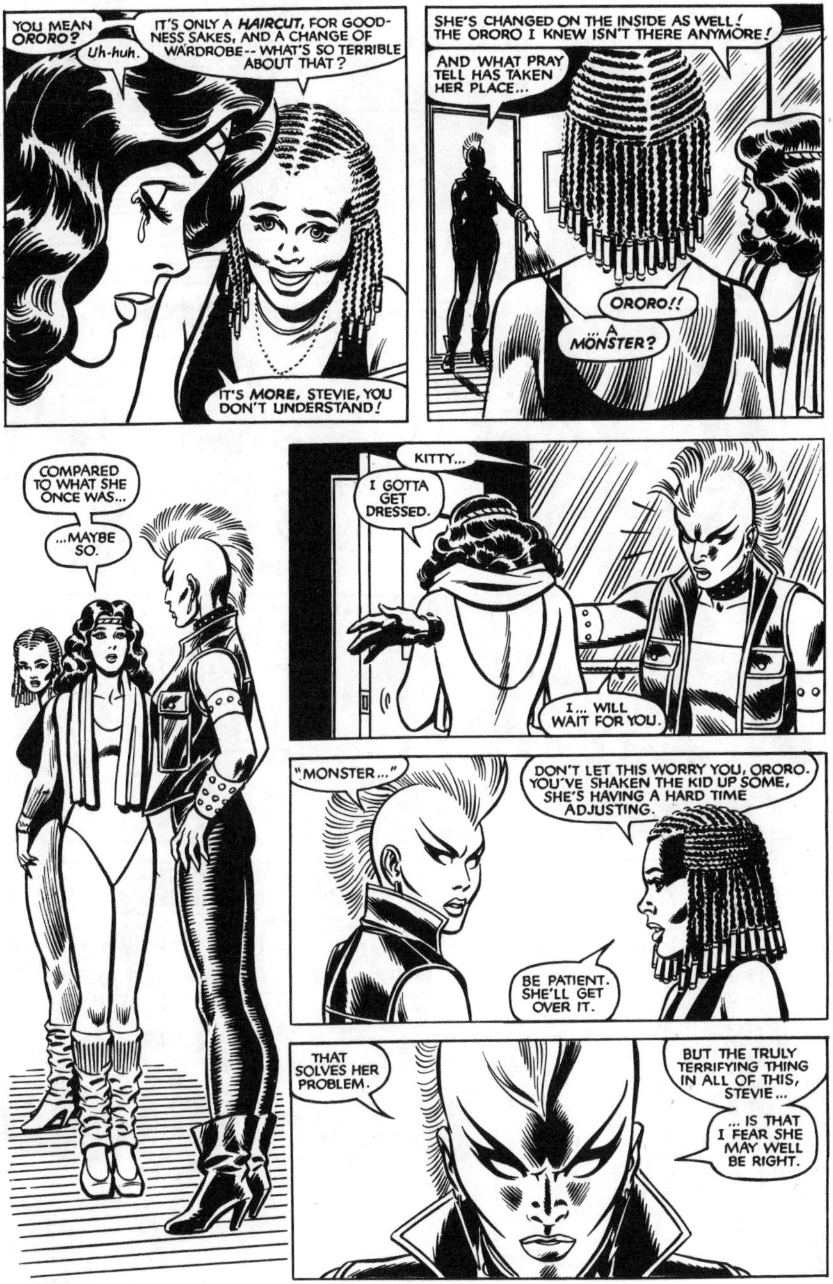
YOU MEAN ORORO?
Uh-huh.
IT'S ONLY A HAIRCUT, FOR GOODNESS SAKES, AND A CHANGE OF WARDROBE-- WHAT'S SO TERRIBLE ABOUT THAT?
IT'S MORE, STEVIE, YOU DON'T UNDERSTAND!
SHE'S CHANGED ON THE INSIDE AS WELL! THE ORORO I KNEW ISN'T THERE ANYMORE!
AND WHAT PRAY TELL HAS TAKEN HER PLACE...
...A MONSTER?
ORORO!!
COMPARED TO WHAT SHE ONCE WAS...
...MAYBE SO.
KITTY...
I GOTTA GET DRESSED.
I... WILL WAIT FOR YOU.
"MONSTER..."
DON'T LET THIS WORRY YOU, ORORO. YOU'VE SHAKEN THE KID UP SOME, SHE'S HAVING A HARD TIME ADJUSTING.
BE PATIENT. SHE'LL GET OVER IT.
THAT SOLVES HER PROBLEM.
BUT THE TRULY TERRIFYING THING IN ALL OF THIS, STEVIE...
...IS THAT I FEAR SHE MAY WELL BE RIGHT.

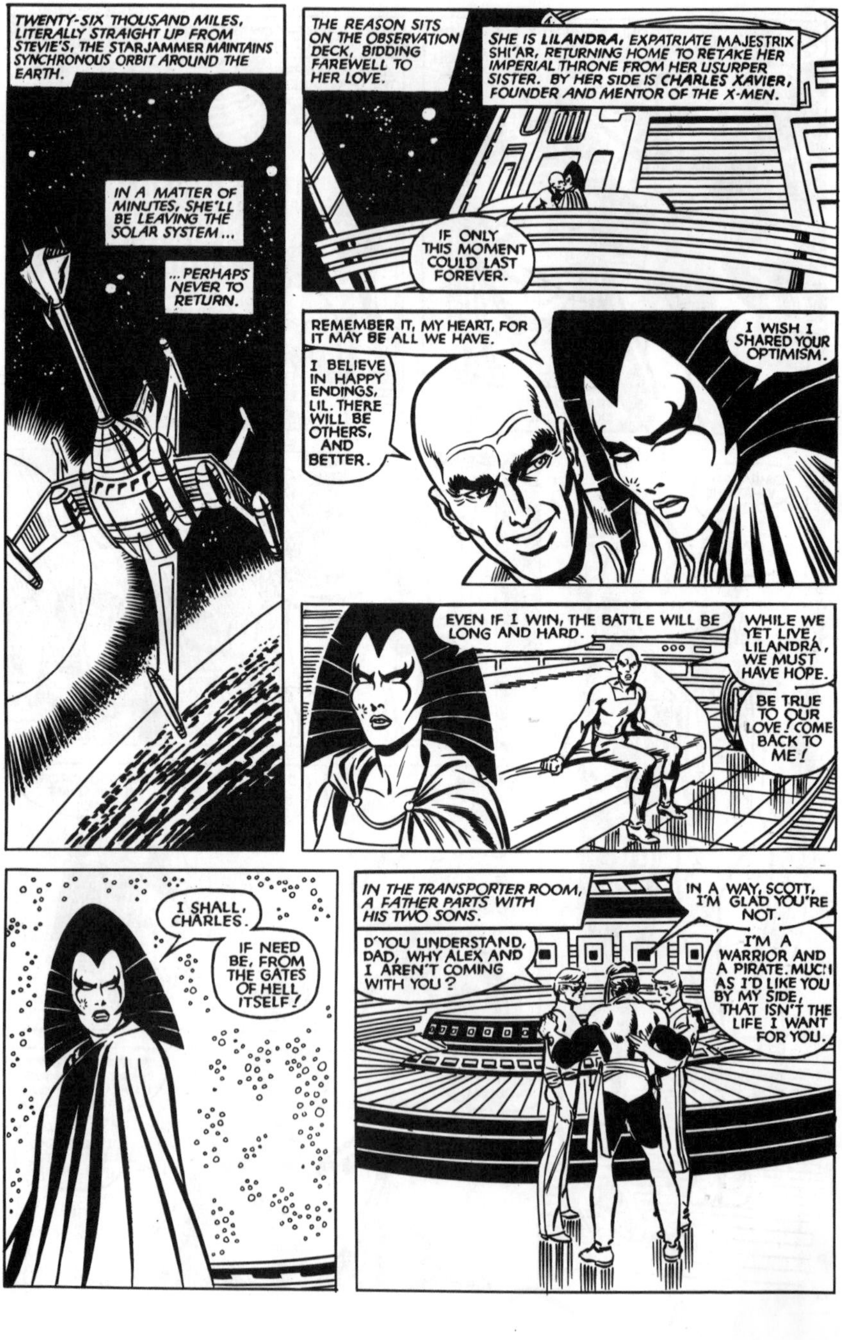
TWENTY-SIX THOUSAND MILES, LITERALLY STRAIGHT UP FROM STEVIE'S, THE STARJAMMER MAINTAINS SYNCHRONOUS ORBIT AROUND THE EARTH.
IN A MATTER OF MINUTES, SHE'LL BE LEAVING THE SOLAR SYSTEM...
...PERHAPS NEVER TO RETURN.
THE REASON SITS ON THE OBSERVATION DECK, BIDDING FAREWELL TO HER LOVE.
SHE IS LILANDRA, EXPATRIATE MAJESTRIX SHI'AR, RETURNING HOME TO RETAKE HER IMPERIAL THRONE FROM HER USURPER SISTER. BY HER SIDE IS CHARLES XAVIER, FOUNDER AND MENTOR OF THE X-MEN.
IF ONLY THIS MOMENT COULD LAST FOREVER.
REMEMBER IT, MY HEART, FOR IT MAY BE ALL WE HAVE.
I BELIEVE IN HAPPY ENDINGS, LIL. THERE WILL BE OTHERS, AND BETTER.
I WISH I SHARED YOUR OPTIMISM.
EVEN IF I WIN, THE BATTLE WILL BE LONG AND HARD.
WHILE WE YET LIVE, LILANDRA, WE MUST HAVE HOPE.
BE TRUE TO OUR LOVE! COME BACK TO ME!
I SHALL, CHARLES.
IF NEED BE, FROM THE GATES OF HELL ITSELF!
IN THE TRANSPORTER ROOM, A FATHER PARTS WITH HIS TWO SONS.
D'YOU UNDERSTAND, DAD, WHY ALEX AND I AREN'T COMING WITH YOU?
IN A WAY, SCOTT, I'M GLAD YOU'RE NOT.
I'M A WARRIOR AND A PIRATE. MUCH AS I'D LIKE YOU BY MY SIDE, THAT ISN'T THE LIFE I WANT FOR YOU.

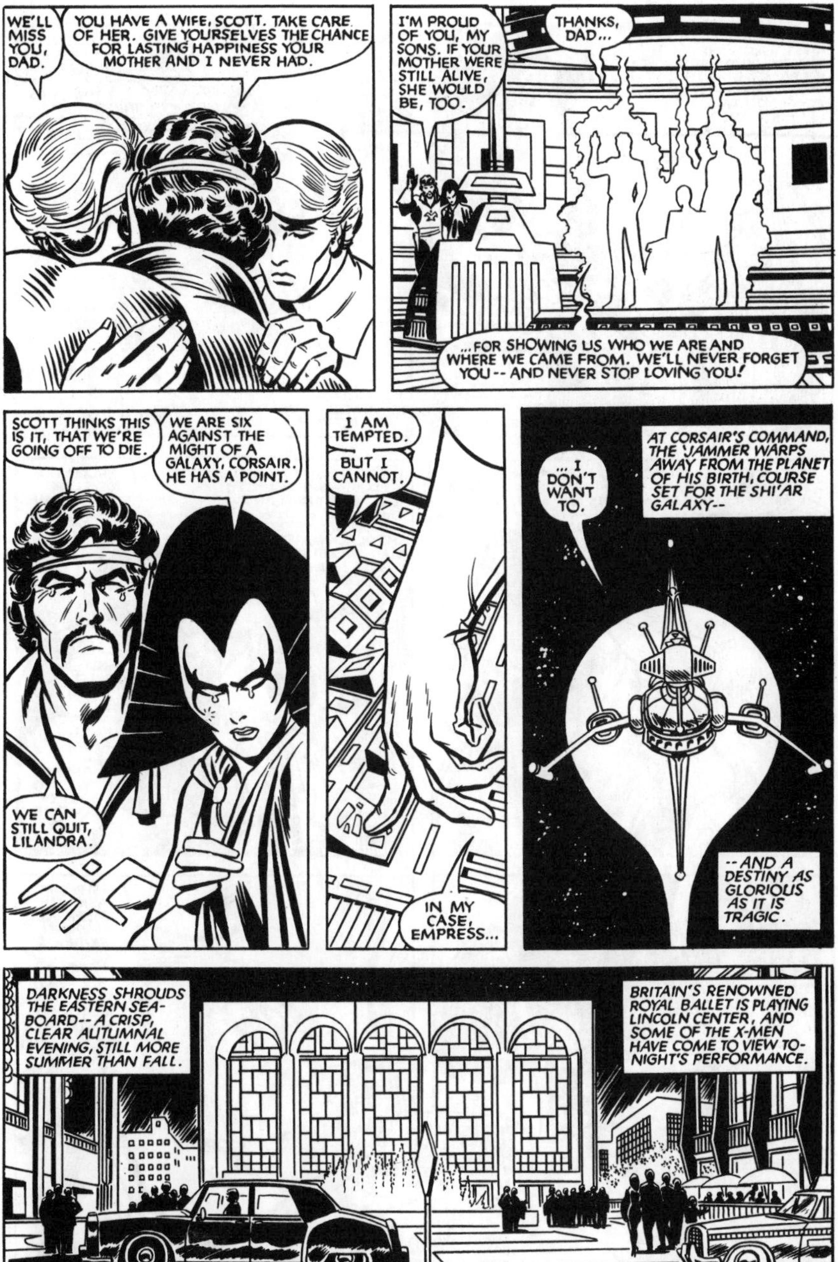
WE'LL MISS YOU, DAD.
YOU HAVE A WIFE, SCOTT. TAKE CARE OF HER. GIVE YOURSELVES THE CHANCE FOR LASTING HAPPINESS YOUR MOTHER AND I NEVER HAD.
I'M PROUD OF YOU, MY SONS. IF YOUR MOTHER WERE STILL ALIVE, SHE WOULD BE, TOO.
THANKS, DAD...
...FOR SHOWING US WHO WE ARE AND WHERE WE CAME FROM. WE'LL NEVER FORGET YOU -- AND NEVER STOP LOVING YOU!
SCOTT THINKS THIS IS IT, THAT WE'RE GOING OFF TO DIE.
WE ARE SIX AGAINST THE MIGHT OF A GALAXY, CORSAIR. HE HAS A POINT.
WE CAN STILL QUIT, LILANDRA.
I AM TEMPTED.
BUT I CANNOT.
IN MY CASE, EMPRESS...
... I DON'T WANT TO.
AT CORSAIR'S COMMAND, THE 'JAMMER WARPS AWAY FROM THE PLANET OF HIS BIRTH, COURSE SET FOR THE SHI'AR GALAXY--
--AND A DESTINY AS GLORIOUS AS IT IS TRAGIC.
DARKNESS SHROUDS THE EASTERN SEA-BOARD-- A CRISP, CLEAR AUTUMNAL EVENING, STILL MORE SUMMER THAN FALL.
BRITAIN'S RENOWNED ROYAL BALLET IS PLAYING LINCOLN CENTER, AND SOME OF THE X-MEN HAVE COME TO VIEW TO-NIGHT'S PERFORMANCE.

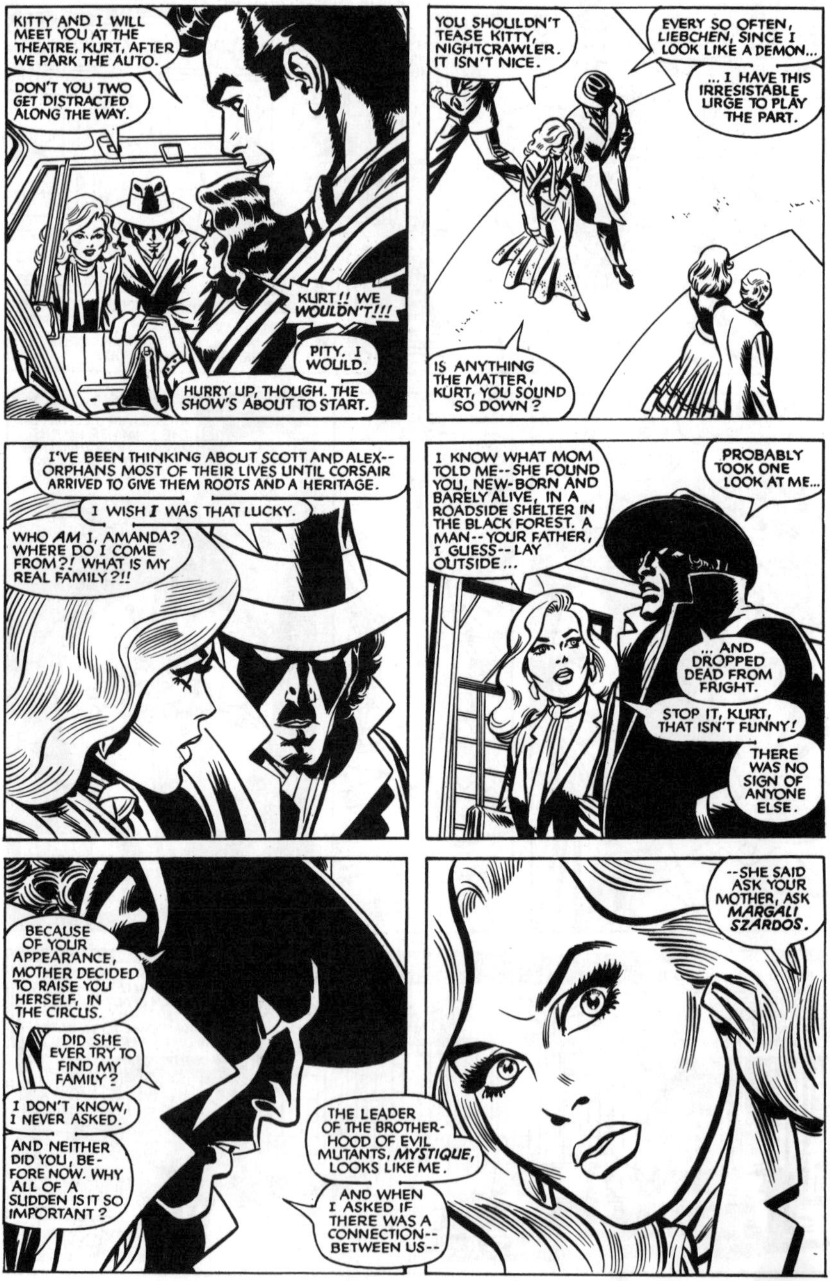
KITTY AND I WILL MEET YOU AT THE THEATRE, KURT, AFTER WE PARK THE AUTO.
DON'T YOU TWO GET DISTRACTED ALONG THE WAY.
KURT!! WE WOULDN'T!!!
PITY. I WOULD.
HURRY UP, THOUGH. THE SHOW'S ABOUT TO START.
YOU SHOULDN'T TEASE KITTY, NIGHTCRAWLER. IT ISN'T NICE.
EVERY SO OFTEN, LIEBCHEN, SINCE I LOOK LIKE A DEMON...
... I HAVE THIS IRRESISTABLE URGE TO PLAY THE PART.
IS ANYTHING THE MATTER, KURT, YOU SOUND SO DOWN?
I'VE BEEN THINKING ABOUT SCOTT AND ALEX-- ORPHANS MOST OF THEIR LIVES UNTIL CORSAIR ARRIVED TO GIVE THEM ROOTS AND A HERITAGE.
I WISH I WAS THAT LUCKY.
WHO AM I, AMANDA? WHERE DO I COME FROM?! WHAT IS MY REAL FAMILY?!!
I KNOW WHAT MOM TOLD ME-- SHE FOUND YOU, NEW-BORN AND BARELY ALIVE, IN A ROADSIDE SHELTER IN THE BLACK FOREST. A MAN-- YOUR FATHER, I GUESS-- LAY OUTSIDE...
PROBABLY TOOK ONE LOOK AT ME...
... AND DROPPED DEAD FROM FRIGHT.
STOP IT, KURT, THAT ISN'T FUNNY!
THERE WAS NO SIGN OF ANYONE ELSE.
BECAUSE OF YOUR APPEARANCE, MOTHER DECIDED TO RAISE YOU HERSELF, IN THE CIRCUS.
DID SHE EVER TRY TO FIND MY FAMILY?
I DON'T KNOW, I NEVER ASKED.
AND NEITHER DID YOU, BE-FORE NOW. WHY ALL OF A SUDDEN IS IT SO IMPORTANT?
THE LEADER OF THE BROTHER-HOOD OF EVIL MUTANTS, MYSTIQUE, LOOKS LIKE ME.
AND WHEN I ASKED IF THERE WAS A CONNECTION-- BETWEEN US--
--SHE SAID ASK YOUR MOTHER, ASK MARGALI SZARDOS.

LIFE'S BEEN SO HECTIC THESE PAST MONTHS, I NEVER GOT THE OPPORTUNITY.

BUT I'VE LET MY QUESTIONS-- AND FEARS-- FESTER FAR TOO LONG. I NEED ANSWERS.

MOM'S IN *GRAFBÜRG.* WE CAN PHONE HER TOMORROW.

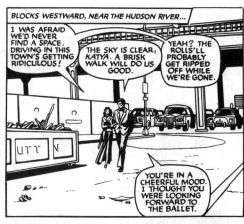

BLOCKS WESTWARD, NEAR THE HUDSON RIVER...

I WAS AFRAID WE'D NEVER FIND A SPACE. DRIVING IN THIS TOWN'S GETTING RIDICULOUS!

THE SKY IS CLEAR, *KATYA.* A BRISK WALK WILL DO US GOOD.

YEAH? THE ROLLS'LL PROBABLY GET RIPPED OFF WHILE WE'RE GONE.

YOU'RE IN A CHEERFUL MOOD. I THOUGHT YOU WERE LOOKING FORWARD TO THE BALLET.

Oh, I AM, PETER. I DON'T MEAN TO BE SUCH A GRUMP. I'VE GOT TOO MUCH ON MY MIND.

WOULD TALKING ABOUT THINGS HELP--?

...I'VE BEGUN WITH *DOUG RAMSEY--* A FRIEND FROM DANCE CLASS-- HE'S INTO COMPUTERS, LIKE ME, ONLY HIS SPECIALTY'S SOFTWARE. I'M THE HARDWARE, NUTS'N' BOLTS FREAK. WE'RE TRYING TO-- AND LEMME KNOW IF I GET TOO TECHNICAL-- WHAT THE *HECK!?!*

IT'S THESE SERIES OF EXPERIMENTS...

LENIN'S GHOST-- AN *EXPLOSION!*

BOOM!!

I CAN HEAR SCREAMS. PEOPLE ARE INJURED-- TRAPPED-- UP THERE!

SUMMON THE FIRE BRIGADE, KITTY--

--WHILE I DO WHAT I CAN TO SAVE THEM!

BE CAREFUL, PETER!

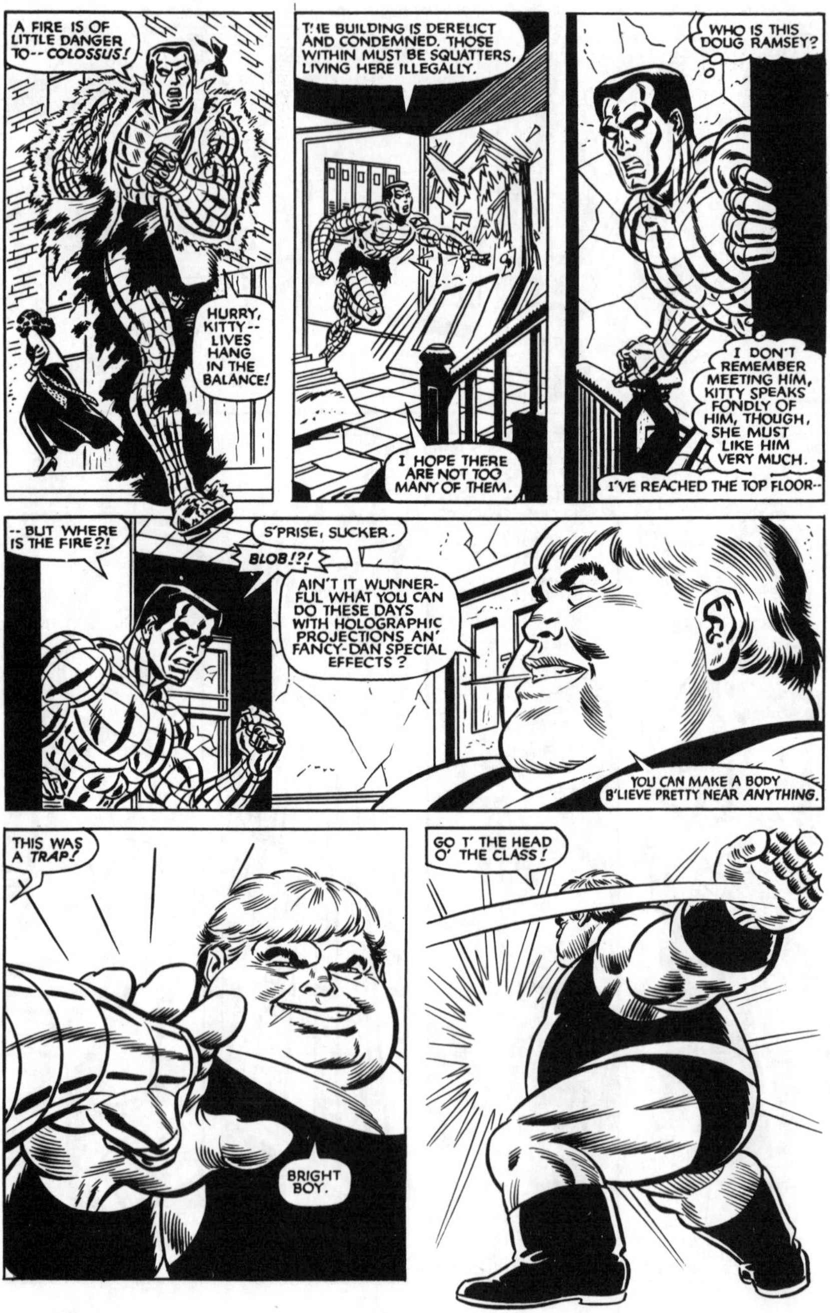
A FIRE IS OF LITTLE DANGER TO-- COLOSSUS!
HURRY, KITTY-- LIVES HANG IN THE BALANCE!
THE BUILDING IS DERELICT AND CONDEMNED. THOSE WITHIN MUST BE SQUATTERS, LIVING HERE ILLEGALLY.
I HOPE THERE ARE NOT TOO MANY OF THEM.
WHO IS THIS DOUG RAMSEY?
I DON'T REMEMBER MEETING HIM, KITTY SPEAKS FONDLY OF HIM, THOUGH, SHE MUST LIKE HIM VERY MUCH.
I'VE REACHED THE TOP FLOOR--
-- BUT WHERE IS THE FIRE?!
S'PRISE, SUCKER.
BLOB!?!
AIN'T IT WUNNERFUL WHAT YOU CAN DO THESE DAYS WITH HOLOGRAPHIC PROJECTIONS AN' FANCY-DAN SPECIAL EFFECTS?
YOU CAN MAKE A BODY B'LIEVE PRETTY NEAR ANYTHING.
THIS WAS A TRAP!
BRIGHT BOY.
GO T' THE HEAD O' THE CLASS!

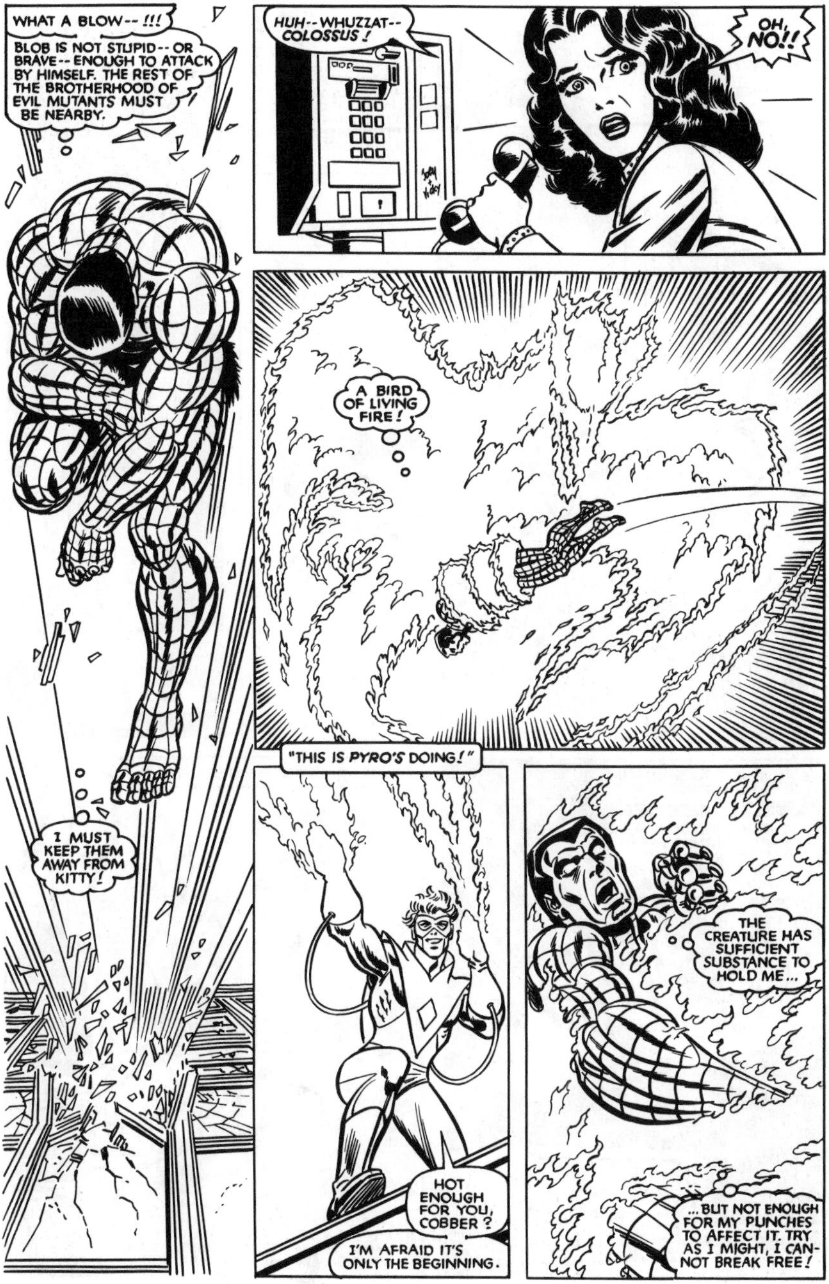
WHAT A BLOW-- !!!
BLOB IS NOT STUPID-- OR BRAVE-- ENOUGH TO ATTACK BY HIMSELF. THE REST OF THE BROTHERHOOD OF EVIL MUTANTS MUST BE NEARBY.
I MUST KEEP THEM AWAY FROM KITTY!
HUH--WHUZZAT-- COLOSSUS!
OH, NO!!
A BIRD OF LIVING FIRE!
"THIS IS PYRO'S DOING!"
HOT ENOUGH FOR YOU, COBBER?
I'M AFRAID IT'S ONLY THE BEGINNING.
THE CREATURE HAS SUFFICIENT SUBSTANCE TO HOLD ME...
...BUT NOT ENOUGH FOR MY PUNCHES TO AFFECT IT. TRY AS I MIGHT, I CANNOT BREAK FREE!

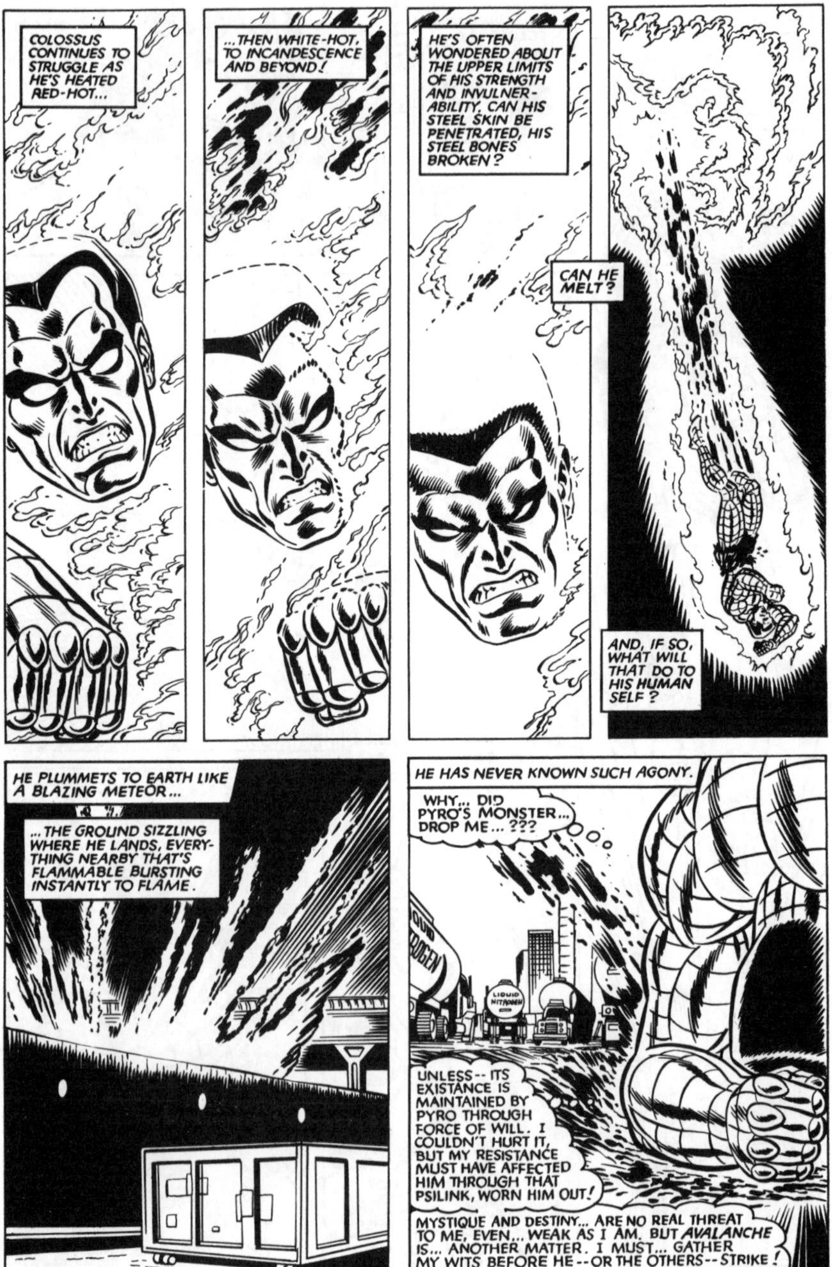

COLOSSUS CONTINUES TO STRUGGLE AS HE'S HEATED RED-HOT...
...THEN WHITE-HOT, TO INCANDESCENCE AND BEYOND!
HE'S OFTEN WONDERED ABOUT THE UPPER LIMITS OF HIS STRENGTH AND INVULNER-ABILITY. CAN HIS STEEL SKIN BE PENETRATED, HIS STEEL BONES BROKEN?
CAN HE MELT?
AND, IF SO, WHAT WILL THAT DO TO HIS HUMAN SELF?
HE PLUMMETS TO EARTH LIKE A BLAZING METEOR...
...THE GROUND SIZZLING WHERE HE LANDS, EVERY-THING NEARBY THAT'S FLAMMABLE BURSTING INSTANTLY TO FLAME.
HE HAS NEVER KNOWN SUCH AGONY.
WHY... DID PYRO'S MONSTER... DROP ME...???
LIQUID NITROGEN
UNLESS--ITS EXISTANCE IS MAINTAINED BY PYRO THROUGH FORCE OF WILL. I COULDN'T HURT IT, BUT MY RESISTANCE MUST HAVE AFFECTED HIM THROUGH THAT PSILINK, WORN HIM OUT!
MYSTIQUE AND DESTINY... ARE NO REAL THREAT TO ME, EVEN... WEAK AS I AM. BUT AVALANCHE IS... ANOTHER MATTER. I MUST... GATHER MY WITS BEFORE HE--OR THE OTHERS--STRIKE!

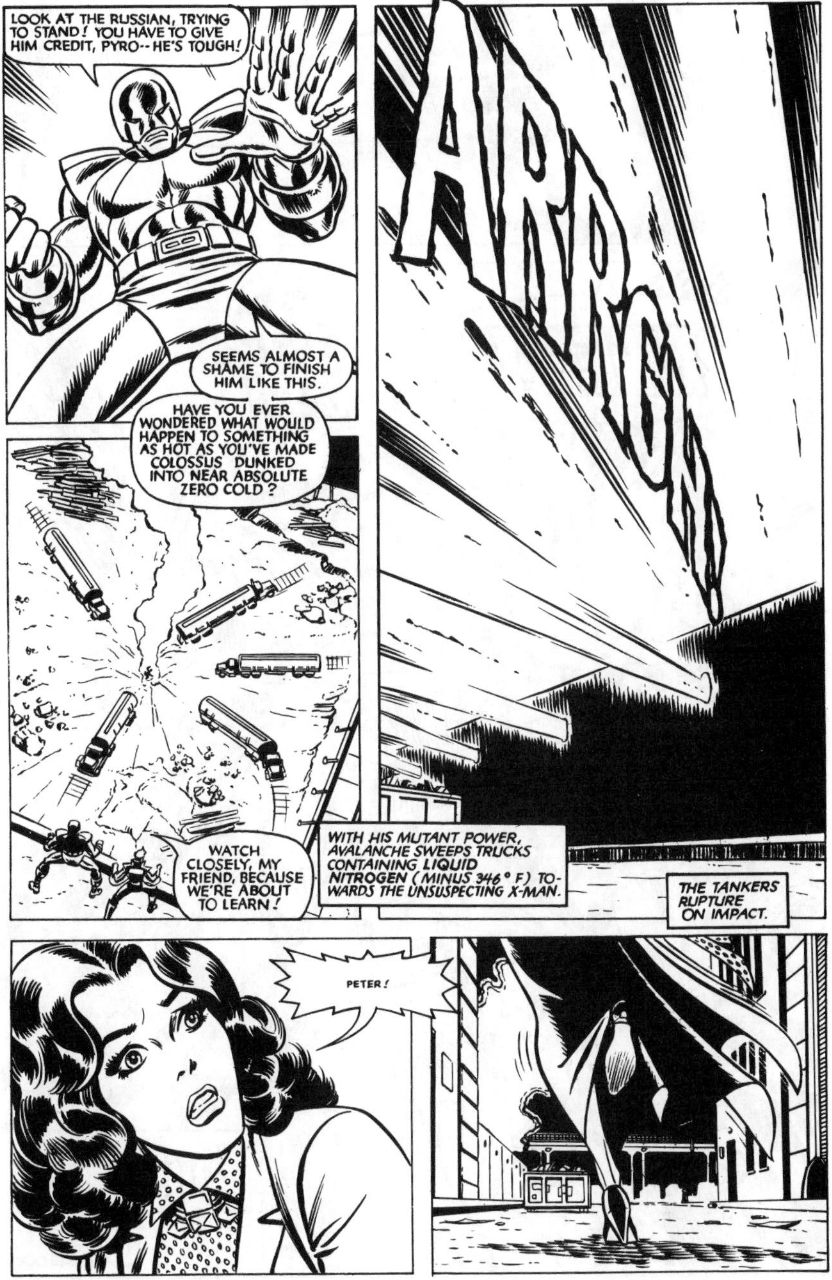
LOOK AT THE RUSSIAN, TRYING TO STAND! YOU HAVE TO GIVE HIM CREDIT, PYRO-- HE'S TOUGH!
SEEMS ALMOST A SHAME TO FINISH HIM LIKE THIS.
HAVE YOU EVER WONDERED WHAT WOULD HAPPEN TO SOMETHING AS HOT AS YOU'VE MADE COLOSSUS DUNKED INTO NEAR ABSOLUTE ZERO COLD?
WATCH CLOSELY, MY FRIEND, BECAUSE WE'RE ABOUT TO LEARN!
WITH HIS MUTANT POWER, AVALANCHE SWEEPS TRUCKS CONTAINING LIQUID NITROGEN (MINUS 346° F) TOWARDS THE UNSUSPECTING X-MAN.
AIRRGGH
THE TANKERS RUPTURE ON IMPACT.
PETER!

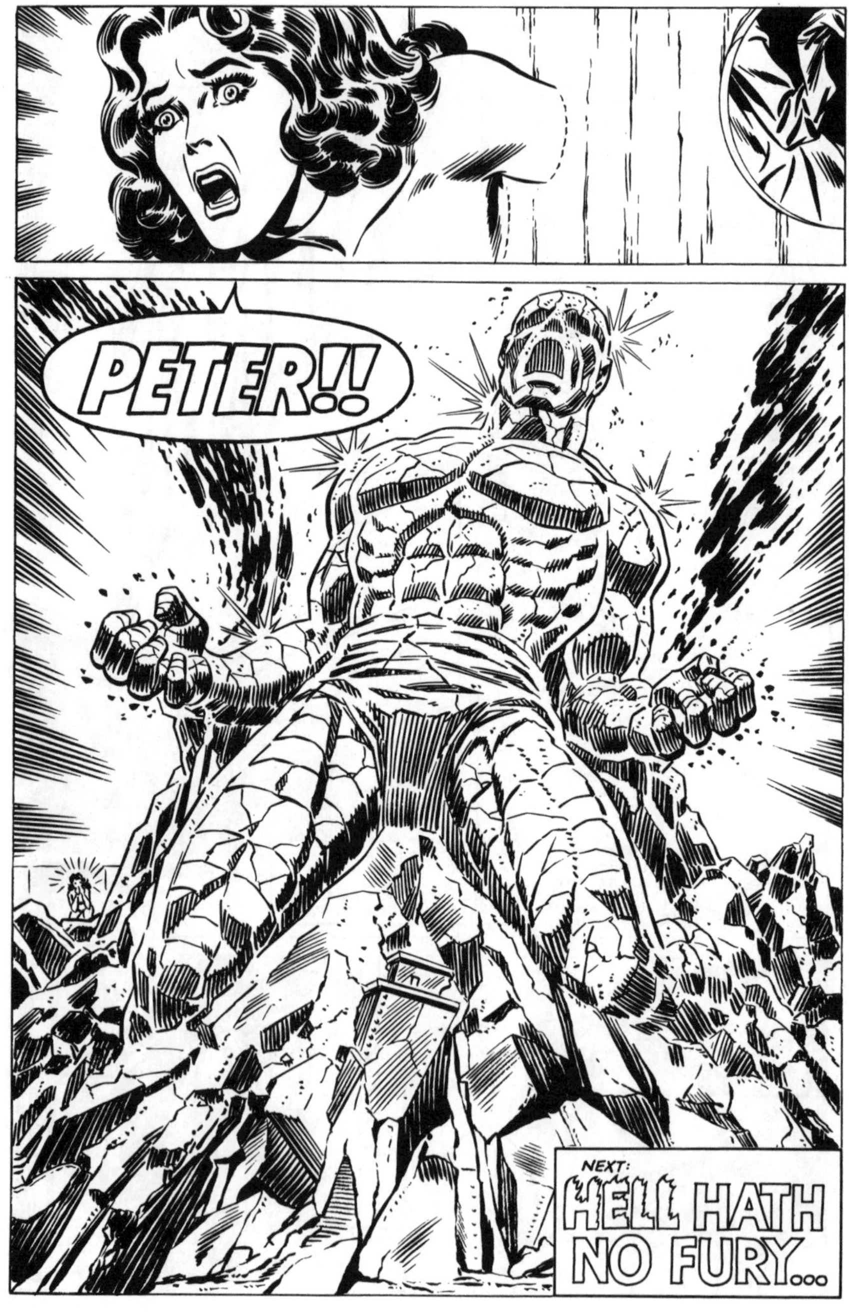
PETER!!
NEXT:
HELL HATH NO FURY...

HEAT METAL WHITE-HOT, THEN SUBJECT IT TO NEAR ABSOLUTE-ZERO COLD -- A TEMPERATURE SO LOW THAT MOLECULAR MOTION VIRTUALLY CEASES -- AND THAT METAL BLISTERS, CRACKS, ULTIMATELY SHATTERS.

THAT IS WHAT'S JUST HAPPENED TO COLOSSUS, IN THIS CONSTRUCTION SITE ON THE WEST SIDE OF MANHATTAN.

FOR A MAN COMPOSED, AS HE IS, OF ORGANIC STEEL, THE PROCESS WOULD SURELY SEEM TO MEAN CERTAIN DEATH.

HELL HATH NO FURY...

A **STAN LEE** PRESENTATION, STARRING THE UNCANNY **X-MEN** -- AS CHRONICLED BY

| CHRIS CLAREMONT writer | JOHN ROMITA, Jr. penciler | BOB WIACEK & BRETT BREEDING inkers | GLYNIS WEIN colorist | TOM ORZECHOWSKI letterer | LOUISE JONES editor | JIM SHOOTER chief |

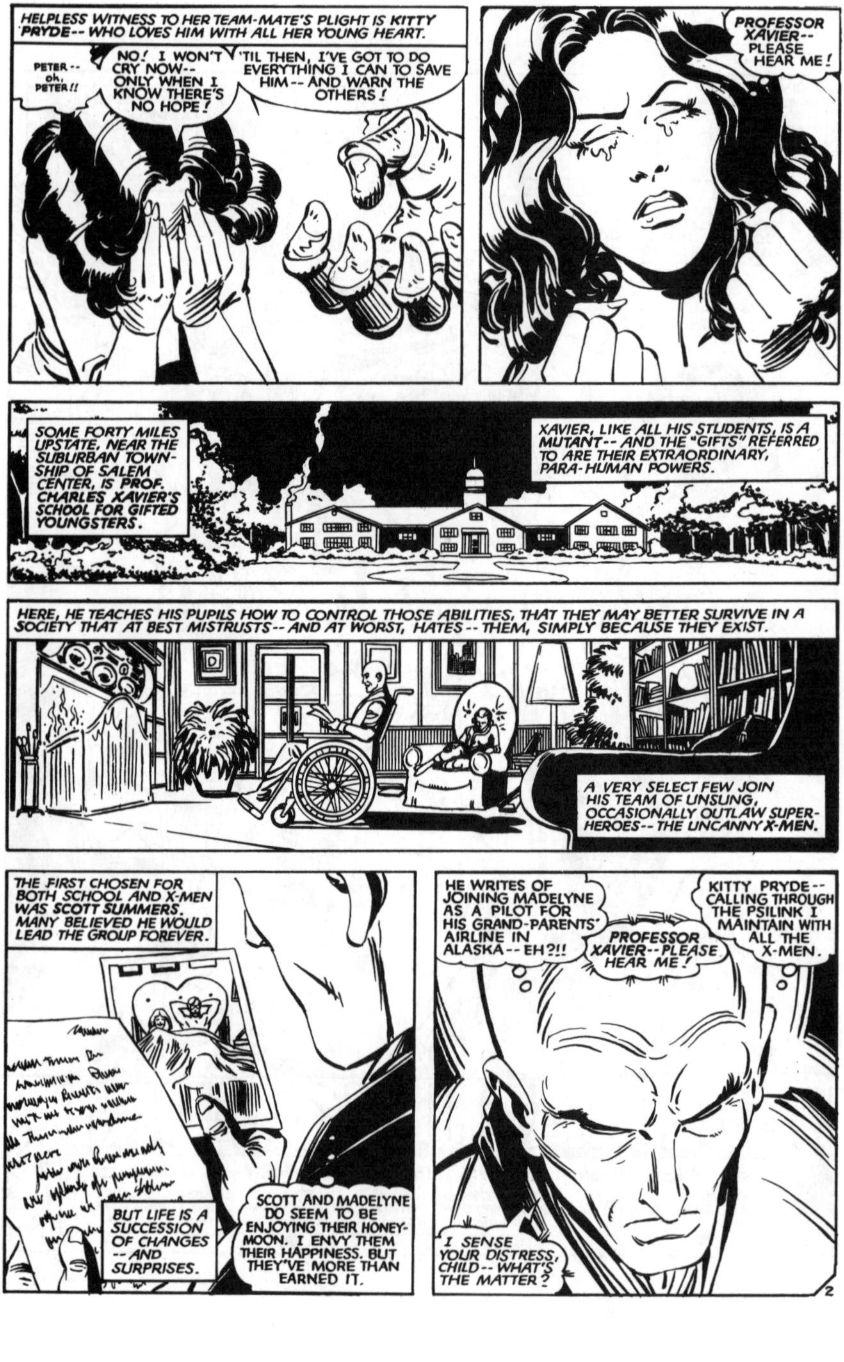
HELPLESS WITNESS TO HER TEAM-MATE'S PLIGHT IS KITTY PRYDE-- WHO LOVES HIM WITH ALL HER YOUNG HEART.
PETER-- oh, PETER!!
NO! I WON'T CRY NOW-- ONLY WHEN I KNOW THERE'S NO HOPE!
'TIL THEN, I'VE GOT TO DO EVERYTHING I CAN TO SAVE HIM-- AND WARN THE OTHERS!
PROFESSOR XAVIER-- PLEASE HEAR ME!
SOME FORTY MILES UPSTATE, NEAR THE SUBURBAN TOWNSHIP OF SALEM CENTER, IS PROF. CHARLES XAVIER'S SCHOOL FOR GIFTED YOUNGSTERS.
XAVIER, LIKE ALL HIS STUDENTS, IS A MUTANT-- AND THE "GIFTS" REFERRED TO ARE THEIR EXTRAORDINARY, PARA-HUMAN POWERS.
HERE, HE TEACHES HIS PUPILS HOW TO CONTROL THOSE ABILITIES, THAT THEY MAY BETTER SURVIVE IN A SOCIETY THAT AT BEST MISTRUSTS-- AND AT WORST, HATES-- THEM, SIMPLY BECAUSE THEY EXIST.
A VERY SELECT FEW JOIN HIS TEAM OF UNSUNG, OCCASIONALLY OUTLAW SUPER-HEROES-- THE UNCANNY X-MEN.
THE FIRST CHOSEN FOR BOTH SCHOOL AND X-MEN WAS SCOTT SUMMERS. MANY BELIEVED HE WOULD LEAD THE GROUP FOREVER.
BUT LIFE IS A SUCCESSION OF CHANGES -- AND SURPRISES.
SCOTT AND MADELYNE DO SEEM TO BE ENJOYING THEIR HONEY-MOON. I ENVY THEM THEIR HAPPINESS. BUT THEY'VE MORE THAN EARNED IT.
HE WRITES OF JOINING MADELYNE AS A PILOT FOR HIS GRAND-PARENTS' AIRLINE IN ALASKA-- EH?!!
PROFESSOR XAVIER-- PLEASE HEAR ME!
KITTY PRYDE-- CALLING THROUGH THE PSILINK I MAINTAIN WITH ALL THE X-MEN.
I SENSE YOUR DISTRESS, CHILD-- WHAT'S THE MATTER?

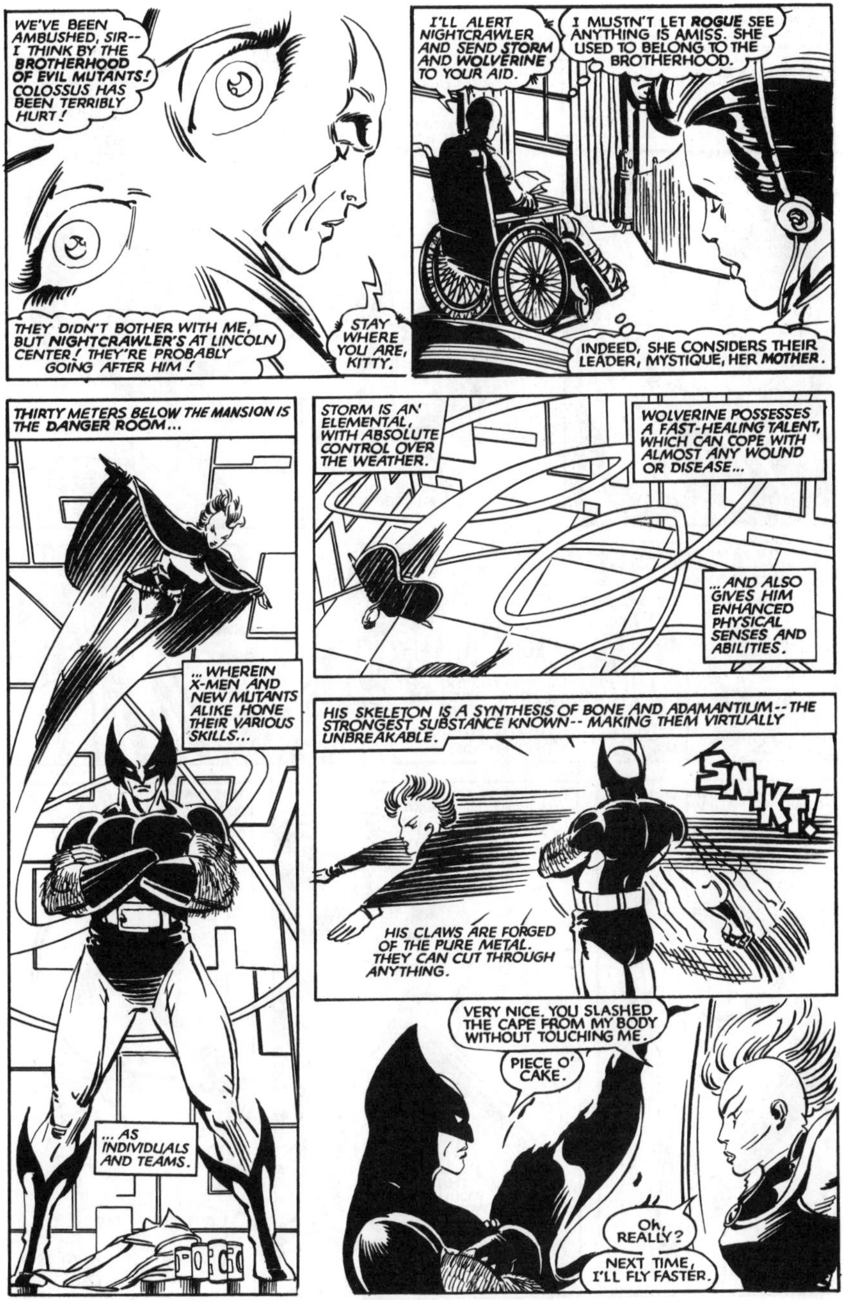
WE'VE BEEN AMBUSHED, SIR-- I THINK BY THE BROTHERHOOD OF EVIL MUTANTS! COLOSSUS HAS BEEN TERRIBLY HURT!
THEY DIDN'T BOTHER WITH ME, BUT NIGHTCRAWLER'S AT LINCOLN CENTER! THEY'RE PROBABLY GOING AFTER HIM!
STAY WHERE YOU ARE, KITTY.
I'LL ALERT NIGHTCRAWLER AND SEND STORM AND WOLVERINE TO YOUR AID.
I MUSTN'T LET ROGUE SEE ANYTHING IS AMISS. SHE USED TO BELONG TO THE BROTHERHOOD.
INDEED, SHE CONSIDERS THEIR LEADER, MYSTIQUE, HER MOTHER.
THIRTY METERS BELOW THE MANSION IS THE DANGER ROOM...
...WHEREIN X-MEN AND NEW MUTANTS ALIKE HONE THEIR VARIOUS SKILLS...
...AS INDIVIDUALS AND TEAMS.
STORM IS AN ELEMENTAL, WITH ABSOLUTE CONTROL OVER THE WEATHER.
WOLVERINE POSSESSES A FAST-HEALING TALENT, WHICH CAN COPE WITH ALMOST ANY WOUND OR DISEASE...
...AND ALSO GIVES HIM ENHANCED PHYSICAL SENSES AND ABILITIES.
HIS SKELETON IS A SYNTHESIS OF BONE AND ADAMANTIUM--THE STRONGEST SUBSTANCE KNOWN-- MAKING THEM VIRTUALLY UNBREAKABLE.
SNIKT!
HIS CLAWS ARE FORGED OF THE PURE METAL. THEY CAN CUT THROUGH ANYTHING.
VERY NICE. YOU SLASHED THE CAPE FROM MY BODY WITHOUT TOUCHING ME.
PIECE O' CAKE.
Oh, REALLY?
NEXT TIME, I'LL FLY FASTER.

A LADY COULD GET HURT THAT WAY.

THE RISK IS WHAT MAKES IT FUN.

THAT'S YUKIO'S LINE-- USUALLY WHEN SHE'S PLAYIN' "CHICKEN" WITH A TWO HUNDRED MILE-AN-HOUR BULLET TRAIN.

ONE COULD HAVE WORSE ROLE MODELS, LOGAN.

X-MEN, WE HAVE AN EMERGENCY.

PROFESSOR, HAVE YOU ALERTED ROGUE?

I BELIEVE, STORM, SHE IS BEST LEFT OUT OF THIS.

A BATTLE WITH THOSE WHO WERE, UNTIL RECENTLY, HER TEAM-MATES AND FRIENDS MIGHT PUT HER LOYALTIES TO AN UNENDURABLE TEST.

I CONCUR.

I'M RECEIVING NO THOUGHT PATTERNS FROM COLOSSUS-- BUT THAT DOESN'T NECESSARILY MEAN THE WORST. HE MAY SIMPLY BE IN DEEP SHOCK.

IF HE IS ALIVE, THOUGH, HOWEVER WILL WE REVIVE--

ARRGH!

A BOLT OF PSIONIC FORCE-- SMASHING THROUGH MY NATURAL DEFENSES LIKE THEY DON'T EXIST!

PROFESSOR, YOU CRIED OUT-- IS EV'RYTHING OKAY?

A SUDDEN... HEADACHE, ROGUE, THAT'S ALL.

WANT SOME ASPIRIN?

THAT WOULD BE WONDERFUL, THANK YOU.

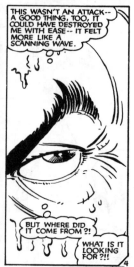

THIS WASN'T AN ATTACK-- A GOOD THING, TOO, IT COULD HAVE DESTROYED ME WITH EASE-- IT FELT MORE LIKE A SCANNING WAVE.

BUT WHERE DID IT COME FROM ?!

WHAT IS IT LOOKING FOR ?!!

4

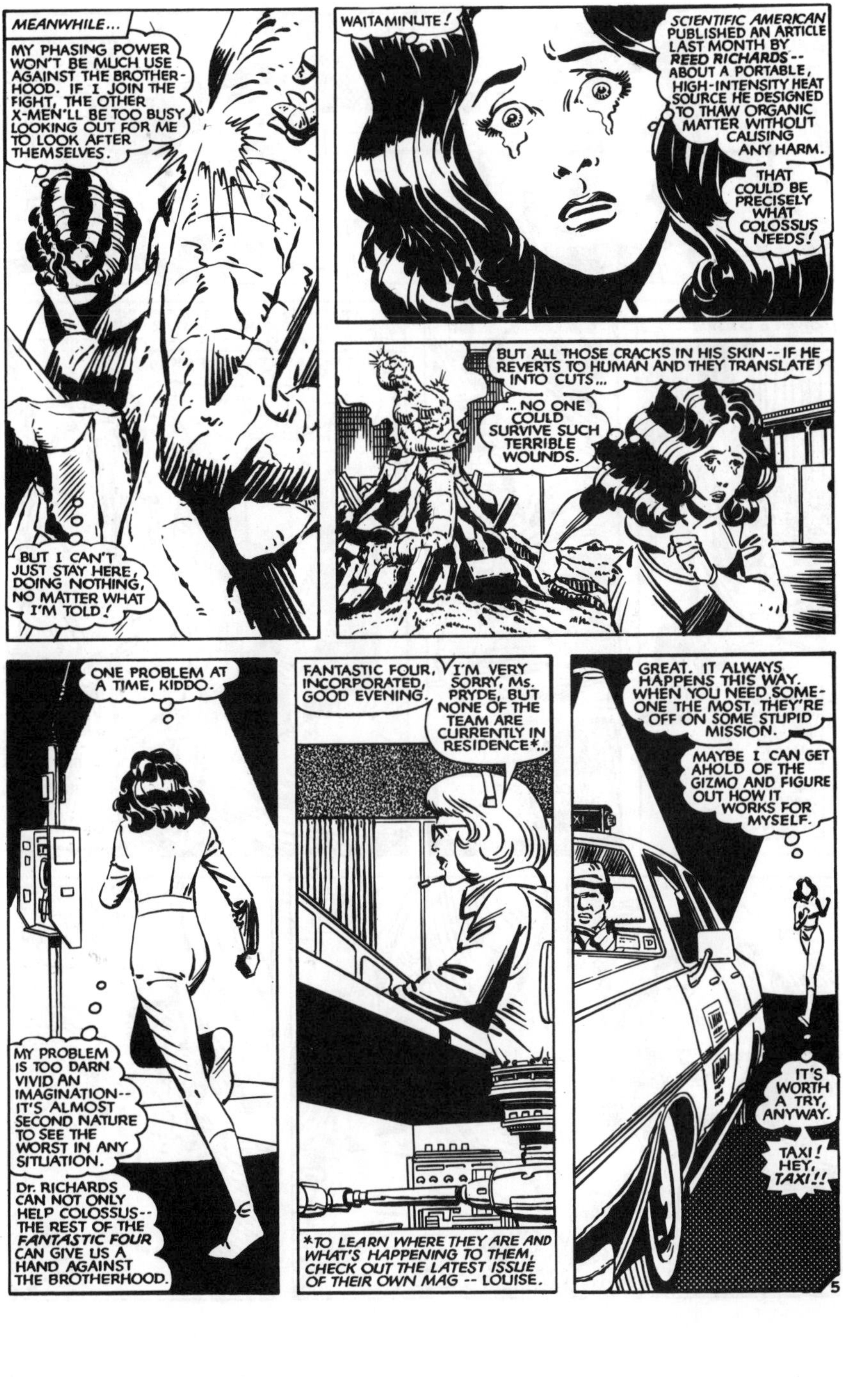
MEANWHILE...
MY PHASING POWER WON'T BE MUCH USE AGAINST THE BROTHERHOOD. IF I JOIN THE FIGHT, THE OTHER X-MEN'LL BE TOO BUSY LOOKING OUT FOR ME TO LOOK AFTER THEMSELVES.
BUT I CAN'T JUST STAY HERE, DOING NOTHING, NO MATTER WHAT I'M TOLD!
WAITAMINUTE!
SCIENTIFIC AMERICAN PUBLISHED AN ARTICLE LAST MONTH BY REED RICHARDS-- ABOUT A PORTABLE, HIGH-INTENSITY HEAT SOURCE HE DESIGNED TO THAW ORGANIC MATTER WITHOUT CAUSING ANY HARM.
THAT COULD BE PRECISELY WHAT COLOSSUS NEEDS!
BUT ALL THOSE CRACKS IN HIS SKIN--IF HE REVERTS TO HUMAN AND THEY TRANSLATE INTO CUTS...
...NO ONE COULD SURVIVE SUCH TERRIBLE WOUNDS.
ONE PROBLEM AT A TIME, KIDDO.
MY PROBLEM IS TOO DARN VIVID AN IMAGINATION-- IT'S ALMOST SECOND NATURE TO SEE THE WORST IN ANY SITUATION.
Dr. RICHARDS CAN NOT ONLY HELP COLOSSUS-- THE REST OF THE FANTASTIC FOUR CAN GIVE US A HAND AGAINST THE BROTHERHOOD.
FANTASTIC FOUR, INCORPORATED, GOOD EVENING.
I'M VERY SORRY, MS. PRYDE, BUT NONE OF THE TEAM ARE CURRENTLY IN RESIDENCE*...
*TO LEARN WHERE THEY ARE AND WHAT'S HAPPENING TO THEM, CHECK OUT THE LATEST ISSUE OF THEIR OWN MAG -- LOUISE.
GREAT. IT ALWAYS HAPPENS THIS WAY. WHEN YOU NEED SOMEONE THE MOST, THEY'RE OFF ON SOME STUPID MISSION.
MAYBE I CAN GET AHOLD OF THE GIZMO AND FIGURE OUT HOW IT WORKS FOR MYSELF.
IT'S WORTH A TRY, ANYWAY.
TAXI! HEY, TAXI!!

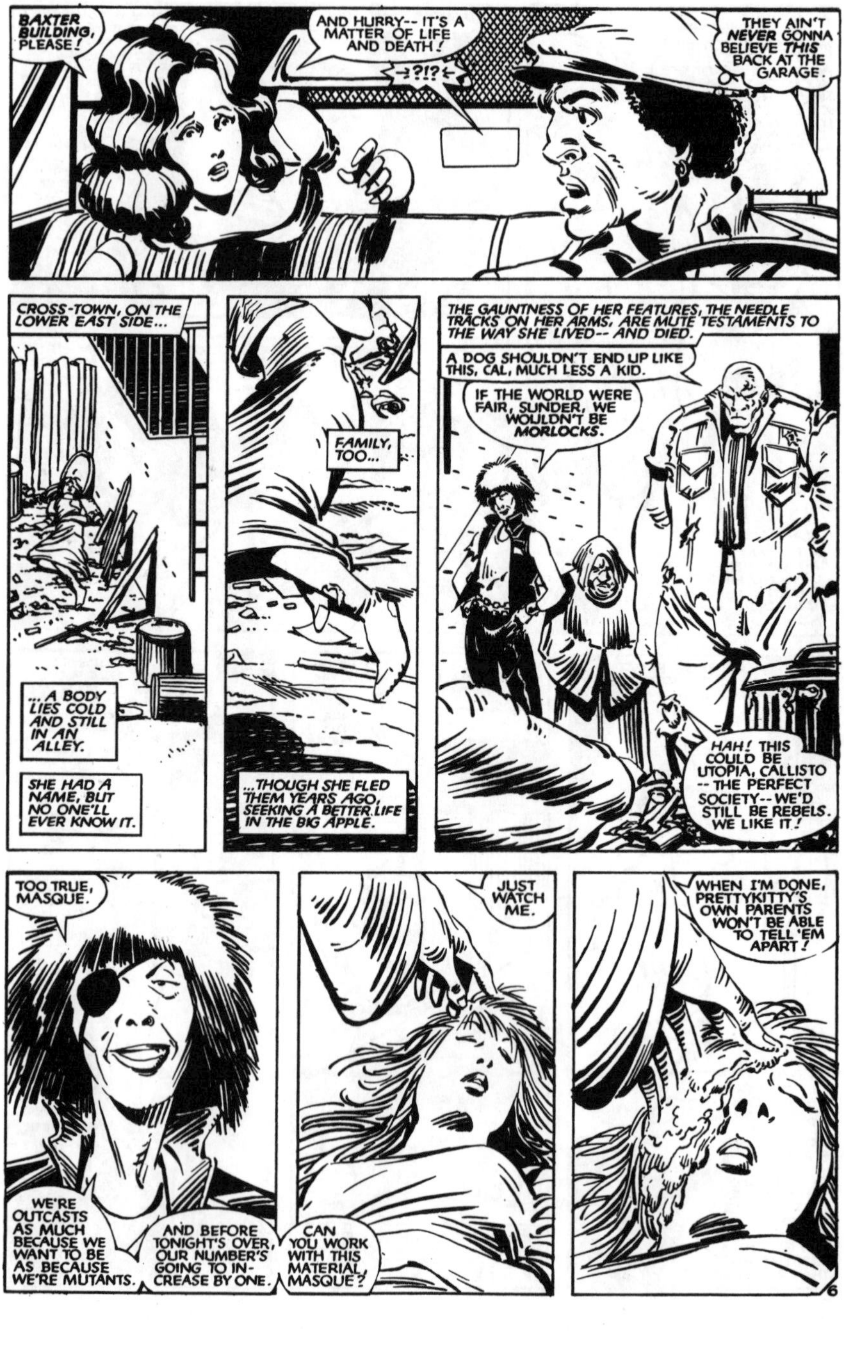
BAXTER BUILDING, PLEASE!
AND HURRY-- IT'S A MATTER OF LIFE AND DEATH!
?!?
THEY AIN'T NEVER GONNA BELIEVE THIS BACK AT THE GARAGE.
CROSS-TOWN, ON THE LOWER EAST SIDE...
...A BODY LIES COLD AND STILL IN AN ALLEY.
SHE HAD A NAME, BUT NO ONE'LL EVER KNOW IT.
FAMILY, TOO...
...THOUGH SHE FLED THEM YEARS AGO, SEEKING A BETTER LIFE IN THE BIG APPLE.
THE GAUNTNESS OF HER FEATURES, THE NEEDLE TRACKS ON HER ARMS, ARE MUTE TESTAMENTS TO THE WAY SHE LIVED-- AND DIED.
A DOG SHOULDN'T END UP LIKE THIS, CAL, MUCH LESS A KID.
IF THE WORLD WERE FAIR, SUNDER, WE WOULDN'T BE MORLOCKS.
HAH! THIS COULD BE UTOPIA, CALLISTO -- THE PERFECT SOCIETY-- WE'D STILL BE REBELS. WE LIKE IT!
TOO TRUE, MASQUE.
WE'RE OUTCASTS AS MUCH BECAUSE WE WANT TO BE AS BECAUSE WE'RE MUTANTS.
AND BEFORE TONIGHT'S OVER, OUR NUMBER'S GOING TO IN-CREASE BY ONE.
CAN YOU WORK WITH THIS MATERIAL, MASQUE?
JUST WATCH ME.
WHEN I'M DONE, PRETTYKITTY'S OWN PARENTS WON'T BE ABLE TO TELL 'EM APART!
6

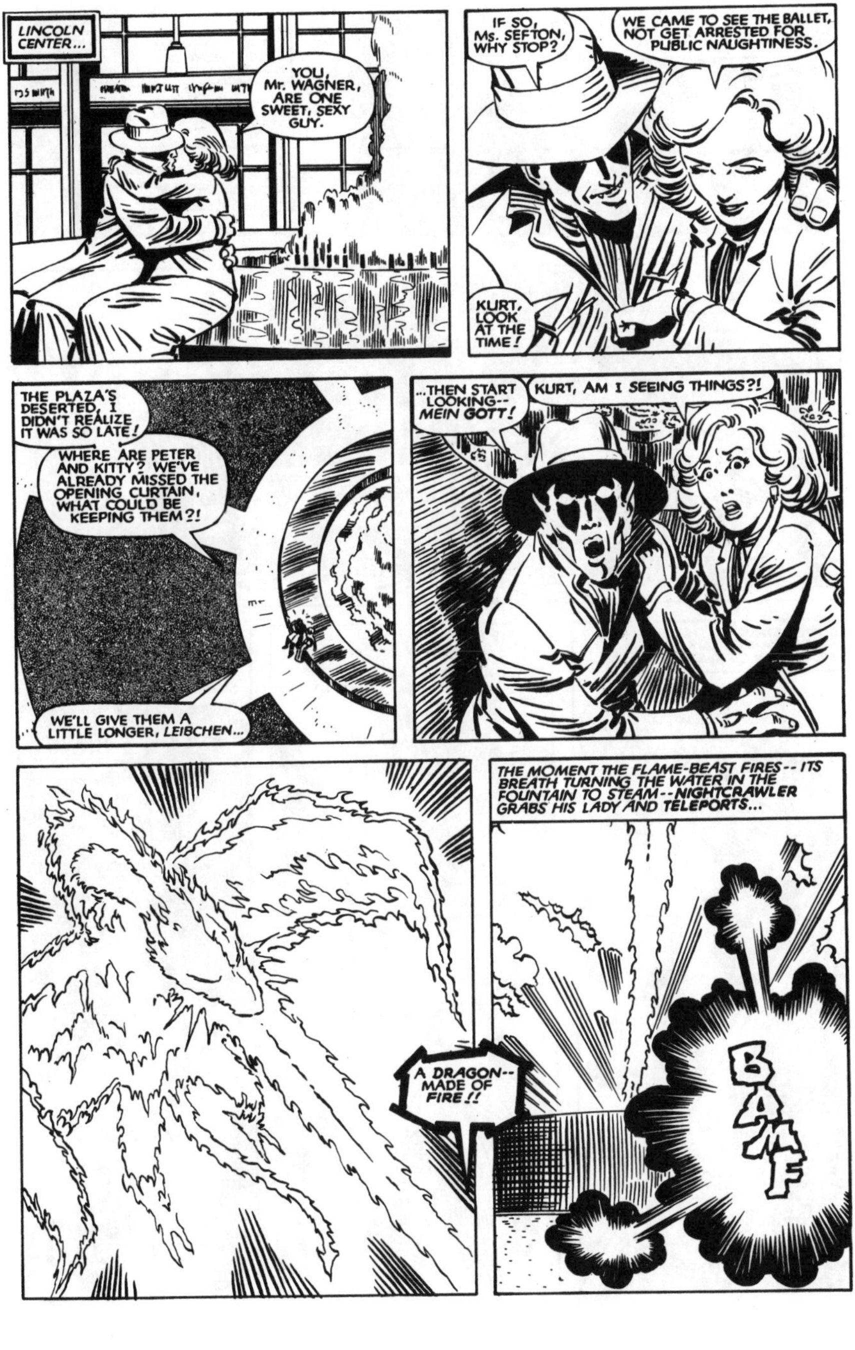
LINCOLN CENTER...
YOU, Mr. WAGNER, ARE ONE SWEET, SEXY GUY.
IF SO, Ms. SEFTON, WHY STOP?
WE CAME TO SEE THE BALLET, NOT GET ARRESTED FOR PUBLIC NAUGHTINESS.
KURT, LOOK AT THE TIME!
THE PLAZA'S DESERTED. I DIDN'T REALIZE IT WAS SO LATE!
WHERE ARE PETER AND KITTY? WE'VE ALREADY MISSED THE OPENING CURTAIN. WHAT COULD BE KEEPING THEM?!
WE'LL GIVE THEM A LITTLE LONGER, LEIBCHEN...
...THEN START LOOKING-- MEIN GOTT!
KURT, AM I SEEING THINGS?!
A DRAGON-- MADE OF FIRE!!
THE MOMENT THE FLAME-BEAST FIRES-- ITS BREATH TURNING THE WATER IN THE FOUNTAIN TO STEAM--NIGHTCRAWLER GRABS HIS LADY AND TELEPORTS...
BAMF

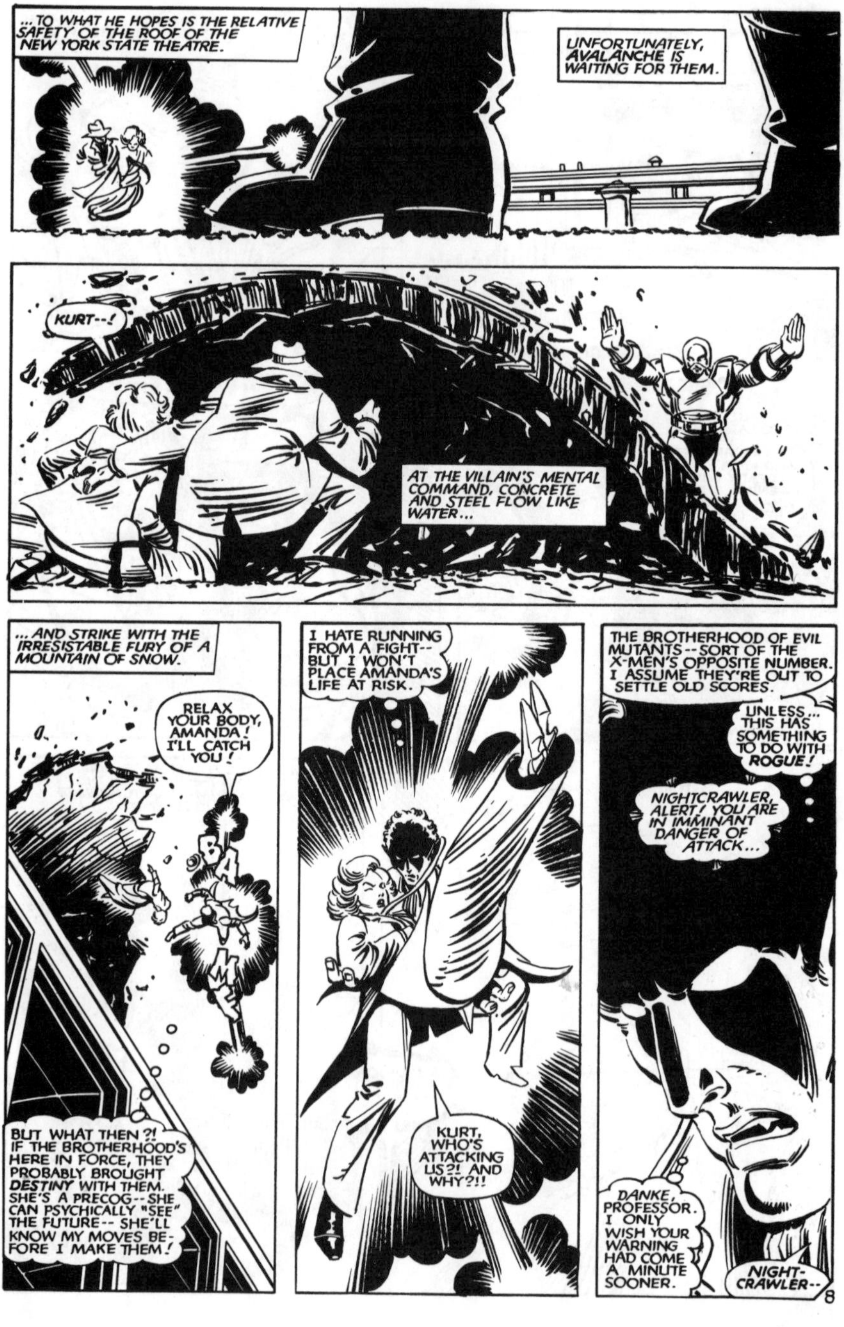
...TO WHAT HE HOPES IS THE RELATIVE SAFETY OF THE ROOF OF THE NEW YORK STATE THEATRE.
UNFORTUNATELY, AVALANCHE IS WAITING FOR THEM.
KURT--!
AT THE VILLAIN'S MENTAL COMMAND, CONCRETE AND STEEL FLOW LIKE WATER...
...AND STRIKE WITH THE IRRESISTABLE FURY OF A MOUNTAIN OF SNOW.
RELAX YOUR BODY, AMANDA! I'LL CATCH YOU!
BAMF
BUT WHAT THEN?! IF THE BROTHERHOOD'S HERE IN FORCE, THEY PROBABLY BROUGHT DESTINY WITH THEM. SHE'S A PRECOG--SHE CAN PSYCHICALLY "SEE" THE FUTURE--SHE'LL KNOW MY MOVES BEFORE I MAKE THEM!
I HATE RUNNING FROM A FIGHT--BUT I WON'T PLACE AMANDA'S LIFE AT RISK.
KURT, WHO'S ATTACKING US?! AND WHY?!!
THE BROTHERHOOD OF EVIL MUTANTS--SORT OF THE X-MEN'S OPPOSITE NUMBER. I ASSUME THEY'RE OUT TO SETTLE OLD SCORES.
UNLESS... THIS HAS SOMETHING TO DO WITH ROGUE!
NIGHTCRAWLER, ALERT! YOU ARE IN IMMINANT DANGER OF ATTACK...
DANKE, PROFESSOR. I ONLY WISH YOUR WARNING HAD COME A MINUTE SOONER.
NIGHT-CRAWLER--

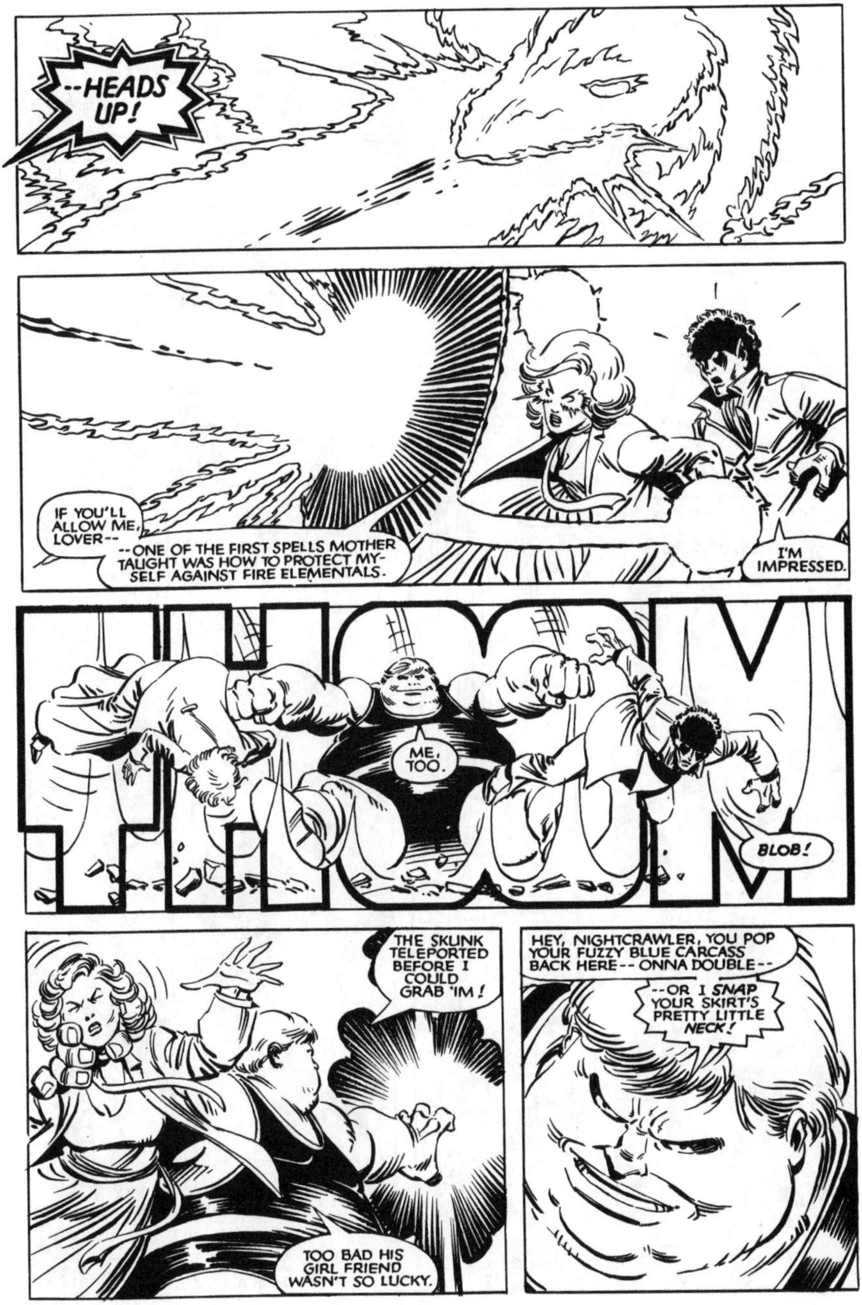
--HEADS UP!
IF YOU'LL ALLOW ME, LOVER--
--ONE OF THE FIRST SPELLS MOTHER TAUGHT WAS HOW TO PROTECT MY-SELF AGAINST FIRE ELEMENTALS.
I'M IMPRESSED.
THOOM
ME, TOO.
BLOB!
THE SKUNK TELEPORTED BEFORE I COULD GRAB 'IM!
TOO BAD HIS GIRL FRIEND WASN'T SO LUCKY.
HEY, NIGHTCRAWLER, YOU POP YOUR FUZZY BLUE CARCASS BACK HERE-- ONNA DOUBLE--
--OR I SNAP YOUR SKIRT'S PRETTY LITTLE NECK!

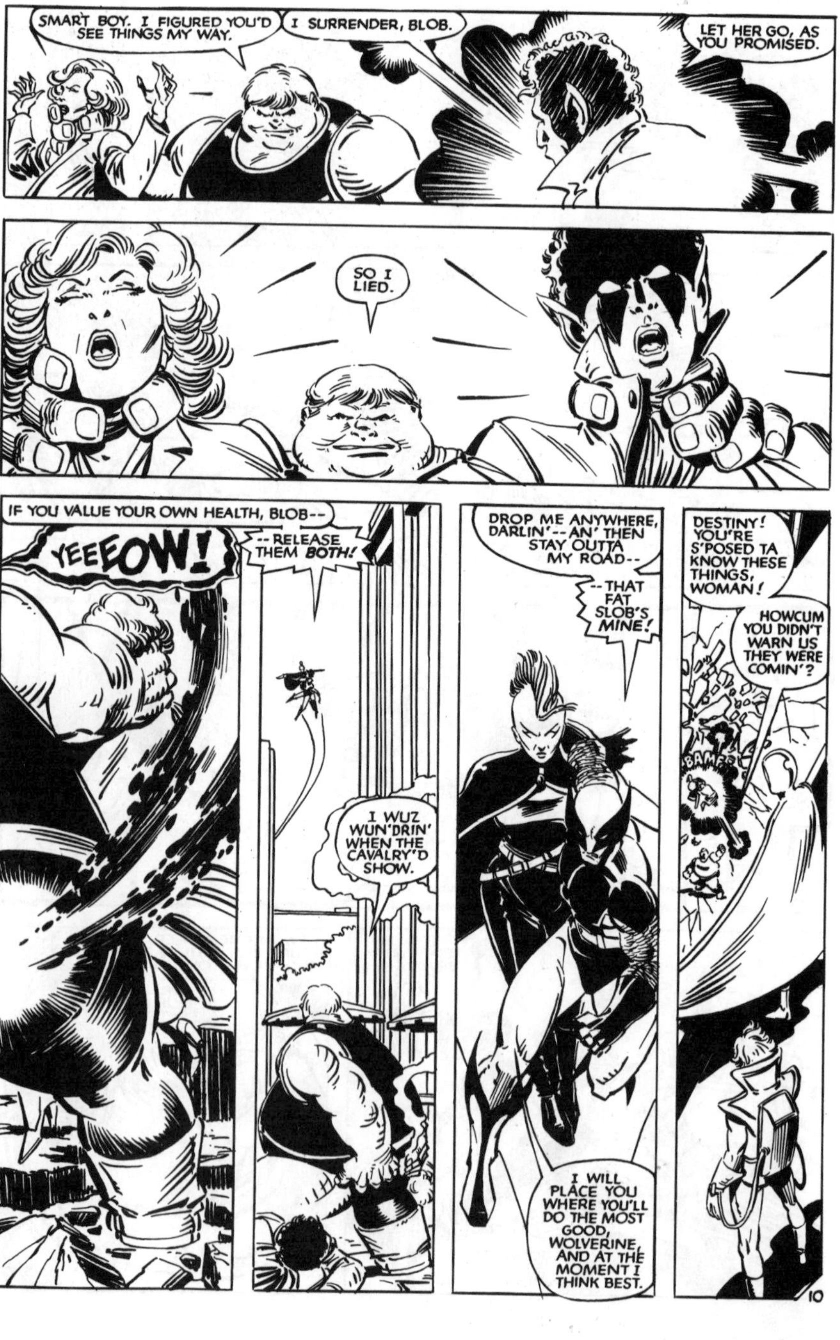
SMART BOY. I FIGURED YOU'D SEE THINGS MY WAY.
I SURRENDER, BLOB.
LET HER GO, AS YOU PROMISED.
SO I LIED.
IF YOU VALUE YOUR OWN HEALTH, BLOB--
YEEEOW!
--RELEASE THEM BOTH!
I WUZ WUN'DRIN' WHEN THE CAVALRY'D SHOW.
DROP ME ANYWHERE, DARLIN'-- AN' THEN STAY OUTTA MY ROAD--
--THAT FAT SLOB'S MINE!
I WILL PLACE YOU WHERE YOU'LL DO THE MOST GOOD, WOLVERINE, AND AT THE MOMENT I THINK BEST.
DESTINY! YOU'RE S'POSED TA KNOW THESE THINGS, WOMAN!
HOWCUM YOU DIDN'T WARN US THEY WERE COMIN'?
BAMF

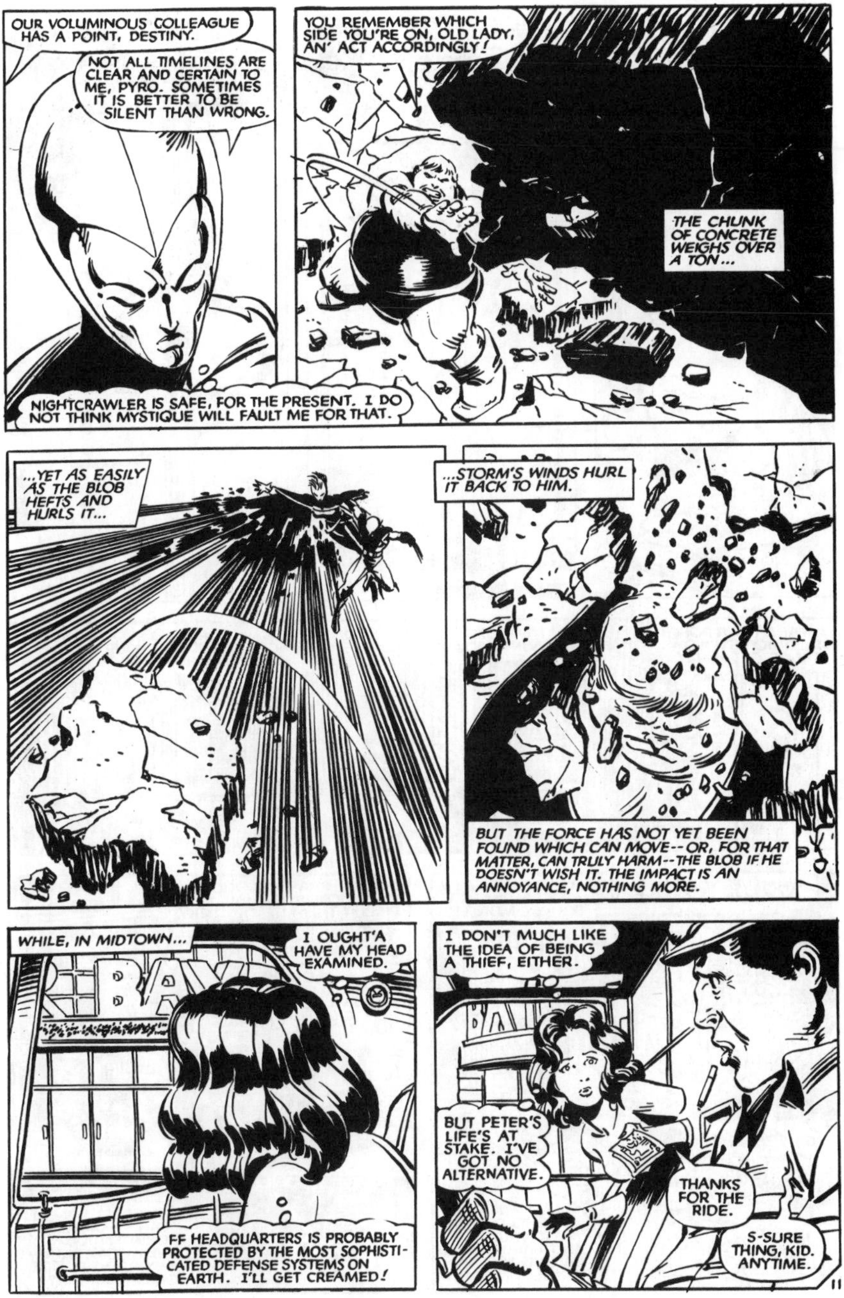
OUR VOLUMINOUS COLLEAGUE HAS A POINT, DESTINY.
NOT ALL TIMELINES ARE CLEAR AND CERTAIN TO ME, PYRO. SOMETIMES IT IS BETTER TO BE SILENT THAN WRONG.
YOU REMEMBER WHICH SIDE YOU'RE ON, OLD LADY, AN' ACT ACCORDINGLY!
THE CHUNK OF CONCRETE WEIGHS OVER A TON...
NIGHTCRAWLER IS SAFE, FOR THE PRESENT. I DO NOT THINK MYSTIQUE WILL FAULT ME FOR THAT.
...YET AS EASILY AS THE BLOB HEFTS AND HURLS IT...
...STORM'S WINDS HURL IT BACK TO HIM.
BUT THE FORCE HAS NOT YET BEEN FOUND WHICH CAN MOVE--OR, FOR THAT MATTER, CAN TRULY HARM--THE BLOB IF HE DOESN'T WISH IT. THE IMPACT IS AN ANNOYANCE, NOTHING MORE.
WHILE, IN MIDTOWN...
I OUGHT'A HAVE MY HEAD EXAMINED.
FF HEADQUARTERS IS PROBABLY PROTECTED BY THE MOST SOPHISTICATED DEFENSE SYSTEMS ON EARTH. I'LL GET CREAMED!
I DON'T MUCH LIKE THE IDEA OF BEING A THIEF, EITHER.
BUT PETER'S LIFE'S AT STAKE. I'VE GOT NO ALTERNATIVE.
THANKS FOR THE RIDE.
S-SURE THING, KID. ANYTIME.

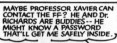

MAYBE PROFESSOR XAVIER CAN CONTACT THE FF? HE AND Dr. RICHARDS ARE BUDDIES-- HE MIGHT KNOW A PASSWORD THAT'LL GET ME SAFELY INSIDE.

I'VE BEEN RUSHING SO FAST-- AND BEEN SO UPSET-- I NEVER THOUGHT TO ASK!

PROFESSOR--?

SO MUCH FOR THAT IDEA, HE ISN'T ANSWERING.

OR CAN'T ANSWER. WE'VE ALL WORRIED FROM THE START THAT ROGUE WOULD TURN OUT TO BE A JUDAS.

HAS SHE SHOWN HER TRUE COLORS AT LAST?!

WHETHER SHE HAS OR NOT, THERE'S NOTHING I CAN DO ABOUT IT.

THIS ELEVATOR'LL TAKE ME TO THE FLOOR BELOW THE FF SECTION.

I'LL PHASE THE REST OF THE WAY.

THERE'S THEIR ROBOT RECEPTIONIST. NOW THINGS GET HAIRY.

ATTENTION! YOU ARE MAKING AN UNAUTHORIZED ENTRY ONTO THE PREMESIS OF FANTASTIC FOUR, INCORPORATED.

PLEASE STATE YOUR BUSINESS AND THEN LEAVE, OR APPROPRIATE SECURITY MEASURES WILL BE TAKEN.

WHATEVER YOU SAY, MISS. I'M KITTY PRYDE, I'M AN X-MAN, I NEED Dr. RICHARDS' ALPHA HEAT SOURCE MODULE...

SQUAWRRRK!

...AN I REALLY HATE TO DO THIS TO YOU, BUT I CAN'T HANG AROUND WAITING FOR HIS PERMISSION. SORRY!

WHEN I PHASE THROUGH ELECTRICAL SYSTEMS, I SHORT-CIRCUIT THEM. IF I'M LUCKY, SHORTING THE RECEPTIONIST'S COMPUTER BRAIN LIKE THAT'LL GIVE ME THE TIME I NEED.

THE LAB IS ON THE THE THIRD LEVEL. BUT I'VE GOTTA BE REAL CAREFUL HOW I GO.

THE LAST THING I CAN AFFORD IS TO UNINTENTIONALLY CRASH SOME ULTRA-IMPORTANT DEVICE OR EXPERIMENT.

12

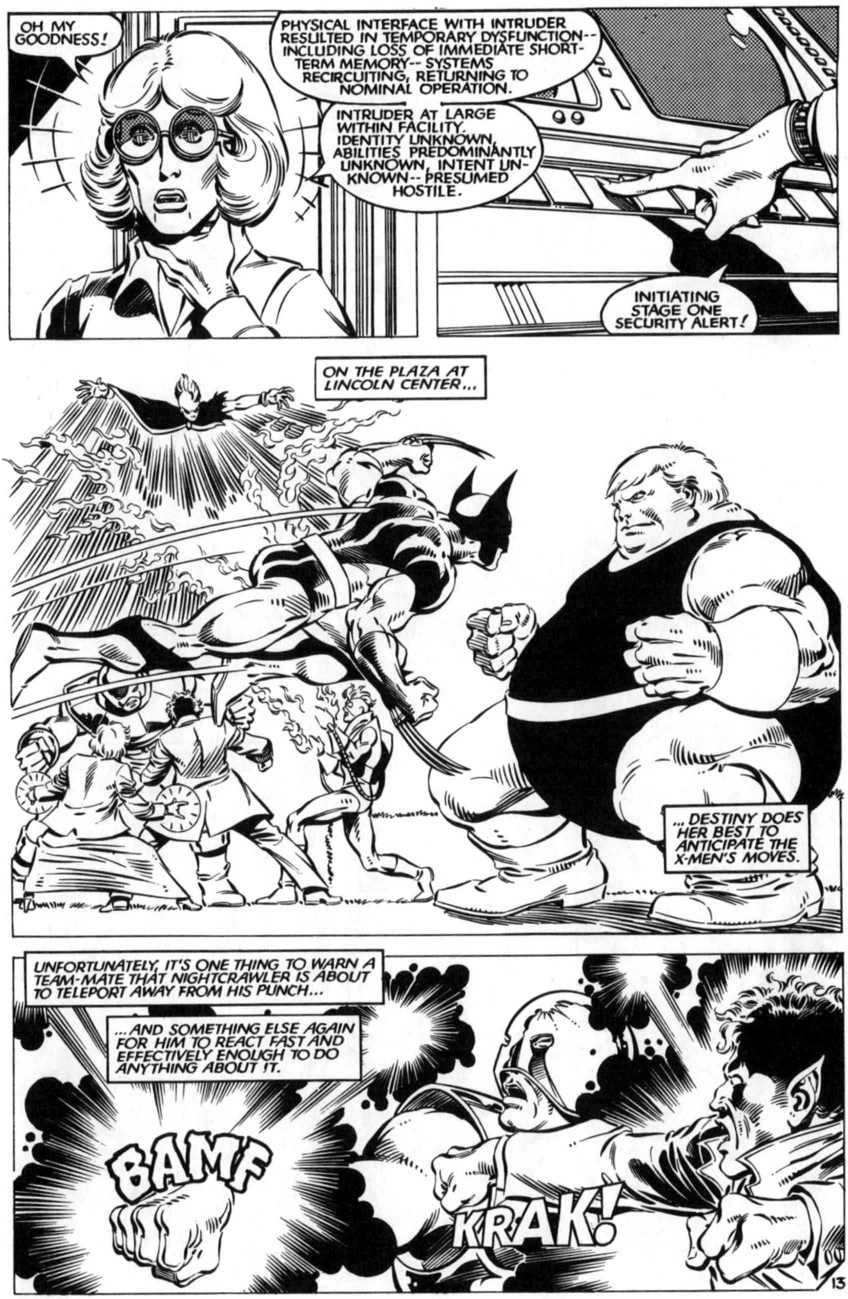

OH MY GOODNESS!
PHYSICAL INTERFACE WITH INTRUDER RESULTED IN TEMPORARY DYSFUNCTION-- INCLUDING LOSS OF IMMEDIATE SHORT-TERM MEMORY-- SYSTEMS RECIRCUITING, RETURNING TO NOMINAL OPERATION.
INTRUDER AT LARGE WITHIN FACILITY. IDENTITY UNKNOWN, ABILITIES PREDOMINANTLY UNKNOWN, INTENT UNKNOWN-- PRESUMED HOSTILE.
INITIATING STAGE ONE SECURITY ALERT!
ON THE PLAZA AT LINCOLN CENTER...
...DESTINY DOES HER BEST TO ANTICIPATE THE X-MEN'S MOVES.
UNFORTUNATELY, IT'S ONE THING TO WARN A TEAM-MATE THAT NIGHTCRAWLER IS ABOUT TO TELEPORT AWAY FROM HIS PUNCH...
...AND SOMETHING ELSE AGAIN FOR HIM TO REACT FAST AND EFFECTIVELY ENOUGH TO DO ANYTHING ABOUT IT.
BAMF
KRAK!

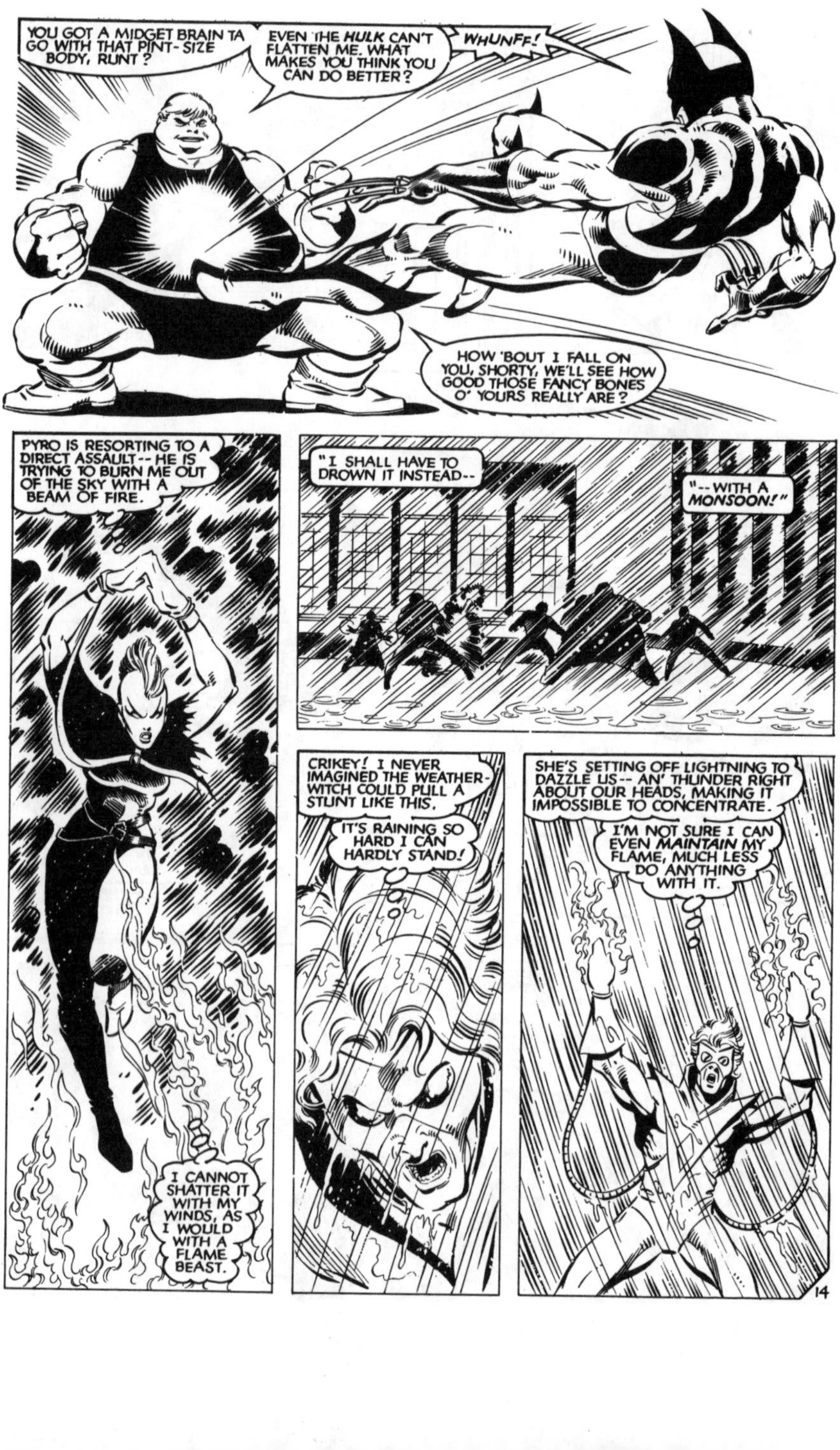

YOU GOT A MIDGET BRAIN TA GO WITH THAT PINT-SIZE BODY, RUNT?
EVEN THE HULK CAN'T FLATTEN ME. WHAT MAKES YOU THINK YOU CAN DO BETTER?
WHUNFF!
HOW 'BOUT I FALL ON YOU, SHORTY, WE'LL SEE HOW GOOD THOSE FANCY BONES O' YOURS REALLY ARE?
PYRO IS RESORTING TO A DIRECT ASSAULT-- HE IS TRYING TO BURN ME OUT OF THE SKY WITH A BEAM OF FIRE.
I CANNOT SHATTER IT WITH MY WINDS, AS I WOULD WITH A FLAME BEAST.
"I SHALL HAVE TO DROWN IT INSTEAD--
"--WITH A MONSOON!"
CRIKEY! I NEVER IMAGINED THE WEATHER-WITCH COULD PULL A STUNT LIKE THIS.
IT'S RAINING SO HARD I CAN HARDLY STAND!
SHE'S SETTING OFF LIGHTNING TO DAZZLE US-- AN' THUNDER RIGHT ABOUT OUR HEADS, MAKING IT IMPOSSIBLE TO CONCENTRATE.
I'M NOT SURE I CAN EVEN MAINTAIN MY FLAME, MUCH LESS DO ANYTHING WITH IT.

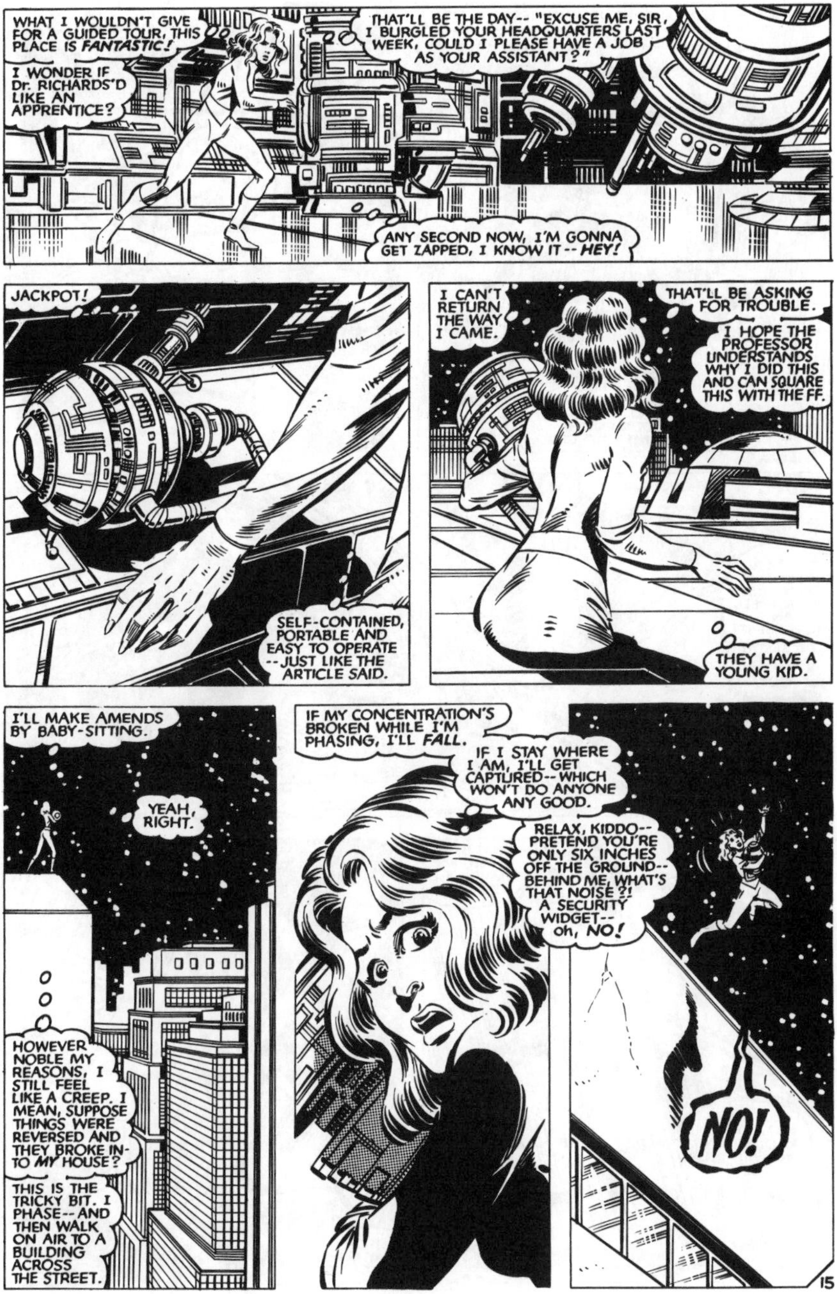
WHAT I WOULDN'T GIVE FOR A GUIDED TOUR, THIS PLACE IS FANTASTIC!
I WONDER IF Dr. RICHARDS'D LIKE AN APPRENTICE?
THAT'LL BE THE DAY-- "EXCUSE ME, SIR, I BURGLED YOUR HEADQUARTERS LAST WEEK, COULD I PLEASE HAVE A JOB AS YOUR ASSISTANT?"
ANY SECOND NOW, I'M GONNA GET ZAPPED, I KNOW IT -- HEY!
JACKPOT!
SELF-CONTAINED, PORTABLE AND EASY TO OPERATE --JUST LIKE THE ARTICLE SAID.
I CAN'T RETURN THE WAY I CAME.
THAT'LL BE ASKING FOR TROUBLE.
I HOPE THE PROFESSOR UNDERSTANDS WHY I DID THIS AND CAN SQUARE THIS WITH THE FF.
THEY HAVE A YOUNG KID.
I'LL MAKE AMENDS BY BABY-SITTING.
YEAH, RIGHT.
HOWEVER NOBLE MY REASONS, I STILL FEEL LIKE A CREEP. I MEAN, SUPPOSE THINGS WERE REVERSED AND THEY BROKE IN-TO MY HOUSE?
THIS IS THE TRICKY BIT. I PHASE--AND THEN WALK ON AIR TO A BUILDING ACROSS THE STREET.
IF MY CONCENTRATION'S BROKEN WHILE I'M PHASING, I'LL FALL.
IF I STAY WHERE I AM, I'LL GET CAPTURED--WHICH WON'T DO ANYONE ANY GOOD.
RELAX, KIDDO-- PRETEND YOU'RE ONLY SIX INCHES OFF THE GROUND-- BEHIND ME, WHAT'S THAT NOISE?! A SECURITY WIDGET-- oh, NO!
NO!

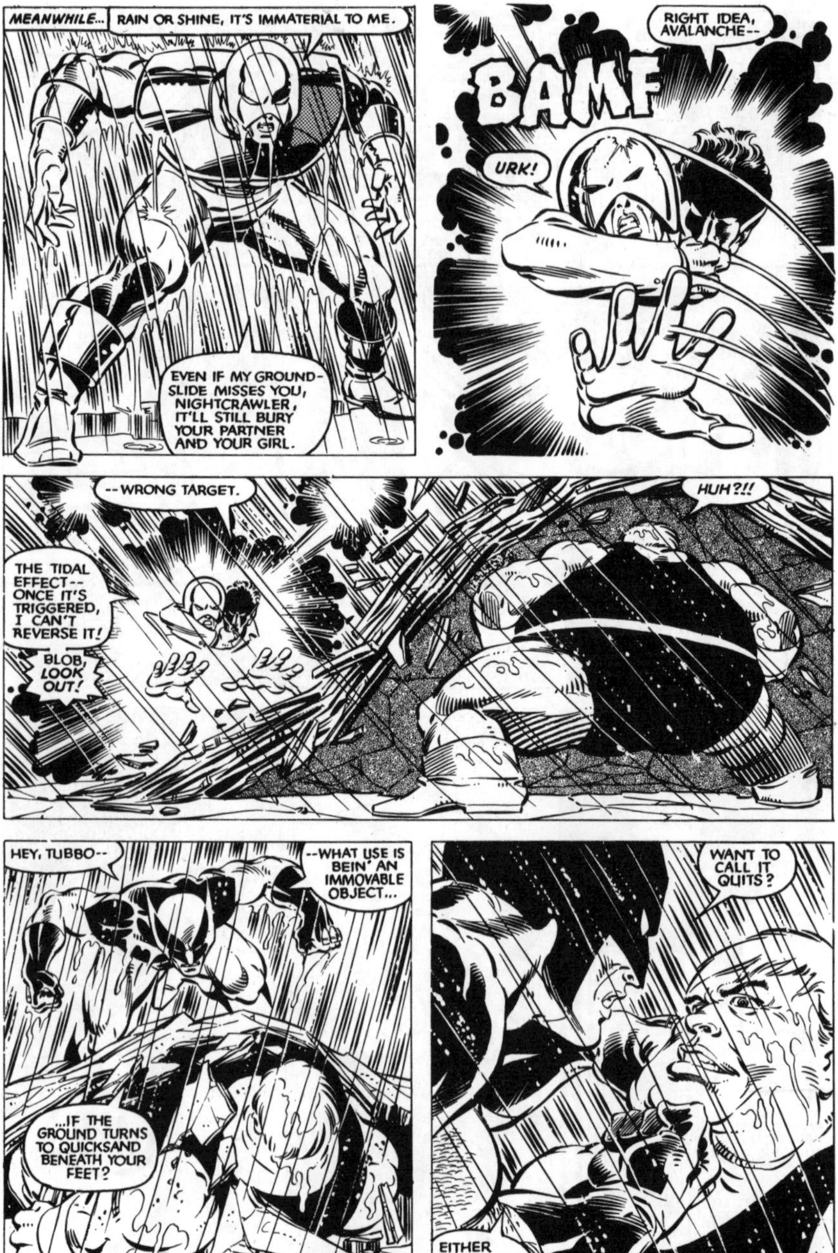
MEANWHILE...
RAIN OR SHINE, IT'S IMMATERIAL TO ME.
EVEN IF MY GROUND-SLIDE MISSES YOU, NIGHTCRAWLER, IT'LL STILL BURY YOUR PARTNER AND YOUR GIRL.
RIGHT IDEA, AVALANCHE--
BAMF
URK!
--WRONG TARGET.
HUH?!!
THE TIDAL EFFECT--ONCE IT'S TRIGGERED, I CAN'T REVERSE IT!
BLOB, LOOK OUT!
HEY, TUBBO--
--WHAT USE IS BEIN' AN IMMOVABLE OBJECT...
...IF THE GROUND TURNS TO QUICKSAND BENEATH YOUR FEET?
WANT TO CALL IT QUITS?
EITHER WAY IS FINE WITH ME.

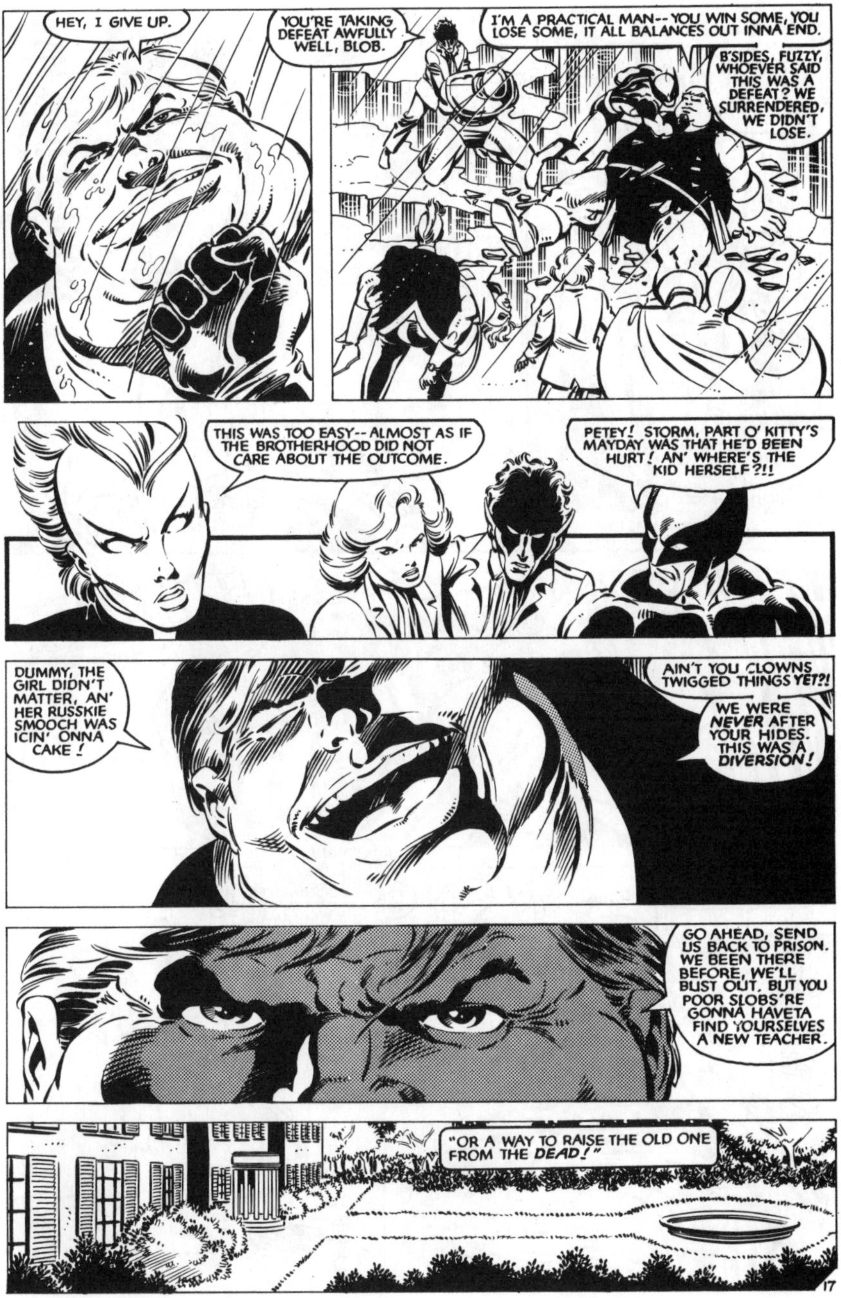

HEY, I GIVE UP.
YOU'RE TAKING DEFEAT AWFULLY WELL, BLOB.
I'M A PRACTICAL MAN-- YOU WIN SOME, YOU LOSE SOME, IT ALL BALANCES OUT INNA END.
B'SIDES, FUZZY, WHOEVER SAID THIS WAS A DEFEAT? WE SURRENDERED, WE DIDN'T LOSE.
THIS WAS TOO EASY-- ALMOST AS IF THE BROTHERHOOD DID NOT CARE ABOUT THE OUTCOME.
PETEY! STORM, PART O' KITTY'S MAYDAY WAS THAT HE'D BEEN HURT! AN' WHERE'S THE KID HERSELF?!!
DUMMY, THE GIRL DIDN'T MATTER, AN' HER RUSSKIE SMOOCH WAS ICIN' ONNA CAKE!
AIN'T YOU CLOWNS TWIGGED THINGS YET?!
WE WERE NEVER AFTER YOUR HIDES. THIS WAS A DIVERSION!
GO AHEAD, SEND US BACK TO PRISON. WE BEEN THERE BEFORE, WE'LL BUST OUT. BUT YOU POOR SLOBS'RE GONNA HAVETA FIND YOURSELVES A NEW TEACHER.
"OR A WAY TO RAISE THE OLD ONE FROM THE DEAD!"

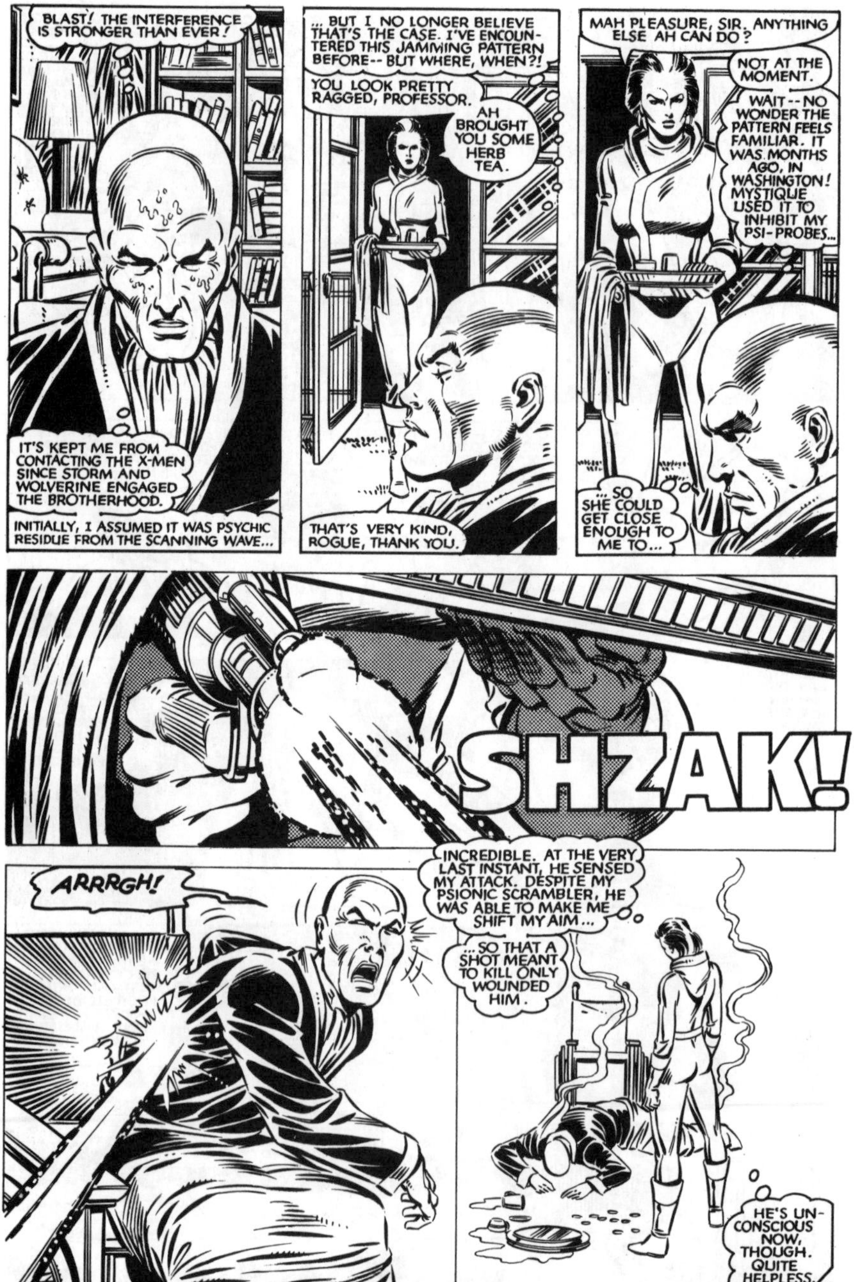
BLAST! THE INTERFERENCE IS STRONGER THAN EVER!
IT'S KEPT ME FROM CONTACTING THE X-MEN SINCE STORM AND WOLVERINE ENGAGED THE BROTHERHOOD.
INITIALLY, I ASSUMED IT WAS PSYCHIC RESIDUE FROM THE SCANNING WAVE...
... BUT I NO LONGER BELIEVE THAT'S THE CASE. I'VE ENCOUNTERED THIS JAMMING PATTERN BEFORE-- BUT WHERE, WHEN?!
YOU LOOK PRETTY RAGGED, PROFESSOR.
AH BROUGHT YOU SOME HERB TEA.
THAT'S VERY KIND, ROGUE, THANK YOU.
MAH PLEASURE, SIR. ANYTHING ELSE AH CAN DO?
NOT AT THE MOMENT.
WAIT -- NO WONDER THE PATTERN FEELS FAMILIAR. IT WAS MONTHS AGO, IN WASHINGTON! MYSTIQUE USED IT TO INHIBIT MY PSI-PROBES...
... SO SHE COULD GET CLOSE ENOUGH TO ME TO...
SHZAK!
ARRRGH!
INCREDIBLE. AT THE VERY LAST INSTANT, HE SENSED MY ATTACK. DESPITE MY PSIONIC SCRAMBLER, HE WAS ABLE TO MAKE ME SHIFT MY AIM...
... SO THAT A SHOT MEANT TO KILL ONLY WOUNDED HIM.
HE'S UNCONSCIOUS NOW, THOUGH. QUITE HELPLESS.

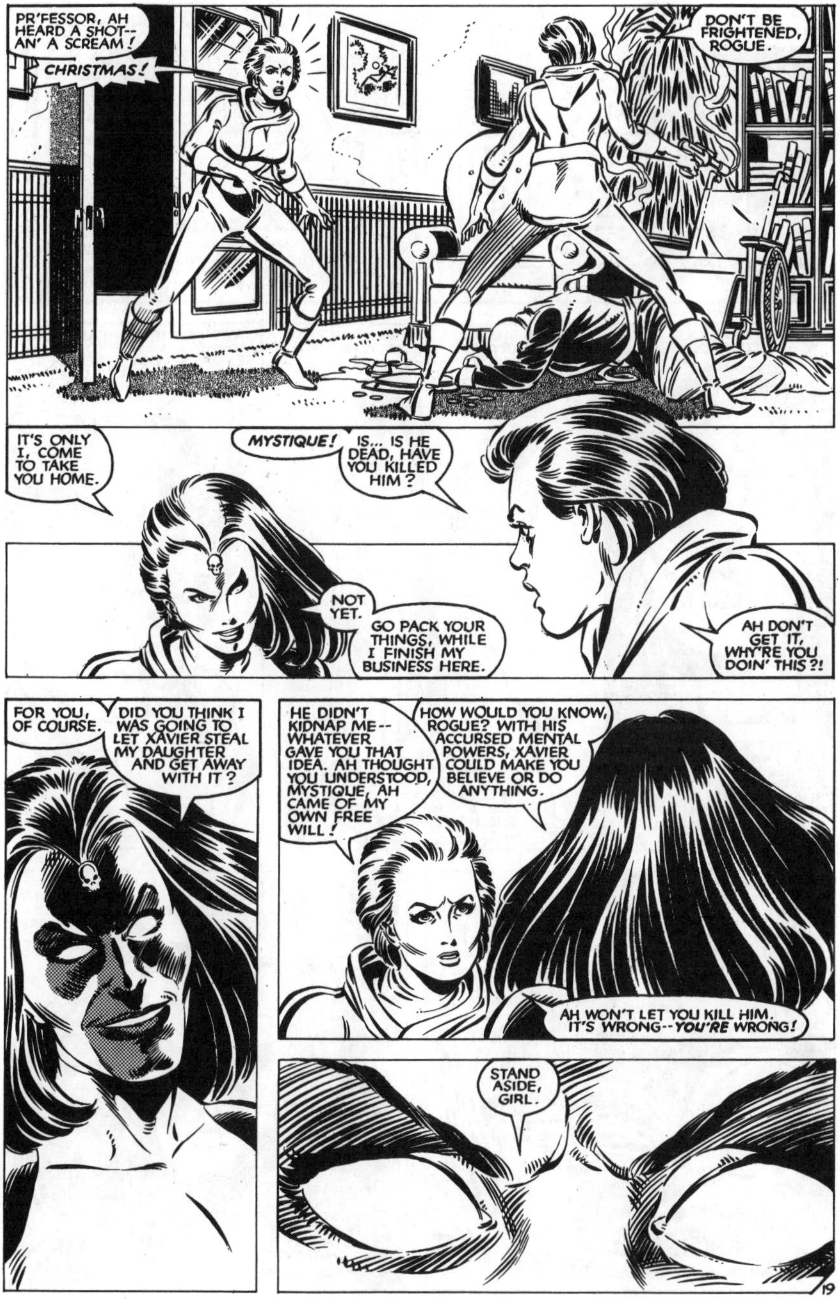
PR'FESSOR, AH HEARD A SHOT-- AN' A SCREAM!
CHRISTMAS!
DON'T BE FRIGHTENED, ROGUE.
IT'S ONLY I, COME TO TAKE YOU HOME.
MYSTIQUE!
IS... IS HE DEAD, HAVE YOU KILLED HIM?
NOT YET.
GO PACK YOUR THINGS, WHILE I FINISH MY BUSINESS HERE.
AH DON'T GET IT, WHY'RE YOU DOIN' THIS?!
FOR YOU, OF COURSE.
DID YOU THINK I WAS GOING TO LET XAVIER STEAL MY DAUGHTER AND GET AWAY WITH IT?
HE DIDN'T KIDNAP ME-- WHATEVER GAVE YOU THAT IDEA. AH THOUGHT YOU UNDERSTOOD, MYSTIQUE, AH CAME OF MY OWN FREE WILL!
HOW WOULD YOU KNOW, ROGUE? WITH HIS ACCURSED MENTAL POWERS, XAVIER COULD MAKE YOU BELIEVE OR DO ANYTHING.
AH WON'T LET YOU KILL HIM. IT'S WRONG--YOU'RE WRONG!
STAND ASIDE, GIRL.
19

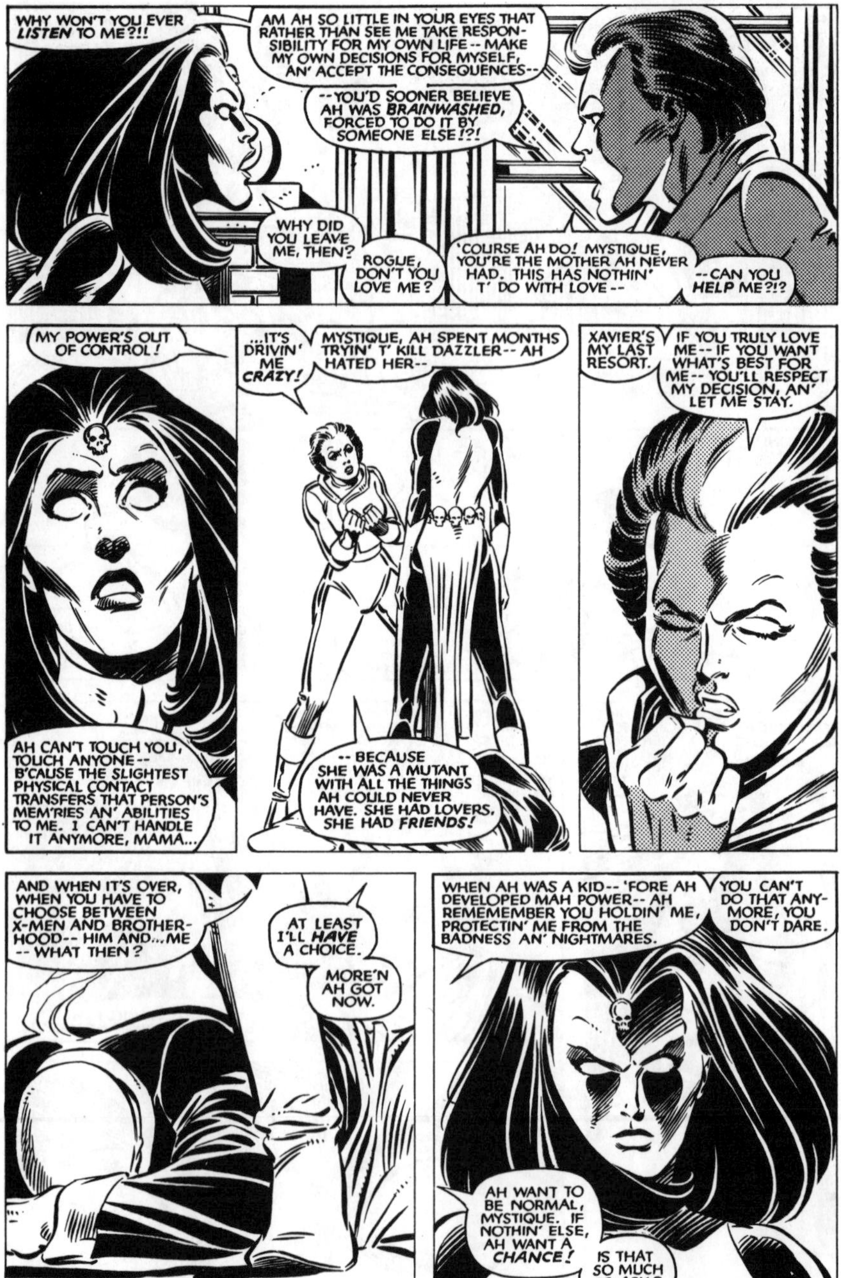
WHY WON'T YOU EVER LISTEN TO ME?!!
AM AH SO LITTLE IN YOUR EYES THAT RATHER THAN SEE ME TAKE RESPONSIBILITY FOR MY OWN LIFE -- MAKE MY OWN DECISIONS FOR MYSELF, AN' ACCEPT THE CONSEQUENCES--
--YOU'D SOONER BELIEVE AH WAS BRAINWASHED, FORCED TO DO IT BY SOMEONE ELSE!?!
WHY DID YOU LEAVE ME, THEN?
ROGUE, DON'T YOU LOVE ME?
'COURSE AH DO! MYSTIQUE, YOU'RE THE MOTHER AH NEVER HAD. THIS HAS NOTHIN' T' DO WITH LOVE --
--CAN YOU HELP ME?!?
MY POWER'S OUT OF CONTROL!
AH CAN'T TOUCH YOU, TOUCH ANYONE-- B'CAUSE THE SLIGHTEST PHYSICAL CONTACT TRANSFERS THAT PERSON'S MEM'RIES AN' ABILITIES TO ME. I CAN'T HANDLE IT ANYMORE, MAMA...
...IT'S DRIVIN' ME CRAZY!
MYSTIQUE, AH SPENT MONTHS TRYIN' T' KILL DAZZLER-- AH HATED HER--
-- BECAUSE SHE WAS A MUTANT WITH ALL THE THINGS AH COULD NEVER HAVE. SHE HAD LOVERS, SHE HAD FRIENDS!
XAVIER'S MY LAST RESORT.
IF YOU TRULY LOVE ME-- IF YOU WANT WHAT'S BEST FOR ME-- YOU'LL RESPECT MY DECISION, AN' LET ME STAY.
AND WHEN IT'S OVER, WHEN YOU HAVE TO CHOOSE BETWEEN X-MEN AND BROTHERHOOD-- HIM AND...ME -- WHAT THEN?
AT LEAST I'LL HAVE A CHOICE.
MORE'N AH GOT NOW.
WHEN AH WAS A KID-- 'FORE AH DEVELOPED MAH POWER-- AH REMEMEMBER YOU HOLDIN' ME, PROTECTIN' ME FROM THE BADNESS AN' NIGHTMARES.
YOU CAN'T DO THAT ANYMORE, YOU DON'T DARE.
AH WANT TO BE NORMAL, MYSTIQUE. IF NOTHIN' ELSE, AH WANT A CHANCE!
IS THAT SO MUCH TO ASK?

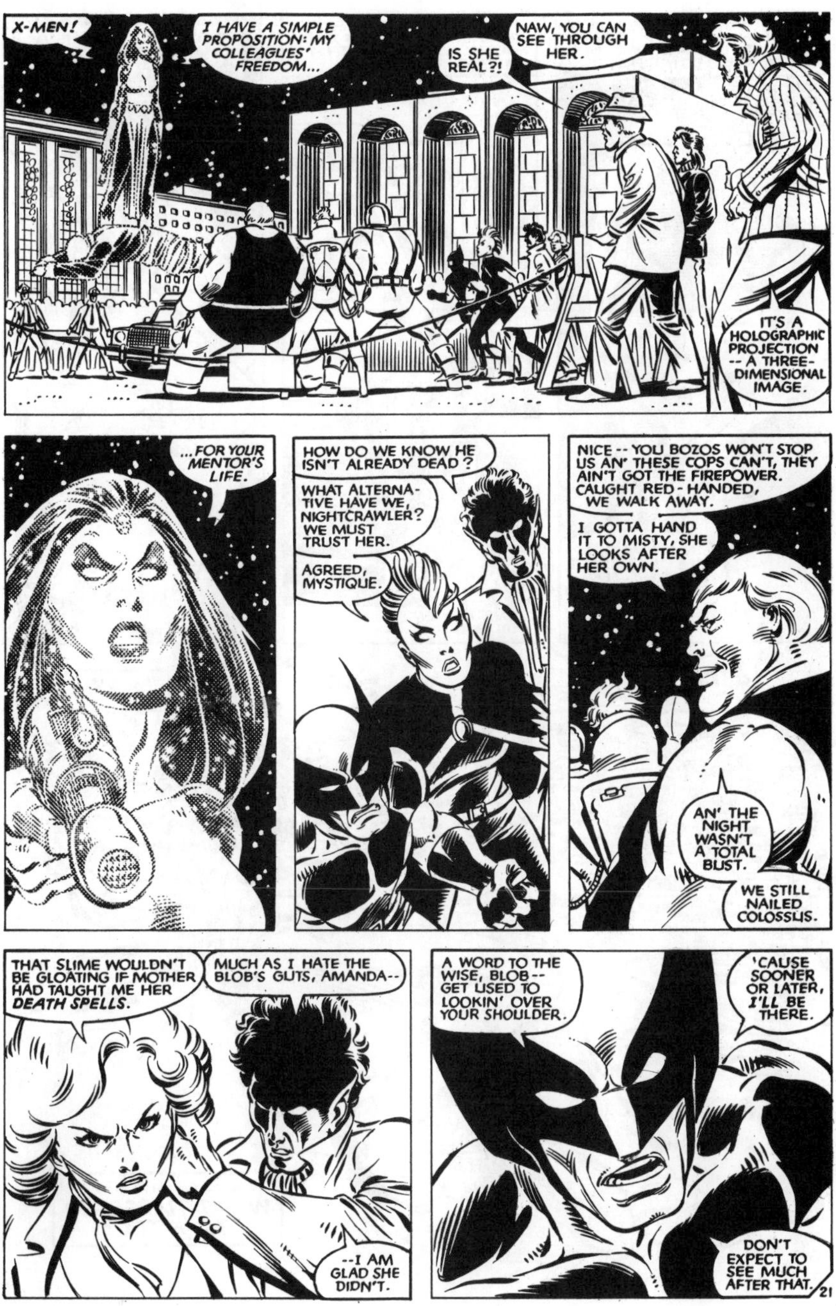
X-MEN!
I HAVE A SIMPLE PROPOSITION: MY COLLEAGUES' FREEDOM...
IS SHE REAL?!
NAW, YOU CAN SEE THROUGH HER.
IT'S A HOLOGRAPHIC PROJECTION -- A THREE-DIMENSIONAL IMAGE.
...FOR YOUR MENTOR'S LIFE.
HOW DO WE KNOW HE ISN'T ALREADY DEAD?
WHAT ALTERNATIVE HAVE WE, NIGHTCRAWLER? WE MUST TRUST HER.
AGREED, MYSTIQUE.
NICE -- YOU BOZOS WON'T STOP US AN' THESE COPS CAN'T, THEY AIN'T GOT THE FIREPOWER. CAUGHT RED-HANDED, WE WALK AWAY.
I GOTTA HAND IT TO MISTY, SHE LOOKS AFTER HER OWN.
AN' THE NIGHT WASN'T A TOTAL BUST.
WE STILL NAILED COLOSSUS.
THAT SLIME WOULDN'T BE GLOATING IF MOTHER HAD TAUGHT ME HER DEATH SPELLS.
MUCH AS I HATE THE BLOB'S GUTS, AMANDA--
--I AM GLAD SHE DIDN'T.
A WORD TO THE WISE, BLOB -- GET USED TO LOOKIN' OVER YOUR SHOULDER.
'CAUSE SOONER OR LATER, I'LL BE THERE.
DON'T EXPECT TO SEE MUCH AFTER THAT.
21

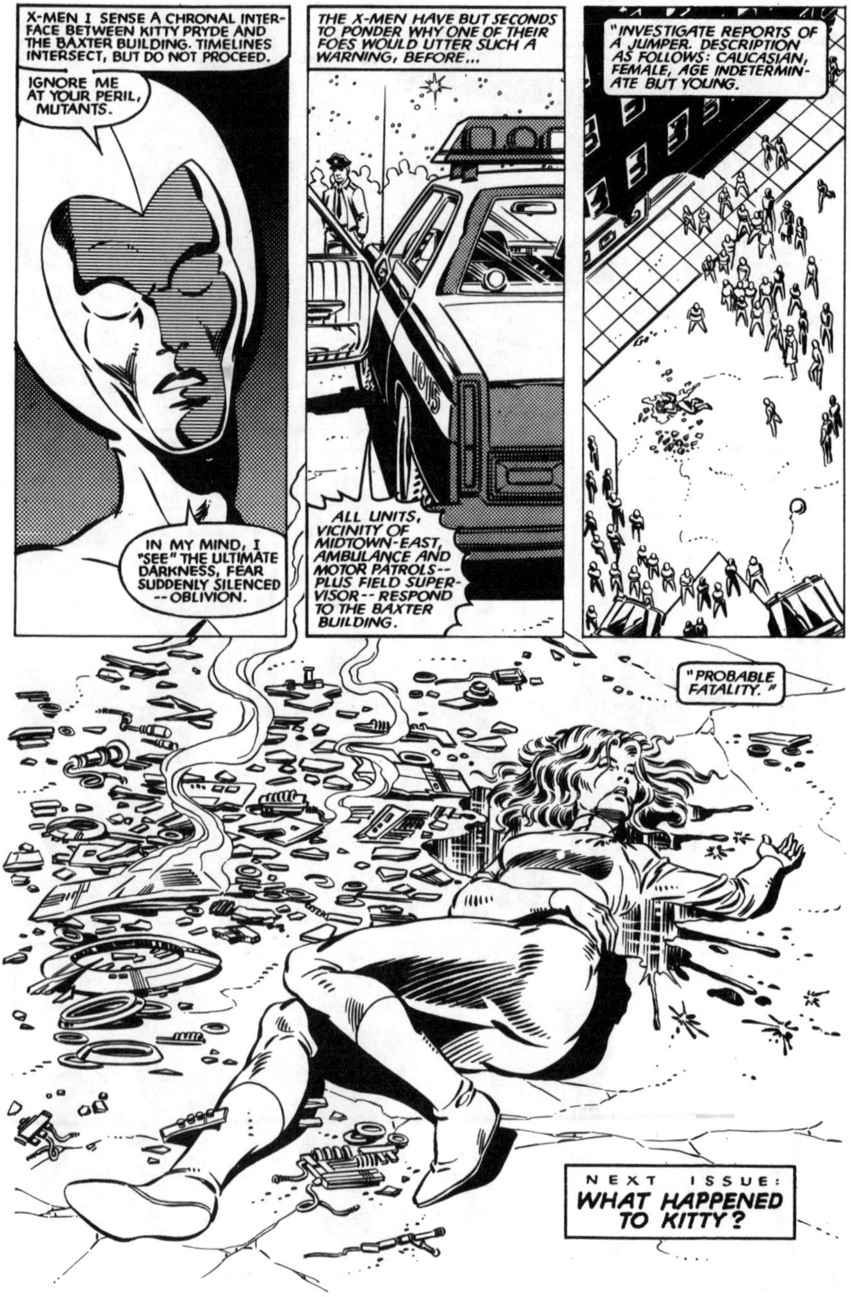
X-MEN I SENSE A CHRONAL INTERFACE BETWEEN KITTY PRYDE AND THE BAXTER BUILDING. TIMELINES INTERSECT, BUT DO NOT PROCEED.
IGNORE ME AT YOUR PERIL, MUTANTS.
IN MY MIND, I "SEE" THE ULTIMATE DARKNESS, FEAR SUDDENLY SILENCED --OBLIVION.
THE X-MEN HAVE BUT SECONDS TO PONDER WHY ONE OF THEIR FOES WOULD UTTER SUCH A WARNING, BEFORE...
ALL UNITS, VICINITY OF MIDTOWN-EAST, AMBULANCE AND MOTOR PATROLS-- PLUS FIELD SUPERVISOR-- RESPOND TO THE BAXTER BUILDING.
"INVESTIGATE REPORTS OF A JUMPER. DESCRIPTION AS FOLLOWS: CAUCASIAN, FEMALE, AGE INDETERMINATE BUT YOUNG.
"PROBABLE FATALITY."
NEXT ISSUE:
WHAT HAPPENED TO KITTY?

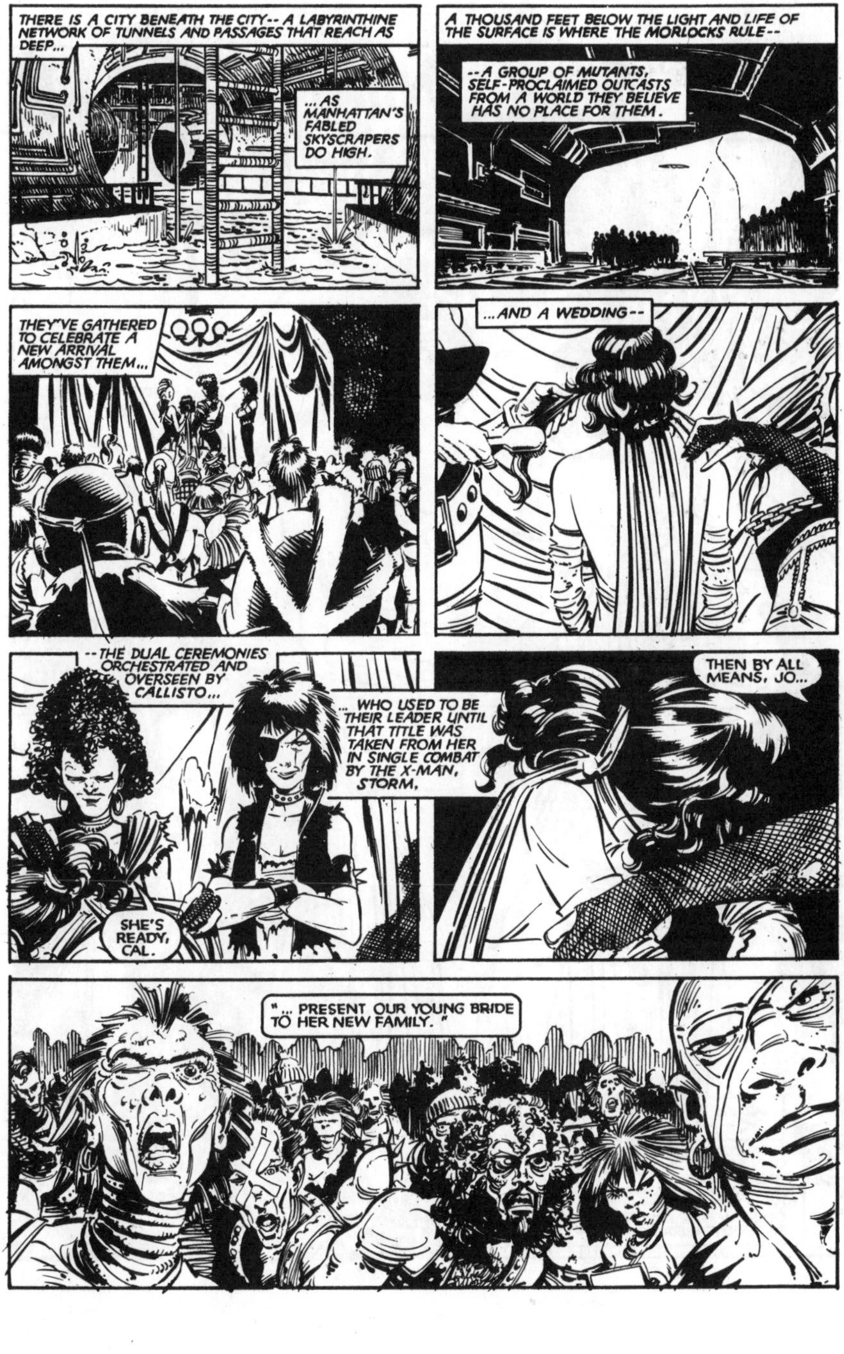
THERE IS A CITY BENEATH THE CITY-- A LABYRINTHINE NETWORK OF TUNNELS AND PASSAGES THAT REACH AS DEEP...
...AS MANHATTAN'S FABLED SKYSCRAPERS DO HIGH.
A THOUSAND FEET BELOW THE LIGHT AND LIFE OF THE SURFACE IS WHERE THE MORLOCKS RULE--
--A GROUP OF MUTANTS, SELF-PROCLAIMED OUTCASTS FROM A WORLD THEY BELIEVE HAS NO PLACE FOR THEM.
THEY'VE GATHERED TO CELEBRATE A NEW ARRIVAL AMONGST THEM...
...AND A WEDDING--
--THE DUAL CEREMONIES ORCHESTRATED AND OVERSEEN BY CALLISTO...
...WHO USED TO BE THEIR LEADER UNTIL THAT TITLE WAS TAKEN FROM HER IN SINGLE COMBAT BY THE X-MAN, STORM.
SHE'S READY, CAL.
THEN BY ALL MEANS, JO...
"...PRESENT OUR YOUNG BRIDE TO HER NEW FAMILY."

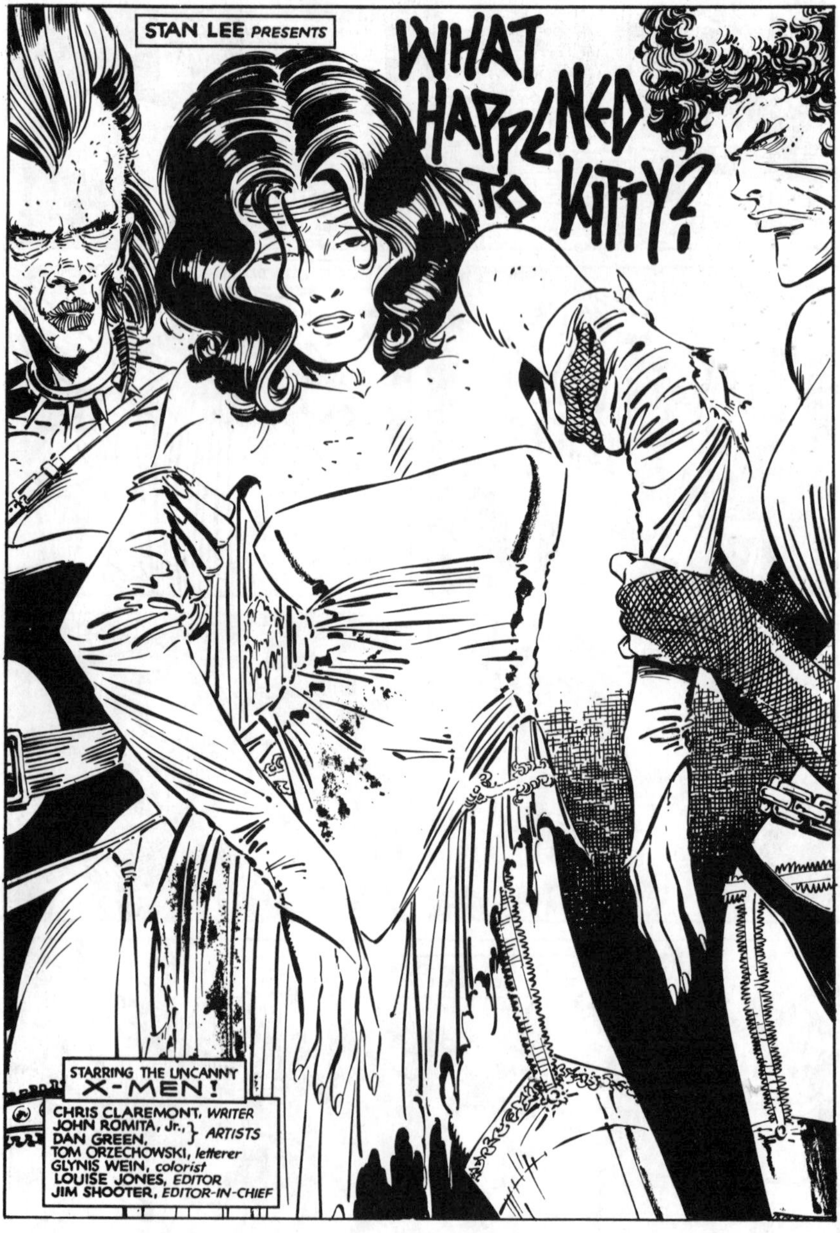
STAN LEE PRESENTS
WHAT HAPPENED TO KITTY?
STARRING THE UNCANNY X-MEN!
CHRIS CLAREMONT, WRITER
JOHN ROMITA, Jr., DAN GREEN, ARTISTS
TOM ORZECHOWSKI, letterer
GLYNIS WEIN, colorist
LOUISE JONES, EDITOR
JIM SHOOTER, EDITOR-IN-CHIEF

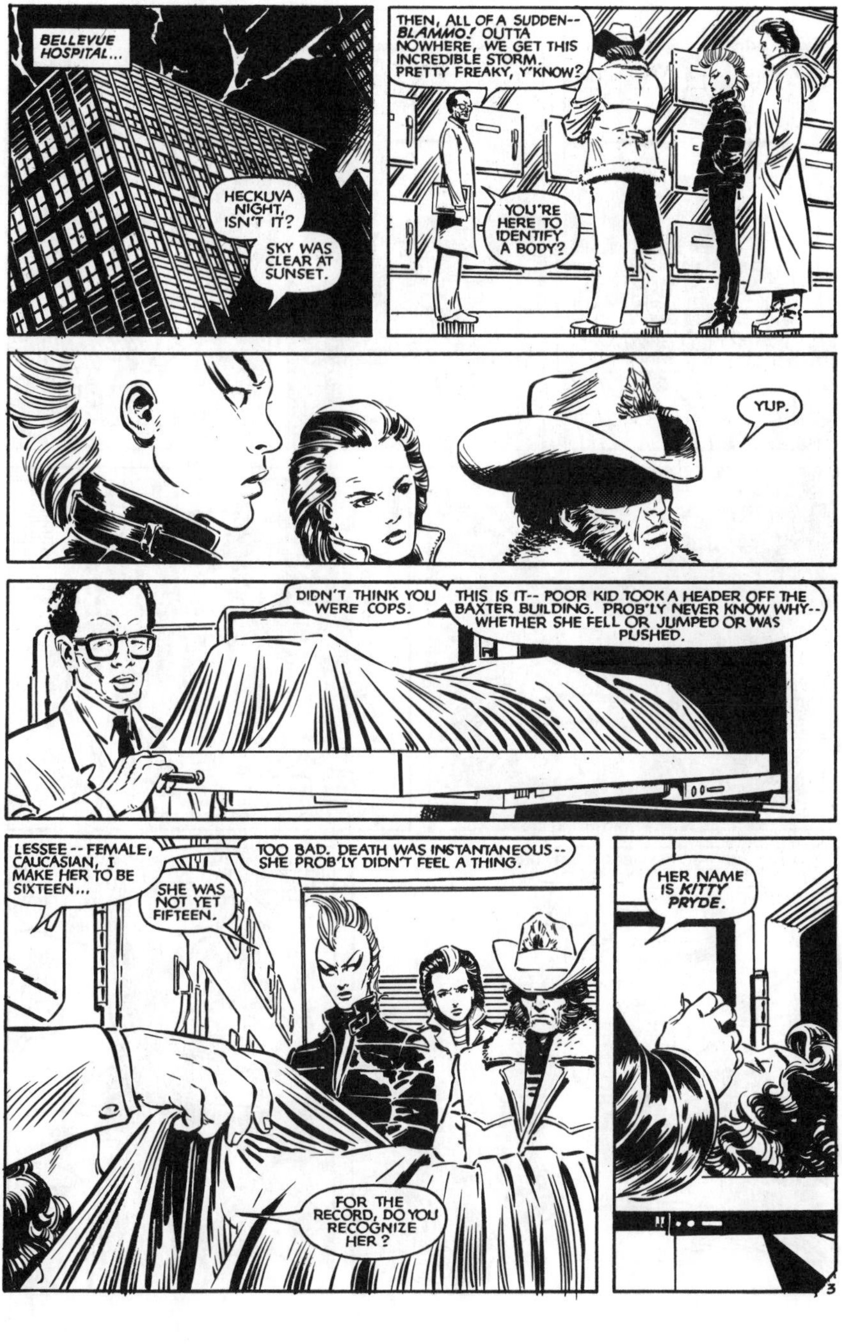

BELLEVUE HOSPITAL...
HECKUVA NIGHT, ISN'T IT?
SKY WAS CLEAR AT SUNSET.
THEN, ALL OF A SUDDEN-- *BLAMMO!* OUTTA NOWHERE, WE GET THIS INCREDIBLE STORM. PRETTY FREAKY, Y'KNOW?
YOU'RE HERE TO IDENTIFY A BODY?
YUP.
DIDN'T THINK YOU WERE COPS.
THIS IS IT-- POOR KID TOOK A HEADER OFF THE BAXTER BUILDING. PROB'LY NEVER KNOW WHY-- WHETHER SHE FELL OR JUMPED OR WAS PUSHED.
LESSEE -- FEMALE, CAUCASIAN, I MAKE HER TO BE SIXTEEN...
SHE WAS NOT YET FIFTEEN.
TOO BAD. DEATH WAS INSTANTANEOUS -- SHE PROB'LY DIDN'T FEEL A THING.
FOR THE RECORD, DO YOU RECOGNIZE HER?
HER NAME IS *KITTY PRYDE*.
3

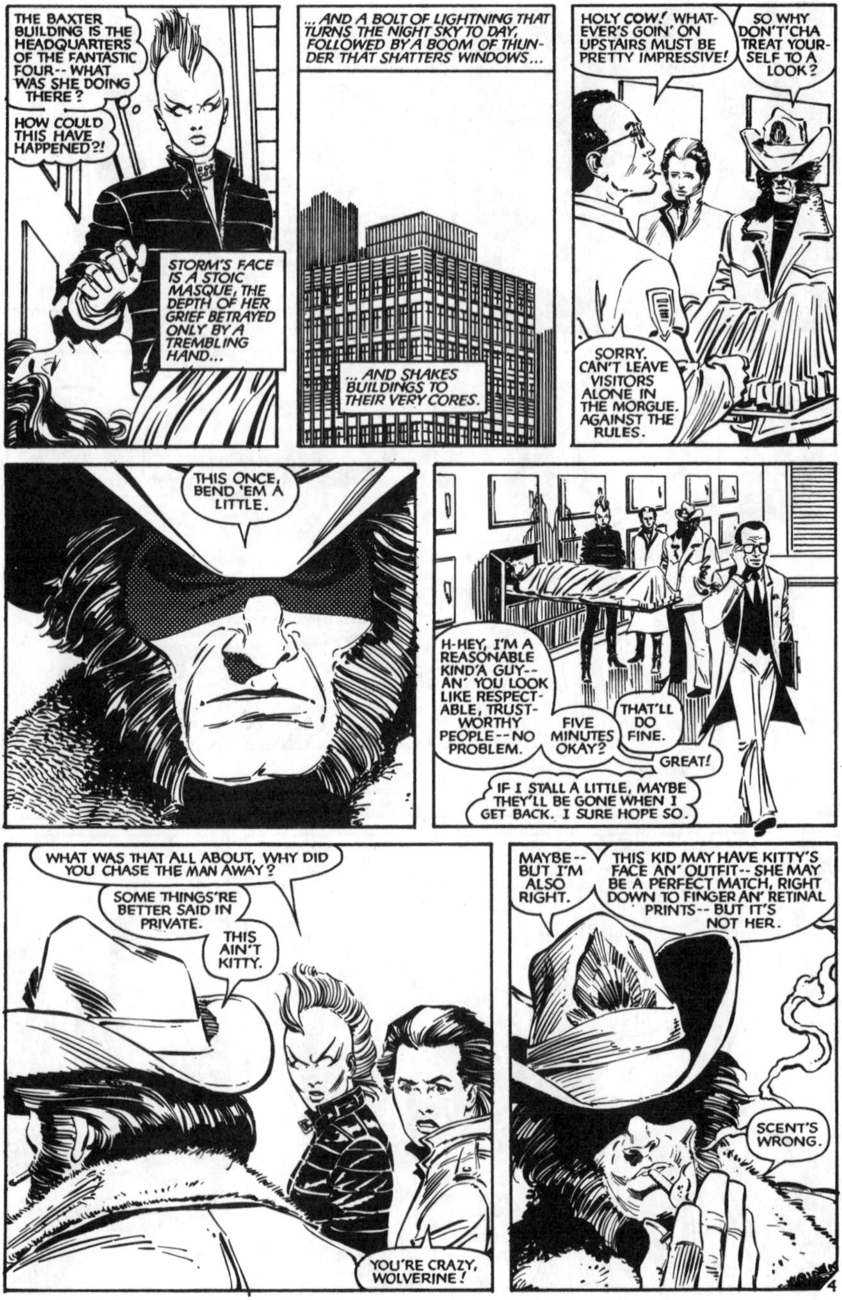
THE BAXTER BUILDING IS THE HEADQUARTERS OF THE FANTASTIC FOUR-- WHAT WAS SHE DOING THERE?
HOW COULD THIS HAVE HAPPENED?!
STORM'S FACE IS A STOIC MASQUE, THE DEPTH OF HER GRIEF BETRAYED ONLY BY A TREMBLING HAND...
...AND A BOLT OF LIGHTNING THAT TURNS THE NIGHT SKY TO DAY, FOLLOWED BY A BOOM OF THUNDER THAT SHATTERS WINDOWS...
...AND SHAKES BUILDINGS TO THEIR VERY CORES.
HOLY COW! WHATEVER'S GOIN' ON UPSTAIRS MUST BE PRETTY IMPRESSIVE!
SO WHY DON'T'CHA TREAT YOURSELF TO A LOOK?
SORRY. CAN'T LEAVE VISITORS ALONE IN THE MORGUE. AGAINST THE RULES.
THIS ONCE, BEND 'EM A LITTLE.
H-HEY, I'M A REASONABLE KIND'A GUY-- AN' YOU LOOK LIKE RESPECTABLE, TRUSTWORTHY PEOPLE--NO PROBLEM.
FIVE MINUTES OKAY?
THAT'LL DO FINE.
GREAT!
IF I STALL A LITTLE, MAYBE THEY'LL BE GONE WHEN I GET BACK. I SURE HOPE SO.
WHAT WAS THAT ALL ABOUT, WHY DID YOU CHASE THE MAN AWAY?
SOME THINGS'RE BETTER SAID IN PRIVATE.
THIS AIN'T KITTY.
YOU'RE CRAZY, WOLVERINE!
MAYBE-- BUT I'M ALSO RIGHT.
THIS KID MAY HAVE KITTY'S FACE AN' OUTFIT-- SHE MAY BE A PERFECT MATCH, RIGHT DOWN TO FINGER AN' RETINAL PRINTS-- BUT IT'S NOT HER.
SCENT'S WRONG.
4

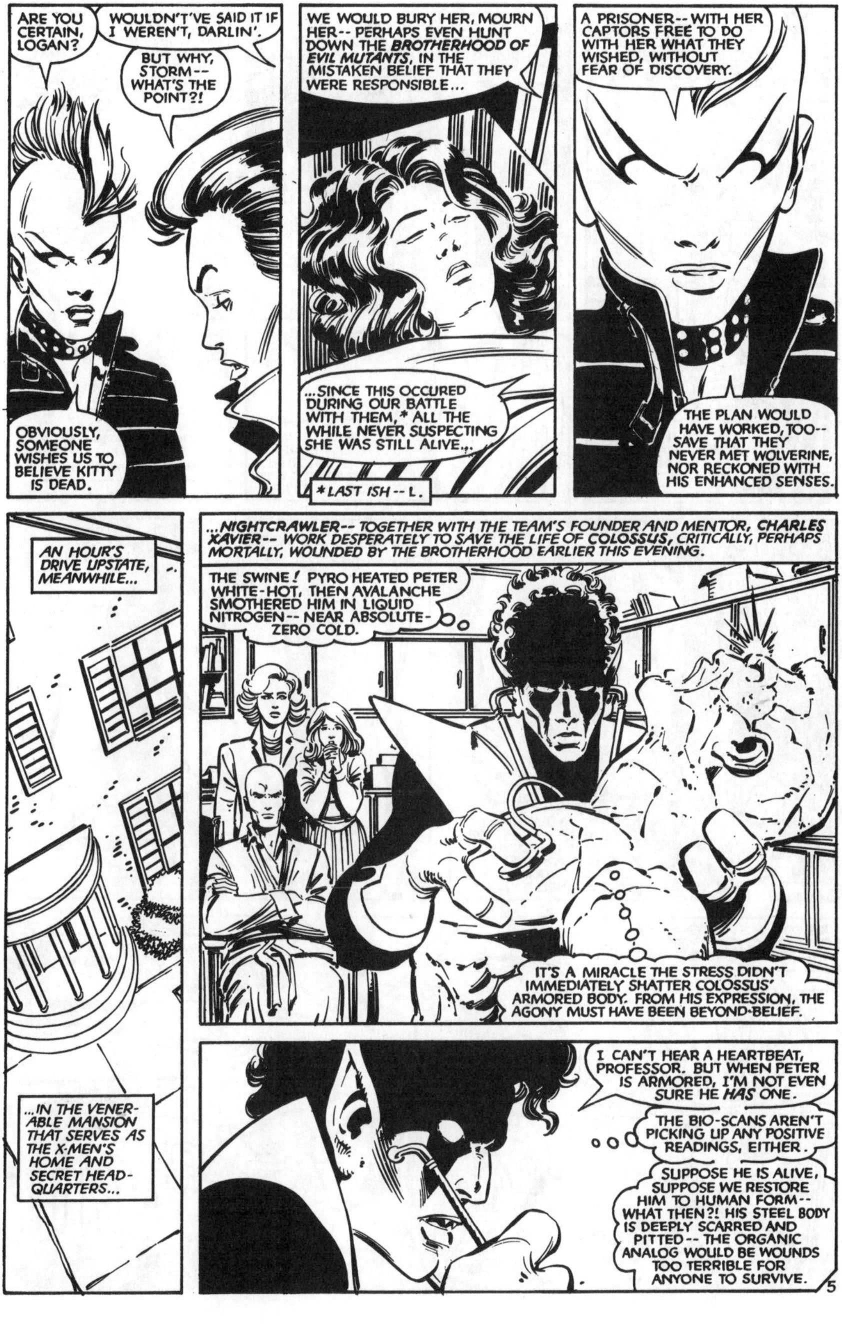
ARE YOU CERTAIN, LOGAN?
WOULDN'T'VE SAID IT IF I WEREN'T, DARLIN'.
BUT WHY, STORM-- WHAT'S THE POINT?!
OBVIOUSLY, SOMEONE WISHES US TO BELIEVE KITTY IS DEAD.
WE WOULD BURY HER, MOURN HER-- PERHAPS EVEN HUNT DOWN THE BROTHERHOOD OF EVIL MUTANTS, IN THE MISTAKEN BELIEF THAT THEY WERE RESPONSIBLE...
...SINCE THIS OCCURED DURING OUR BATTLE WITH THEM,* ALL THE WHILE NEVER SUSPECTING SHE WAS STILL ALIVE...
*LAST ISH -- L.
A PRISONER-- WITH HER CAPTORS FREE TO DO WITH HER WHAT THEY WISHED, WITHOUT FEAR OF DISCOVERY.
THE PLAN WOULD HAVE WORKED, TOO-- SAVE THAT THEY NEVER MET WOLVERINE, NOR RECKONED WITH HIS ENHANCED SENSES.
AN HOUR'S DRIVE UPSTATE, MEANWHILE...
...IN THE VENERABLE MANSION THAT SERVES AS THE X-MEN'S HOME AND SECRET HEADQUARTERS...
...NIGHTCRAWLER-- TOGETHER WITH THE TEAM'S FOUNDER AND MENTOR, CHARLES XAVIER-- WORK DESPERATELY TO SAVE THE LIFE OF COLOSSUS, CRITICALLY, PERHAPS MORTALLY, WOUNDED BY THE BROTHERHOOD EARLIER THIS EVENING.
THE SWINE! PYRO HEATED PETER WHITE-HOT, THEN AVALANCHE SMOTHERED HIM IN LIQUID NITROGEN-- NEAR ABSOLUTE-ZERO COLD.
IT'S A MIRACLE THE STRESS DIDN'T IMMEDIATELY SHATTER COLOSSUS' ARMORED BODY. FROM HIS EXPRESSION, THE AGONY MUST HAVE BEEN BEYOND-BELIEF.
I CAN'T HEAR A HEARTBEAT, PROFESSOR. BUT WHEN PETER IS ARMORED, I'M NOT EVEN SURE HE HAS ONE.
THE BIO-SCANS AREN'T PICKING UP ANY POSITIVE READINGS, EITHER.
SUPPOSE HE IS ALIVE, SUPPOSE WE RESTORE HIM TO HUMAN FORM-- WHAT THEN?! HIS STEEL BODY IS DEEPLY SCARRED AND PITTED-- THE ORGANIC ANALOG WOULD BE WOUNDS TOO TERRIBLE FOR ANYONE TO SURVIVE.

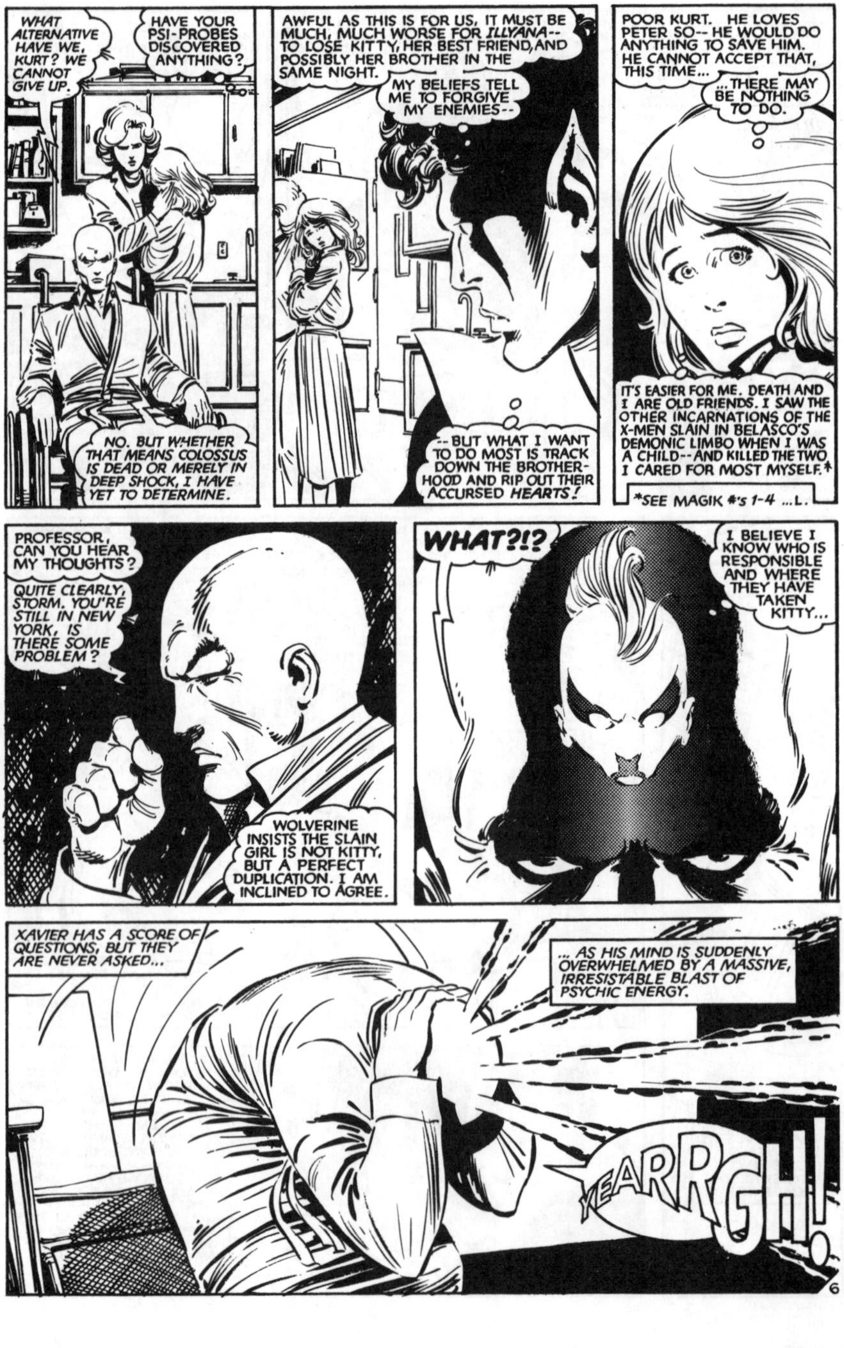
WHAT ALTERNATIVE HAVE WE, KURT? WE CANNOT GIVE UP.
HAVE YOUR PSI-PROBES DISCOVERED ANYTHING?
NO. BUT WHETHER THAT MEANS COLOSSUS IS DEAD OR MERELY IN DEEP SHOCK, I HAVE YET TO DETERMINE.
AWFUL AS THIS IS FOR US, IT MUST BE MUCH, MUCH WORSE FOR ILLYANA-- TO LOSE KITTY, HER BEST FRIEND, AND POSSIBLY HER BROTHER IN THE SAME NIGHT.
MY BELIEFS TELL ME TO FORGIVE MY ENEMIES--
--BUT WHAT I WANT TO DO MOST IS TRACK DOWN THE BROTHER-HOOD AND RIP OUT THEIR ACCURSED HEARTS!
POOR KURT. HE LOVES PETER SO-- HE WOULD DO ANYTHING TO SAVE HIM. HE CANNOT ACCEPT THAT, THIS TIME...
...THERE MAY BE NOTHING TO DO.
IT'S EASIER FOR ME. DEATH AND I ARE OLD FRIENDS. I SAW THE OTHER INCARNATIONS OF THE X-MEN SLAIN IN BELASCO'S DEMONIC LIMBO WHEN I WAS A CHILD--AND KILLED THE TWO I CARED FOR MOST MYSELF.*
*SEE MAGIK #'s 1-4 ...L.
PROFESSOR, CAN YOU HEAR MY THOUGHTS?
QUITE CLEARLY, STORM. YOU'RE STILL IN NEW YORK, IS THERE SOME PROBLEM?
WOLVERINE INSISTS THE SLAIN GIRL IS NOT KITTY, BUT A PERFECT DUPLICATION. I AM INCLINED TO AGREE.
WHAT?!?
I BELIEVE I KNOW WHO IS RESPONSIBLE AND WHERE THEY HAVE TAKEN KITTY...
XAVIER HAS A SCORE OF QUESTIONS, BUT THEY ARE NEVER ASKED...
... AS HIS MIND IS SUDDENLY OVERWHELMED BY A MASSIVE, IRRESISTABLE BLAST OF PSYCHIC ENERGY.
YEARRRGH!

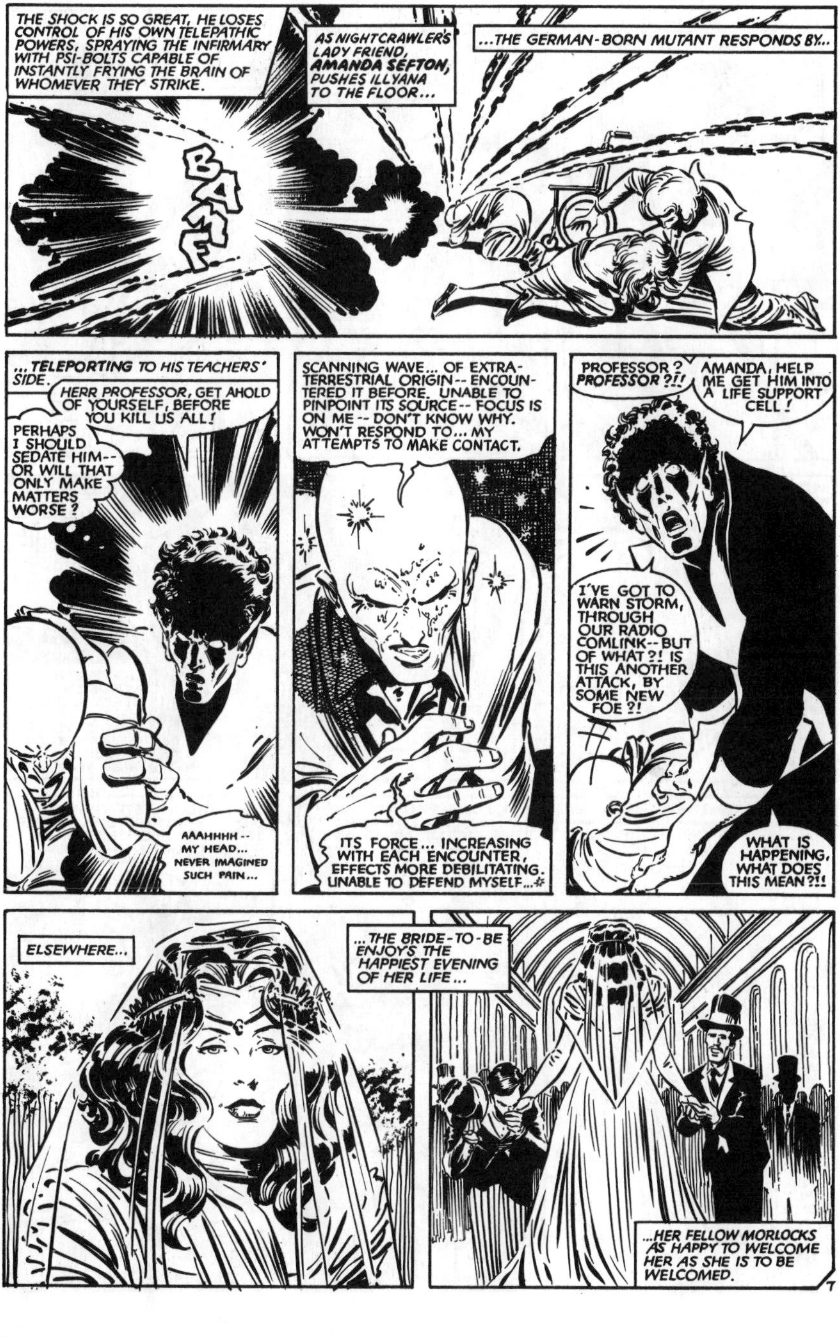
THE SHOCK IS SO GREAT, HE LOSES CONTROL OF HIS OWN TELEPATHIC POWERS, SPRAYING THE INFIRMARY WITH PSI-BOLTS CAPABLE OF INSTANTLY FRYING THE BRAIN OF WHOMEVER THEY STRIKE.
AS NIGHTCRAWLER'S LADY FRIEND, AMANDA SEFTON, PUSHES ILLYANA TO THE FLOOR...
...THE GERMAN-BORN MUTANT RESPONDS BY...
BAMF
...TELEPORTING TO HIS TEACHERS' SIDE.
HERR PROFESSOR, GET AHOLD OF YOURSELF, BEFORE YOU KILL US ALL!
PERHAPS I SHOULD SEDATE HIM-- OR WILL THAT ONLY MAKE MATTERS WORSE?
AAAHHHH-- MY HEAD... NEVER IMAGINED SUCH PAIN...
SCANNING WAVE... OF EXTRA-TERRESTRIAL ORIGIN-- ENCOUNTERED IT BEFORE. UNABLE TO PINPOINT ITS SOURCE-- FOCUS IS ON ME-- DON'T KNOW WHY. WON'T RESPOND TO... MY ATTEMPTS TO MAKE CONTACT.
ITS FORCE... INCREASING WITH EACH ENCOUNTER, EFFECTS MORE DEBILITATING. UNABLE TO DEFEND MYSELF...
PROFESSOR? PROFESSOR?!!
AMANDA, HELP ME GET HIM INTO A LIFE SUPPORT CELL!
I'VE GOT TO WARN STORM, THROUGH OUR RADIO COMLINK-- BUT OF WHAT?! IS THIS ANOTHER ATTACK, BY SOME NEW FOE?!
WHAT IS HAPPENING, WHAT DOES THIS MEAN?!!
ELSEWHERE...
...THE BRIDE-TO-BE ENJOYS THE HAPPIEST EVENING OF HER LIFE...
...HER FELLOW MORLOCKS AS HAPPY TO WELCOME HER AS SHE IS TO BE WELCOMED.

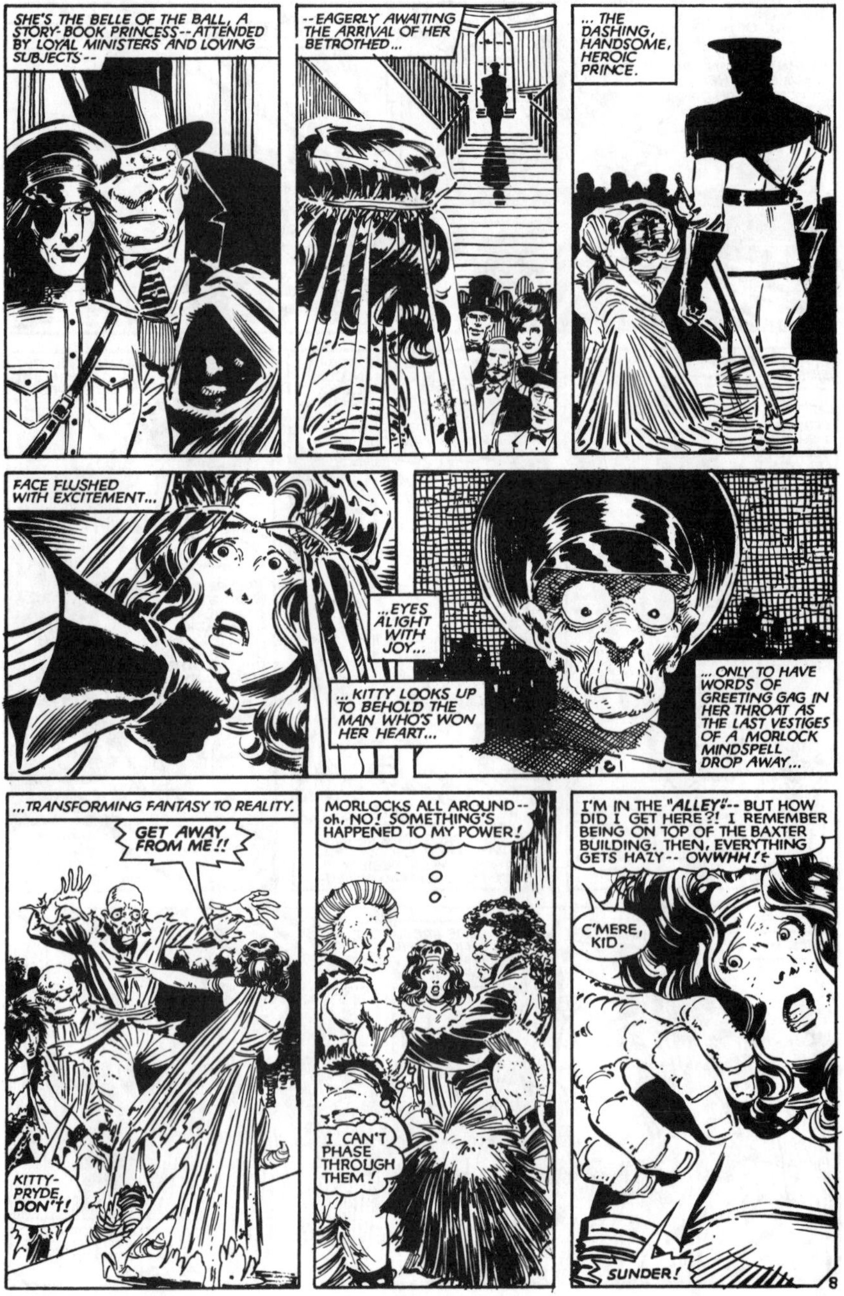
SHE'S THE BELLE OF THE BALL, A STORY-BOOK PRINCESS--ATTENDED BY LOYAL MINISTERS AND LOVING SUBJECTS--
--EAGERLY AWAITING THE ARRIVAL OF HER BETROTHED...
... THE DASHING, HANDSOME, HEROIC PRINCE.
FACE FLUSHED WITH EXCITEMENT...
...EYES ALIGHT WITH JOY...
...KITTY LOOKS UP TO BEHOLD THE MAN WHO'S WON HER HEART...
... ONLY TO HAVE WORDS OF GREETING GAG IN HER THROAT AS THE LAST VESTIGES OF A MORLOCK MINDSPELL DROP AWAY...
...TRANSFORMING FANTASY TO REALITY.
GET AWAY FROM ME!!
KITTY-PRYDE, DON'T!
MORLOCKS ALL AROUND-- oh, NO! SOMETHING'S HAPPENED TO MY POWER!
I CAN'T PHASE THROUGH THEM!
I'M IN THE "ALLEY"-- BUT HOW DID I GET HERE?! I REMEMBER BEING ON TOP OF THE BAXTER BUILDING. THEN, EVERYTHING GETS HAZY-- OWWHH!
C'MERE, KID.
SUNDER!

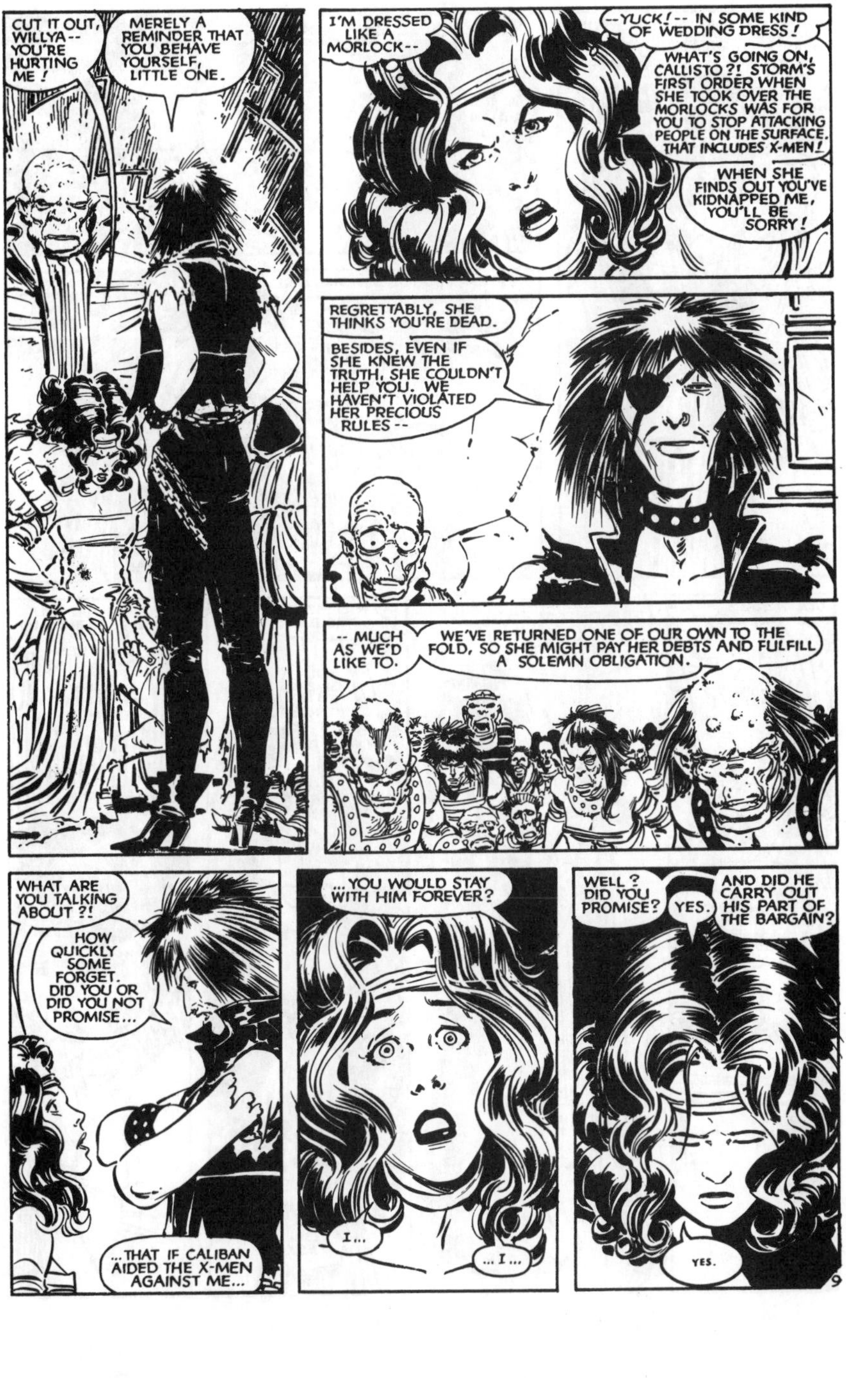

CUT IT OUT, WILLYA-- YOU'RE HURTING ME!
MERELY A REMINDER THAT YOU BEHAVE YOURSELF, LITTLE ONE.
I'M DRESSED LIKE A MORLOCK--
--YUCK!-- IN SOME KIND OF WEDDING DRESS!
WHAT'S GOING ON, CALLISTO?! STORM'S FIRST ORDER WHEN SHE TOOK OVER THE MORLOCKS WAS FOR YOU TO STOP ATTACKING PEOPLE ON THE SURFACE. THAT INCLUDES X-MEN!
WHEN SHE FINDS OUT YOU'VE KIDNAPPED ME, YOU'LL BE SORRY!
REGRETTABLY, SHE THINKS YOU'RE DEAD.
BESIDES, EVEN IF SHE KNEW THE TRUTH, SHE COULDN'T HELP YOU. WE HAVEN'T VIOLATED HER PRECIOUS RULES --
-- MUCH AS WE'D LIKE TO.
WE'VE RETURNED ONE OF OUR OWN TO THE FOLD, SO SHE MIGHT PAY HER DEBTS AND FULFILL A SOLEMN OBLIGATION.
WHAT ARE YOU TALKING ABOUT?!
HOW QUICKLY SOME FORGET. DID YOU OR DID YOU NOT PROMISE...
...THAT IF CALIBAN AIDED THE X-MEN AGAINST ME...
...YOU WOULD STAY WITH HIM FOREVER?
I...
...I...
WELL? DID YOU PROMISE?
YES.
AND DID HE CARRY OUT HIS PART OF THE BARGAIN?
YES.

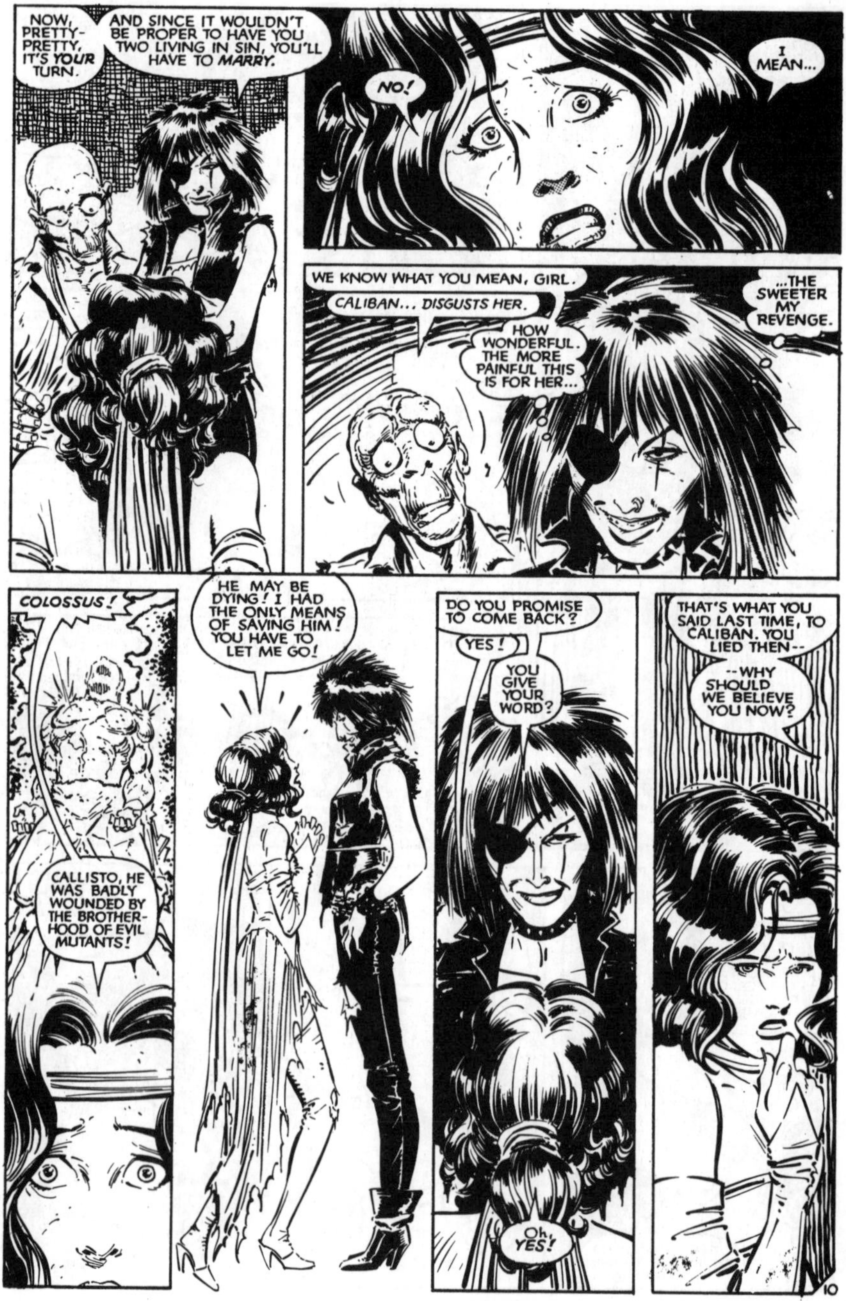
NOW, PRETTY-PRETTY, IT'S YOUR TURN.
AND SINCE IT WOULDN'T BE PROPER TO HAVE YOU TWO LIVING IN SIN, YOU'LL HAVE TO MARRY.
NO!
I MEAN...
WE KNOW WHAT YOU MEAN, GIRL.
CALIBAN... DISGUSTS HER.
HOW WONDERFUL. THE MORE PAINFUL THIS IS FOR HER...
...THE SWEETER MY REVENGE.
COLOSSUS!
CALLISTO, HE WAS BADLY WOUNDED BY THE BROTHER-HOOD OF EVIL MUTANTS!
HE MAY BE DYING! I HAD THE ONLY MEANS OF SAVING HIM! YOU HAVE TO LET ME GO!
DO YOU PROMISE TO COME BACK?
YES!
YOU GIVE YOUR WORD?
Oh, YES!
THAT'S WHAT YOU SAID LAST TIME, TO CALIBAN. YOU LIED THEN--
--WHY SHOULD WE BELIEVE YOU NOW?

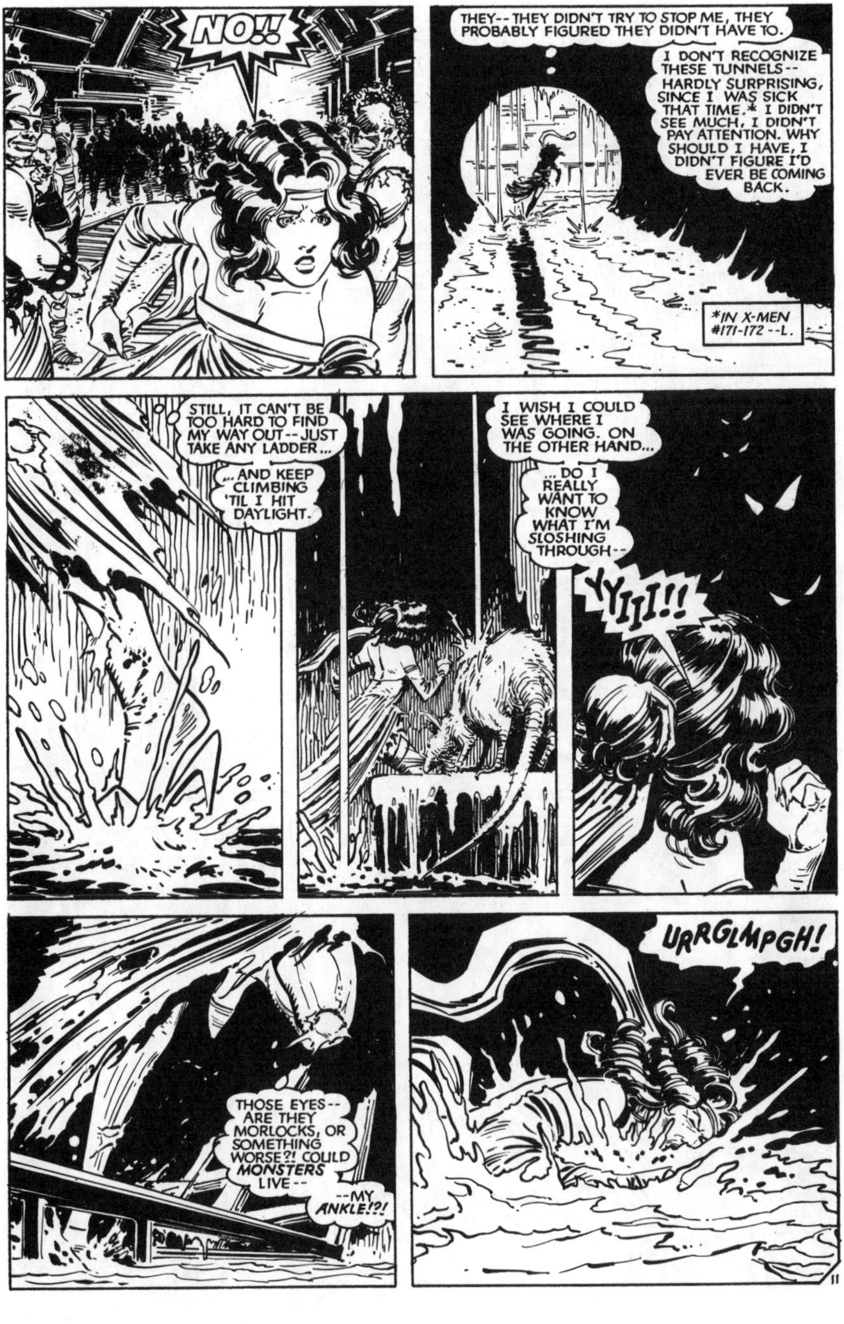
NO!!
THEY-- THEY DIDN'T TRY TO STOP ME, THEY PROBABLY FIGURED THEY DIDN'T HAVE TO.
I DON'T RECOGNIZE THESE TUNNELS-- HARDLY SURPRISING, SINCE I WAS SICK THAT TIME.* I DIDN'T SEE MUCH, I DIDN'T PAY ATTENTION. WHY SHOULD I HAVE, I DIDN'T FIGURE I'D EVER BE COMING BACK.
*IN X-MEN #171-172 --L.
STILL, IT CAN'T BE TOO HARD TO FIND MY WAY OUT-- JUST TAKE ANY LADDER...
...AND KEEP CLIMBING 'TIL I HIT DAYLIGHT.
I WISH I COULD SEE WHERE I WAS GOING. ON THE OTHER HAND...
...DO I REALLY WANT TO KNOW WHAT I'M SLOSHING THROUGH--
YYIII!!
THOSE EYES-- ARE THEY MORLOCKS, OR SOMETHING WORSE?! COULD MONSTERS LIVE--
--MY ANKLE!?!
URRGLMPGH!

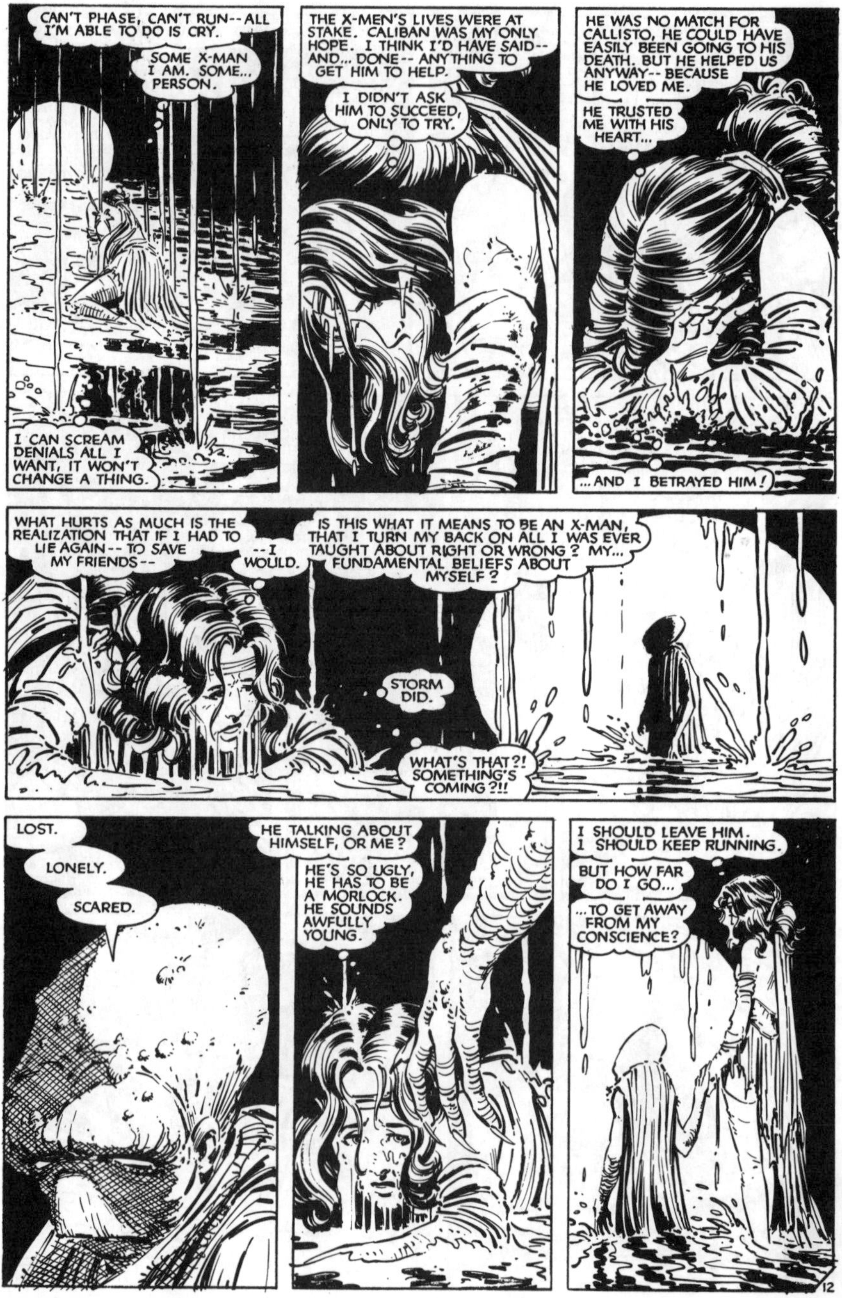
CAN'T PHASE, CAN'T RUN--ALL I'M ABLE TO DO IS CRY.
SOME X-MAN I AM. SOME... PERSON.
I CAN SCREAM DENIALS ALL I WANT, IT WON'T CHANGE A THING.
THE X-MEN'S LIVES WERE AT STAKE. CALIBAN WAS MY ONLY HOPE. I THINK I'D HAVE SAID--AND... DONE--ANYTHING TO GET HIM TO HELP.
I DIDN'T ASK HIM TO SUCCEED, ONLY TO TRY.
HE WAS NO MATCH FOR CALLISTO, HE COULD HAVE EASILY BEEN GOING TO HIS DEATH. BUT HE HELPED US ANYWAY--BECAUSE HE LOVED ME.
HE TRUSTED ME WITH HIS HEART...
...AND I BETRAYED HIM!
WHAT HURTS AS MUCH IS THE REALIZATION THAT IF I HAD TO LIE AGAIN--TO SAVE MY FRIENDS--
--I WOULD.
IS THIS WHAT IT MEANS TO BE AN X-MAN, THAT I TURN MY BACK ON ALL I WAS EVER TAUGHT ABOUT RIGHT OR WRONG? MY... FUNDAMENTAL BELIEFS ABOUT MYSELF?
STORM DID.
WHAT'S THAT?! SOMETHING'S COMING?!!
LOST.
LONELY.
SCARED.
HE TALKING ABOUT HIMSELF, OR ME?
HE'S SO UGLY, HE HAS TO BE A MORLOCK. HE SOUNDS AWFULLY YOUNG.
I SHOULD LEAVE HIM. I SHOULD KEEP RUNNING.
BUT HOW FAR DO I GO...
...TO GET AWAY FROM MY CONSCIENCE?
12

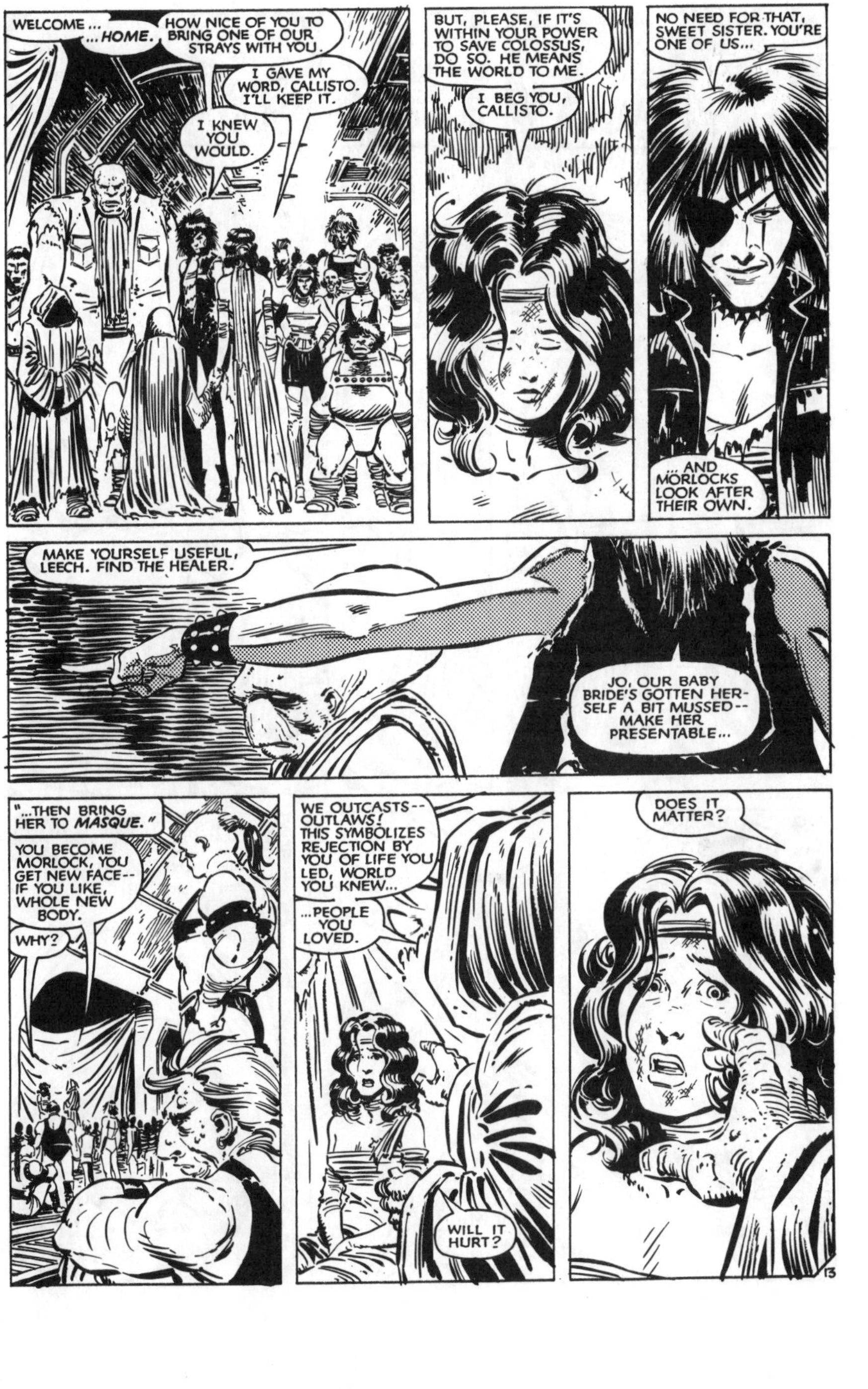
WELCOME ...
... HOME.
HOW NICE OF YOU TO BRING ONE OF OUR STRAYS WITH YOU.
I GAVE MY WORD, CALLISTO. I'LL KEEP IT.
I KNEW YOU WOULD.
BUT, PLEASE, IF IT'S WITHIN YOUR POWER TO SAVE COLOSSUS, DO SO. HE MEANS THE WORLD TO ME.
I BEG YOU, CALLISTO.
NO NEED FOR THAT, SWEET SISTER. YOU'RE ONE OF US...
... AND MORLOCKS LOOK AFTER THEIR OWN.
MAKE YOURSELF USEFUL, LEECH. FIND THE HEALER.
JO, OUR BABY BRIDE'S GOTTEN HERSELF A BIT MUSSED-- MAKE HER PRESENTABLE...
"...THEN BRING HER TO MASQUE."
YOU BECOME MORLOCK, YOU GET NEW FACE-- IF YOU LIKE, WHOLE NEW BODY.
WHY?
WE OUTCASTS-- OUTLAWS! THIS SYMBOLIZES REJECTION BY YOU OF LIFE YOU LED, WORLD YOU KNEW...
...PEOPLE YOU LOVED.
WILL IT HURT?
DOES IT MATTER?

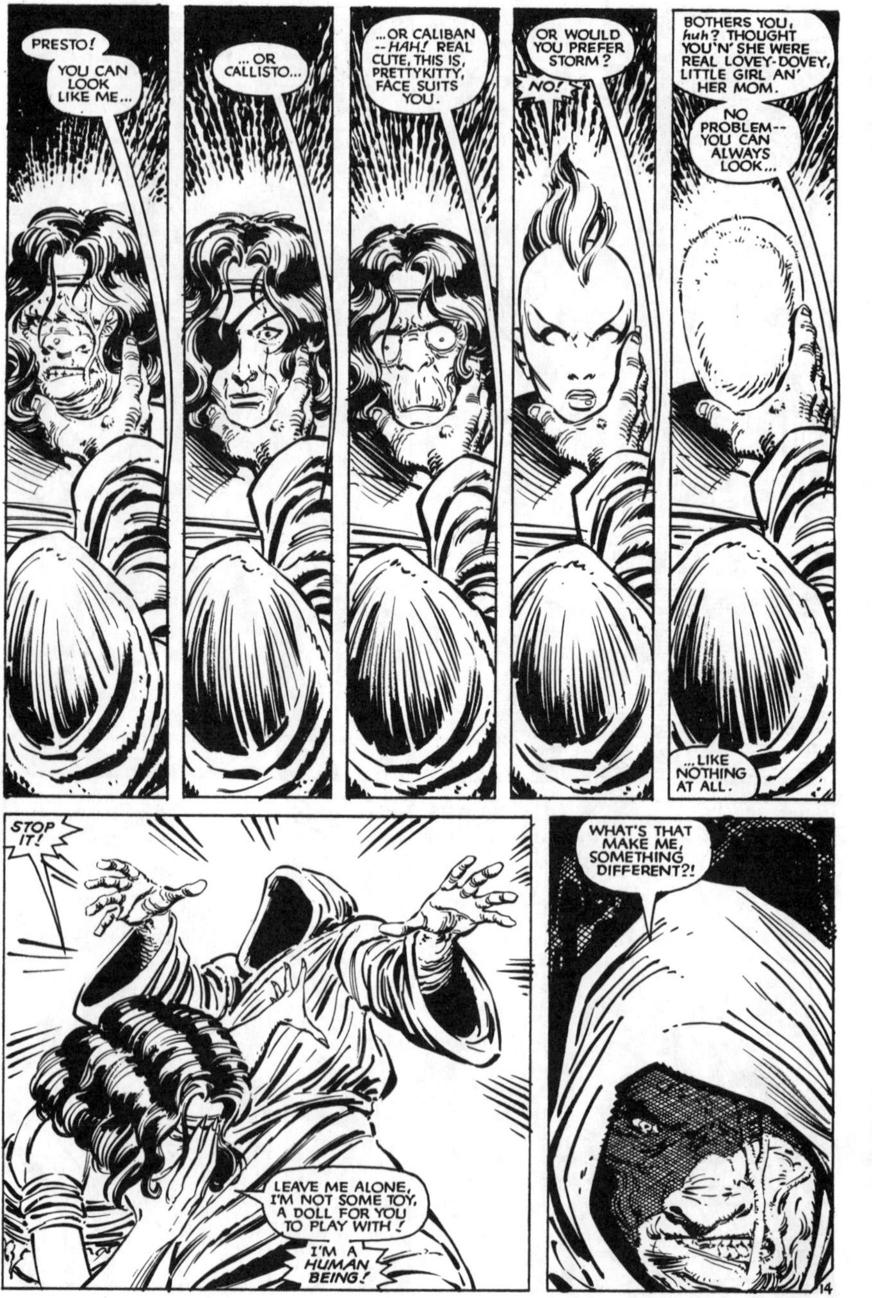
PRESTO!
YOU CAN LOOK LIKE ME...
...OR CALLISTO...
...OR CALIBAN --HAH! REAL CUTE, THIS IS, PRETTYKITTY, FACE SUITS YOU.
OR WOULD YOU PREFER STORM?
NO!
BOTHERS YOU, huh? THOUGHT YOU'N' SHE WERE REAL LOVEY-DOVEY, LITTLE GIRL AN' HER MOM.
NO PROBLEM-- YOU CAN ALWAYS LOOK...
...LIKE NOTHING AT ALL.
STOP IT!
LEAVE ME ALONE, I'M NOT SOME TOY, A DOLL FOR YOU TO PLAY WITH!
I'M A HUMAN BEING!
WHAT'S THAT MAKE ME, SOMETHING DIFFERENT?!

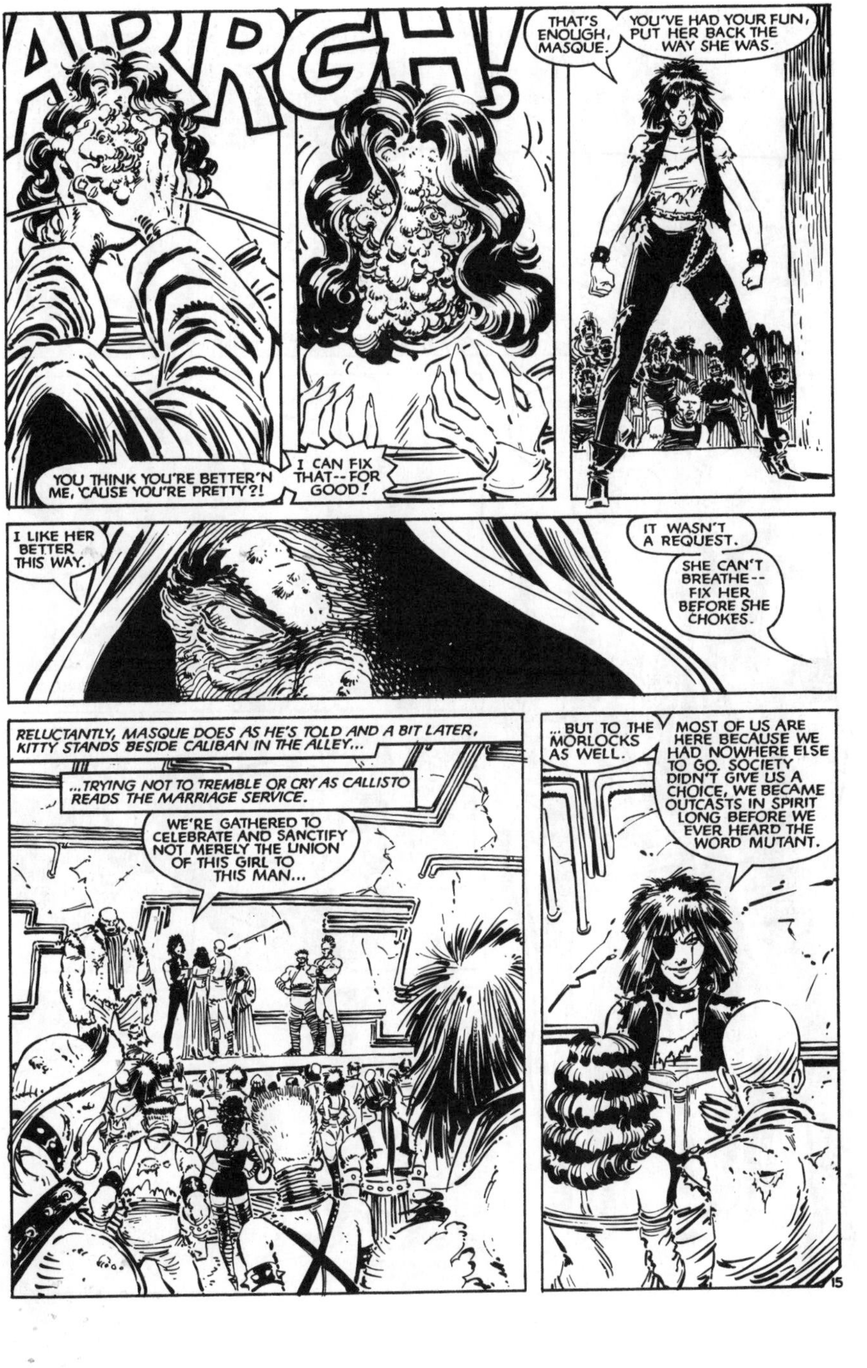
ARRGH!
YOU THINK YOU'RE BETTER'N ME, 'CAUSE YOU'RE PRETTY?!
I CAN FIX THAT--FOR GOOD!
THAT'S ENOUGH, MASQUE.
YOU'VE HAD YOUR FUN, PUT HER BACK THE WAY SHE WAS.
I LIKE HER BETTER THIS WAY.
IT WASN'T A REQUEST.
SHE CAN'T BREATHE--FIX HER BEFORE SHE CHOKES.
RELUCTANTLY, MASQUE DOES AS HE'S TOLD AND A BIT LATER, KITTY STANDS BESIDE CALIBAN IN THE ALLEY...
...TRYING NOT TO TREMBLE OR CRY AS CALLISTO READS THE MARRIAGE SERVICE.
WE'RE GATHERED TO CELEBRATE AND SANCTIFY NOT MERELY THE UNION OF THIS GIRL TO THIS MAN...
...BUT TO THE MORLOCKS AS WELL.
MOST OF US ARE HERE BECAUSE WE HAD NOWHERE ELSE TO GO. SOCIETY DIDN'T GIVE US A CHOICE, WE BECAME OUTCASTS IN SPIRIT LONG BEFORE WE EVER HEARD THE WORD MUTANT.

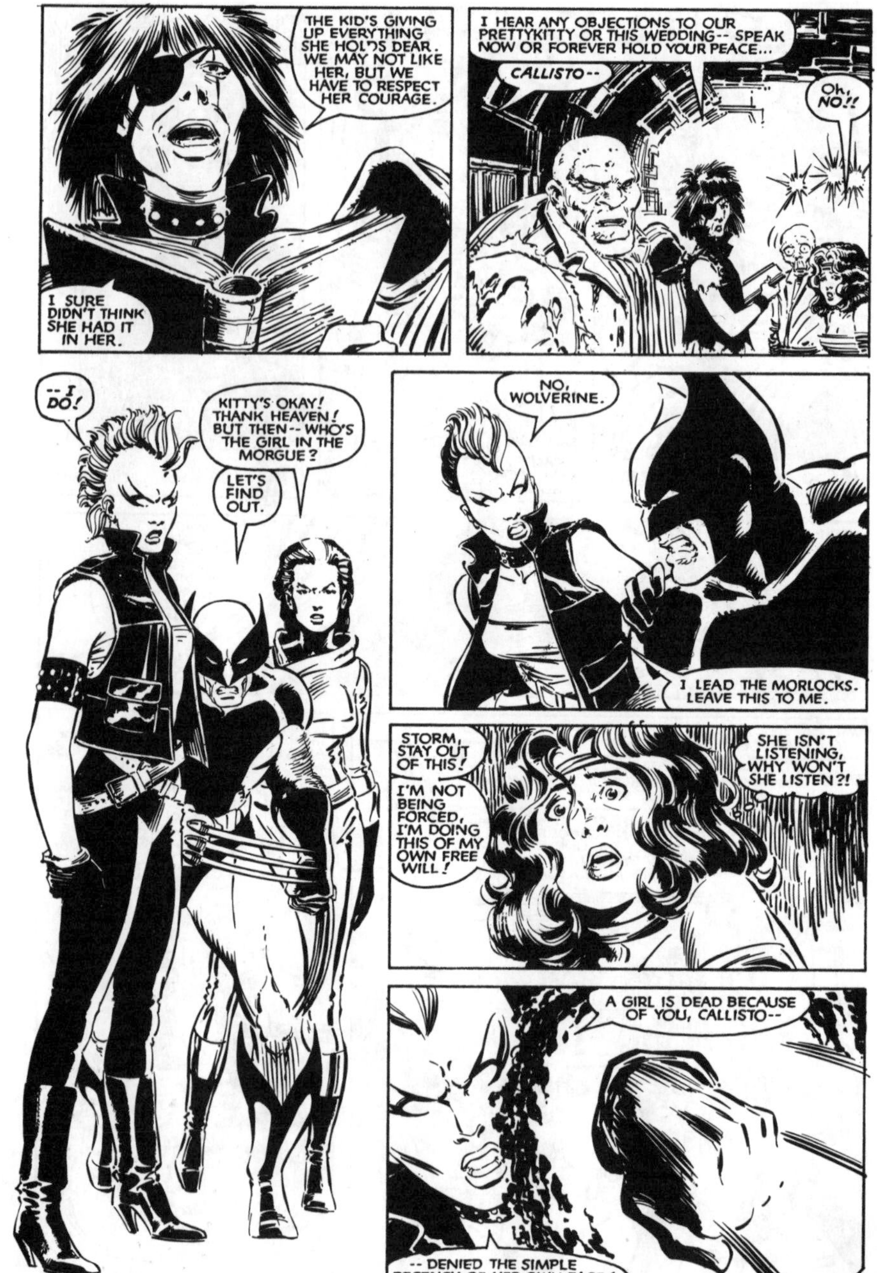
THE KID'S GIVING UP EVERYTHING SHE HOLDS DEAR. WE MAY NOT LIKE HER, BUT WE HAVE TO RESPECT HER COURAGE.
I SURE DIDN'T THINK SHE HAD IT IN HER.
I HEAR ANY OBJECTIONS TO OUR PRETTYKITTY OR THIS WEDDING-- SPEAK NOW OR FOREVER HOLD YOUR PEACE...
CALLISTO--
Oh, NO!!
--I DO!
KITTY'S OKAY! THANK HEAVEN! BUT THEN--WHO'S THE GIRL IN THE MORGUE?
LET'S FIND OUT.
NO, WOLVERINE.
I LEAD THE MORLOCKS. LEAVE THIS TO ME.
STORM, STAY OUT OF THIS!
I'M NOT BEING FORCED, I'M DOING THIS OF MY OWN FREE WILL!
SHE ISN'T LISTENING, WHY WON'T SHE LISTEN?!
A GIRL IS DEAD BECAUSE OF YOU, CALLISTO--
--DENIED THE SIMPLE DECENCY OF HER OWN FACE!

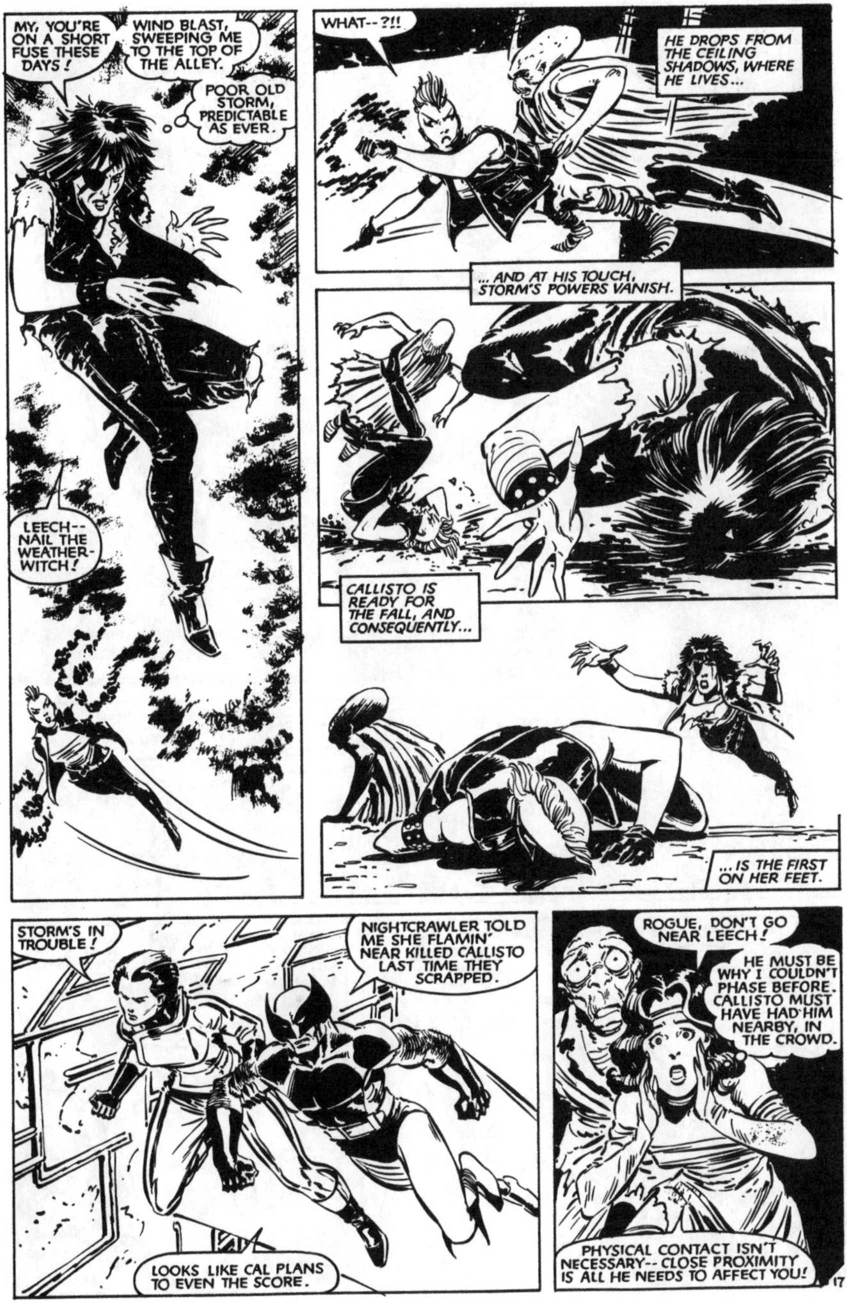
MY, YOU'RE ON A SHORT FUSE THESE DAYS!
WIND BLAST, SWEEPING ME TO THE TOP OF THE ALLEY.
POOR OLD STORM, PREDICTABLE AS EVER.
LEECH-- NAIL THE WEATHER-WITCH!
WHAT--?!!
HE DROPS FROM THE CEILING SHADOWS, WHERE HE LIVES...
...AND AT HIS TOUCH, STORM'S POWERS VANISH.
CALLISTO IS READY FOR THE FALL, AND CONSEQUENTLY...
...IS THE FIRST ON HER FEET.
STORM'S IN TROUBLE!
NIGHTCRAWLER TOLD ME SHE FLAMIN' NEAR KILLED CALLISTO LAST TIME THEY SCRAPPED.
LOOKS LIKE CAL PLANS TO EVEN THE SCORE.
ROGUE, DON'T GO NEAR LEECH!
HE MUST BE WHY I COULDN'T PHASE BEFORE. CALLISTO MUST HAVE HAD HIM NEARBY, IN THE CROWD.
PHYSICAL CONTACT ISN'T NECESSARY-- CLOSE PROXIMITY IS ALL HE NEEDS TO AFFECT YOU!

UNFORTUNATELY...

OWW!

BEIN' INVULNERABLE SPOILED ME. AH'D FORGOTTEN WHAT IT WAS LIKE T'HURT MYSELF.

I WANT WHAT'S MINE...

... BY RIGHT!

I NEEDED NO POWERS TO BEAT YOU BEFORE, CALLISTO. AND I WAS A GENTLER WOMAN THEN.

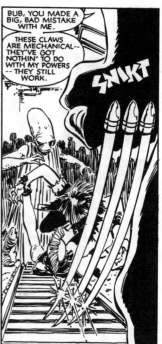

BUB, YOU MADE A BIG, BAD MISTAKE WITH ME.

THESE CLAWS ARE MECHANICAL-- THEY'VE GOT NOTHIN' TO DO WITH MY POWERS -- THEY STILL WORK.

SNIKT

WHAT SHOULD WE DO?

CALLISTO NEEDS OUR HELP!

NO, THIS IS A LEADERSHIP DUEL, SHE'S ON HER OWN.

WHAT ABOUT THE RUNT?

WE GET TOO CLOSE, LEECH'LL ZAP OUR POWERS, WE WON'T STAND A CHANCE.

NEVER LIKED THAT MISERABLE BUGGER ANYWAY.

WOLVERINE -- LOGAN -- SHEATHE YOUR CLAWS!!

WHY'RE YOU GIVIN' ME GRIEF, PUN'KIN? WE'VE COME TO RESCUE YOU?

DID YOU EVER CONSIDER ASKING IF I WANTED TO BE RESCUED?!

OR IS THIS JUST A CONVENIENT EXCUSE...

...TO BASH IN SOME SKULLS?!

18

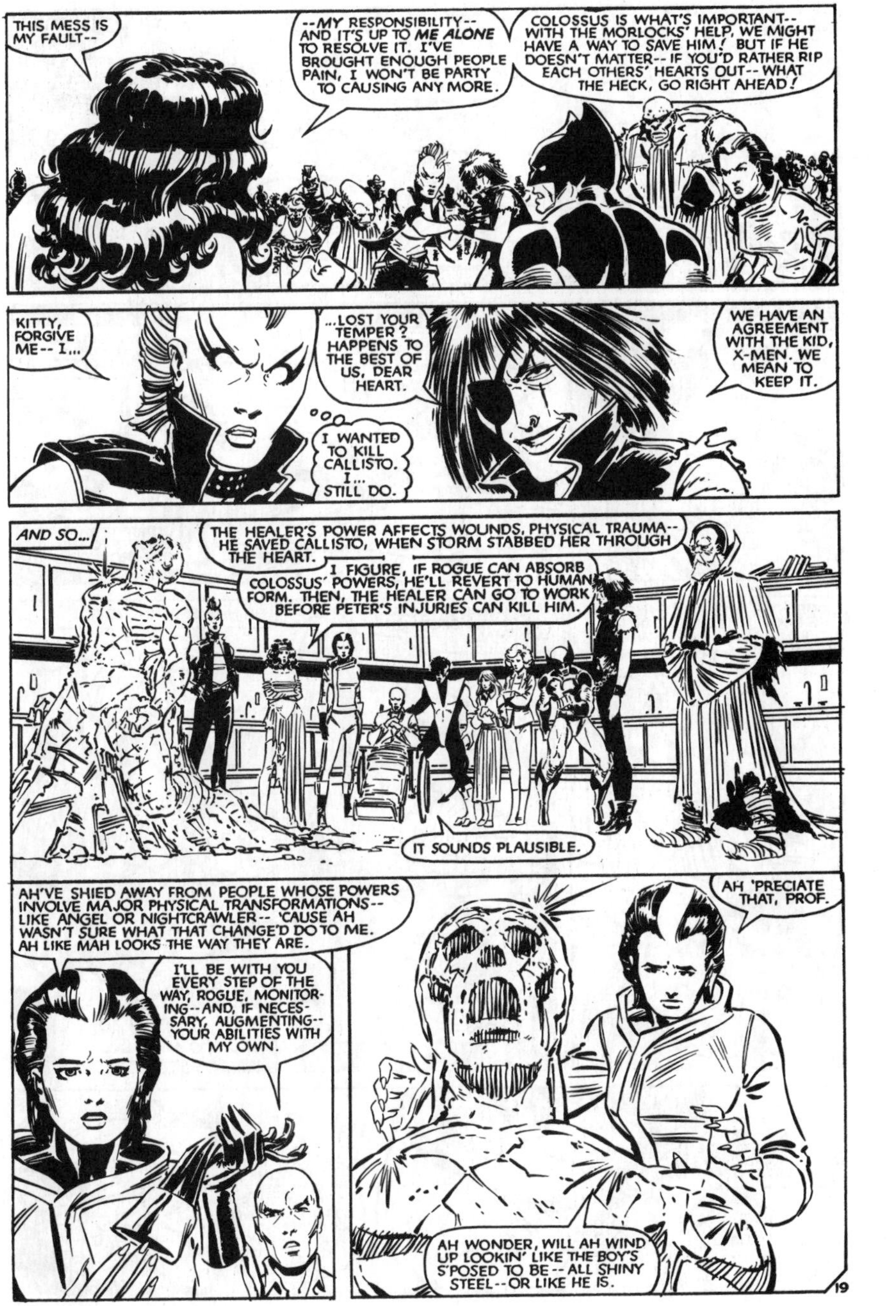
THIS MESS IS MY FAULT--
--MY RESPONSIBILITY-- AND IT'S UP TO ME ALONE TO RESOLVE IT. I'VE BROUGHT ENOUGH PEOPLE PAIN, I WON'T BE PARTY TO CAUSING ANY MORE.
COLOSSUS IS WHAT'S IMPORTANT-- WITH THE MORLOCKS' HELP, WE MIGHT HAVE A WAY TO SAVE HIM! BUT IF HE DOESN'T MATTER-- IF YOU'D RATHER RIP EACH OTHERS' HEARTS OUT-- WHAT THE HECK, GO RIGHT AHEAD!
KITTY, FORGIVE ME-- I...
I WANTED TO KILL CALLISTO. I... STILL DO.
...LOST YOUR TEMPER? HAPPENS TO THE BEST OF US, DEAR HEART.
WE HAVE AN AGREEMENT WITH THE KID, X-MEN. WE MEAN TO KEEP IT.
AND SO...
THE HEALER'S POWER AFFECTS WOUNDS, PHYSICAL TRAUMA-- HE SAVED CALLISTO, WHEN STORM STABBED HER THROUGH THE HEART.
I FIGURE, IF ROGUE CAN ABSORB COLOSSUS' POWERS, HE'LL REVERT TO HUMAN FORM. THEN, THE HEALER CAN GO TO WORK BEFORE PETER'S INJURIES CAN KILL HIM.
IT SOUNDS PLAUSIBLE.
AH'VE SHIED AWAY FROM PEOPLE WHOSE POWERS INVOLVE MAJOR PHYSICAL TRANSFORMATIONS-- LIKE ANGEL OR NIGHTCRAWLER-- 'CAUSE AH WASN'T SURE WHAT THAT CHANGE'D DO TO ME. AH LIKE MAH LOOKS THE WAY THEY ARE.
I'LL BE WITH YOU EVERY STEP OF THE WAY, ROGUE, MONITORING--AND, IF NECESSARY, AUGMENTING-- YOUR ABILITIES WITH MY OWN.
AH 'PRECIATE THAT, PROF.
AH WONDER, WILL AH WIND UP LOOKIN' LIKE THE BOY'S S'POSED TO BE-- ALL SHINY STEEL--OR LIKE HE IS.
19

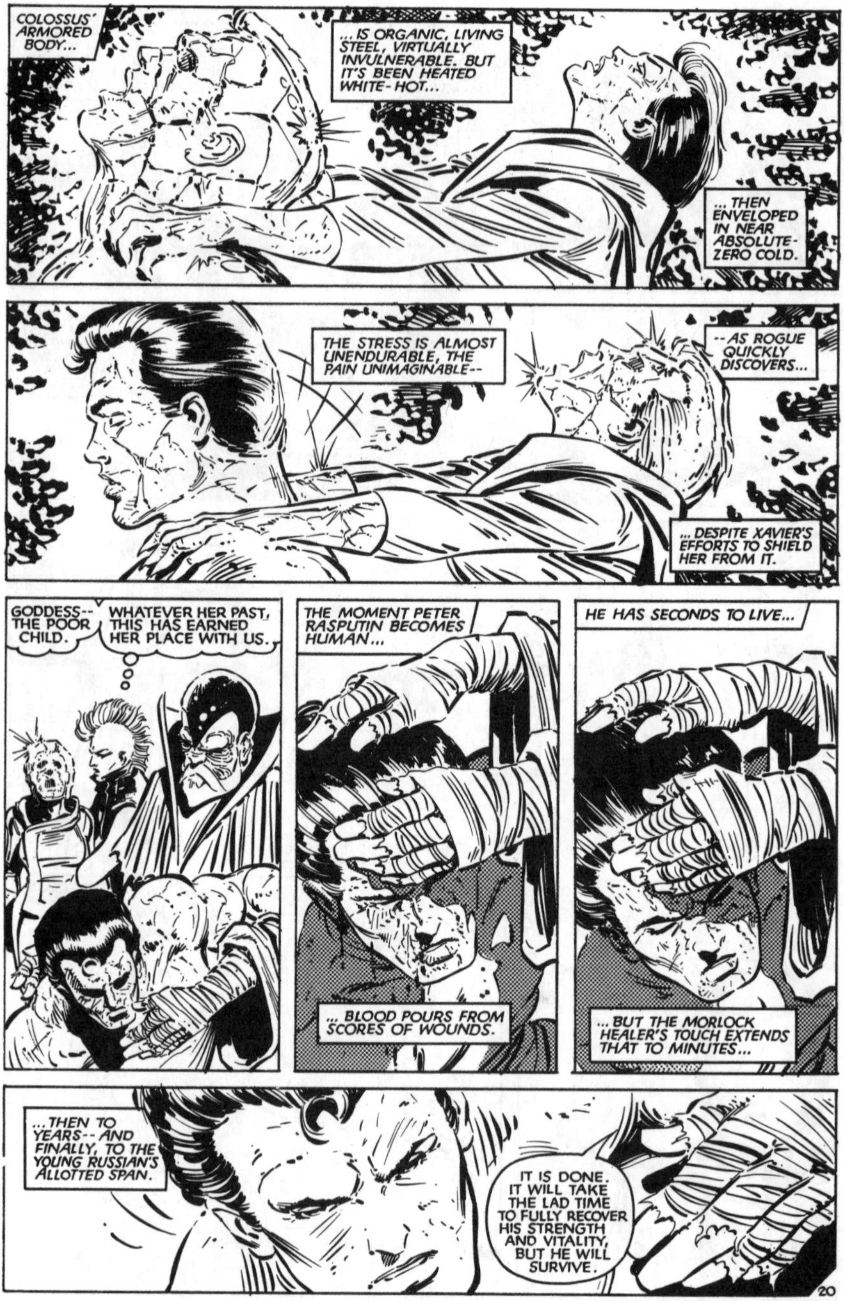

COLOSSUS' ARMORED BODY...
...IS ORGANIC, LIVING STEEL, VIRTUALLY INVULNERABLE. BUT IT'S BEEN HEATED WHITE-HOT...
...THEN ENVELOPED IN NEAR ABSOLUTE-ZERO COLD.
THE STRESS IS ALMOST UNENDURABLE, THE PAIN UNIMAGINABLE--
--AS ROGUE QUICKLY DISCOVERS...
...DESPITE XAVIER'S EFFORTS TO SHIELD HER FROM IT.
GODDESS-- THE POOR CHILD.
WHATEVER HER PAST, THIS HAS EARNED HER PLACE WITH US.
THE MOMENT PETER RASPUTIN BECOMES HUMAN...
...BLOOD POURS FROM SCORES OF WOUNDS.
HE HAS SECONDS TO LIVE...
...BUT THE MORLOCK HEALER'S TOUCH EXTENDS THAT TO MINUTES...
...THEN TO YEARS-- AND FINALLY, TO THE YOUNG RUSSIAN'S ALLOTTED SPAN.
IT IS DONE. IT WILL TAKE THE LAD TIME TO FULLY RECOVER HIS STRENGTH AND VITALITY, BUT HE WILL SURVIVE.

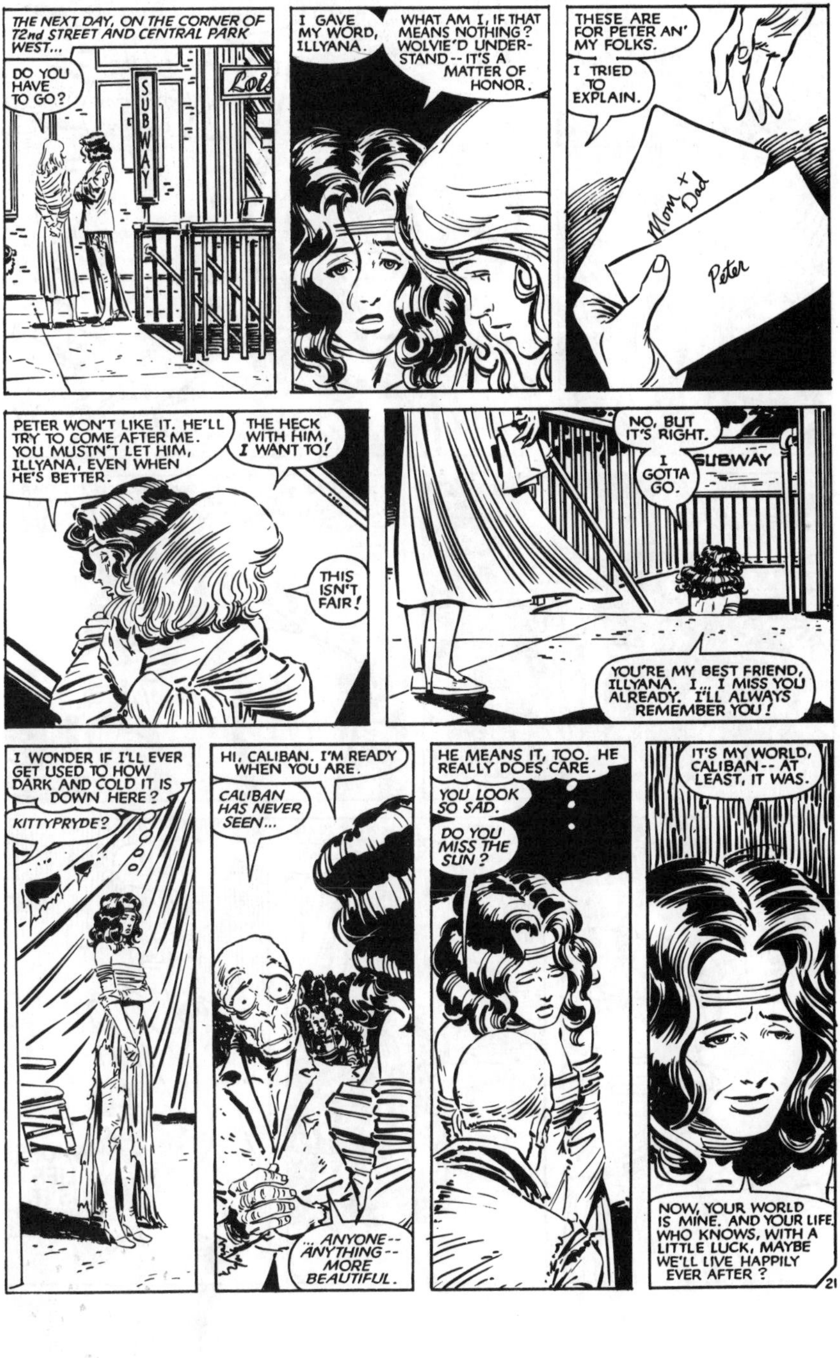

THE NEXT DAY, ON THE CORNER OF 72nd STREET AND CENTRAL PARK WEST...
DO YOU HAVE TO GO?
SUBWAY
I GAVE MY WORD, ILLYANA.
WHAT AM I, IF THAT MEANS NOTHING? WOLVIE'D UNDERSTAND-- IT'S A MATTER OF HONOR.
THESE ARE FOR PETER AN' MY FOLKS.
I TRIED TO EXPLAIN.
Mom + Dad
Peter
PETER WON'T LIKE IT. HE'LL TRY TO COME AFTER ME. YOU MUSTN'T LET HIM, ILLYANA, EVEN WHEN HE'S BETTER.
THE HECK WITH HIM, I WANT TO!
THIS ISN'T FAIR!
NO, BUT IT'S RIGHT.
I GOTTA GO.
SUBWAY
YOU'RE MY BEST FRIEND, ILLYANA. I... I MISS YOU ALREADY. I'LL ALWAYS REMEMBER YOU!
I WONDER IF I'LL EVER GET USED TO HOW DARK AND COLD IT IS DOWN HERE?
KITTYPRYDE?
HI, CALIBAN. I'M READY WHEN YOU ARE.
CALIBAN HAS NEVER SEEN...
...ANYONE-- ANYTHING-- MORE BEAUTIFUL.
HE MEANS IT, TOO. HE REALLY DOES CARE.
YOU LOOK SO SAD.
DO YOU MISS THE SUN?
IT'S MY WORLD, CALIBAN-- AT LEAST, IT WAS.
NOW, YOUR WORLD IS MINE. AND YOUR LIFE. WHO KNOWS, WITH A LITTLE LUCK, MAYBE WE'LL LIVE HAPPILY EVER AFTER?

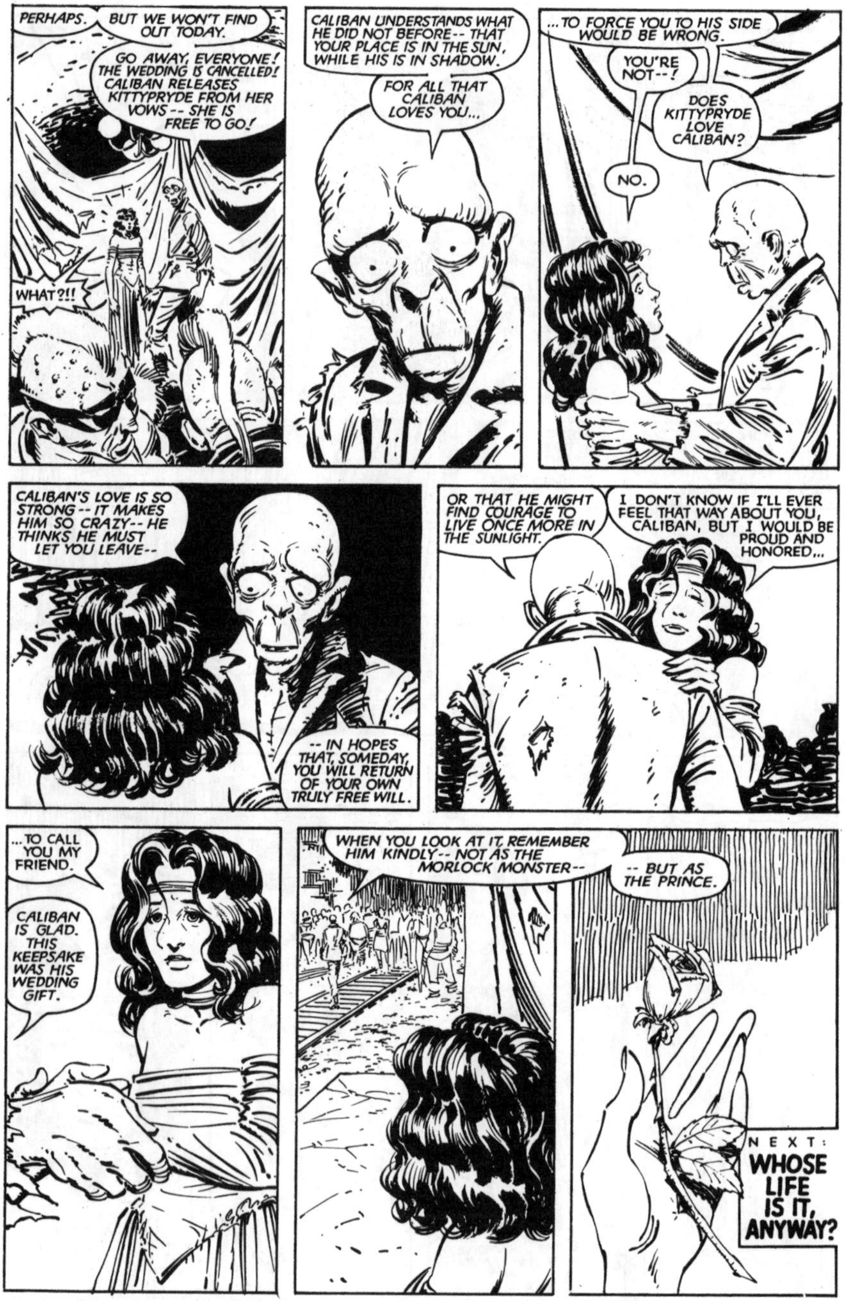

PERHAPS.
BUT WE WON'T FIND OUT TODAY.
GO AWAY, EVERYONE! THE WEDDING IS CANCELLED! CALIBAN RELEASES KITTYPRYDE FROM HER VOWS -- SHE IS FREE TO GO!
WHAT?!!
CALIBAN UNDERSTANDS WHAT HE DID NOT BEFORE -- THAT YOUR PLACE IS IN THE SUN, WHILE HIS IS IN SHADOW.
FOR ALL THAT CALIBAN LOVES YOU...
...TO FORCE YOU TO HIS SIDE WOULD BE WRONG.
YOU'RE NOT--!
DOES KITTYPRYDE LOVE CALIBAN?
NO.
CALIBAN'S LOVE IS SO STRONG -- IT MAKES HIM SO CRAZY -- HE THINKS HE MUST LET YOU LEAVE --
-- IN HOPES THAT, SOMEDAY, YOU WILL RETURN OF YOUR OWN TRULY FREE WILL.
OR THAT HE MIGHT FIND COURAGE TO LIVE ONCE MORE IN THE SUNLIGHT.
I DON'T KNOW IF I'LL EVER FEEL THAT WAY ABOUT YOU, CALIBAN, BUT I WOULD BE PROUD AND HONORED...
...TO CALL YOU MY FRIEND.
CALIBAN IS GLAD. THIS KEEPSAKE WAS HIS WEDDING GIFT.
WHEN YOU LOOK AT IT, REMEMBER HIM KINDLY -- NOT AS THE MORLOCK MONSTER --
-- BUT AS THE PRINCE.
NEXT: WHOSE LIFE IS IT, ANYWAY?

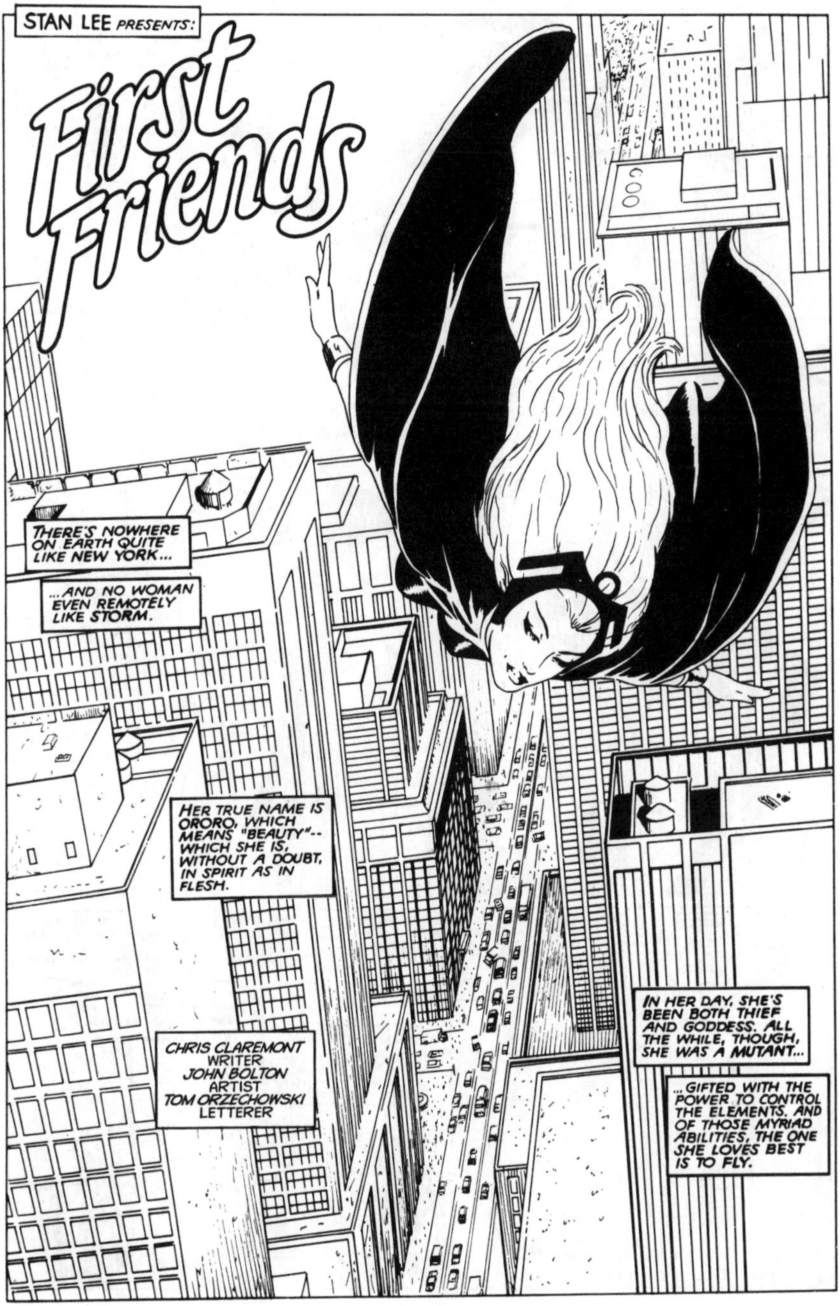

STAN LEE PRESENTS:
First Friends
THERE'S NOWHERE ON EARTH QUITE LIKE NEW YORK...
...AND NO WOMAN EVEN REMOTELY LIKE STORM.
HER TRUE NAME IS ORORO, WHICH MEANS "BEAUTY"-- WHICH SHE IS, WITHOUT A DOUBT, IN SPIRIT AS IN FLESH.
CHRIS CLAREMONT WRITER
JOHN BOLTON ARTIST
TOM ORZECHOWSKI LETTERER
IN HER DAY, SHE'S BEEN BOTH THIEF AND GODDESS. ALL THE WHILE, THOUGH, SHE WAS A MUTANT...
...GIFTED WITH THE POWER TO CONTROL THE ELEMENTS. AND OF THOSE MYRIAD ABILITIES, THE ONE SHE LOVES BEST IS TO FLY.

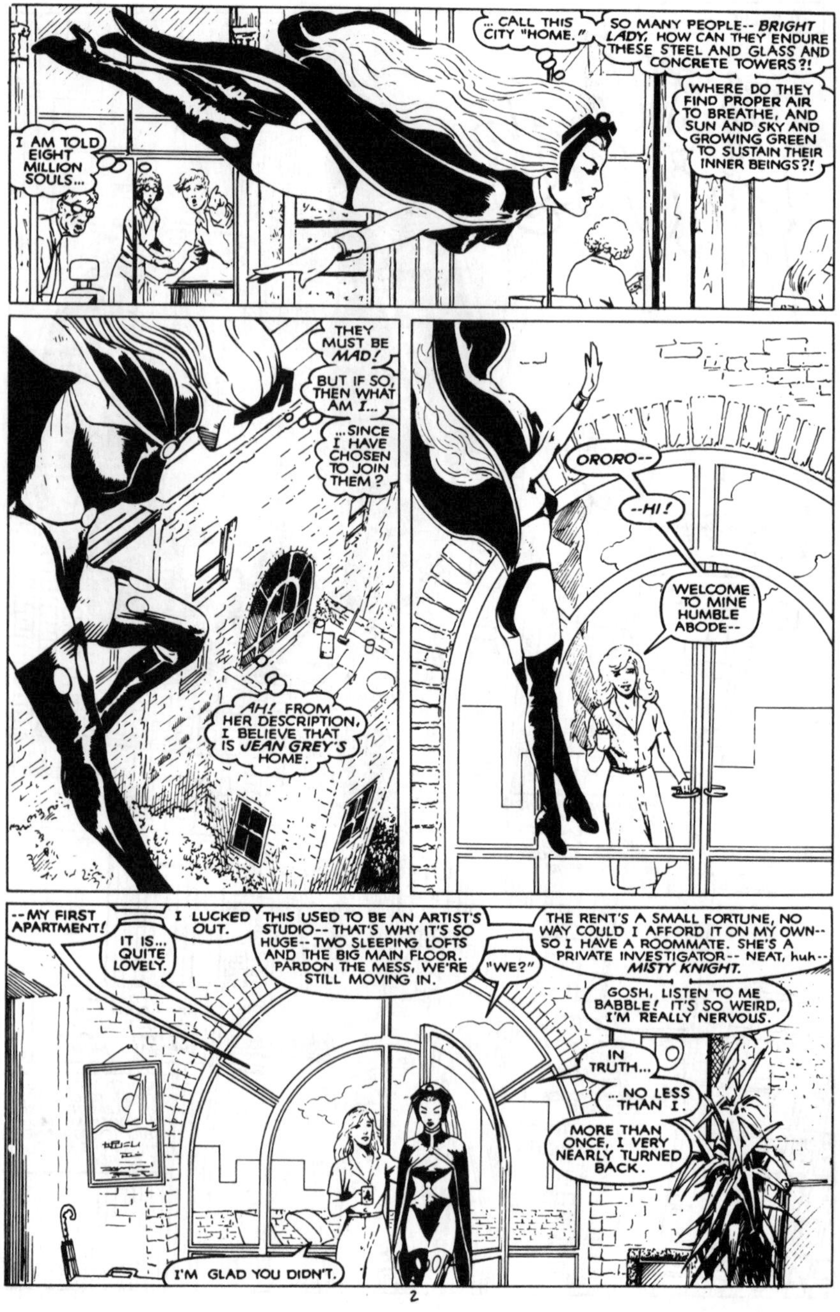
I AM TOLD EIGHT MILLION SOULS...
... CALL THIS CITY "HOME."
SO MANY PEOPLE-- BRIGHT LADY, HOW CAN THEY ENDURE THESE STEEL AND GLASS AND CONCRETE TOWERS?!
WHERE DO THEY FIND PROPER AIR TO BREATHE, AND SUN AND SKY AND GROWING GREEN TO SUSTAIN THEIR INNER BEINGS?!
THEY MUST BE MAD!
BUT IF SO, THEN WHAT AM I...
...SINCE I HAVE CHOSEN TO JOIN THEM?
AH! FROM HER DESCRIPTION, I BELIEVE THAT IS JEAN GREY'S HOME.
ORORO--
--HI!
WELCOME TO MINE HUMBLE ABODE--
--MY FIRST APARTMENT!
IT IS... QUITE LOVELY.
I LUCKED OUT.
THIS USED TO BE AN ARTIST'S STUDIO-- THAT'S WHY IT'S SO HUGE-- TWO SLEEPING LOFTS AND THE BIG MAIN FLOOR. PARDON THE MESS, WE'RE STILL MOVING IN.
"WE?"
THE RENT'S A SMALL FORTUNE, NO WAY COULD I AFFORD IT ON MY OWN-- SO I HAVE A ROOMMATE. SHE'S A PRIVATE INVESTIGATOR-- NEAT, huh-- MISTY KNIGHT.
GOSH, LISTEN TO ME BABBLE! IT'S SO WEIRD, I'M REALLY NERVOUS.
IN TRUTH...
...NO LESS THAN I.
MORE THAN ONCE, I VERY NEARLY TURNED BACK.
I'M GLAD YOU DIDN'T.

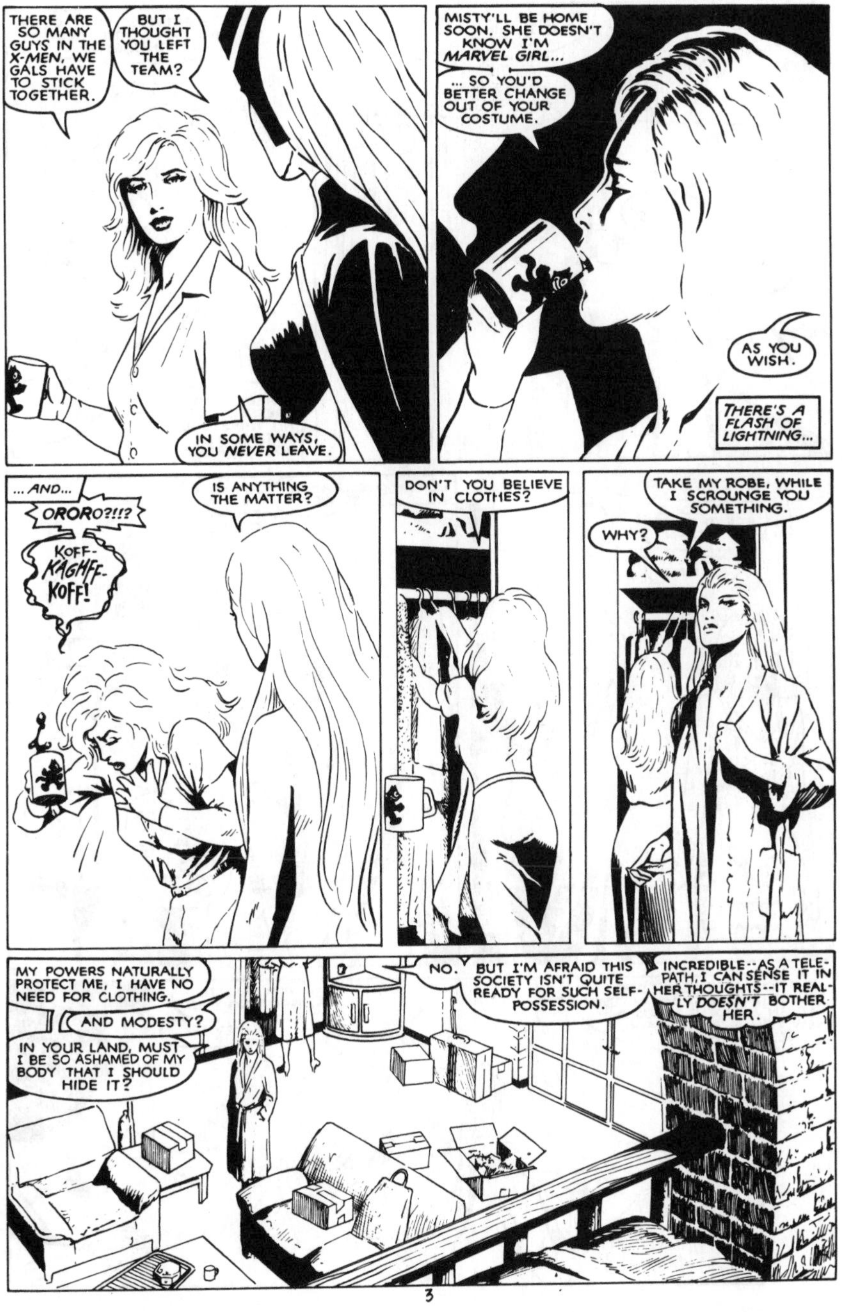
THERE ARE SO MANY GUYS IN THE X-MEN, WE GALS HAVE TO STICK TOGETHER.
BUT I THOUGHT YOU LEFT THE TEAM?
IN SOME WAYS, YOU *NEVER* LEAVE.
MISTY'LL BE HOME SOON. SHE DOESN'T KNOW I'M *MARVEL GIRL*...
... SO YOU'D BETTER CHANGE OUT OF YOUR COSTUME.
AS YOU WISH.
THERE'S A FLASH OF LIGHTNING...
... AND...
ORORO?!!?
KOFF-KAGHFF-KOFF!
IS ANYTHING THE MATTER?
DON'T YOU BELIEVE IN CLOTHES?
TAKE MY ROBE, WHILE I SCROUNGE YOU SOMETHING.
WHY?
MY POWERS NATURALLY PROTECT ME, I HAVE NO NEED FOR CLOTHING.
AND MODESTY?
IN YOUR LAND, MUST I BE SO ASHAMED OF MY BODY THAT I SHOULD HIDE IT?
NO.
BUT I'M AFRAID THIS SOCIETY ISN'T QUITE READY FOR SUCH SELF-POSSESSION.
INCREDIBLE--AS A TELEPATH, I CAN SENSE IT IN HER THOUGHTS--IT REALLY *DOESN'T* BOTHER HER.

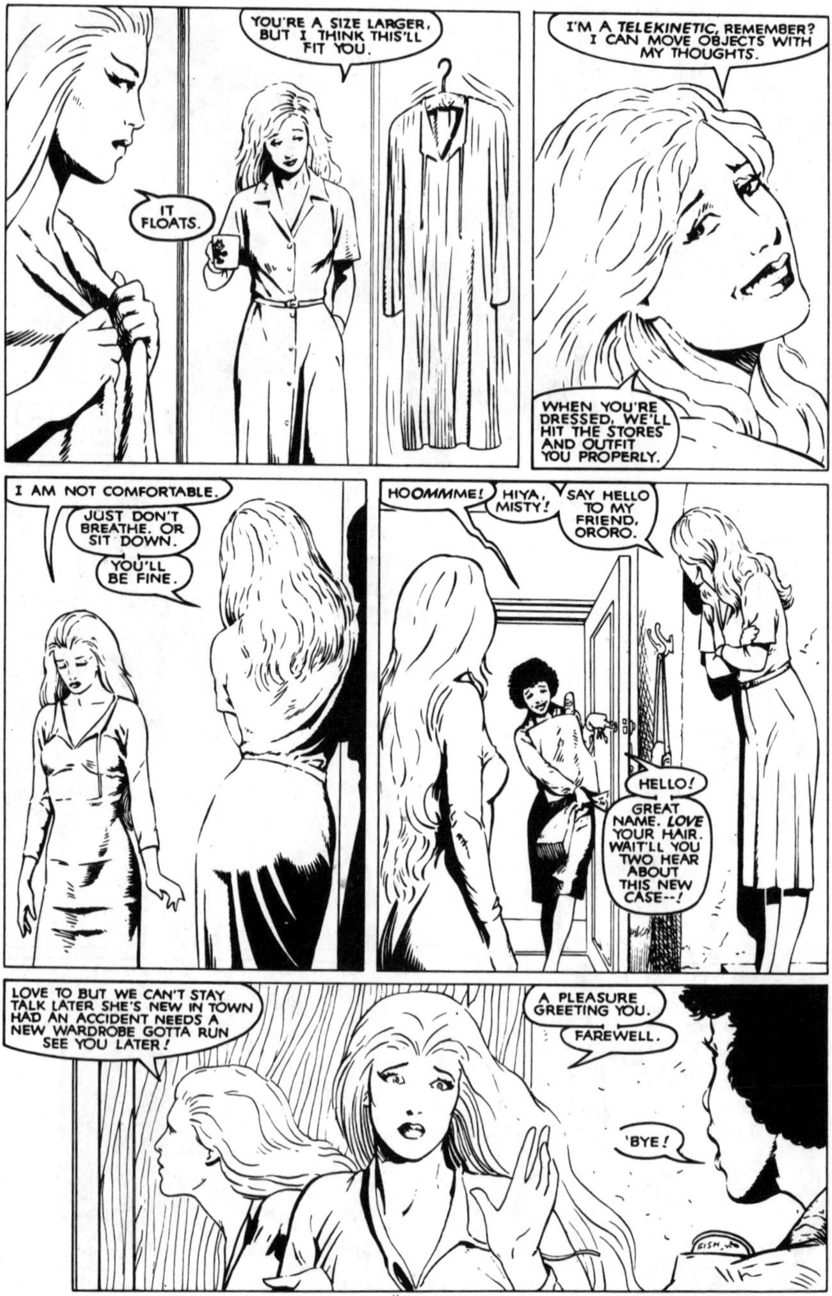
YOU'RE A SIZE LARGER, BUT I THINK THIS'LL FIT YOU.
IT FLOATS.
I'M A TELEKINETIC, REMEMBER? I CAN MOVE OBJECTS WITH MY THOUGHTS.
WHEN YOU'RE DRESSED, WE'LL HIT THE STORES AND OUTFIT YOU PROPERLY.
I AM NOT COMFORTABLE.
JUST DON'T BREATHE. OR SIT DOWN.
YOU'LL BE FINE.
HOOMMME!
HIYA, MISTY!
SAY HELLO TO MY FRIEND, ORORO.
HELLO!
GREAT NAME. LOVE YOUR HAIR. WAIT'LL YOU TWO HEAR ABOUT THIS NEW CASE--!
LOVE TO BUT WE CAN'T STAY TALK LATER SHE'S NEW IN TOWN HAD AN ACCIDENT NEEDS A NEW WARDROBE GOTTA RUN SEE YOU LATER!
A PLEASURE GREETING YOU.
FAREWELL.
'BYE!

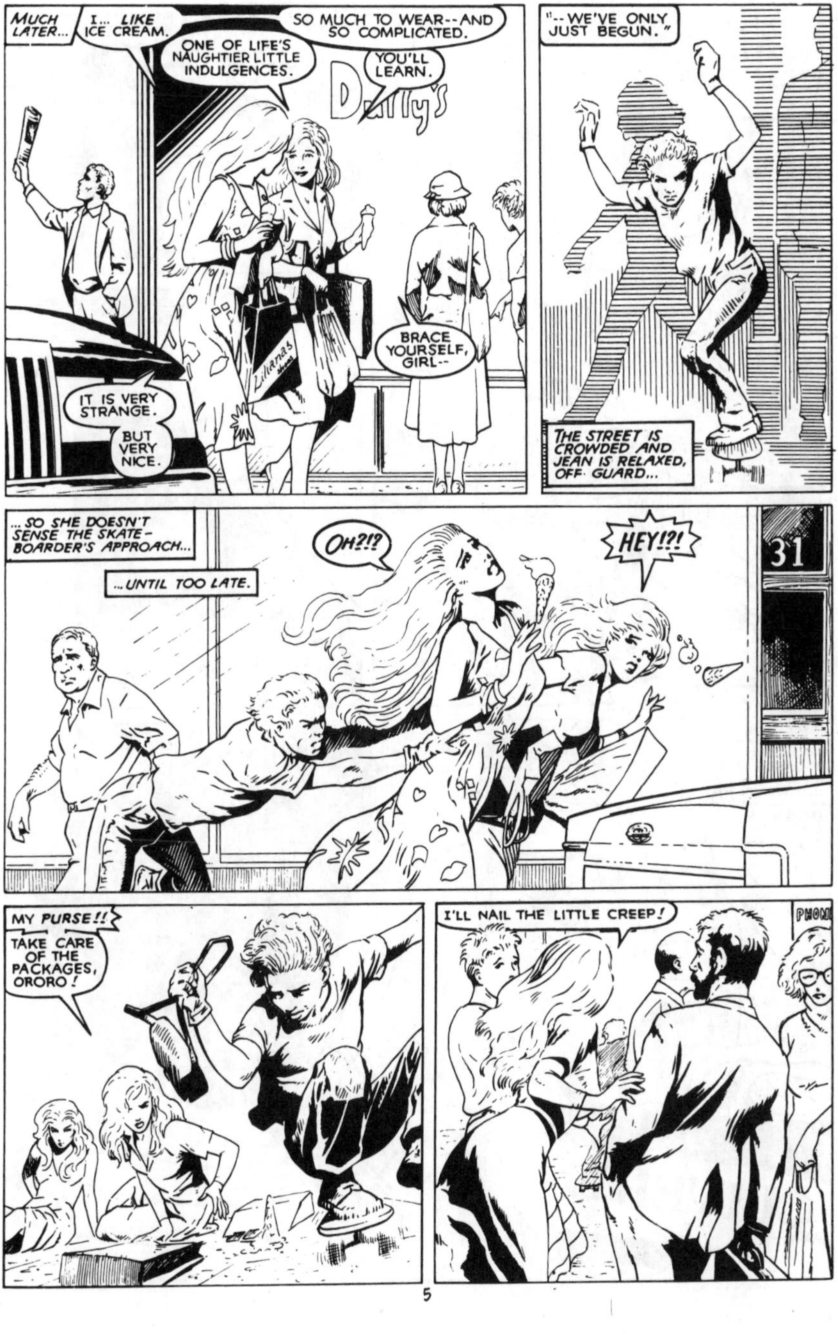
MUCH LATER...
I... LIKE ICE CREAM.
ONE OF LIFE'S NAUGHTIER LITTLE INDULGENCES.
SO MUCH TO WEAR--AND SO COMPLICATED.
YOU'LL LEARN.
Darly's
Liliana's
BRACE YOURSELF, GIRL--
IT IS VERY STRANGE.
BUT VERY NICE.
"--WE'VE ONLY JUST BEGUN."
THE STREET IS CROWDED AND JEAN IS RELAXED, OFF GUARD...
...SO SHE DOESN'T SENSE THE SKATE-BOARDER'S APPROACH...
...UNTIL TOO LATE.
OH?!?
HEY!?!
31
MY PURSE!!
TAKE CARE OF THE PACKAGES, ORORO!
I'LL NAIL THE LITTLE CREEP!

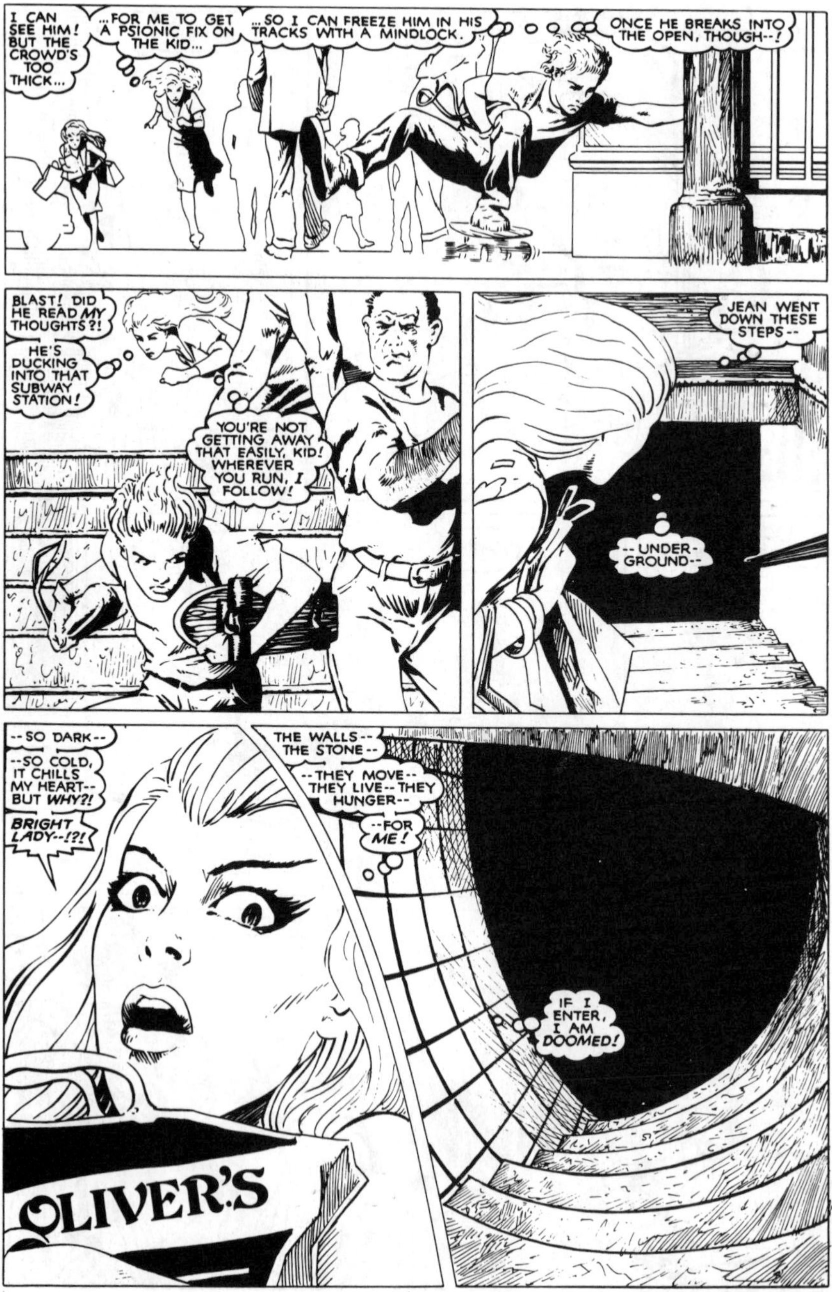
I CAN SEE HIM! BUT THE CROWD'S TOO THICK...
...FOR ME TO GET A PSIONIC FIX ON THE KID...
...SO I CAN FREEZE HIM IN HIS TRACKS WITH A MINDLOCK.
ONCE HE BREAKS INTO THE OPEN, THOUGH--!
BLAST! DID HE READ MY THOUGHTS?!
HE'S DUCKING INTO THAT SUBWAY STATION!
YOU'RE NOT GETTING AWAY THAT EASILY, KID! WHEREVER YOU RUN, I FOLLOW!
JEAN WENT DOWN THESE STEPS--
--UNDER-GROUND--
--SO DARK--
--SO COLD, IT CHILLS MY HEART-- BUT WHY?!
BRIGHT LADY--!?!
THE WALLS-- THE STONE--
--THEY MOVE-- THEY LIVE-- THEY HUNGER--
--FOR ME!
IF I ENTER, I AM DOOMED!
OLIVER'S

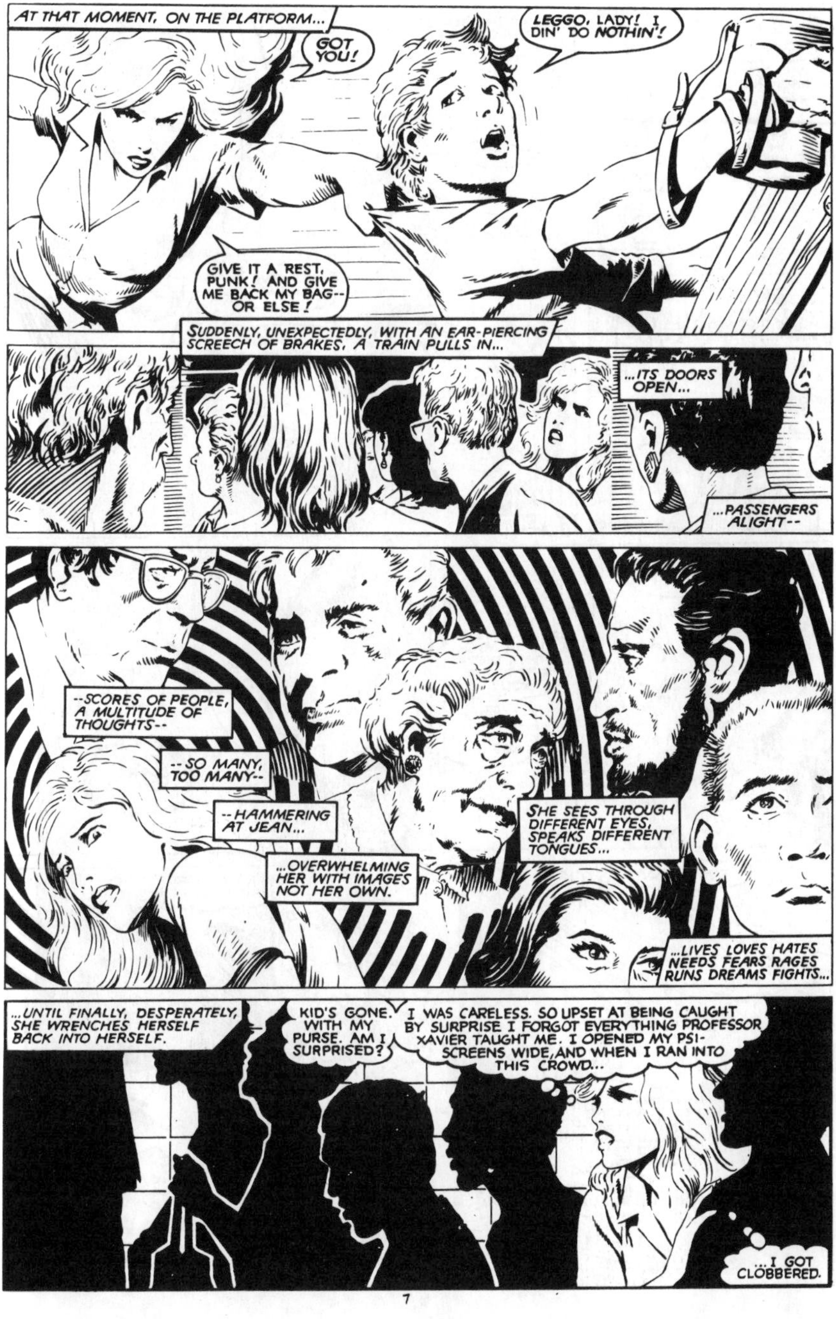
AT THAT MOMENT, ON THE PLATFORM...
GOT YOU!
LEGGO, LADY! I DIN' DO NOTHIN'!
GIVE IT A REST, PUNK! AND GIVE ME BACK MY BAG-- OR ELSE!
SUDDENLY, UNEXPECTEDLY, WITH AN EAR-PIERCING SCREECH OF BRAKES, A TRAIN PULLS IN...
...ITS DOORS OPEN...
...PASSENGERS ALIGHT--
--SCORES OF PEOPLE, A MULTITUDE OF THOUGHTS--
--SO MANY, TOO MANY--
--HAMMERING AT JEAN...
...OVERWHELMING HER WITH IMAGES NOT HER OWN.
SHE SEES THROUGH DIFFERENT EYES, SPEAKS DIFFERENT TONGUES...
...LIVES LOVES HATES NEEDS FEARS RAGES RUNS DREAMS FIGHTS...
...UNTIL FINALLY, DESPERATELY, SHE WRENCHES HERSELF BACK INTO HERSELF.
KID'S GONE. WITH MY PURSE. AM I SURPRISED?
I WAS CARELESS. SO UPSET AT BEING CAUGHT BY SURPRISE I FORGOT EVERYTHING PROFESSOR XAVIER TAUGHT ME. I OPENED MY PSI-SCREENS WIDE, AND WHEN I RAN INTO THIS CROWD...
...I GOT CLOBBERED.

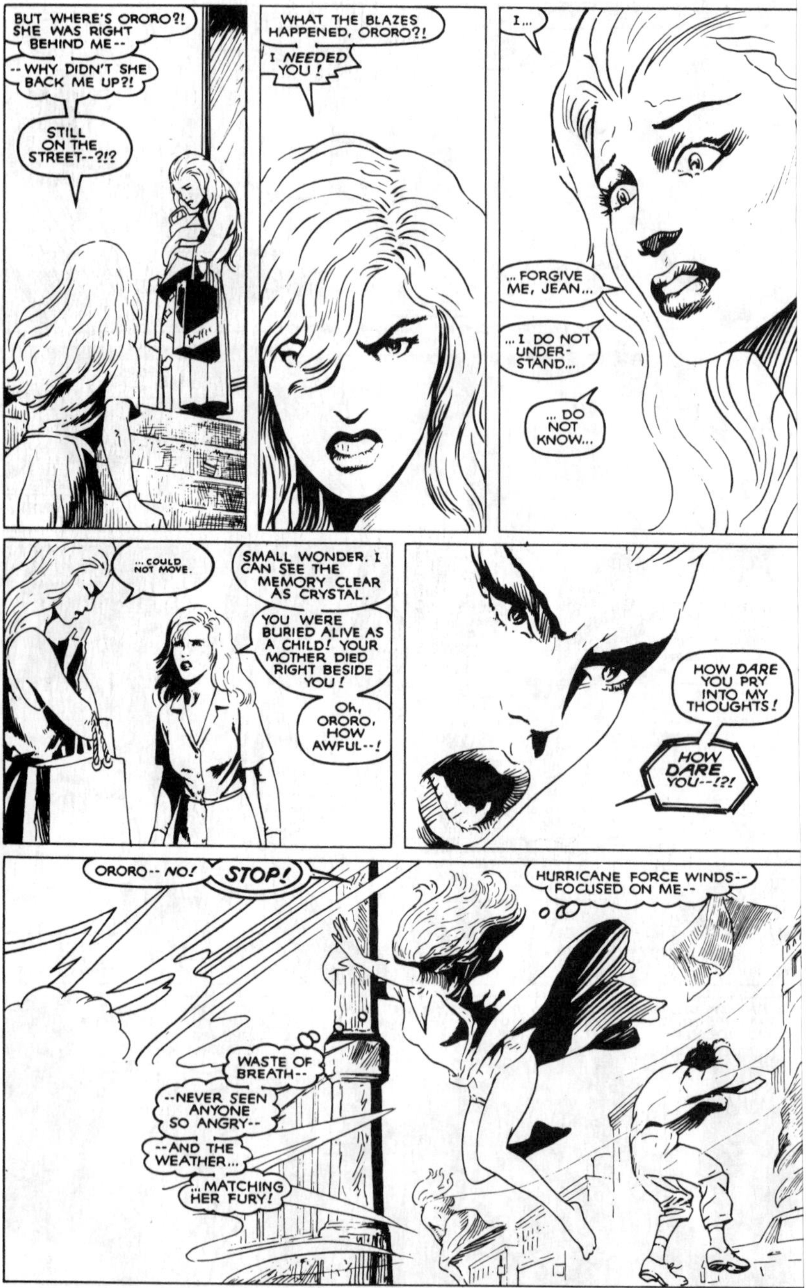
BUT WHERE'S ORORO?! SHE WAS RIGHT BEHIND ME--
--WHY DIDN'T SHE BACK ME UP?!
STILL ON THE STREET--?!?
WHAT THE BLAZES HAPPENED, ORORO?!
I NEEDED YOU!
I...
...FORGIVE ME, JEAN...
...I DO NOT UNDER-STAND...
...DO NOT KNOW...
...COULD NOT MOVE.
SMALL WONDER. I CAN SEE THE MEMORY CLEAR AS CRYSTAL.
YOU WERE BURIED ALIVE AS A CHILD! YOUR MOTHER DIED RIGHT BESIDE YOU!
Oh, ORORO, HOW AWFUL--!
HOW DARE YOU PRY INTO MY THOUGHTS!
HOW DARE YOU--!?!
ORORO-- NO!
STOP!
HURRICANE FORCE WINDS-- FOCUSED ON ME--
WASTE OF BREATH--
--NEVER SEEN ANYONE SO ANGRY--
--AND THE WEATHER...
...MATCHING HER FURY!

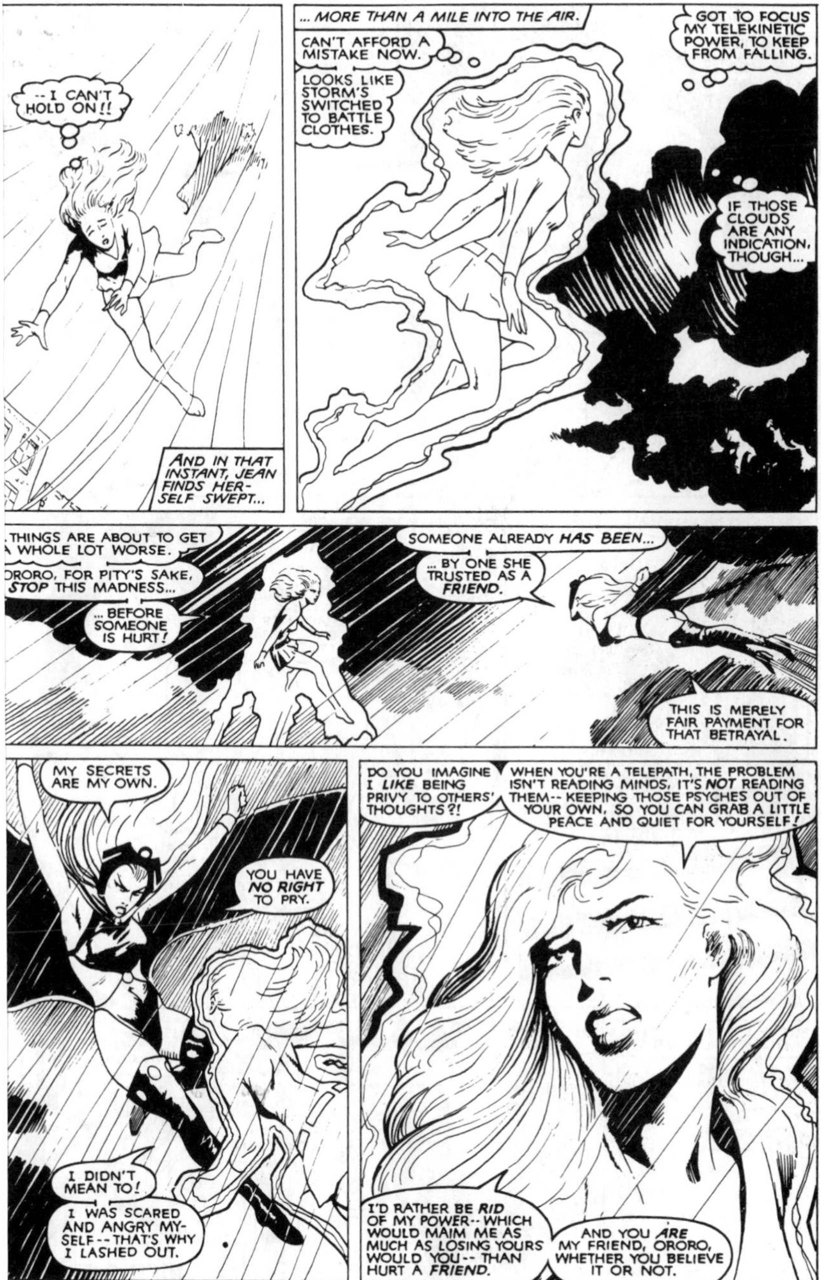
-- I CAN'T HOLD ON!!
AND IN THAT INSTANT, JEAN FINDS HER-SELF SWEPT...
... MORE THAN A MILE INTO THE AIR.
CAN'T AFFORD A MISTAKE NOW.
LOOKS LIKE STORM'S SWITCHED TO BATTLE CLOTHES.
GOT TO FOCUS MY TELEKINETIC POWER, TO KEEP FROM FALLING.
IF THOSE CLOUDS ARE ANY INDICATION, THOUGH...
THINGS ARE ABOUT TO GET A WHOLE LOT WORSE.
ORORO, FOR PITY'S SAKE, STOP THIS MADNESS...
... BEFORE SOMEONE IS HURT!
SOMEONE ALREADY HAS BEEN...
... BY ONE SHE TRUSTED AS A FRIEND.
THIS IS MERELY FAIR PAYMENT FOR THAT BETRAYAL.
MY SECRETS ARE MY OWN.
YOU HAVE NO RIGHT TO PRY.
I DIDN'T MEAN TO!
I WAS SCARED AND ANGRY MY-SELF -- THAT'S WHY I LASHED OUT.
DO YOU IMAGINE I LIKE BEING PRIVY TO OTHERS' THOUGHTS?!
WHEN YOU'RE A TELEPATH, THE PROBLEM ISN'T READING MINDS, IT'S NOT READING THEM-- KEEPING THOSE PSYCHES OUT OF YOUR OWN, SO YOU CAN GRAB A LITTLE PEACE AND QUIET FOR YOURSELF!
I'D RATHER BE RID OF MY POWER-- WHICH WOULD MAIM ME AS MUCH AS LOSING YOURS WOULD YOU-- THAN HURT A FRIEND.
AND YOU ARE MY FRIEND, ORORO, WHETHER YOU BELIEVE IT OR NOT.

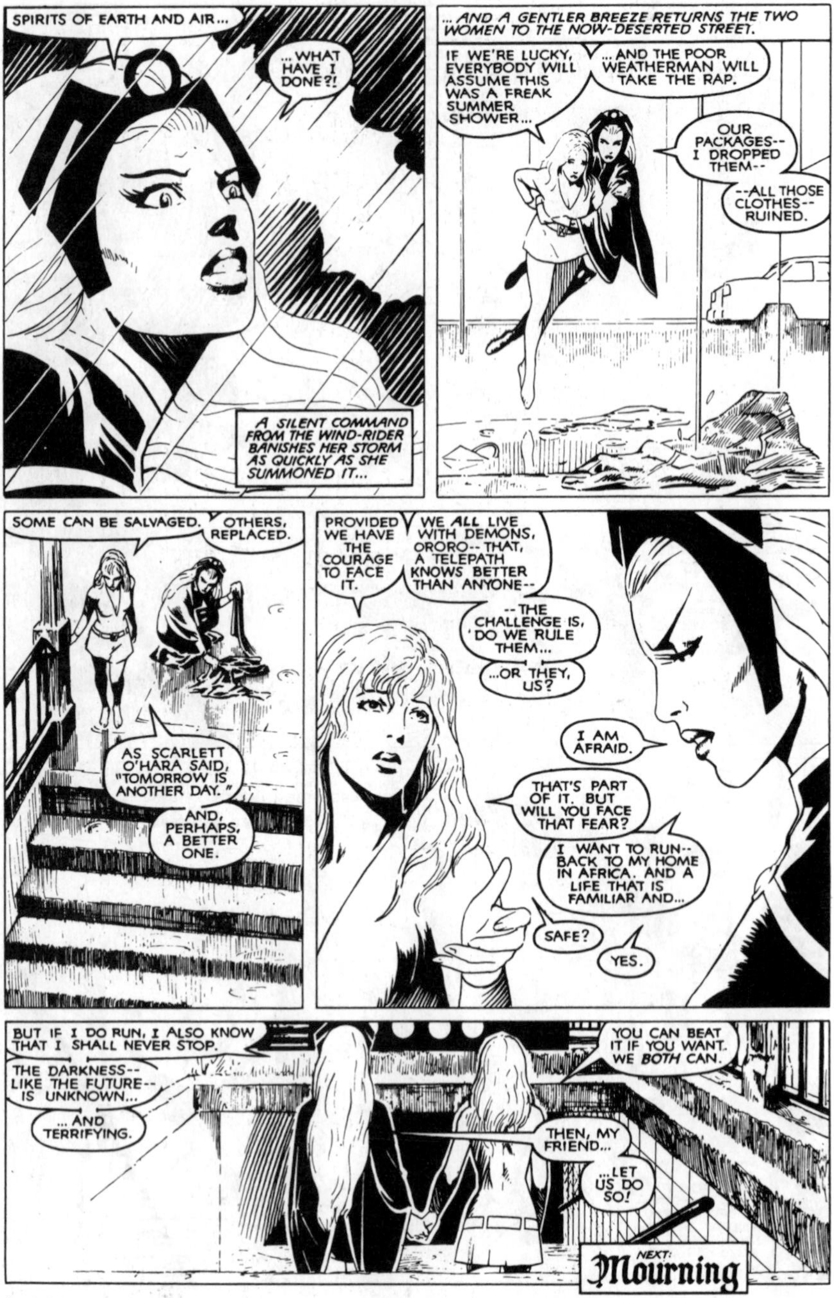
SPIRITS OF EARTH AND AIR...
...WHAT HAVE I DONE?!
A SILENT COMMAND FROM THE WIND-RIDER BANISHES HER STORM AS QUICKLY AS SHE SUMMONED IT...
...AND A GENTLER BREEZE RETURNS THE TWO WOMEN TO THE NOW-DESERTED STREET.
IF WE'RE LUCKY, EVERYBODY WILL ASSUME THIS WAS A FREAK SUMMER SHOWER...
...AND THE POOR WEATHERMAN WILL TAKE THE RAP.
OUR PACKAGES-- I DROPPED THEM--
--ALL THOSE CLOTHES-- RUINED.
SOME CAN BE SALVAGED.
OTHERS, REPLACED.
AS SCARLETT O'HARA SAID, "TOMORROW IS ANOTHER DAY."
AND, PERHAPS, A BETTER ONE.
PROVIDED WE HAVE THE COURAGE TO FACE IT.
WE ALL LIVE WITH DEMONS, ORORO-- THAT, A TELEPATH KNOWS BETTER THAN ANYONE--
--THE CHALLENGE IS, DO WE RULE THEM...
...OR THEY, US?
I AM AFRAID.
THAT'S PART OF IT. BUT WILL YOU FACE THAT FEAR?
I WANT TO RUN-- BACK TO MY HOME IN AFRICA. AND A LIFE THAT IS FAMILIAR AND...
SAFE?
YES.
BUT IF I DO RUN, I ALSO KNOW THAT I SHALL NEVER STOP.
THE DARKNESS-- LIKE THE FUTURE-- IS UNKNOWN...
...AND TERRIFYING.
YOU CAN BEAT IT IF YOU WANT. WE BOTH CAN.
THEN, MY FRIEND...
...LET US DO SO!
NEXT: Mourning